Asset Valuation Theory
资产估值原理

〔美〕Frank Hugh Koger Ⅲ 著

图书在版编目(CIP)数据

资产估值原理：英文 / (美)弗兰克·休·科格尔三世(Frank Hugh Koger Ⅲ)著. —北京：北京大学出版社，2017.3
ISBN 978-7-301-28527-5

Ⅰ. ①资… Ⅱ. ①弗… Ⅲ. ①资产价值—估价—英文 Ⅳ. ①F273.4

中国版本图书馆 CIP 数据核字(2017)第 159941 号

书　　　名	资产估值原理 ZICHAN GUZHI YUANLI
著作责任者	〔美〕Frank Hugh Koger Ⅲ 著
责任编辑	张　燕
标准书号	ISBN 978-7-301-28527-5
出版发行	北京大学出版社
地　　　址	北京市海淀区成府路 205 号　100871
网　　　址	http://www.pup.cn　新浪微博：@北京大学出版社
电子信箱	zpup@pup.cn
电　　　话	邮购部 62752015　发行部 62750672　编辑部 62762926
印　刷　者	三河市北燕印装有限公司
经　销　者	新华书店
	787 毫米 × 1092 毫米　16 开本　22 印张　439 千字 2017 年 3 月第 1 版　2017 年 3 月第 1 次印刷
定　　　价	49.00 元

未经许可，不得以任何方式复制或抄袭本书之部分或全部内容。
版权所有，侵权必究
举报电话：010-62752024　电子信箱：fd@pup.pku.edu.cn
图书如有印装质量问题，请与出版部联系，电话：010-62756370

Asset Valuation Theory

Frank Hugh Koger III[1]

---
[1] Peking University, HSBC Business School; fritzkoger@phbs.pku.edu.cn

For Kelly, Lynn, Kiel

and for CQG MM YY.

Preface

It is with great pleasure that I offer this textbook regarding a subject of general interest. My goal is to impart to the student not only relevant financial knowledge, but also improved abilities regarding how to approach and to solve related problems. Furthermore, I hope to enhance the readers enthusiasm for the subject. The material is relevant for not only professional purposes to those working in finance, but also personal reasons regarding management of one's private wealth. Hence, the student should have great motivation for studying this book.

The purpose of this text is to offer a mathematically rigorous approach to valuing assets. That is to say, the book is not overly technical, as it does not offer math for the sake of math. The subject is treated in such a manner that the student can learn how to use valuation techniques and apply them to assets beyond those included in this book. As the book is primarily intended to offer theory, little reference is made directly to current topics and issues. Hence, I hope that the book will be somewhat timeless.

As the book stresses theory, numerical examples are chosen judiciously. They are offered where they are able to help drive home relevant intuition and/or for concepts not covered in other textbooks. However, to strike a balance for those desiring a focus on applications, problem sets primarily feature numerical examples. A generous helping of exhibits enhances the book, as I believe that these are great in exposing intuition. Liberal usage of comparative statics analysis aids the student in developing her/his ability to extract key relationships between value and its drivers.

Knowledge of multi-variable calculus is helpful as it is used in developing comparative statics. Familiarity with probability & statistics also enhances the students' ability to comprehend the material. However, stochastic processes are generally beyond this textbook's scope.

This textbook was borne from my own lecture notes used to teach a course of the same name. Given the relative technical strength of our masters of finance and masters of quantitative finance students, I was afforded the opportunity to develop lectures with a higher level of mathematical treatment than that which is covered in many textbooks. I cover most of the material in this book in a 36-hour course, but realistically the book should probably be covered in two courses. (Again, our masters students are technically very talented and have taken several pre-requisite courses such as financial economics prior to my course. Hence, this allows me to proceed at a brisk pace.) The results have been rewarding, with the course very well received by students. Many who have subsequently passed CFA examinations have commented on how helpful the course is in pursuing this valuable professional designation.

Intended Market

The book is appropriate for both advanced undergraduate students and graduate students with reasonably strong math skills. The book is also relevant for practitioners looking for tools and techniques to enhance their abilities to tackle new challenges. As previously mentioned, the level of treatment in the textbook is more mathematically rigorous than that of many other financial textbooks. The student with knowledge of multi-variable calculus and probability & statistics will be able to follow derivations of results and will benefit on a more profound level. Nonetheless, even for those who lack this level of mathematical sophistication, the book can still be helpful given its extensive exposition of summary results, detailed explanations and related diagrams.

Key Features

Knowledge regarding valuation of assets is critically important to those who desire to work in the world of finance. It is also invaluable in managing one's own personal wealth. The book offers a sound grounding not only in valuation, but also in its application to assets not included here.

Part I reviews financial basics such as discounting cash flows, future values of cash flows and value additivity. Special cases of the latter are included, such as growing perpetuities and annuities. This part also shows the most common metrics used for historical performance of asset returns.

Part II discusses metrics of risk and how these impact corresponding rewards that investors may expect. Future asset rates of return are modeled via random variables, and investors preferences are modeled via utility functions. Investors optimal frontier of risky asset portfolios is identified, and introduction of a risk-free asset allows identification of the capital market line. An intuitive development of the security market line is derived, and the market model is introduced. The arbitrage pricing theory is reviewed, and its implementation via detailed numerical examples is shown.

Part III focuses on equity valuation. Financial accounting statements are introduced, and many ratios used to analyze a firm's financial health are reviewed. Relative valuation of a firm's equity is discussed. Several techniques of absolute valuation via discounted cash flows are also covered. The earnings multiplier model, a hybrid of both relative valuation via price-to-earnings ratio and absolute valuation via dividend discount model, is explored in detail.

Part IV examines valuation of fixed-income securities, focusing on fixed coupon bonds. Initially bond pricing is reviewed, breaking down components of value. Various yield metrics are explored. Comparative statics are performed in order to determine the drivers of bond value. These relationships allow subsequent calculation of useful simplified price-yield approximations. Pricing of bonds between coupon dates is subsequently covered in more detail than in other books. Lastly, given a set of benchmark rates such as those of the US Treasury, useful implicit future periodic rates are determined, e.g., spot rates and forward rates.

Part V deals with options. Expiration date payoffs of options, of combinations of options, and of portfolios of securities including options are reviewed. A derivation of put-call spot parity utilizing the critically important no-arbitrage principle is developed. Utilizing a binomial stock pricing model, option valuations via replicating portfolio, via delta hedge, and via risk-neutral valuation are derived. The flexibility of a multi-period binomial model in valuing American options as well as path-dependent options is shown. A sketch of an outline of the development of the Black-Scholes model is presented. Corresponding comparative statics results are performed.

Acknowledgements

Many people have played a part in developing this book. In particular, feedback from students, including many talented teaching assistants through the years, has been critical to this book's production. I am particularly grateful to Tiffany Bai, who read the original manuscript in its entirety and provided valuable comments. Other students who have provided particularly useful input include Mona Zhou, Cathy Liu, Ginger Huang, Michael Ma and Hazel Wang.

I'd also like to thank PHBS Dean, professor Wen Hai, for his encouragement and support in authoring this textbook. Additionally, Annie Jin of PHBS helped coordinate publication, and the staff at Peking University Press was instrumental with its enthusiasm and advice.

About The Author

Koger holds the position of assistant professor at Peking University, Shenzhen, PRC. He received a B.S. in Chemical Engineering from Louisiana State University, where he was a member of Phi Beta Kappa and Phi Kappa Phi honor societies. He received his International MBA from the Darla Moore School of Business at the University of South Carolina, where he graduated 1st of 92 students. He was the only student in his cohort to conclude his studies with a perfect grade point average of 4.0/4.0. Koger received a Ph.D. in finance from Tulane University. Professor Koger also holds a charter from the Institute of Chartered Financial Analysts.

Professor Koger has vast teaching experience. While a Ph.D. student at Tulane, he taught financial management, advanced financial management and managerial accounting at the undergraduate level. At the masters level, he taught corporate financial policy and fixed income analytics.

At Peking University (PKU), Koger currently teaches asset valuation theory, financial modeling, advanced financial modeling and financial modeling in Excel. None of these courses existed prior to his arrival, as he has initiated and developed all these from scratch. He has also taught corporate finance at PKU. Professor Koger has consistently earned some of the highest teaching evaluations at PKU. Furthermore, he has received teaching awards, not only from the PKU HSBC Business School (PHBS), but also at the campus-wide level of PKU Shenzhen.

During his time at PKU, Koger has been invited to teach individual courses at other universities. He has taught fixed income: models and applications at South University of Science and Technology in Shenzhen, China. Koger has instructed financial modeling in multiple summer sessions at Ruhr University, Bochum International Summer Session (BISS) in Bochum, Germany, where he received the highest evaluation of the 16 courses offered during BISS 2015.

Koger has been active in relevant service to PHBS. He was solely responsible for securing academic partnerships with both the CFA Institute as well as the Global Association of Risk Professionals. Koger has given his time via volunteer review sessions for CFA examinations. At PHBS, he has also served on both the curriculum committee as well as the teaching quality committee. Professor Koger established PHBS first exchange program, that with Tulane University, and subsequently has helped in developing other exchange programs. He has also volunteered his time with lectures of introductory finance at Shenzhen High School (Shenzhen Zhong Xue).

Prior to working in academia, Koger was the general manager of Filtration Group Technical Media, a manufacturer of media for air filters and a former stand-alone division of Filtration Group. Prior to this, he has worked for 15 years for Hoechst A.G. in numerous capacities of increasing responsibility and in several locations, including the USA (Texas, Kentucky, New Jersey, Michigan and South Carolina) and Germany (Bavaria).

Common Variable Definitions

APr	annualized percentage rate of return, compounded $m\frac{\text{periods}}{\text{year}}$
c_0	current European call option premium or price
c_1^u	call value after one period in up state of binomial model
c_1^d	call value after one period in down state of binomial model
C_0	current American call option premium or price
C_T	call option payoff at expiration, date T
C_t	coupon interest payment from a bond received at date t
CF_t	cash flow received at date t
D_0	current value of debt
d_t	dividend per share received at date t
E	earnings, or net income, NI
Eq_0	current value of equity
EAr	effective annualized rate of return, on a discrete basis
EV	enterprise value, or loosely, firm value, V
$E[X]$	expected value of random variable X
F	face value of a bond, received at maturity, date T
FCF_t	free cash flow for period t evaluated at date t
$FCFE_t$	free cash flow to equity holders for period t
FV_t	future value at date t of cash flows received before date t
$f(x)$	probability density function of random variable X at $X = x$
$F(x)$	cumulative probability distribution function of X at $X = x$
g^i	annualized growth rate of entity i, e.g., g^{CF} or g^{Eq}
GMR	geometric mean gross return
GMr	geometric mean rate of return
$h'(x_0)$	derivative of function $h(x)$ with respect to x evaluated at x_0
$h''(x_0)$	second derivative of function $h(x)$ with respect to x at $x = x_0$

IRR	annualized rate implied by cost (price) and future CFs
IV_0	current intrinsic value of cash flows
K	option strike or exercise price
M	market portfolio of all risky assets
NI	net income, or earnings, E
P_0	current price of a security; American put premium
p_0	current European put option premium or price
p_1^d	put value one period in down state of binomial model
p_1^u	put value one period in up state of binomial model
P_T	put option payoff at expiration, date T
PV_0	current (date $t=0$) present value of future CF(s)
R_t	annualized gross return for period t
r_t	annualized rate of return, or yield, for period t
r^E	annualized rate of return demanded by equity holders
r^D	annualized rate of return demanded by debt holders
r^f	annualized rate demanded by investors of risk-free asset
r^i	annualized rate demanded by investors of asset i
r^m	annualized rate demanded by investors of market portfolio
$s(R^x)$	historical standard deviation of gross return of security x
$s^2(R^x)$	historical variance of gross return of security x
$s(r^x)$	historical standard deviation of rate of return of security x
$s^2(r^x)$	historical variance of rate of return of security x
S_0	current stock price
S_1^d	stock price after one period in down state of binomial model
S_1^u	stock price after one period in up state of binomial model
T	maturity or terminal date of security, or date of final CF
T^C	corporate tax rate
V_t	value at date t of CF, package of CFs, security or firm
w^i	weight of component i in weighted average calculations
$WACC$	weighted average cost of capital
y	yield to maturity, an annualized percentage rate of return
β^x	regression slope coefficient: x returns on market returns
$\sigma(R^x)$	expected standard deviation of return of security x
$\sigma^2(R^x)$	expected variance of return of security x

Brief Contents

Part I The Basics — 1
Chapter 1 Review of Financial Basics — 3
Chapter 2 Historical Returns — 10

Part II Risk, Reward, Portfolio Theory and Capital Market Equilibrium — 25
Chapter 3 Future (Next Period) Return — 27
Chapter 4 Optimal Portfolio Identification — 36
Chapter 5 Capital Market Line, Market Model and Security Market Line — 43
Chapter 6 Arbitrage Pricing Theory — 55

Part III Equity Valuation — 69
Chapter 7 Review of Financial Accounting Statements — 71
Chapter 8 Financial Statement Analysis and Relative Valuation — 85
Chapter 9 Absolute Valuation: Discounting Cash Flows — 108
Chapter 10 Earnings Multiplier Model — 135

Part IV Bond Theory — 143
Chapter 11 Introduction to Bonds — 145
Chapter 12 March to Maturity and Malkiel Results — 155
Chapter 13 Approximations to Price-yield Relations — 166
Chapter 14 Pricing Bonds Between Coupon Dates — 177
Chapter 15 Rate and Yield Metrics — 187

Part V Options   203

Chapter 16 Expiration Date Option Payoffs and Profits   205

Chapter 17 Option Valuation: Single Period Binomial Model   224

Chapter 18 Option Valuation: Multi-period Model   248

Chapter 19 American Binomial Option Pricing Model   257

Chapter 20 Option Valuation: Black-Scholes Model   271

Solutions to Selected End-of-chapter Problems   285

References and Suggested Readings   319

Index   323

Contents

Part I The Basics — 1

Chapter 1 Review of Financial Basics — 3
- 1.1 Timelines, Stock Variables and Flow Variables — 3
- 1.2 Moving Cash Flows Through Time — 4
- 1.3 Evenly Spaced Cash Flows Growing at Rate g — 6
- Problems — 8

Chapter 2 Historical Returns — 10
- 2.1 Single Period Gross Return and Rate of Return — 10
- 2.2 Multi-period Historical Returns — 11
- 2.3 Means and Variances of Historical Returns — 12
- 2.4 Linear Relationship of Two-asset Historical Returns — 14
- 2.5 Historical Portfolio Returns — 15
- 2.6 Continuously Compounded Returns — 17
- 2.7 Continuously Compounded Historical Portfolio Returns — 18
- 2.8 Returns When Security Cash Flows Are Not Reinvested — 18
- 2.9 Continuously Compounded Returns if Nonreinvestment — 20
- Problems — 21

Part II Risk, Reward, Portfolio Theory and Capital Market Equilibrium — 25

Chapter 3 Future (Next Period) Return — 27
- 3.1 Future (Next Period) Return for a Single Asset — 27
- 3.2 Expectation and Variance of Future Return — 27
- 3.3 Linear Relation Between Future Returns of Two Assets — 28
- 3.4 Future (Next Period) Portfolio Return — 29
    - 3.4.1 Benefit of Asset Diversification in a Portfolio — 30

	3.4.2 Special Cases: Future Return of Two-asset Portfolios	32
Problems		34

Chapter 4 Optimal Portfolio Identification — 36
4.1 Markowitz Theory of Risky-Asset Efficient Portfolios — 36
4.2 Investor Preferences over Risk and Expected Reward — 39
Problems — 42

Chapter 5 Capital Market Line, Market Model and Security Market Line — 43
5.1 Capital Market Line — 43
5.2 Idiosyncratic Risk, Systematic Risk, and Market Model — 46
5.3 Security Market Line — 48
5.4 Comparing and Contrasting the CML and the SML — 50
Problems — 53

Chapter 6 Arbitrage Pricing Theory — 55
6.1 Demanded, Expected and Implied Rates of Return — 59
6.2 *APT* Continued: How to Make a Profit — 60
6.3 Implementing an Arbitrage Portfolio per *APT* — 62
    6.3.1 Example: Three Assets, Two Systematic Risk Factors — 63
    6.3.2 Example: Four Assets, Two Systematic Risk Factors — 64
Problems — 66

Part III Equity Valuation — 69

Chapter 7 Review of Financial Accounting Statements — 71
7.1 Income Statement — 71
7.2 Balance Sheet — 74
7.3 Statement of Cash Flows — 75
7.4 Free Cash Flows and Free Cash Flows to Equity — 78
Problems — 83

Chapter 8 Financial Statement Analysis and Relative Valuation — 85
8.1 Common Size Financial Accounting Statements — 86
8.2 Internal Liquidity Ratios — 88
8.3 Operating Performance Ratios — 92
8.4 Financial Risk Ratios — 94
8.5 Operational Risk Ratios — 98

8.6	Sustainable Growth of Equity	102
8.7	External Liquidity Ratios	102
8.8	Relative Valuation	103
	8.8.1 Price to Sales Ratio	104
	8.8.2 Price to Cash Flow Ratio	105
	8.8.3 Price to Book Value Ratio	105
	8.8.4 Price to Earnings Ratio	106
8.9	Relative Valuation Versus Absolute Valuation	106
	Problems	107

Chapter 9 Absolute Valuation: Discounting Cash Flows — 108

9.1	Growth Rate Calculations	109
9.2	Historical Relationships: Income Statement	110
9.3	Historical Relationships: Balance Sheet	113
9.4	Future Pro-forma Statements for DCF Analysis	118
9.5	Costs of Capital: $WACC$ and Others	119
9.6	Hypothetical Demanded Rate of Return: No Debt	124
9.7	Discounted Cash Flow (DCF) Techniques	125
9.8	Scenario Analyses: $WACC$ and Growth of FCFs Impact Enterprise Value	130
	Problems	133

Chapter 10 Earnings Multiplier Model — 135

10.1	Developing the Model	135
10.2	Comparative Statics	137
	10.2.1 Impact of Initial Equity, Eq_0	138
	10.2.2 Impact of Equity Holders' Demanded Rate of Return, r^E	138
	10.2.3 Impact of Equity Holders' ROE	139
	10.2.4 Impact of Plowback Ratio, b	139
	Problems	141

Part IV Bond Theory — 143

Chapter 11 Introduction to Bonds — 145

11.1	Time-lines and Basics	147
11.2	Sources of Bond Return	148
11.3	Promised Cash Flows Versus Expected Cash Flows	149

11.4	Yield to Maturity, Nominal Yield, Current Yield	150
11.5	Price-yield Curve	151
	Problems	153

Chapter 12 March to Maturity and Malkiel Results 155

12.1	March to Maturity	155
12.2	Malkiel Results	158
	12.2.1 Impact of Yield to Maturity, y	158
	12.2.2 Impact of Coupon Rate	162
	12.2.3 Impact of Time to Maturity, T	163
	Problems	165

Chapter 13 Approximations to Price-yield Relations 166

13.1	Macaulay Duration and Modified Duration	166
13.2	Convexity	168
13.3	Price-yield Approximations	170
13.4	Effective Duration and Effective Convexity	172
13.5	Empirical Duration	174
13.6	Other Price-yield Metrics	175
	Problems	175

Chapter 14 Pricing Bonds Between Coupon Dates 177

14.1	A New Time-line	177
14.2	Dirty Price	178
14.3	Accrued Interest and Clean Price	180
14.4	Theoretical Accrued Interest	185
	Problems	186

Chapter 15 Rate and Yield Metrics 187

15.1	Spot Rates	187
15.2	Forward Rates	190
	15.2.1 Single Period Forward Rates	190
	15.2.2 Multi-period Forward Rates	192
15.3	Realized Holding Period Yield	194
15.4	Yield to Worst	198
15.5	Other Yield Metrics	199
	Problems	201

Part V Options   203

Chapter 16 Expiration Date Option Payoffs and Profits   205

  16.1 Option Basics   205

  16.2 Long Call Payoff and Profit at Expiration   206

  16.3 Short Call Payoff and Profit at Expiration   208

  16.4 Long Put Payoff and Profit at Expiration   210

  16.5 Short Put Payoff and Profit at Expiration   212

  16.6 Expiration Payoffs of Portfolios Containing Options   214

   16.6.1 Protective Put   214

   16.6.2 Covered Call   215

   16.6.3 Long Straddle   216

   16.6.4 Short Straddle   217

   16.6.5 Collar   218

  16.7 Put-Call Spot Parity   220

  Problems   222

Chapter 17 Option Valuation: Single Period Binomial Model   224

  17.1 Arbitrage and Bounds on Option Premiums   224

   17.1.1 A European Call Lower Bound   224

   17.1.2 A European Call Upper Bound   225

   17.1.3 Summary of Bounds on European Options   226

  17.2 Binomial Stock Price Model   227

   17.2.1 Call Value via Delta Hedge   228

   17.2.2 Put Value via Delta Hedge   231

   17.2.3 Call Replicating Portfolio   232

   17.2.4 Put Replicating Portfolio   235

   17.2.5 Risk-Neutral Valuation   236

   17.2.6 Comparative Statics   239

  Problems   245

Chapter 18 Option Valuation: Multi-period Model   248

  18.1 Two-period Binomial Stock Price Model   248

  18.2 Two-period Binomial Option Pricing Model   250

  18.3 Multi-period Binomial Stock Price Model   251

  18.4 Multi-period Binomial Option Pricing Model   252

  Problems   254

Chapter 19 American Binomial Option Pricing Model — 257
  19.1 American Call Option Valuation — 257
  19.2 American Put Option Valuation — 258
  19.3 Summary of American Option Valuation — 258
  19.4 American Put Valuation: An Example — 259
  19.5 Impact of Ability to Exercise Early — 259
    19.5.1 Value Creation — 259
    19.5.2 Digging Deeper into Timing — 264
    19.5.3 Probability of Exercise as Time Passes — 267
  Problems — 268

Chapter 20 Option Valuation: Black-Scholes Model — 271
  20.1 European Call Option Value — 272
  20.2 European Put Option Value — 273
  20.3 Comparative Statics — 276
  Problems — 282

Solutions to Selected End-of-chapter Problems — 285
References and Suggested Readings — 319
Index — 323

PART I   The Basics

In chapter 1 we begin by reviewing how values of cash flows vary through time. We develop timelines used throughout the text and define different types of variables. We show how the principle of value additivity can be used to value packages of cash flows, giving additional consideration to specials cases such as annuities and perpetuities.

In chapter 2 we review different types of calculations used to measure historical performances of assets. Metrics for both risk and reward are introduced. we show how to perform such calculations for individual assets as well as portfolios of assets. We also consider discrete returns versus continuously compounded returns. Finally, the impact of dividend reinvestment is addressed.

CHAPTER 1

Review of Financial Basics

This chapter reviews introductory financial concepts. We first examine how one values cash flows at different points in time. For such calculations, we need an investor's demanded (or equivalently, required) rate of return, the so-called discount rate. In this chapter, we treat these rates as exogenous, i.e., as given. In a later chapter, we explore how to derive discount rates, which depend critically on the perceived riskiness of cash flows being discounted.

1.1 Timelines, Stock Variables and Flow Variables

This book shows several timelines. Figure 1.1 shows part of one, starting at the current date ($t = 0$) and ending T years from now, date T. Each vertical hash mark corresponds to a date, t, in years. Unless otherwise noted, today's date (present time) is always $t = 0$. Periods of time (in years) are denoted below the timeline as needed, in between the hash marks, as period t begins at date $t-1$ and ends at date t. Figure 1.2 shows a more complete timeline.

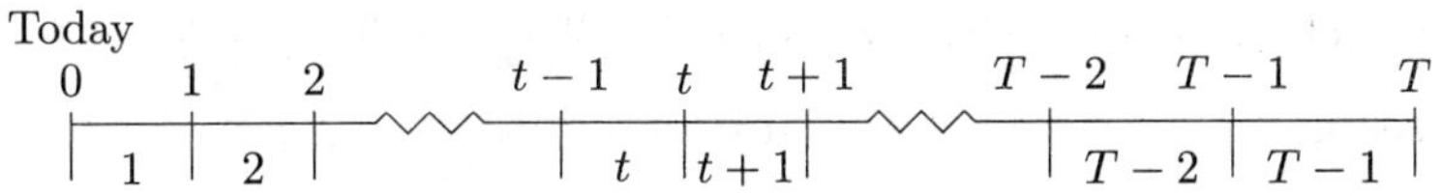

Figure 1.1 Basic timeline for T years, starting with today, $t = 0$

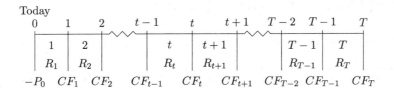

Figure 1.2 Basic timeline, including stock variables and flow variables

Variables are shown below the timeline. Cash flows (CF_t), indexed with dates via subscripts, are positive if received and negative if paid. (Note that $-P_0$ indicates purchase of a security at $t = 0$ for a current price of P_0.) Gross returns (R_t, defined later) are indexed with periods via subscripts.

Future cash flows are unknown except for a risk-free asset. Though we note them simply CF_t, $t > 0$, we should consider them as expected cash flows. For a risk-free asset, expected cash flows equal **promised cash flows**. For risky assets with promised cash flows (e.g., risky bonds), **expected cash flows** are less than those promised, i.e., $E[CF_t] = \int_0^{CF_t^P} f(x)x\,dx < CF_t^P$, where $f(x)$ is the density function of CF_t and CF_t^P is the promised cash flow at date t. As $f(x)$ places positive probability on weights of cash flows less than that promised, then $E[CF_t] < CF_t^P$.

In order to understand why some variables are shown directly below a hash mark (corresponding to a date) while others are between them (corresponding to a period), we need to understand the difference between a **stock variable** and a **flow variable**. The former is measured at a specific *point in time*, i.e., at a date. One can think of this metric as one taken via still photograph. In contrast, the latter is measured *over a duration of time*, i.e., for a period. One can think of this metric as one taken via video. As examples, consider a country's debt versus its budget deficit. Debt is a stock variable, measuring the cumulative net borrowing at a point in time. In contrast, deficit is a flow variable, measuring the change in debt over a duration of time (e.g., for a year). In some sense, we can "convert" stock variables to flow variables by taking differences. As flow variables are measured per period of time, or $/\Delta$ time, then the difference a stock variable at two different points in time "looks like" a flow variable, i.e., $\frac{\Delta \text{ stock variable}}{\Delta \text{ time}}$. To continue our example, the difference in the USA's debt between end of year t and end of year $t-1$, which coincides with period t, is $\frac{\text{debt}_t(\$) - \text{debt}_{t-1}(\$)}{\text{end year}_t - \text{end year}_{t-1}} = \frac{\text{debt}_t(\$) - \text{debt}_{t-1}(\$)}{1\ \text{year}_t}$. This has dimensions of $\frac{\$}{\text{year}_t}$, and by definition equals the deficit for year_t. So referring to figure 1.2, cash flows are stock variables, received at a particular date, and returns are flow variables, corresponding to a particular period or duration of time.[1]

1.2 Moving Cash Flows Through Time

Consider a cash flow received one year from now, CF_1. Given an investor's de-

---

[1] Regarding common variables, present value (PV_0), time 1 value (V_1), time 2 equity value (Eq_2), time $t-1$ asset value (A_{t-1}), time t cash flow (CF_t), time $t+1$ weight of asset i (w_{t+1}^i) and time T future value (FV_T) are stock variables. Period 1 rate of return (r_1), period 2 gross return (R_2), period $t+1$ sales (S_{t+1}) and period $T-1$ net income (NI_{T-1}) are flow variables. These variables will be soon defined.

manded rate of return (i.e., her discount rate) of $r > 0$, then she calculates the present value ($t = 0$) of CF_1 as $PV_0 = \frac{CF_1}{1+r}$, where PV_0 is the **present value** of CF_1, as in figure 1.3.

```
              Today
                0                                  1
                |——————————————————————————————————|
                                                  CF₁
                                 1/(1+r)¹
        PV₀ = CF₁/(1+r)¹
```

Figure 1.3 Discounting a single cash flow received 1 year from today

As $r > 0$, then a dollar received a year from today is worth less than a dollar today. Why is $PV_0 < CF_1$? As an investor is impatient, she would rather spend a dollar today versus a dollar a year from now. Equivalently, a potential saver of capital must be induced to save (invest) capital for a year (i.e., paid a rate of return of $r > 0$) versus consuming (spending) it today.

Now consider a single cash flow, CF_2, received two years from today. Analogous to before, our investor's value one year prior to receipt of CF_2 (i.e., value at $t = 1$) is $V_1 = \frac{CF_2}{1+r} < CF_2$. From $PV_0 = \frac{V_1}{1+r}$, then $PV_0 = \frac{CF_2}{(1+r)^2}$, as shown in figure 1.4.

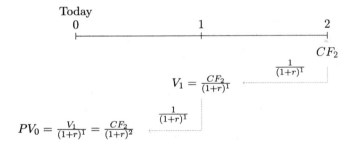

Figure 1.4 Discounting a single cash flow received 2 years from today

Analogously, for any CF_t, then $PV_0 = \frac{CF_t}{(1+r)^t} < CF_t$. Reversing the process, we can calculate the **future value** at time t of a given value today, V_0, as follows: $FV_t = V_0(1+r)^t$. In short, as an investor demands a rate of return $r > 0$, then she expects to have a greater value in the future, FV_t, than she has today, or $FV_t > V_0$.

Generalizing, cash flows in different currencies are not *directly* comparable. Analogously, cash flows at different points in time are not *directly* comparable. Just as one may not *directly* add 1 USD plus 1 RMB yielding "2" of something, one may not *directly* add 1 USD received at $t = 1$ plus 1 USD received at $t = 0$ yielding 2 USD. In the first case, one must convert 1 USD to RMB (approximately 6 RMB) and add it to 1 RMB (yielding approximately 7 RMB). Alternatively, one may convert 1 RMB to USD (approximately 0.17 USD) and add it to 1 USD, yielding approximately 1.17 USD. In either case, the result is the same: 7 RMB is approximately 1.17 USD.

In the second case, one must convert CF_1 to $PV_0 = \frac{CF_1}{(1+r)^1}$ and add it to CF_0, yielding $\frac{CF_1}{(1+r)^1} + CF_0$. Alternatively, one may convert CF_0 to $FV_1 = CF_0(1+r)^1$ and add it to CF_1, yielding $V_1 = CF_0(1+r)^1 + CF_1$. As this is the combined value at time 1, we need to divide it by $(1+r)^1$ in order to compare it to the previous $t = 0$ value calculated. Thus, $PV_0 = \frac{V_1}{(1+r)^1} = \frac{CF_0(1+r)^1 + CF_1}{(1+r)^1} = CF_0 + \frac{CF_1}{(1+r)^1}$, which matches the previous calculation.

The key result of the above is the concept, **value additivity**. Once an investor converts multiple cash flows received at different points in time to a common point in time (i.e., once they are converted to a common basis), then she may add them. It is perfectly analogous to cash flows in multiple currencies. Just as one may add/subtract cash flows in different currencies once they are all converted to a common currency, one may add/subtract cash flows occuring at different times once they are all converted to a common time (i.e., common date). Whereas the "conversion factor" across a geographical border is currency exchange rate, the "conversion factor" across time is the factor $(1+r)^t > 1$. In moving cash flows forward in time, one multiplies by this factor, increasing value. In moving cash flows backward in time, one divides by this factor, decreasing value. Finally, once one has a single converted value at a given point in time for a summation of several values occuring at different points in time, the single collective value can be moved around on the timeline in lieu of moving around individual values of which the collective value is comprised.

1.3 Evenly Spaced Cash Flows Growing at Rate g

Figure 1.5 shows a series of evenly spaced cash flows, each arriving at the end of the respective period, e.g., the first cash flow, CF_1, arrives one period (year) from now. In general, the **intrinsic value** (IV) of a series of T cash flows is the sum of their

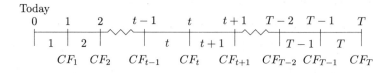

Figure 1.5 Series of evenly spaced cash flows, each at the end of a period

present values, or

$$IV = \sum_{t=1}^{T} \frac{CF_t}{(1+r)^t} = \frac{CF_1}{(1+r)^1} + \frac{CF_2}{(1+r)^2} + \ldots + \frac{CF_T}{(1+r)^T}. \quad (1.1)$$

Let's assume that the first cash flow one period from now is CF_1 and that cash flows grow at constant rate g, where $g < r$.[2] Then the second cash flow, received two periods from now, is $CF_2 = CF_1(1+g)$. Continuing, $CF_3 = CF_2(1+g)$ and so forth. Let's define $Z \equiv \frac{CF_1}{1+g}$. This implies that $CF_t = Z(1+g)^t, \forall t \in 1, 2, \ldots, T$. So

$$IV = \sum_{t=1}^{T} \frac{CF_t}{(1+r)^t} = \frac{Z(1+g)}{(1+r)} + \frac{Z(1+g)^2}{(1+r)^2} + \ldots + \frac{Z(1+g)^T}{(1+r)^T}. \quad (1.2)$$

Let $z \equiv \frac{1+g}{1+r}$. By dividing equation (1.2) by z, then adding and subtacting z^T to the right hand side, equation (1.2) becomes $\frac{IV}{z} = IV + Z(1 - z^T)$. Thus, algebraically solving for IV and replacing z with $\frac{1+g}{1+r}$ and Z with $\frac{CF_1}{1+g}$ yields the following expression for the intrinsic value of a **growing annuity** (T is finite; $g > 0$):

$$IV(\text{Growing Annuity}) = \frac{CF_1}{r-g}\left[1 - \left(\frac{1+g}{1+r}\right)^T\right]. \quad (1.3)$$

In addtion to equation (1.3), consider three special cases. The intrinsic values of an **annuity** (T is finite; $g = 0$), a **growing perpetuity** ($T \to \infty$; $g > 0$), and a **perpetuity** ($T \to \infty$; $g = 0$) are as follows.[3]

$$IV(\text{Annuity}) = \frac{CF}{r}\left[1 - \left(\frac{1}{1+r}\right)^T\right]. \quad (1.4)$$

$$IV(\text{Growing Perpetuity}) = \frac{CF_1}{r-g}. \quad (1.5)$$

$$IV(\text{Perpetuity}) = \frac{CF}{r}. \quad (1.6)$$

For intrinsic values of an annuity and of a perpetuity, no subscript is needed on the cash flow, as all cash flows are the same, given $g = 0$.

Let's drive home a point made earlier. Once cash flows are converted to a single date and added, this single collective value may be evaluated at any other date. In doing so, it is far more convenient to move around in time a single value versus multiple component cash flows. Consider the future value at maturity ($t = T$) of a growing

---

[2]Otherwise, value is unbounded if cash flows last forever, i.e., as $T \to \infty$ as in the case of a growing perpetuity, discussed later.

[3]For the growing perpetuity, as $g < r$, then as $T \to \infty$, $\left(\frac{1+g}{1+r}\right)^T \to 0$.

annuity, shown in figure 1.6. $FV_T = CF_1(1+r)^{T-1} + CF_2(1+r)^{T-2} + ... + CF_{T-1}(1+r)^{T-(T-1)} + CF_T(1+r)^{T-T}$. Dividing by $(1+r)^T$, then $\frac{FV_T}{(1+r)^T} = CF_1(1+r)^{-1} + CF_2(1+r)^{-2} + ... + CF_{T-1}(1+r)^{-(T-1)} + CF_T(1+r)^{-T}$. The right hand side is simply PV_0, so in short, $\frac{FV_T}{(1+r)^T} = PV_0$. As claimed, once we calculate the collective present value of the growing annuity's stream of cash flows, PV_0, we can revalue the entire cash flow stream at maturity via $FV_T = PV_0(1+r)^T$. Running the process in reverse, we can first calculate $FV_T = \frac{CF_1}{r-g}[(1+r)^T - (1+g)^T]$ and then revalue the entire stream via $PV_0 = \frac{FV_T}{(1+r)^T}$.[4]

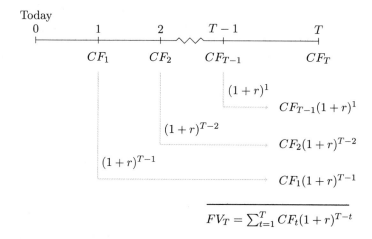

Figure 1.6 **Future value at date T of a series of evenly spaced cash flows**

Problems

1. Today is the first day of 2016. Suppose you win a cake eating game, and you can choose to receive either $10,000$ today or $30,000$ at the end of 2026. Given a discount rate of 10%, which one do you prefer? (Ignore taxes.)

2. You are evaluating a new project. The project has an initial cost of $10,000$, and then generates revenues at the end of the following 2 years of $5,000$ and $6,000$, respectively. If the discount rate is 10%, would you accept this project? (i.e., Is its intrinsic value positive (accept) or negative (reject)?)

3. (*Continue Problem 2*) What discount rate makes the project's intrinsic value equal to zero, i.e., what is the project's internal rate of return (IRR)?

---

[4]The expression for FV_T follows from $PV_0(1+r)^T = \frac{CF_1}{r-g}\left[1 - \frac{(1+g)^T}{(1+r)^T}\right](1+r)^T$. Analogously, $FV_t = PV_0(1+r)^t, \forall t \in \{1, 2, ..., T\}$.

4. You deposit $5,000 into your bank account on the first day of this year. How many years will it take to double your savings if the interest rate is 8%?

5. You plan to save money in a bank for 5 years and hope to have a value of $10,000 5 years from now. How much do you need to deposit at the end of each year to achieve this goal if the bank pays 5% interest rate? (Assume that the $10,000 value includes the final deposit at the end of year 5.)

6. You received an assignment from your boss to value stock A. It paid a $20 dividend yesterday and you believe that the dividend will grow at an annual rate of 5% over the next 5 years. If investors demand a rate of return of 10%, what is its intrinsic value? (Assume that the dividend is paid at the end of each year.)

7. You invest in a special bond with no maturity (i.e., cash flows forever), and it pays a fixed interest coupon of $40 at the end of each year. If the current price of this bond is $1000, what is the discount rate used by investors for this bond?

8. A stock has a current price of $100. The company paid $10 dividend yesterday. Investors expect its dividend to grow at a constant rate each year. If investors require a rate of return for this stock of 12%, what constant growth rate for these dividends is being assumed by investors?

CHAPTER 2

Historical Returns

There are many types of returns in finance. In this chapter we define gross return, rate of return, means (central tendency) and variances (dispersions) of returns using historical data. In the next chapter, we turn to analogous concepts couched in the future.

2.1 Single Period Gross Return and Rate of Return

Gross return, R, or simply **return** is the ratio of cash flows received to capital invested. Per the left half of figure 2.1, consider a single security (e.g., one share of stock) bought one year ago for P_{-1} which pays a cash flow per security (e.g., dividend per share) today of d_0 and immediately afterward is sold for its present *ex-dividend* price (i.e., *post*-dividend, or price excluding the dividend) of P_0. Then the gross return during period 0 is $R_0 = \frac{d_0 + P_0}{P_{-1}}$. Loosely speaking, $R_t = \frac{\text{initial investment}_{t-1} + \text{profit}_t}{\text{initial investment}_{t-1}} = 1 + \frac{\text{profit}_t}{\text{initial investment}_{t-1}}$. **Net return** or **rate of return** equals gross return minus one, or net return$_t = \frac{\text{profit}_t}{\text{initial investment}_{t-1}}$. Generally, for *period t* the gross return, R_t, and net return (rate of return), r_t, in terms of prices per security and cash flows per security shown in the right half of figure 2.1 are

$$R_t = \frac{CF_t + P_t}{P_{t-1}} \quad \text{and} \quad r_t = \frac{CF_t + P_t - P_{t-1}}{P_{t-1}} = \frac{CF_t + P_t}{P_{t-1}} - 1 = R_t - 1. \qquad (2.1)$$

```
                    Today
    -1                0                 t-1                  t
    ├────────────────┤                  ├──────────────────┤
   -P_{-1}         R_0, r_0    d_0     -P_{t-1}     R_t, r_t    CF_t
                              P_0                              P_t
```

Figure 2.1 Single period gross return and rate of return

2.2 Multi-period Historical Returns

Figure 2.2 shows a single security purchased T periods ago with the following cash flows per security (e.g., stock dividends/share) and *ex-post* prices per share, i.e., prices immediately after the cash flow per security is dispensed (e.g., *ex*-dividend price). As

```
           -T      -T+1    -T+2              -2       -1       Today
                                                                 0
           |--------|-------|------ ~ ------|--------|---------|
              R_{-T+1}  R_{-T+2}              R_{-1}   R_0
              CF_{-T+1} CF_{-T+2}           CF_{-2}  CF_{-1}  CF_0
           P_{-T}  P_{-T+1} P_{-T+2}        P_{-2}   P_{-1}   P_0
```

Figure 2.2 Historical timeline for T years, ending with today, $t = 0$

we are dealing with historical data, dates are negative, starting at year $-T$ and ending with today, year 0. At date $-T$, immediately after CF_{-T} is paid (if there exists such a cash flow), an investor makes an initial dollar investment of I^i_{-T} in security i at it's *ex-post* price of P_{-T}. In what follows, we assume **reinvestment of cash flows** (e.g., dividends). For example, given an initial dollar investment of I^i_{-T} in a stock, then the **shares owned** at each date t are as follows.

$$sh^i_{-T} \equiv \frac{I^i_{-T}}{P_{-T}}, \quad \text{and}$$

$$sh^i_t \equiv sh^i_{-T} \prod_{n=-T+1}^{t} \left(1 + \frac{CF^i_n}{P^i_n}\right),$$

$$sh^i_t = sh^i_{t-1} \left(1 + \frac{CF^i_t}{P^i_t}\right), \forall t \in \{-T+1, -T+2, ..., -1, 0\}. \tag{2.2}$$

The first expression for sh^i_t is in terms of exogenous parameters (i.e., cash flows per security and price per security), whereas the second one, a recursive formula for sh^i_t in terms of sh^i_{t-1}, is perhaps more convenient in execution, e.g., in an Excel spreadsheet. So at any given date t after the initial date $-T$, the number of shares owned, sh^i_t, equals the initial number purchased, sh^i_{-T}, plus those subsequently purchased via reinvestment of cash flows generated by the security until date t. With the number of shares determined, then value simply equals the product of shares and price, or

$$V^i_{-T} \equiv \left(P^i_{-T}\right) sh^i_{-T} = I^i_{-T}, \quad \text{and}$$

$$V^i_t \equiv P^i_t \left[sh^i_t\right] = P^i_t \left[sh^i_{-T} \prod_{n=-T+1}^{t} \left(1 + \frac{CF^i_n}{P^i_n}\right)\right] = P^i_t \left[sh^i_{t-1}\left(1 + \frac{CF^i_t}{P^i_t}\right)\right], \tag{2.3}$$

$\forall t \in \{-T+1, -T+2, ..., -1, 0\}$. So the ratio $\frac{sh^i_t}{sh^i_{-T}}$ is the product expression in equation (2.3). Note that if there are no cash flows generated by the security, the ratio $\frac{sh^i_t}{sh^i_{-T}}$ equals one: the shares owned remain constant. With the above definitions, we can rewrite equation (2.1) as[1]

$$R^i_t = \frac{V^i_t}{V^i_{t-1}} \quad \text{and} \quad r^i_t = \frac{V^i_t - V^i_{t-1}}{V^i_{t-1}} = \frac{V^i_t}{V^i_{t-1}} - 1 = R^i_t - 1. \tag{2.4}$$

Consider a stock with the series of dividends per share and prices per share shown in figure 2.3. Suppose an investor purchases \$20 of this stock three periods ago. First,

```
        -3              -2              -1            Today
                                                         0
        |---------------|---------------|---------------|
     d_{-3}=2       d_{-2}=1         d_{-1}=6        d_0=4
               period_{-2}     period_{-1}      period_0
     P_{-3}=10       P_{-2}=11       P_{-1}=9        P_0=12
               R_{-2}, r_{-2}   R_{-1}, r_{-1}    R_0, r_0
```

Figure 2.3 Multi-period cash flows and prices of a security

$I^i_{-3} = \$20$, and the initial number of shares purchased was $sh_{-3} = \frac{20}{10} = 2$ shares. Next per equation (2.2), $sh_{-2} = 2\left[\left(1+\frac{1}{11}\right)\right] = 2.18$ shares, $sh_{-1} = 2\left[\left(1+\frac{1}{11}\right)\left(1+\frac{6}{9}\right)\right] = 3.64$ shares, and $sh_0 = 2\left[\left(1+\frac{1}{11}\right)\left(1+\frac{6}{9}\right)\left(1+\frac{4}{12}\right)\right] = 4.85$ shares. So per equation (2.3), $V_{-3}=20$, $V_{-2}=11(2.18)=24$, $V_{-1}=9(3.64)=32.73$ and $V_0=12(4.85)=58.18$. Finally, per equation (2.4), regarding period returns, $R_{-2} = \frac{24}{20} = 1.20$, $R_{-1} = \frac{32.73}{24} = 1.36$, and $R_0 = \frac{58.18}{32.73} = 1.78$.[2]

2.3 Means and Variances of Historical Returns

Given T periods, we can calculate T different single-period returns. Using index t in the summation sign that follows to reference *periods*, the **arithmetic mean return** is

$$AMR = \frac{1}{T}\sum_{t=-T+1}^{0} R_t = \frac{1}{T}\sum_{t=-T+1}^{0} \frac{CF_t + P_t}{P_{t-1}} = \frac{1}{T}\sum_{t=-T+1}^{0} \frac{V_t}{V_{t-1}}, \quad \text{and} \tag{2.5}$$

$$AMr = \frac{1}{T}\sum_{t=-T+1}^{0} r_t = \frac{1}{T}\sum_{t=-T+1}^{0} \frac{CF_t + P_t}{P_{t-1}} - 1 = \frac{1}{T}\sum_{t=-T+1}^{0} \frac{V_t}{V_{t-1}} - 1. \tag{2.6}$$

Of course, $AMr = AMR - 1$. Another metric for mean multi-period return is the **geometric mean return** (GMR), which solves the following: $V_{-T}(1+GMR)^T = V_0$,

---
[1] Per equation (2.3), $\frac{V^i_t}{V^i_{t-1}} = \frac{P^i_t}{P^i_{t-1}}\left[1 + \frac{CF^i_t}{P^i_t}\right] = \frac{P^i_t + CF^i_t}{P^i_{t-1}}$, consistent with our defintion for gross return per equation (2.1).

[2] Analogously, $r_{-2} = 1.20 - 1 = 0.20$, $r_{-1} = 1.36 - 1 = 0.36$, and $r_0 = 1.78 - 1 = 0.78$.

or[3]

$$GMR = \left(\frac{V_0}{V_{-T}}\right)^{1/T} = \left(\frac{P_0}{P_{-T}}\left[\prod_{n=-T+1}^{0}\left(1+\frac{CF_n}{P_n}\right)\right]\right)^{1/T}, \qquad (2.7)$$

and $GMr = GMR - 1$. Note that while AMr may be calculated directly per equation (2.6), there is no corresponding *direct* calculation for GMr, which can only be calculated via $GMr = GMR - 1$.

In contrast to the AMR, which considers periodic interim security values, GMR does *not*, as GMR only considers the initial value and final value. Also, $GMR < AMR$, as AMR tends to capture volatility of value changes.[4] Regarding usages of AMR versus GMR, some practitioners prefer AMR for expectation of next period return and prefer GMR as an historical metric. As a simple example of how different the two metrics can be, consider two securities, A and B, with the following prices over the past two years: $P^A_{-2} = 10$, $P^A_{-1} = 5$ and $P^A_0 = 10$, while $P^B_{-2} = 10$, $P^B_{-1} = 10$ and $P^B_0 = 10$. For ease of exposition, assume no cash flows for either security A or B during these two periods. As prices of A and B both begin and end at the same level of 10, $GMR^A = GMR^B = \left(\frac{10}{10}\right)^{\frac{1}{2}} = 1$. However, in stark contrast to $GMR^A = GMR^B$, $AMR^A > AMR^B$, as A is more volatile than B, all else equal, or $\left(\frac{10}{5} + \frac{5}{10}\right)/2 = 1.25 = AMR^A > AMR^B = \left(\frac{10}{10} + \frac{10}{10}\right)/2 = 1$.

Holding period return is the multi-period equivalent of gross return.

$$HPR = \frac{V_0}{V_{-T}} = (GMR)^T = \frac{P_0}{P_{-T}}\left[\prod_{n=-T+1}^{0}\left(1+\frac{CF_n}{P_n}\right)\right], \qquad (2.8)$$

and $HPr = HPR - 1$. Continuing with the example shown in figure 2.3, $HPR = \frac{V_0}{V_{-3}} = \frac{58.18}{20} = 2.91$, $GMR = HPR^{1/T} = 2.91^{1/3} = 1.43$, and $GMr = GMR - 1 = 43\%$.

The advantage of GMR versus HPR (and of GMr versus HPr) is that GMR (GMr) normalizes HPR (HPr) by converting it to an *annualized* metric. As a simple numerical example, consider two investments, A and B. Each has an HPR of 1.2, but A was purchased one year ago and B was purchased 10 years ago. Then $(1.2)^{1/1} - 1 = 20\% = GMr^A > GMr^B \approx 2\% = (1.2)^{1/10} - 1$. Though $HPr^A = HPr^B$, A's superior performance is reflected via $GMr^A > GMr^B$, as A required only a fraction of the time relative to B to earn the same HPR.

---

[3]From equation (2.3), $V_0 = P_0 \frac{I_{-T}}{P_{-T}}[\prod_{n=-T+1}^{0}(1+\frac{CF_n}{P_n})]$. Recall that $V_{-T} = I_{-T}$.

[4]The only exception is the trivial case in which each period return, R_t, is exactly the same, R, $\forall t \in \{1, 2, ..., T\}$, in which case $R = AMR = GMR$ and $r = AMr = GMr$.

AMR and *GMR* are metrics of central tendency. In finance, risk-averse investors are also particularly concerned with metrics of dispersion. Using the historical first moment of gross return (*AMR*), the second moment calculation is the **variance** of gross return, $s^2(R)$. Given historical data for security x,[5]

$$s^2(R^x) = \frac{1}{T-1} \sum_{t=-T+1}^{0} (R_t^x - AMR^x)^2$$

$$= s^2(r^x) = \frac{1}{T-1} \sum_{t=-T+1}^{0} (r_t^x - AMr^x)^2 \geqslant 0. \quad (2.9)$$

Variance has dimensions of $(R_t^x)^2$. In order to put variance on the same basis as AMR, which has the same dimension as R_t^x, take the square root of variance to calculate **standard deviation** of return, or $s(R^x) = \sqrt{s^2(R^x)}$. As dispersion of return, $s(R^x)$, is a metric for risk, and as mean return, AMR^x, is a metric for reward, then the **coefficient of variation** of asset x, $CV^x = \frac{s(R^x)}{AMR^x}$, is the ratio of $\frac{\text{risk}}{\text{reward}}$. All else equal, a risk-averse investor would prefer a smaller value.

2.4 Linear Relationship of Two-asset Historical Returns

Prices of risky assets, i.e., those whose returns are not guaranteed with certainty, do not move perfectly in tandem. As we will explore later, the degree to which assets move in tandem (or not) is critical in determining the riskiness of a portfolio. A metric which caputures the degree of linear co-movement of returns between pairs of assets x and y is the **covariance**.

$$s^2(R^x, R^y) = \frac{1}{T-1} \sum_{t=-T+1}^{0} (R_t^x - AMR^x)(R_t^y - AMR^y)$$

$$= \frac{1}{T-1} \sum_{t=-T+1}^{0} R_t^x (R_t^y - AMR^y) = \frac{1}{T-1} \sum_{t=-T+1}^{0} (R_t^x - AMR^x) R_t^y$$

$$= s^2(r^x, r^y) = \frac{1}{T-1} \sum_{t=-T+1}^{0} (r_t^x - AMr^x)(r_t^y - AMr^y)$$

$$= \frac{1}{T-1} \sum_{t=-T+1}^{0} r_t^x (r_t^y - AMr^y) = \frac{1}{T-1} \sum_{t=-T+1}^{0} (r_t^x - AMr^x) r_t^y. \quad (2.10)$$

Of the above array of equations, the third and fourth lines, which utilize rates of return, correspond precisely to the first and second lines, respectively, which utilize

---

[5] Variance is strictly positive except for the trivial case where R_t^x is the same for each period, in which case $R_t^x = AMR^x, \forall t \in \{-T+1, -T+2, ..., 0\}$. In this case, $s^2(R^x) = 0$.

gross returns. As rate of return equals gross return minus one, then $\sigma^2(R) = \sigma^2(r)$.[6] The equivalence between the first and second lines (and respectively, between the third and fourth lines) follows from the definition of AMR.[7]

Covariance of R^x and R^y is positive (negative) if asset values of x and y tend to move in tandem (in opposite directions). The more in tandem or more in opposition the asset values move, the larger is the magnitude of $s^2(R^x, R^y)$. If asset values move relatively linearly independently of one another, $s^2(R^x, R^y)$ is close to zero.[8] While covariance is useful in subsequent calculations, it is somewhat difficult to interpret. As a result, **correlation coefficient** as a stand-alone metric is calculated as

$$r(R^x, R^y) = \frac{s^2(R^x, R^y)}{s(R^x)s(R^y)} = r(r^x, r^y) = \frac{s^2(r^x, r^y)}{s(r^x)s(r^y)} \in [-1, +1]. \tag{2.11}$$

In the hypothetical case where two risky asset values move perfectly linearly in tandem (in opposite directions) over time, $r(R^x, R^y) = +1(-1)$. If asset values move relatively linearly independently of one another, $r(R^x, R^y)$ is close to zero.[9]

2.5 Historical Portfolio Returns

Consider a portfolio P comprised of I assets, each referenced by superscript i. For each asset i, its beginning value for period t is V^i_{t-1}, giving a beginning portfolio value of[10]

$$V^P_{t-1} = \sum_{i=1}^{I} V^i_{t-1}. \tag{2.12}$$

---

[6] Adding a constant to a random variable impacts neither its variance nor its covariance with another random variable.

[7] Note: $\frac{1}{T-1}\sum_{t=-T+1}^{0}(R^x_t - AMR^x)(R^y_t - AMR^y) = \frac{1}{T-1}\sum_{t=-T+1}^{0} R^x_t(R^y_t - AMR^y) - \frac{1}{T-1}\sum_{t=-T+1}^{0} AMR^x(R^y_t - AMR^y)$. In the latter sum, AMR^x is not a function of t and thus can be pulled out of the summation, which is indexed by period t. Finally, this sum equals $\frac{AMR^x}{T-1}\sum_{t=-T+1}^{0}(R^y_t - AMR^y) = 0$, by defintion of AMR^y.

[8] If R^x and R^y move independently of one another, then $s^2(R^x, R^y) = 0$. However, $s^2(R^x, R^y) = 0$ does *not* mean that R^x and R^y are indepdenent of one another.

[9] In a linear regression of R^y on R^x, the metric "goodness of fit", R^2, equals $(r(R^y, R^x))^2$.

[10] We continue to use our definition of value per equation (2.3), which assumes reinvestment of cash flows generated by the security.

Let's define **portfolio weights** for each asset i as follows, where obviously, $\sum_{i=1}^{I} w_{t-1}^i = 1$.[11]

$$w_{t-1}^i \equiv \frac{V_{t-1}^i}{V_{t-1}^P} \quad (2.13)$$

Using asset market values, the weight of each asset i is its fraction of total portfolio value. Next **portfolio gross return** in period t is

$$R_t^P = \frac{V_t^P}{V_{t-1}^P} = \frac{\sum_{i=1}^{I} V_t^i \frac{V_{t-1}^i}{V_{t-1}^i}}{V_{t-1}^P} = \sum_{i=1}^{I} \frac{V_t^i}{V_{t-1}^i} \frac{V_{t-1}^i}{V_{t-1}^P} = \sum_{i=1}^{I} \left(R_t^i\right) w_{t-1}^i, \quad (2.14)$$

as $\frac{V_t^i}{V_{t-1}^i} = R_t^i$ and $\frac{V_{t-1}^i}{V_{t-1}^P} = w_{t-1}^i$. Of course, the **portfolio rate of return** is $r_t^P = R_t^P - 1$. Analogously, portfolio rate of return can also be calculated directly as $r_t^P = \sum_{i=1}^{I} \left(r_t^i\right) w_{t-1}^i$.

Now consider T periods, from dates $-T$ to 0. Analogous to the single asset case, **portfolio holding period return** is[12]

$$HPR^P = \frac{V_0^P}{V_{-T}^P} = \prod_{t=-T+1}^{0} \frac{V_t^P}{V_{t-1}^P} = \prod_{t=-T+1}^{0} R_t^P = \prod_{t=-T+1}^{0} \left[\sum_{i=1}^{I} \left(R_t^i\right) w_{t-1}^i\right]$$

$$= \frac{1}{V_{-T}^P} \sum_{i=1}^{I} V_0^i \frac{V_{-T}^i}{V_{-T}^i} = \sum_{i=1}^{I} \frac{V_0^i}{V_{-T}^i} \frac{V_{-T}^i}{V_{-T}^P} = \sum_{i=1}^{I} \left(HPR^i\right) w_{-T}^i, \quad (2.15)$$

as $\frac{V_0^i}{V_{-T}^i} = HPR^i$ and $\frac{V_{-T}^i}{V_{-T}^P} = w_{-T}^i$. On the first line above, HPR^P is defined as the ratio of ending portfolio value to initial value, which also equals the product of all period portfolio gross returns. On the second line, we see that it also equals the weighted average of individual asset holding period returns, where the weight for each asset is its initial fractional value relative to the entire portfolio value. Thus, the HPR^P can be calculated either via aggregating at the portfolio level first (by calculating each period's R_t^P) followed by aggregating over time (the first line above) or via aggregating all time periods at the individual asset level first (by calculating each asset's HPR^i) followed by aggregating at the asset level (the second line above).

Consistent with other calculations, $GMR^P = (HPR^P)^{1/T}$, $GMr^P = GPR^P - 1$,

---

[11] Dividing equation (2.12) by V_{t-1}^P, then $1 = \frac{\sum_{i=1}^{I} V_{t-1}^i}{V_{t-1}^P} = \sum_{i=1}^{I} \frac{V_{t-1}^i}{V_{t-1}^P} = \sum_{i=1}^{I} w_{t-1}^i$. We can pull V_{t-1}^P into the summation indexed by i since V_{t-1}^P is *not* a function of index i. Analogously, any factor not indexed by i that is inside the summation may be pulled outside. We take advantage of such manipulations later as well.

[12] HPR^P can also be written as $\sum_{i=1}^{I} \left[\prod_{t=-T+1}^{0} \left(R_t^i\right) w_t^i\right]$.

and $HPr^P = HPR^P - 1$.[13] Next, portfolio AMR is[14]

$$AMR^P = \frac{1}{T}\sum_{t=-T+1}^{0} R_t^P = \frac{1}{T}\sum_{t=-T+1}^{0}\frac{V_t^P}{V_{t-1}^P} = \frac{1}{T}\sum_{t=-T+1}^{0}\frac{\sum_{i=1}^{I} V_t^i \frac{V_{t-1}^i}{V_{t-1}^i}}{V_{t-1}^P}$$

$$= \frac{1}{T}\sum_{t=-T+1}^{0}\left[\sum_{i=1}^{I}\left(R_t^i\right) w_{t-1}^i\right], \qquad (2.16)$$

and $AMr^P = AMR^P - 1$.[15] Finally, **portfolio variance** and **portfolio standard deviation** of gross return are calculated, respectively, as $s^2(R^P) = \frac{1}{T-1}\sum_{t=-T+1}^{0}(R_t^P - AMR^P)^2$ and $s(R^P) = \sqrt{s^2(R^P)}$.[16] Of course, $s^2(r^P) = s^2(R^P)$ and $s(r^P) = s(R^P)$, as $r^P = R^P - 1$.

2.6 Continuously Compounded Returns

Until now we have calculated returns on a discrete basis per equations (2.1) and (2.4). Often in finance we use continuously compounded returns, where $P_t + CF_t = V_t = P_{t-1}e^{r_t|cc} = V_{t-1}e^{r_t|cc}$. Rearranging,

$$r_t|cc = \log\left(\frac{CF_t + P_t}{P_{t-1}}\right) = \log\left(\frac{V_t}{V_{t-1}}\right) \text{ and}$$

$$R_t|cc = 1 + \log\left(\frac{CF_t + P_t}{P_{t-1}}\right) = 1 + \log\left(\frac{V_t}{V_{t-1}}\right) = 1 + r_t|cc. \qquad (2.17)$$

Using the above recursively, $V_0 = V_{-T}(e^{r_{-T+1}|cc})(e^{r_{-T+2}|cc})\ldots(e^{r_0|cc})$. As $AMr|cc = \frac{1}{T}\sum_{-T+1}^{0} r_t|cc = \ln(\frac{V_0}{V_{-T}})/T$, then $V_0 = V_{-T}e^{T(AMr|cc)}$. Interestingly, $AMr|cc$ can be calculated from just two data points, V_0 and V_{-T}. This is in stark contrast to AMr of discrete returns, where all interim security values must be used. Next, from $HPR = \frac{V_0}{V_{-T}}$, then it can also be written as $HPR = e^{T(AMr|cc)}$.[17] Finally, $s^2(r|cc)$

---

[13] Directly, $HPr^P = \frac{V_0^P}{V_{-T}^P} - 1 = \prod_{t=-T+1}^{0}\left[\frac{V_t^P}{V_{t-1}^P}\right] - 1 = \sum_{i=1}^{I}\left(HPr^i\right)w_{-T}^i$.

[14] AMR^P also equals $\frac{1}{T}\sum_{i=1}^{I}\left[\sum_{t=-T+1}^{0}\left(R_t^i\right) w_{t-1}^i\right]$.

[15] In contrast to the portfolio HPR calculation, it makes little sense to aggregate across time and then across assets in calculating portfolio AMR. One should aggregate across assets and then through time. The key difference is the final expression of equation (2.15), which contains w_{-T}^i, versus that of equation (2.16), which contains w_{t-1}^i. In calculating portfolio HPR, w_{-T}^i is *independent* of index t, so it is calculated just once, at date $-T$. In contrast, if one were to choose to calculate portfolio AMR via time aggregation at the asset level followed by aggregation aross assets, w_{t-1}^i is *dependent* on index t, so it must recalculated for each period t.

[16] Equivalently, $s^2(r^P) = \frac{1}{T-1}\sum_{t=-T+1}^{0}(r_t^P - AMr^P)^2$ and $s(r^P) = \sqrt{s^2(r^P)}$.

[17] As before, $HPr = HPR - 1$, $GMR = (HPR)^{1/T}$, and $GMr = GMR - 1$.

$= \frac{1}{T-1}\sum_{-T+1}^{0}(r_t|cc - AMr|cc)^2$, $s^2(r^x, r^y|cc) = \frac{1}{T-1}\sum_{-T+1}^{0}(r_t^x|cc - AMr^x|cc)(r_t^y|cc - AMr^y|cc)$, and $r(r^x, r^y|cc) = \frac{s^2(r^x,r^y|cc)}{s(r^x|cc)s(r^y|cc)}$.

Consider again the example in figure 2.3. For continuously compounded returns, $r_{-2} = \log(\frac{1+11}{10}) = 18.23\%$, $r_{-1} = \log(\frac{6+9}{11}) = 31.02\%$, and $r_0 = \log(\frac{4+12}{9}) = 57.54\%$. Note that $r_t|cc < r_t, \forall t \in \{-2, -1, 0\}$, which implies that $AMr|cc = 35.59\% < 44.71\% = AMr$. Finally, $s(r|cc) = 20.0\% < 29.8\% = s(r)$.

2.7 Continuously Compounded Historical Portfolio Returns

From $V_{t-1}^P = \sum_{i=1}^{I} V_{t-1}^i = \sum_{i=1}^{I} w^i V_{t-1}^P$ and $r_t|cc = \log(\frac{V_t}{V_{t-1}})$, then

$$r_t^P|cc = \log\left(\frac{V_t^P}{V_{t-1}^P}\right) = \log\left(\frac{\sum_{i=1}^{I} V_t^i}{V_{t-1}^P}\right) = \log\left(\frac{\sum_{i=1}^{I} V_{t-1}^i e^{r_t^i|cc}}{V_{t-1}^P}\right)$$

$$= \log\left(\frac{\sum_{i=1}^{I} w_{t-1}^i V_{t-1}^P e^{r_t^i|cc}}{V_{t-1}^P}\right) = \log\left(\sum_{i=1}^{I} w_{t-1}^i e^{r_t^i|cc}\right). \quad (2.18)$$

Analogous to the single asset case, $V_0^P = V_{-T}^P e^{T(AMr^P|cc)}$ and $HPR^P = e^{T(AMr^P|cc)}$. Also, $s^2(r^P|cc) = \frac{1}{T-1}\sum_{t=-T+1}^{0}(r_t^P|cc - AMr^P|cc)^2$.

2.8 Returns When Security Cash Flows Are Not Reinvested

In this chapter, we have assumed reinvestment of interim cash flows generated by a security, e.g., dividends generated by a stock. However, if they are *not* reinvested, then value bleeds offs, and some types of returns are lower than those previously calculated. Equation (2.1) remains the same: $R_t = \frac{CF_t + P_t}{P_{t-1}}$ and $r_t = R_t - 1$, for all periods $t \in \{-T+1, -T+2, ..., -1, 0\}$. However, equation (2.2) is no longer valid, as the product term becomes 1; if there is no reinvestment, then the number of shares never changes and always equals the initial value. So $sh_{-T}^i = \frac{I_{-T}^i}{P_{-T}} = sh_t^i|NR$, $\forall t \in \{-T+1, -T+2, ..., -1, 0\}$, where NR stands for "non-reinvestment". Also, equation (2.3) can no longer be used to calculate returns. While $V_t^i = P_t^i[sh_t^i] = P_t^i[sh_{-T}^i]$ still captures value of investment at any time t, it fails to recognize that value bleeds off when cash flows are not reinvested. So $R_t|NR = R_t = \frac{CF_t + P_t}{P_{t-1}}$ is still valid, but $R_t|NR \neq \frac{V_t}{V_{t-1}}$.

One metric for central tendency, AMR, can still be used as was previously done when we considered reinvestment of cash flows. As before,

$$AMR|NR = \frac{1}{T}\sum_{t=-T+1}^{0} R_t = \frac{1}{T}\sum_{t=-T+1}^{0} \frac{CF_t + P_t}{P_{t-1}}, \quad (2.19)$$

and $AMr|NR = AMR|NR - 1$. However, $AMR|NR \neq \frac{1}{T}\sum_{t=-T+1}^{0}\frac{V_t}{V_{t-1}}$. The reason why AMR remains valid even when cash flows are not reinvested is that it utilizes each period's return, which is independent of size of investment, i.e., of number of shares owned. So in some sense, value is "reset" in each period's calculation. Per equation (2.1), an individual period return includes the cash flow, even though that cash flow may be subsequently consumed or invested elsewhere. Next, the metric of dispersion corresponding to AMR, variance of return (equation (2.9)), can also be used in the non-reinvestment case. Additionally, equations (2.10) and (2.11) for covariance and correlation coefficient between pairs of asset returns, respectively, are still valid.

While AMR remains valid, another metric for centrial tendency, GMR, does not remain valid when cash flows are not reinvested. (As $HPR = GMR^{1/T}$, then HPR also becomes invalid.) As previously defined in equation (2.7), GMR assumes no leakage of value, so it is unable to account for the step drop in value each time a cash flow is dispensed. One way to handle this leakage of value in a calculation similar to GMR (and hence, similar to $HPR = GMR^T$) is to ignore the time value of money for interim cash flows received due to security ownership. From the perspective that these cash flows do not subsequently contribute to value creation with respect to investment in the security that generates them, then one option is to treat them as if they were received at the end of the holding period, i.e., today. By "changing" their timing to today's date, then they will have had no opportunity to generate additional value as of today. So let's define **holding period return given non-reinvestment** as the solution to $P_{-T}(HPR|NR) = (\sum_{t=-T+1}^{0} CF_t) + P_0$, or

$$HPR|NR = \frac{(\sum_{t=-T+1}^{0} CF_t) + P_0}{P_{-T}}, \qquad (2.20)$$

and $HPr|NR = HPR|NR - 1$. Thus, the **geometric mean rate of return given non-reinvestment** is $GMR|NR = (HPR|NR)^{1/T}$, and $GMr|NR = GMR|NR - 1$. Again, equation (2.20) treats all interim security cash flows as if they were received at the end of the evaluation period, today ($t = 0$).[18] Finally, due to leakage of value, $HPR|NR < HPR$, $HPr|NR < HPr$, $GMR|NR < GMR$, and $GMr|NR < GMr$.

Continuing with the example in figure 2.3, $HPR|NR = \frac{(\sum_{t=-T+1}^{0} CF_t)+P_0}{P_{-T}} = \frac{(1+6+4)+12}{10} = 2.30$, $GMR|NR = (HPR|NR)^{1/T} = 2.3^{1/3} = 1.32$, and $GMr|NR = GMR|NR - 1 = 32\%$. Note that $2.30 = HPR|NR < HPR = 2.91$ and $32\% =$

---

[18]It would be inappropriate to use an internal rate of return type of calculation, as this implicitly assumes reinvestment of cash flows at a reinvestment rate of IRR. Consider this: $P_{-T} = \sum_{t=-T+1}^{-1} \frac{(CF_t)}{(1+IRR)^t} + \frac{P_0+CF_0}{(1+IRR)^T}$. Comparing this to $P_{-T} = \frac{(\sum_{t=-T+1}^{0} CF_t)+P_0}{(1+GMr^{NR})^T}$, it is obvious that $IRR > GMr^{NR}$, as IRR mistakenly overstates the security's return by implicitly assuming reinvestement of interim cash flows.

2.9 Continuously Compounded Returns if Nonreinvestment

Regarding continuous compounding, $r_t|(NR,cc) = r_t|cc$, analogous to the discrete case where non-reinvestment of interim cash flows does not impact single-period returns. Thus, it follows that $AMr|(NR,cc) = AMr|cc = \frac{1}{T}\sum_{-T+1}^{0} r_t|cc$, but $AMr|(NR,cc) \neq \ln(\frac{V_0}{V_{-T}})/T$ due to leakage of value.[19] Next, we can define an **average continuously compounded return given nonreinvestment** as[20]

$$\bar{r}|(NR,cc) \equiv \frac{\log(HPR|NR)}{T} = \frac{1}{T}\log\left(\frac{\left(\sum_{t=-T+1}^{0} CF_t\right) + P_0}{P_{-T}}\right). \quad (2.21)$$

So $\bar{r}|(NR,cc) < AMr|(NR,cc) = AMr|cc$.[21]

For a portfolio, $AMr^P|(NR,cc) = AMr^P|cc = \frac{1}{T}\sum_{t=-T+1}^{0} r_t^P|cc$, but $AMr^P|(NR,cc) \neq \ln(\frac{V_0^P}{V_{-T}^P})/T$ due to leakage of value.

Finally, $s^2(r^P|NR,cc) = s^2(r^P|cc)$ and $\bar{r}^P|(NR,cc) = \frac{\log(HPR^P|NR)}{T} = \frac{1}{T}\log\left(\frac{\sum_{i=1}^{I}(\sum_{t=-T+1}^{0} CF_t^i) + P_0^i}{\sum_{i=1}^{I} P_{-T}^i}\right)$.

Considering again the example in figure 2.3, $\bar{r}|(NR,cc) = \log(\frac{1+6+4+12}{10})/3 = 27.76\%$, which, due to leakage of value, is less than $AMr|(NR,cc) = AMr|cc = 35.59\%$. In figure 2.4, we summarize metrics related to single-period rates of return (or net returns) from the example in figure 2.3.

This chapter has focused on metrics for historical means and variances of returns. In the next chapter, we will consider metrics that quantify future returns, i.e., expected means and variances.

---

[19] So as in analogous discrete cases, $s^2(r|NR,cc) = s^2(r|cc)$, $s^2(r^x, r^y|NR,cc) = s^2(r^x, r^y|cc)$, and $r(r^x, r^y|NR,cc) = r(r^x, r^y|cc)$.

[20] This average return solves the following: $(\sum_{-T+1}^{0} CF_t) + P_0 = P_{-T}e^{T(\bar{r}|NR,cc)}$.

[21] While concepts of HPR and GMR are impacted by reinvestment of interim cash flows, they are distinct from whether or not returns are calculated discretely or compounded continuously.

Metric	Calculation	Value
Discrete Returns		
AMr	$= \frac{1}{T}\sum_{-T+1}^{0} r_t = \frac{1}{T}\sum_{-T+1}^{0} \frac{CF_t + P_t}{P_{t-1}} - 1$	44.71%
$AMr\|NR$	$= \frac{1}{T}\sum_{-T+1}^{0} r_t = \frac{1}{T}\sum_{-T+1}^{0} \frac{CF_t + P_t}{P_{t-1}} - 1$	44.71%
Continuously Compounded Returns		
$AMr\|cc$	$= \frac{1}{T}\sum_{-T+1}^{0} r_t\|cc = \frac{1}{T}\sum_{-T+1}^{0} \log\left(\frac{CF_t + P_t}{P_{t-1}}\right)$	35.59%
$AMr\|(NR, cc)$	$= \frac{1}{T}\sum_{-T+1}^{0} r_t\|cc = \frac{1}{T}\sum_{-T+1}^{0} \log\left(\frac{CF_t + P_t}{P_{t-1}}\right)$	35.59%
$\bar{r}\|(NR, cc)$	$= \frac{1}{T}\log\left(\frac{(\sum_{-T+1}^{0} CF_t) + P_0}{P_{-T}}\right)$	27.76%
Geometric Mean Returns		
GMr	$HPR^{\frac{1}{T}} - 1 = \left(\frac{V_0}{V_{-T}}\right)^{\frac{1}{T}} - 1$	42.75%
$GMr\|NR$	$\left(\frac{(\sum_{-T+1}^{0} CF_t) + P_0}{P_{-T}}\right)^{\frac{1}{T}} - 1$	32.00%
Dispersions of Returns		
$s(r)$	$= \sqrt{\frac{1}{T}\sum_{-T+1}^{0}(r_t - AMr)^2}$	29.8%
$s(r\|NR)$	$= \sqrt{\frac{1}{T}\sum_{-T+1}^{0}(r_t - AMr\|NR)^2}$	29.8%
$s(r\|cc)$	$= \sqrt{\frac{1}{T}\sum_{-T+1}^{0}(r_t\|cc - AMr\|cc)^2}$	20.0%
$s(r\|NR, cc)$	$= \sqrt{\frac{1}{T}\sum_{-T+1}^{0}(r_t\|cc - AMr\|NR, cc)^2}$	20.0%

Figure 2.4 Summary calculations of example given in figure 2.3

Problems

Unless otherwise noted, assume reinvestment of interim cash flows.

1. A stock has a current price of $100 and pays a dividend of $5 at the end of each year. If you bought this stock at $95 last year and sell it now, what is your holding period return and yield?

2. (*Continue Problem 1*) If you bought this stock for $98 three years ago and sell it now, what is your holding period return and yield?

3. A stock has an historical price path as follows: $P_{-3} = \$20, P_{-2} = \$25, P_{-1} = \$10, P_0 = \$30$. If you bought this stock 3 years ago, calculate each single period rate of

return. Assume that the stock paid no dividends during this time.

4. (*Continue Problem 3*) What's your arithmetic mean rate of return and geometric mean yield?

5. (*Continue Problem 3*) What's the variance and standard deviation of the return of this stock?

6. There are two assets X and Y, and their historical rate of return data are shown in the following table:

Period	r^x	r^y
-5	$+10\%$	$+20\%$
-4	-15%	-20%
-3	$+20\%$	-10%
-2	$+25\%$	$+30\%$
-1	-30%	-20%
0	$+20\%$	$+60\%$

Calculate the two assets' arithmetic mean yields, AMr^x and AMr^y, their standard deviations of returns, $s(r^x)$ and $s(r^y)$, the covariance of their returns, $s^2(r^x, r^y)$, and the correlation coefficient between their returns, $r(r^x, r^y)$.

7. A portfolio is comprised of three assets A, B and C. The portfolio is comprised of 2 shares of A, 1 share of B and 3 shares of C. Their prices in the past are as follows (assume no interim cash flows).

Year	P^A	P^B	P^C
-2	5	5	5
-1	6	4	4.33
0	7.5	8	3

For each period, calculate the weights of the three assets in the portfolio and their net returns.

8. (*Continue Problem 7*) Using previous answers, calculate the portfolio's net return in each period.

9. (*Continue Problem 7*) Using previous answers, calculate the portfolio's geometric net return.

10. (*Continue Problem 7*) Use another method to calculate the portfolio's geometric period net return. (Hint: calculate each asset's HPR first.)

11. Two years ago, you invested $15 in Stock A, $20 in Stock B and $15 in Stock C. Each stock has an annual year-end dividend payment. Then you used these stocks to construct a portfolio. The three stocks' historical ex-dividend prices and dividend payments are shown in the table below.

Year	P^A	P^B	P^C	d^A	d^B	d^C
−2	5	4	3	3	2	1
−1	10	8	2	5	6	1
0	4	10	6	1	2	4

Based on these data, for each stock, calculate their gross returns, shares owned on each date, HPR, HPr, GMR, GMr, AMR, AMr, $s^2(R)$ and $s(R)$. Then calculate the same values excluding shares owned for the portfolio. (Hint: as for calculations of the portfolio returns, you can calculate portfolio values on each date first.)

12. (*Continue Problem 11*) Assume there is no reinvestment of the interim cash flows, calculate the weights of each stock (on date −2 and date −1) and the values required in Problem 11.

PART II Risk, Reward, Portfolio Theory and Capital Market Equilibrium

In chapter 3 we begin by reviewing how future asset returns can be modeled via random variables. We show how creating portfolios of assets via diversification reduces risk. Specifically, combining risky assets whose correlations of returns are imperfect reduces risk.

In chapter 4 we review the portfolio work of Harry Markowitz. We identify the optimal investment opportunity set, i.e., the combinations of assets that maximize expected return for a given level of acceptable risk. Introducing investor preferences over risk and reward, we can then identify an individual investor's optimal portfolio.

In chapter 5 we introduce a risk-free asset into the investment opportunity set, resulting in the capital market line. Using the market model, we then give an intuitive development of the security market line. The similarities and differences of the capital market line and security market line are discussed.

Finally in chapter 6 we explore the arbitrage pricing theory. After sketching a development of the model, we give detailed simple examples of its implementation.

CHAPTER 3

Future (Next Period) Return

In the previous chapter, we examined the past. Now we look forward, where calculations are more interesting: investors compete for future risk-adjusted returns. Our beliefs regarding the future are modeled via probability distributions of random variables representing asset returns. We show how to estimate means and variances of returns during the next period for not only individual assets, but also portfolios of assets.

3.1 Future (Next Period) Return for a Single Asset

For an asset x, consider an investor's belief regarding the **cumulative probability distribution function**, or simply distribution, of next period's gross return, $R^x \in [\underline{R^x}, \overline{R^x}]$, of $F_x(z) \equiv Pr(R^x \leqslant z)$.[1] For simplicity, further assume that $F_x(z)$ is continuous such that its derivative $f_x(z) = \frac{dF_x(z)}{dz}$, the **probability density function**, or simply density, exists and is positive $\forall R^x \in [\underline{R^x}, \overline{R^x}]$. So $F_x(z)$ is strictly increasing over its support, $[\underline{R^x}, \overline{R^x}]$. Figure 3.1 shows an example, the standard normal distribution, where $(\mu, \sigma^2) = (0, 1)$, defined on support $R^x \in \Re$.

3.2 Expectation and Variance of Future Return

Next period's **expected gross return** and **variance of gross return** are, respectively,

$$E[R^x] = \mu(R^x) = \int_{z=\underline{R^x}}^{z=\overline{R^x}} f_x(z)z\,dz \quad \text{and}$$

$$\sigma^2(R^x) = \int_{z=\underline{R^x}}^{z=\overline{R^x}} f_x(z)(z - E[R^x])^2\,dz. \tag{3.1}$$

---

[1] Equivalently, we could model rate of return, $r^x \in [\underline{r^x}, \overline{r^x}]$, where $\underline{r^x} = \underline{R^x} - 1$ and $\overline{r^x} = \overline{R^x} - 1$, using the same $F_x(z) \equiv Pr(r^x \leqslant z - 1)$.

Comparable to the historical case, **standard deviation** of gross return is $\sigma(R^x) = \sqrt{\sigma^2(R^x)}$.[2]

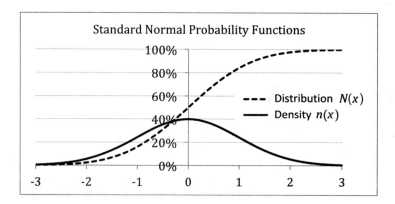

Figure 3.1 **Standard normal density function and distribution function**

For simplicity, returns are sometimes modeled using discrete random variables, i.e., where the distribution is characterized by a discontinuous jump function. For discrete cases, given S possible states, $s \in [1, 2, ..., S]$, let mass be represented by $Pr(s)$, the probability of state s occuring. Given return $R^x(s)$ for asset x in state s, then

$$E[R^x] = \mu(R^x) = \sum_{s=1}^{S} Pr(s) R^x(s), \text{ and} \quad (3.2)$$

$$\sigma^2(R^x) = \sum_{s=1}^{S} Pr(s) \left(R^x(s) - E[R^x]\right)^2, \quad (3.3)$$

and $\sigma(R^x) = \sqrt{\sigma^2(R^x)}$. In comparing earlier equations for historical mean and variance, respectively, to equations (3.2) and (3.3) for analogous metrics regarding future discrete returns, it is obvious that past metrics resemble those of the future, given that a uniform distribution is "assigned" to historical data points, i.e., each is assigned an equal "probability" weight of $\frac{1}{T}$. Figure 3.2 shows an example probability mass function for a random variable whose value can take on one of five possible values, each with 20% probability. Figure 3.3 shows the corresponding distribution function.

3.3 Linear Relation Between Future Returns of Two Assets

Consider two assets x and y whose returns are modeled via continuous random variables, R^x and R^y, respectively. Given a joint density function of $f_{xy}(R^x, R^y)$, the

---

[2] Of course, $E[r^x] = \mu(r^x) = E[R^x] - 1 = \mu(R^x) - 1$, and $\sigma(r^x) = \sigma(R^x)$. The latter follows as $r^x = R^x - 1$.

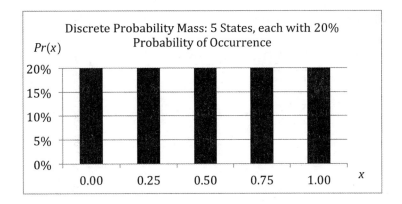

Figure 3.2   Discrete probability mass function

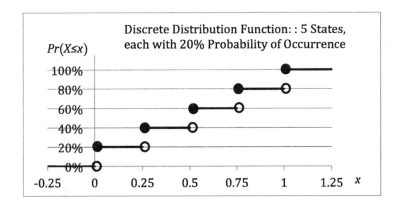

Figure 3.3   Discrete cumulative probability distribution function

covariance of gross returns is

$$\sigma^2(R^x, R^y) = \int_{z=\underline{R^x}}^{z=\overline{R^x}} \int_{v=\underline{R^y}}^{v=\overline{R^y}} f_{xy}(z,v)\,[z - \mu(R^x)]\,[v - \mu(R^y)]\,dv\,dz. \quad (3.4)$$

Given two assets x and y whose returns are modeled via discrete random variables, the covariance of gross returns is $\sigma^2(R^x, R^y) = \sum_{s=1}^{S} Pr(s)\,[R^x(s) - \mu(R^x)][R^y(s) - \mu(R^y)]$. Finally, the correlation coefficient between a pair of asset returns is $\rho(R^x, R^y) = \frac{\sigma^2(R^x, R^y)}{\sigma(R^x)\sigma(R^y)}$.

3.4   Future (Next Period) Portfolio Return

Using historical metrics, we showed that a portfolio's return is a weighted average of individual asset returns. Analogously, for the next period,

$$E\left[R^P\right] = \sum_{i=1}^{I} w^i E\left[R^i\right], \quad (3.5)$$

and next period's portfolio variance is given by,

$$\sigma^2\left(R^P\right) = \sum_{i=1}^{I}\sum_{j=1}^{I} w^i w^j \sigma^2\left(R^i, R^j\right)$$

$$= \sum_{i=1}^{I}\left(w^i\right)^2 \sigma^2\left(R^i\right) + \sum_{i=1}^{I}\sum_{j\neq i}^{I} w^i w^j \sigma^2(R^i, R^j)$$

$$= \sum_{i=1}^{I}\left(w^i\right)^2 \sigma^2\left(R^i\right) + 2\sum_{i=1}^{I}\sum_{j>i}^{I} w^i w^j \sigma^2(R^i, R^j), \quad (3.6)$$

where $\sigma^2(R^i, R^j)$ is interpreted as $\sigma^2(R^i)$ if $i = j$.

3.4.1 Benefit of Asset Diversification in a Portfolio

Let's explore implications of equation (3.6). In its final expression, the single sum contains variance terms, while the nested set of sums contains covariance terms. In $\sigma^2\left(R^P\right)$, there are I^2 total terms: I variance terms, and thus, $I^2 - I = I(I-1)$ covariance terms.[3] The variance-covariance matrix is shown in figure 3.4, and variance terms are underlined to highlight them. For illustrative purposes, let's assume that all assets have equal weights, so each $w^i = \frac{1}{I}$. Furthermore, assume that all variances, $\sigma^2(R^i)$, are the same, and that all covariances, $\sigma^2(R^i, R^j) = \rho(R^i, R^j)\sigma(R^i)\sigma(R^j)$, are also equal to each other. Combining these last two assumptions, then for each pair of assets i and j, $\rho(R^i, R^j)$ is always the same. Thus, for notational ease during this discussion, let $\rho(R^i, R^j) = \rho$, and let $\sigma^2(R^i, R^j) = \rho\sigma(R^i)\sigma(R^j) = \rho\sigma^2(R^i)$. In the final line of equation (3.6), the expression with I variance terms sums to $I[(\frac{1}{I})^2\sigma^2(R^i)] = \frac{\sigma^2(R^i)}{I}$, and the expression with $I(I-1)$ covariance terms sums to $I(I-1)[(\frac{1}{I})^2\rho\sigma^2(R^i)]$. Thus, given these assumptions, equation (3.6) simplifies to

$$\sigma^2(R^P) = \frac{\sigma^2(R^i)}{I}\left[1 + (I-1)\rho\right]. \quad (3.7)$$

The ratio of the contribution of the portfolio's variance due to the covariance terms, $\sigma^2(R^i)\frac{(I-1)\rho}{I}$, to that due to the variance terms, $\frac{\sigma^2(R^i)}{I}$, is $(I-1)\rho$. In a large portfolio with many assets (i.e., large I), then the average ρ is likely to be positive. Thus, as one continues to add more assets (i.e., increases I) without bound, then $(I-1)\rho$ also increases without bound. In a portfolio with many assets, the portfolio's variance is dominated by the covariances of returns between pairs of assets. Equivalently, variances of individual asset returns become relatively unimportant.

---

[3] There exist $I(I-1)/2$ distinct covariance terms, as for each pair of assets i and j, $\sigma^2(R^i, R^j) = \sigma^2(R^j, R^i)$.

$$\begin{pmatrix} \underline{\sigma^2(R^1)} & \sigma^2(R^1,R^2) & \cdots & \sigma^2(R^1,R^I) \\ \sigma^2(R^2,R^1) & \underline{\sigma^2(R^2)} & \cdots & \sigma^2(R^2,R^I) \\ \vdots & \vdots & & \vdots \\ \sigma^2(R^{I-1},R^1) & \sigma^2(R^{I-1},R^2) & \cdots & \sigma^2(R^{I-1},R^I) \\ \sigma^2(R^I,R^1) & \sigma^2(R^1,R^2) & \cdots & \underline{\sigma^2(R^I)} \end{pmatrix}$$

Figure 3.4 Variance-covariance matrix as part of $\sigma(R^P)$ calculation

Another insight from equation (3.7) is that as ρ decreases, so does portfolio variance, all else equal. Thus, combining assets whose prices tend to move less in tandem (i.e., small ρ) reduces portfolio variance. Figure 3.5 depicts equation (3.7) and its implications, showing $\sigma(R^P)$ as a function of I, while parameterizing ρ.[4]

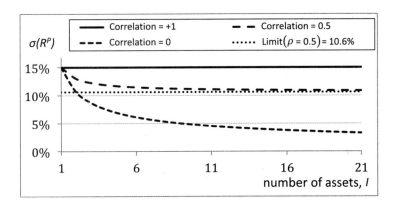

Figure 3.5 Diversification: reduction of return variance via adding assets

From equation (3.7), as $I \to \infty$, then $\sigma(R^P) \to \sigma(R^i)\sqrt{\rho}$. In figure 3.5, the limiting value of $\sigma(R^P|\rho = 0.5)$ as $I \to \infty$ is shown as $15\%\sqrt{0.5} = 10.6\%$. So in going from one asset ($\sigma(R^P) = \sigma(R^i) = 15\%$) to many assets, it is possible to reduce $\sigma(R^P)$ by an *absolute* amount of 4.4%, from 15% to 10.6%. Note that with only five assets, 77% of this total possible absolute reduction is obtained.[5] With 10 (20) assets, 88% (94%) of the total possible absolute reduction is obtained. Numerical results shown in figure 3.6 correspond to the curve ($\rho = 0.5$) of figure 3.5. So the good news is that significant portfolio diversification (i.e., elimination of idiosyncratic risk) is possible with just a few assets.

---

[4] For each asset i, $\sigma(R^i) = 15\%$. Between all pairs of assets, ρ is constant.

[5] The calculation is as follows: $\frac{15\% - 11.6\%}{15\% - 10.6\%} = \frac{3.4}{4.4} = 77\%$.

Number of assets, I	$\sigma(R^P)$	Relative reduction of $\sigma(R^P)$ from $\sigma(R^i) = 15\%$
5	11.6%	77%
10	11.1%	88%
20	10.9%	94%
∞	10.6%	100%

Figure 3.6 Impact of number of assets (I) on portfolio variance; $\rho = 0.5$

Portfolio diversification is related to a couple of distinct ideas. First, by putting together many assets, then as some may have performances worse than expected due to firm specific issues (i.e., **idiosyncratic risk**), others should have performances better than expected. This is an application of the **law of large numbers**. Second, by putting together assets with relatively low correlation among them (i.e., by reducing **systematic risk**), variance of return should be reduced. We see both of these ideas in figure 3.5. Refering back to equation (3.6), then loosely speaking, the summation of variance terms is related to idiosyncratic risk, and the summation of covariance terms is related to systematic risk.

3.4.2 Special Cases: Future Return of Two-asset Portfolios

To further illustrate previous calculations, consider a portfolio of two assets, x and y.

$$E\left[R^P\right] = w^x E\left[R^x\right] + w^y E\left[R^y\right], \quad \text{and}$$
$$\sigma^2\left(R^P\right) = (w^x)^2 \sigma^2\left(R^x\right) + (w^y)^2 \sigma^2\left(R^y\right) + 2w^x w^y \sigma^2\left(R^x, R^y\right), \quad (3.8)$$

where $\sigma^2(R^x, R^y) = \rho(R^x, R^y)\sigma(R^x)\sigma(R^y)$. To drive home the point that portfolio variance increases (decreases) as asset prices move more (less) in tandem, $\frac{\partial \sigma^2(R^P)}{\partial \rho(R^x, R^y)} = 2w^x w^y \sigma(R^x)\sigma(R^y) > 0$, assuming long positions in both x and y, i.e., $w^x > 0$ and $w^y > 0$. Let's consider three special cases of portfolios containing two risky assets each, i.e., $\sigma^2(R^x) > 0$ and $\sigma^2(R^y) > 0$.

$$\rho(R^x, R^y) = +1 \Rightarrow \sigma^2\left(R^P\right) = (w^x \sigma\left(R^x\right) + w^y \sigma\left(R^y\right))^2 > 0. \quad (3.9)$$
$$\rho(R^x, R^y) = 0 \Rightarrow \sigma^2\left(R^P\right) = (w^x \sigma\left(R^x\right))^2 + (w^y \sigma\left(R^y\right))^2 > 0. \quad (3.10)$$
$$\rho(R^x, R^y) = -1 \Rightarrow \sigma^2\left(R^P\right) = (w^x \sigma\left(R^x\right) - w^y \sigma\left(R^y\right))^2 \geqslant 0. \quad (3.11)$$

Equation (3.11), where $\rho(R^x, R^y) = -1$, has an interesting implication. Given two risky assets, each with positive variance of return, then if they are perfectly *negatively* correlated, it is possible to construct a risk-free portfolio, i.e., one with zero variance.[6]

In addition to figure 3.5, figure 3.7 also graphically shows the impact of ρ upon $\sigma(r^P)$.[7] The three curves in figure 3.7 are generated by varying w^x (and $w^y = 1 - w^x$.) Point x (y) represents asset x (y), where $w^x = 1$ ($w^y = 1$).[8] When $w^i < 0$, then asset i is shorted.

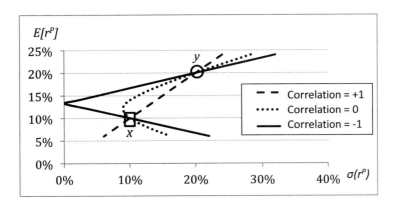

Figure 3.7   Impact of correlation coefficient upon portfolio variance

Regarding any two-asset portfolio that is *long* both assets, then for a given expected return (i.e., given fixed weights $w^x > 0$ and $w^y > 0$ such that $E[r^P] \in (10\%, 20\%)$ in this example is held constant), its variance is increasing in correlation coefficient, as proven earlier. One can confirm this by traveling horizontally from left to right across figure 3.7, holding fixed any $E[r^P] \in (10\%, 20\%)$. (Recall that expected return is linear in asset weights.) Any curve in $(\sigma(r^P), E[r^P])$ space generated by varying weights of assets is called a **frontier**. In a world with only two risky assets x and y, then for a given $\rho(r^x, r^y)$, this frontier represents the investors' **investment opportunity set**. Note that it only considers the realm of possibilities given *all* available assets; specifically, it does *not* include investor preferences.

In the next chapter, we consider portfolios with more than two risky assets. Determining the frontier or investment opportunity set of such portfolios is mathematically more challenging, as optimization is involved. We also introduce a risk-free asset, which

---

[6]Setting $\sigma^2(R^P) = 0$ in equation (3.11), and recognizing that $w^x = 1 - w^y$, then $w^x = \frac{\sigma(R^y)}{\sigma(R^x) + \sigma(R^y)}$, so $w^y = 1 - w^x = \frac{\sigma(R^x)}{\sigma(R^x) + \sigma(R^y)}$. The weights are intuitive; the weight of each asset is increasing in the variance of the other asset and decreasing in its own variance. To create a portfolio with zero variance of return, less (more) weight should be placed on the asset with the greater (lesser) variance.

[7]Note: $(\sigma(r^x), E[r^x]) = (10\%, 10\%)$, and $(\sigma(r^y), E[r^y]) = (20\%, 20\%)$. As a reminder, $\sigma(R^i) = \sigma(r^i)$, so we can use them interchangeably. Analogously, $\rho(r^x, r^y) = \rho(R^x, R^y)$.

[8]We allow w^x ($w^y = 1 - w^x$) to range from -0.5 to $+1.5$ ($+1.5$ to -0.5).

expands the asset opportunity set. Combining this with investors' preferences, we can nail down each individual's optimal portfolio selection. Finally, by disentangling idiosyncratic risk from systematic risk, we deliver the much celebrated Capital Asset Pricing Model, or CAPM.

Problems

1. Consider an asset whose future return r^x is modeled as a continuous random variable with probability density function of $f_x(z) = 1$ on support $[0, 1]$. What is the expected return and standard deviation of r^x?

2. Consider an asset whose future return r^x is modeled as a discrete random variable with probability mass function as follows.

Return	-20%	5%	30%
Probability	0.2	0.5	0.3

What is the expected return and standard deviation of r^x?

3. Consider two assets, X and Y. Their rate of returns are modeled via continuous random variables and follow the same density function of $f_x(z) = f_y(v) = 1$, with support on $[0, 1]$. If they are independent, what is the covariance of the two assets' returns? (Hint: if two variables are independent, their joint density function is simply the product of their respective density functions.) Consider using the following general covariance relation: $\sigma^2(R^x, R^y) = E(R^x R^y) - E(R^x)E(R^y)$.

4. A portfolio consists of two assets, X and Y. Asset X's expected return and standard deviation are 10% and 0.3, respectively. Asset Y's expected return and standard deviation are 20% and 0.6, respectively. If the two assets have the same weights in the portfolio (i.e., $w^x = w^y = 0.5$), and if their returns are independent (which implies that the correlation coefficient between the two assets' return is zero), calculate the portfolio's expected return and standard deviation.

5. (*Continue Problem 4*) If these two assets' correlation coefficient is $+1$, what is the standard deviation of the portfolio?

6. (*Continue Problem 4*) If these two assets' correlation coefficient is -1, what is the standard deviation of the portfolio?

Compare and contrast the results to problems 4, 5 and 6. Comment on the relationships between these three answers.

7. (*Continue Problem 4*) To assets X and Y, let's add an additional asset Z into this portfolio. Its expected return and standard deviation are 6% and 0%, respectively. Assume that the three assets' returns are all independent of one another. Assuming equal weights for all three equal to $\frac{1}{3}$ each, what is the new portfolio's expected return and standard deviation?

Compared with your answers in Problem 4, what can you conclude?

8. A portfolio consists of only two assets X and Y, where $E[r^x] = 8\%$, $E[r^y] = 20\%$, $\sigma(r^x) = 0.1$, $\sigma(r^y) = 0.6$ and $\rho(r^x, r^y) = -1$. What weights should we assign to assets X and Y in order to minimize the standard deviation of return of this portfolio?

And what is this value of the minimum standard deviation? (Assume that $w^x + w^y = 1$.)

9. Consider again the parameters of problem 4, where $\rho(R^x, R^y) = 0$. What are the assets' weights that minimize the portfolio's standard deviation of return?

Can the portfolio achieve the same minimum standard deviation of return as in your previous answer?

If not, what is the new minimum value?

Is it larger or smaller than that of problem 8?

Explain the relationship between the two answers (i.e., to problems 8 and 9).

CHAPTER 4

Optimal Portfolio Identification

We concluded the previous chapter by generating the investment opportunity set (or frontier) in a world with only two risky assets. In this chapter, we consider the optimal investment opportunity set given many risky assets. Then we turn our attention to an investor's preferences. In short, even though all investors face the same optimal investment opportunity set, they will choose different portfolios due to their varying degrees of risk aversion.

4.1 Markowitz Theory of Risky-Asset Efficient Portfolios

Refer back to figure 3.7. Specifically, consider the curve corresponding to a correlation coefficient equal to zero, $\rho(R^x, R^y) = 0$. To risky assets x and y, we introduce risky asset z, where $(\sigma(r^z), E[r^z]) = (25\%, 15\%)$. For illustration purposes, assume that all three correlations between pairs of two assets is zero, or $\rho(R^x, R^y) = \rho(R^x, R^z) = \rho(R^y, R^z) = 0$. In figure 4.1, we continue to generate portfolios in which each involves only two assets. Thus, three frontiers are possible: xy (as before in figure 3.7, where $\rho(R^x, R^y) = 0$), xz and yz. Note that in portfolios involving only two assets, the frontier in $(\sigma(r^P), E[r^P])$ space is generated simply by changing portfolio weights. There is *no* optimization performed in generating these three investment opportunity sets. Let's be clear: generally speaking, investment opportunity sets include *all* available assets. So the correct interpretation of figure 4.1 is to consider 3 different worlds, where each investor may only invest in assets that exist in her world. So in one world, only assets x and y exist, and in a second (third) world, only assets x and z (y and z) exist.

Now consider a world where all three assets exist. Beyond two assets, determination of an optimal investment opportunity set is more challenging, as optimization is required. Figure 4.2 adds to figure 4.1 the frontier generated when considering all three risky assets simultaneously. How is this generated? We follow the guidance of Harry Markowitz, the American Nobel Prize winner. We solve a constrained optimization

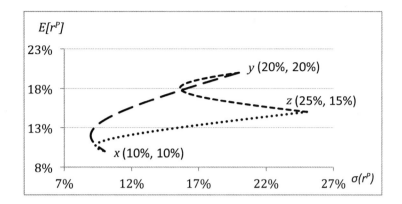

Figure 4.1 Three distinct portfolio frontiers, each of two risky assets

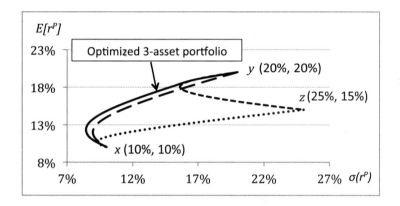

Figure 4.2 Optimized portfolio of three risky assets

problem. Obviously, given $(\sigma(r^P), E[r^P])$ space, a rational risk-averse investor desires to "travel northwest". We are implicitly assuming that investors care only about the first two moments of portfolio return.[1] For a desired level of expected reward, $E[r^P]$, a risk-averse investor desires the lowest risk possible, $\sigma(r^P)$, i.e., to "travel west" as far as possible. From another perspective, for a given acceptable level of risk, $\sigma(r^P)$, a rational investor desires the highest expected reward possible, $E[r^P]$, i.e., to "travel north" as far as possible.[2] So any movement in the 90 degree quadrant bounded by

---

[1] If returns are assumed to be normally distributed, then using only the first two moments is appropriate. In reality, returns are not necessarily normally distributed, but rather may exhibit asymmetry and/or "fat tails". Though investors are concerned with higher moments such as the third (a metric for skewness or lack of symmetry) and fourth (kurtosis, a metric to identify "fat tails"), these are beyond the scope of this text.

[2] Minimizing risk for a given expected reward generates the entire outer frontier in figure 4.2. Maximizing expected reward for a given level of risk generates *only* the upper (i.e., positive sloping) portion of this frontier.

due west and by due north is unambiguously desired by a rational risk-averse investor. The entire outer frontier in figure 4.2 is identified via

$$\min_{w^1, w^2, \ldots, w^I} \sigma^2(r^P) = \sum_{i=1}^{I} \sum_{j=1}^{I} w^i w^j \sigma^2(r^i, r^j),$$

$$\text{s.t. } E\left[r^P\right] = \sum_{i=1}^{I} w^i E\left[r^i\right] \geqslant k_{E[r^P]},$$

$$\text{s.t. } \sum_{i=1}^{I} w^i = 1, \quad \text{(budget constraint)} \quad \text{and}$$

$$\text{s.t. } w^i \geqslant 0, \forall i \in \{1, 2, \ldots, I\}, \quad \text{(no short sales)} \tag{4.1}$$

where $k_{E[r^P]}$ is a pre-determined parameter corresponding to the minimum desired expected return of the investor.[3] In terms of the above discussion, *minimizing* risk, $\sigma(r^P)$, for a given level of expected reward, $E[r^P]$, means "travelling due west" as far as possible. The budget constraint means that the investor's total level of investment is pre-determined (i.e., she will invest neither more nor less than what she has to invest), and the no short sales constraint prevents short-selling (i.e., borrowing an asset in order to sell it without owning it).[4]

Consider the portfolio on the outer envelope with minimum variance, called the **global minimum variance portfolio**, *GMVP*, as shown in figure 4.3. Consistent with appearances in figure 4.3, the identified outer frontier above the *GMVP* is strictly

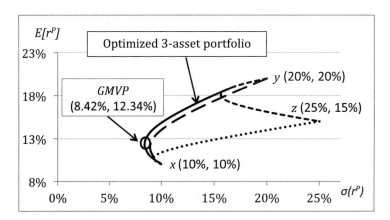

Figure 4.3 Global minimum variance portfolio, GMVP

---

[3] In equilibrium, the constraint with $k_{E[r^P]}$ binds, i.e., is an equality.

[4] Of course, an investor with a short position must not only repay all interim cash flows generated by the security, but also close out her position (i.e., purchase a replacement for the loaned asset in the market and return it to the lender) at some future point in time.

increasing. As such, this upper section of the frontier above the $GMVP$ is uniquely invertible, i.e., there is a one-to-one mapping between $\sigma(r^P)$ and $E[r^P]$. Thus, we can equivalently determine the upper section of the Markowitz frontier via a *maximization* program (versus minimization above) as

$$\max_{w^1,w^2,\ldots,w^I} E\left[r^P\right] = \sum_{i=1}^{I} w^i E\left[r^i\right],$$

$$\text{s.t.} \quad \sigma^2(r^P) = \sum_{i=1}^{I}\sum_{j=1}^{I} w^i w^j \sigma^2(r^i, r^j) \leqslant k_\sigma,$$

$$\text{s.t.} \quad \sum_{i=1}^{I} w^i = 1, \quad \text{(budget constraint) and}$$

$$\text{s.t.} \quad w^i \geqslant 0, \forall i \in \{1, 2, \ldots, I\}, \quad \text{(no short sales)} \tag{4.2}$$

where k_σ is a pre-determined parameter corresponding to the maximum risk acceptable to the investor.[5] In terms of the above discussion, maximizing expected reward ($E[r^P]$) for a given level of risk ($\sigma(r^P)$) means "travelling due north" as far as possible. Compared to the first program (i.e., minimization of $\sigma(r^P)$ subject to (a) desired $E[r^P]$, (b) budget constraint and (c) no short sales constraint), the constrained maximization of $E[r^P]$ has the advantage of identifying *only* the upper portion of the outer frontier above the $GMVP$. This upper segment is the **efficient frontier**, comprised exclusively of **efficient portfolios**, i.e., the **optimal investment opportunity set of risky assets**.

4.2 Investor Preferences over Risk and Expected Reward

As the efficient frontier is a continuous function in $(\sigma(r^P), E[r^P])$ space, an investor has an infinite number of efficient portfolios of risky assets from which to choose. Which one does she select? In addition to the set of available assets, we need to model an **investor's preferences** (i.e., her risk/reward tradeoffs) from which she can determine her "best" portfolio. We model her preferences via **utility function** $U(\sigma(r^P), E[r^P])$. As our investor is rational (i.e. more wealth is better, all else equal), then $U'(E[r^P]|\sigma(r^P)) > 0$. As economists typically assume decreasing marginal return of wealth, then $U''(E[r^P]|\sigma(r^P)) < 0$. Consistent with classic economic thought, we assume that our investor is risk-averse, or $U'(\sigma(r^P)|E[r^P]) < 0$, and that her marginal cost of risk is increasing in risk ($U''(\sigma(r^P)|E[r^P]) < 0$). Finally, we assume that at

---
[5]In equilibrium, the constraint with k_σ binds, i.e., is an equality.

higher levels of risk (i.e., increased $\sigma(r^P)$), a risk-averse investor experiences lower sensitivity to increasing wealth, or $\frac{\partial^2 U(\sigma(r^P), E[r^P])}{\partial E[r^P]\partial \sigma(r^P)} < 0$.[6]

We have framed figures 3.7, 4.1, 4.2, 4.3 and 4.4 in $(\sigma(r^P), E[r^P])$ space. Thus, to plot the three-dimensional surface $U(\sigma(r^P), E[r^P])$ onto the two-dimensional $(\sigma(r^P), E[r^P])$ space, we need to use the same strategy that map makers use via topological maps. In such a map, lines are drawn which represent constant height above sea level. This is an effective technique to project a third dimension (i.e., height above sea level) onto a two-dimensional map (i.e., longitude and latitude). Analogously, given our two dimensions, $\sigma(r^P)$ and $E[r^P]$, we can draw lines which respresent "constant height", i.e., constant utility for an investor. From $U(\sigma(r^P), E[r^P])$, then

$$dU = U'\left(\sigma(r^P)|E[r^P]\right) d\sigma(r^P) + U'\left(E[r^P]|\sigma(r^P)\right) dE\left[r^P\right],$$

or setting this equal to zero in order to identify an **iso-utility** (i.e., $dU = 0$), then

$$\frac{dE\left[r^P\right]}{d\sigma(r^P)} = -\frac{U'\left(\sigma(r^P)|E[r^P]\right)}{U'\left(E[r^P]|\sigma(r^P)\right)} > 0. \tag{4.3}$$

This is positive because $U'(\sigma(r^P)|E[r^P]) < 0$ and $U'(E[r^P]|\sigma(r^P)) > 0$, so iso-utility curves for a risk-averse investor are increasing in $(\sigma(r^P), E[r^P])$ space. Next, differentiating equation (4.3) with respect to $\sigma(r^P)$, then[7]

$$\frac{d^2 E\left[r^P\right]}{(d\sigma(r^P))^2} = -\frac{1}{(U'(r))^2}\left[U''(\sigma)U'(r) - U'(\sigma)\left(\frac{\partial^2 U(r,\sigma)}{\partial r \partial \sigma}\right)\right] > 0. \tag{4.4}$$

The positive sign follows from assumptions above. Together, equations (4.3) and (4.4) imply that iso-utilities are increasing and convex in $(\sigma(r^P), E[r^P])$ space. This is an important result, as it implies that the highest possible iso-utility for each investor, a convex function in $(\sigma(r^P), E[r^P])$ space, must be uniquely tangential at a single point to the optimal asset opportunity set, which is a concave function in the same space. In other words, for any given investor, she identifies with a unique optimal portfolio.

Consider figure 4.4. Iso-utilities of investors x (more risk averse) and y (less risk averse) are shown along with the efficient frontier. How do we know that in $(\sigma(r^P), E[r^P])$ space the more risk averse investor's iso-utilities are steeper than those of the less risk averse investor? Holding $U'(E[r^P]|\sigma(r^P))$ fixed, then $U'(\sigma(r^P)|E[r^P]) < 0$

---

[6]We further assume a continuous utility function where $\frac{\partial^2 U(\sigma(r^P), E[r^P])}{\partial E[r^P]\partial \sigma(r^P)} = \frac{\partial^2 U(\sigma(r^P), E[r^P])}{\partial \sigma(r^P)\partial E[r^P]} < 0$.

[7]For notational ease, on the right hand side of equation (4.4) we use "r" for "$E[r^P|\sigma(r^P)]$" and "σ" for "$\sigma(r^P)|E[r^P]$".

is more (less) negative for the more (less) risk-averse investor, x (y). Thus, per equation (4.3), then $\frac{dE[r^P]}{d\sigma(r^P)}$ must be greater (lesser) for the more (less) risk-averse investor. Again, as each investor desires the highest utility possible, one will choose the most "northwest" iso-utility among her set of achievable iso-utilities, i.e., those which intersect the efficient frontier. In figure 4.4, we show three iso-utilities for each investor, x and y. For each investor, two iso-utilities are achievable, whereas the highest one is not. Thus, investor x's (y's) highest achievable iso-utility is $x1$ ($y1$), as she chooses tangential portfolio x (y).

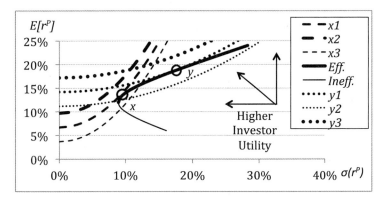

Figure 4.4 Investor iso-utilities for different degrees of risk aversion

Finally, figure 4.5 shows the equilibrium results. Note that the outer envelope, identified via minimization program on page 38, is drawn with two fonts. The upper half, the efficient frontier identified via maximization program on page 39, is drawn with a heavy solid font. The lower half, an *inefficient* frontier (identified only by the minimization program on page 38), is drawn with a thin solid font. The interface between these two fonts on the outer envelope identifies the $GMVP$.

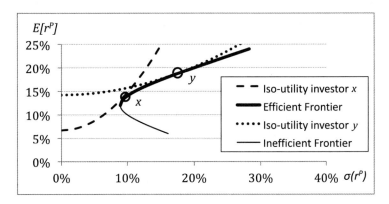

Figure 4.5 Investor optimal portfolios for different degrees of risk aversion

Problems

1. Consider a portfolio that consists of three assets, X, Y and Z. Asset X's (Y's, Z's) expected return and standard deviation are 10% and 0.3, respectively (20% and 0.5 for Y, 35% and 0.7 for Z). The correlations of returns between pairs of assets are all zero: $\rho(r^x, r^y) = \rho(r^y, r^z) = \rho(r^x, r^z) = 0$. Respecting the budget constraint, $w^x + w^y + w^z = 1$, then what is the optimal portfolio for an investor who desires a standard deviation of return of 45% (i.e., what are her optimal w^x, w^y and w^z)? Short sales are allowed.

What is the optimal portfolio's expected return?

2. Given assets and parameters of problem 1, what is the optimal portfolio when short sales are *not* allowed? (i.e., what are the optimal w^x, w^y and w^z)?

What is this optimal constrained portfolio's expected return?

Contrast expected returns of the portfolios in this problem and problem 1.

Explain the relationship of these two results.

3. Assume your personal utility function is $u(\sigma, E[r]) = E[r] - a\sigma^2$. The investment opportunity set has a Markowitz efficient portfolio frontier of $E[r] = 4b\sigma^{0.5} + c$, given $\sigma > \sigma^{\min}$, where a, b and c are positive constants. (There is no risk-free asset available.) What is the expected return of your optimal risky portfolio, where your answer should be in terms of parameters a, b and c?

4. Given the result of problem 3, is your optimal expected return increasing or decreasing in parameter a? in b? in c? Explain each result.

CHAPTER

Capital Market Line, Market Model and Security Market Line

In the previous chapter, we generated the frontier of efficient portfolios of risky assets. Afterwards, we showed that an investor considers her own preferences over risk and expected reward via utility function to identify her optimal portfolio. In this chapter, we recognize the existence of a risk-free asset. This dramatically impacts the investment opportunity set in the sense that for essentially any degree of risk an investor is willing to accept, her expected return increases. As before, each investor combines her preferences over risk and expected reward with the optimal investment opportunity set of assets, expanded due to the risk-free asset, to determine her optimal portfolio. Finally, we disentangle systematic risk from idiosyncratic risk to deliver the capital asset pricing model, $CAPM$.

5.1 Capital Market Line

We now recognize the existence of a risk-free asset.[1] How do we develop an expanded investment opportunity set of assets by adding the risk-free asset to the efficient frontier of risky assets? Consider combining a risk-free asset, defined by coordinates in $(\sigma(r^P), E[r^P])$ space of $(0, r^f)$, with an arbitrary efficient portfolio of risky assets, e, defined by $(\sigma(r^e), E[r^e])$.[2] The weights are w^e and $w^f = 1 - w^e$, respectively, per the budget constraint. Using two-asset portfolio relationships previously derived, $E[r^P] = w^e E[r^e] + (1 - w^e) r^f = r^f + w^e (E[r^e] - r^f)$, and $\sigma^2(r^P) = (w^e)^2 \sigma^2(r^e) + (1 - w^e)^2 \sigma^2(r^f) + 2 w^e w^f \sigma^2(r^e, r^f)$. By definition of a risk-free asset, $\sigma^2(r^f) = 0$. Thus, $\sigma^2(r^e, r^f) = \rho(r^e, r^f) \sigma(r^e) \sigma(r^f) = 0$. So $\sigma^2(r^P) = (w^e)^2 \sigma^2(r^e)$.

---

[1] As an example, short-term maturity U.S. Treasury securities can serve as a proxy.
[2] Note that $r^f < E[r^e]$, as $0 = \sigma(r^f) < \sigma(r^e)$, for any efficient portfolio of risky assets, e. In other words, investors demand higher expected reward for higher risk accepted.

Substituting $w^e = \frac{\sigma(r^P)}{\sigma(r^e)}$ into $E[r^P] = r^f + w^e(E[r^e] - r^f)$, then

$$E[r^P] = r^f + \frac{\sigma(r^P)}{\sigma(r^e)}\left(E[r^e] - r^f\right). \tag{5.1}$$

In $(\sigma(r^P), E[r^P])$ space, equation (5.1) is linear with intercept r^f and slope $\frac{E[r^e]-r^f}{\sigma(r^e)} > 0$. But which of the infinite number of efficient portfolios does an investor choose for e? Given that she desires to "travel northwest", and given that the intercept of the line in equation (5.1) is fixed at $(0, r^f)$, she rotates counter-clockwise the line "northwest" as far as possible. In other words, holding the intercept fixed at $(0, r^f)$, she maximizes the slope, $\frac{E[r^e]-r^f}{\sigma(r^e)} > 0$. As the efficient frontier of risky portfolios is convex in $(\sigma(r^P), E[r^P])$ space, then it intersects the most "northwest" straight line represented by equation (5.1) at a single point of tangency. As all rational risk-averse investors follow this same optimization process, all arrive at this same efficient portfolio of risky assets e represented by the point of tangency.[3]

The line in equation (5.1) is everywhere strictly "northwest" of the efficient frontier of risky assets (except at the one point of tangency, efficient portfolio e, where the two functions share a common point). Thus, all investors invest along this line. Determination of an investor's optimal portfolio is determined as before. She overlays her iso-utilities, which quantify her preferences over risk and expected reward, onto this linear expanded set of investment asset opportunities. As iso-utilities are convex in $(\sigma(r^P), E[r^P])$ space, the highest achievable one is tangent to this line. This point of tangency is her optimal portfolio.

Each investor selects her optimal portfolio, which is a convex combination of the risk-free asset and efficient portfolio of risky assets e. Above we showed that $w^e = \frac{\sigma(r^P)}{\sigma(r^e)}$, and $w^f = 1 - w^e = 1 - \frac{\sigma(r^P)}{\sigma(r^e)}$. So $w^e = 0$ ($w^e = 1$) corresponds to the risk-free asset (portfolio e). A weight w^e equal to $x\%$ corresponds to a distance of $x\%$ along the line away from the risk-free asset at coordinates $(0, r^f)$ toward portfolio e at coordinates $(\sigma(r^e), E[r^e])$. So for example, $w^e = 50\%$ corresponds to coordinatates in $(\sigma(r^P), E[r^P])$ space of $(\frac{\sigma(r^e)}{2}, r^f + \frac{E[r^e]-r^f}{2}) = (\frac{\sigma(r^e)}{2}, \frac{E[r^e]+r^f}{2})$, i.e., at the point on the line 50% of the way from the risk-free asset toward portfolio e.

For all points along the line between $(0, r^f)$ and $(\sigma(r^e), E[r^e])$, both weights w^e

---

[3] An assumption of this is that all investors have the same view of the world with respect to model parameters. Specifically, investors have homogeneous expectations regarding means and variances of all asset returns. If investors have heterogeneous expectations, then they will derive different Markowitz risky asset efficient portfolio frontiers and thus, they will not agree on tangential portfolio e.

and w^f are in the interval $(0,1)$. In such cases, an investor purchases (i.e., establishes long positions) in both e and the risk-free asset. Is it possible to invest in portfolios along the line beyond e? Yes, and such portfolios imply that $w^e = \frac{\sigma(r^P)}{\sigma(r^e)} > 1$, corresponding to $w^f = 1 - w^e < 0$. In short, an investor borrows money (i.e., establishes a short position in the risk-free asset) at the risk-free rate of return, r^f, and invests that money plus her initital investment in portfolio e.

Figure 5.1 shows iso-utilities of investors x (more risk averse) and y (less risk averse) along with the expanded investment opportunity set. Recall that in $(\sigma(r^P), E[r^P])$ space, iso-utilities of the more risk averse investor (x) are steeper than those of the less risk averse investor (y). Again, as each investor desires the highest utility possible, she will choose the most "northwest" iso-utility among her set of achievable iso-utilities, i.e., among those that intersect the efficient frontier. So in figure 5.1, investor x's (y's) highest achievable iso-utility is $x1$ ($y1$). Also, investor x invests 50% in efficient portfolio e (i.e., long position, where $w^e = \frac{\sigma(r^x)}{\sigma(r^e)} = \frac{7.5\%}{15\%} = 0.5$) and 50% in the risk-free asset (also a long position, where $w^f = 1 - w^e = 1 - 0.5 = 0.5$). In contrast, investor y invests 160% in efficient portfolio e (long position, where $w^e = \frac{\sigma(r^y)}{\sigma(r^e)} = \frac{25\%}{15\%} = 1.60$) and -60% in the risk-free asset (short position, where $w^f = 1 - w^e = 1 - 1.60 = -0.60$). For each dollar that y has to invest, she borrows $\frac{6}{10}$ of a dollar at the risk-free rate and purchases 1.60 dollars of portfolio e. As expected, investor y (x), the less (more) risk-averse investor, sets up an optimal portfolio that engages in higher (lower) risk, i.e., $25\% = \sigma(r^y) > \sigma(r^x) = 7.5\%$. As investor y (x) accepts higher (lower) risk, she enjoys higher (settles for lower) expected reward, i.e., $17\% = E[r^y] > E[r^x] = 7\%$.

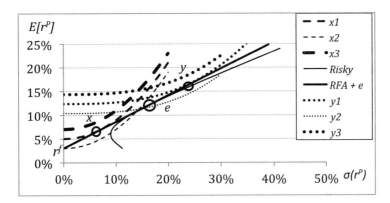

Figure 5.1 Investors' iso-utilities and investment opportunity set

As previously mentioned, the portfolio selected by every rational risk-averse investor is a combination of only two building blocks: the risk-free asset and efficient risky portfolio e.[4] Recognizing this allows us to argue that e must be the **market portfolio**, M, i.e., the hypothetical portfolio consisting of all risky assets. Using a contradiction argument, presume that portfolio e excludes an arbitrary risky asset, x. As the risky component of all investors' portfolios is composed *only* of portfolio e, then no investor has a position (either long or short) in x, But this contradicts the existence of asset x. So the presumption that arbitrary risky asset x is excluded from efficient portfolio e is false, i.e., e must include all risky assets. Thus, by definition, e must be the market portfolio, M. So equation (5.1) can be re-written as the **capital market line**, or CML,

$$E\left[r^P\right] = r^f + \sigma\left(r^P\right)\left[\frac{E\left[r^m\right] - r^f}{\sigma\left(r^m\right)}\right]. \qquad (5.2)$$

The difference $E[r^m] - r^f$ is called the **market risk premium**, the incremental return demanded by investors who invest in the risky market portfolio relative to a risk-free asset. The slope of the CML in $(\sigma(r^P), E[r^P])$ space, $\frac{E[r^m] - r^f}{\sigma(r^m)} > 0$, is called the **market price of risk**. Relative to investment in a risk-free asset, it's the incremental return demanded, $E[r^m] - r^f$, per incremental total risk accepted, $\sigma(r^m) - \sigma(r^f) = \sigma(r^m)$, for those who invest in risky portfolio M. The relevant risk metric in the CML is $\sigma(r^P)$, total portfolio risk.[5] Figure 5.2 graphically depicts the CML.

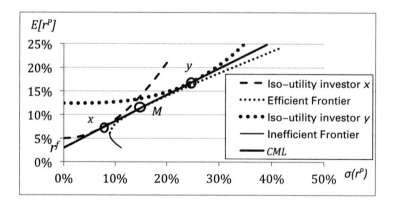

Figure 5.2 Capital market line, CML

5.2 Idiosyncratic Risk, Systematic Risk, and Market Model

The CML gives us a relationship between $E[r^P]$ and $\sigma(r^P)$ for portfolios that are convex combinations of a risk-free asset and the well diversified portfolio of all risky assets, the market portfolio, M. As neither the risk-free asset nor M have idiosyncratic

---

[4]This is the **monetary separation theorem** of portfolio investment.
[5]As discussed later, total risk equals systematic risk plus idiosyncratic risk.

risk, then any portfolio along the CML has zero idiosyncratic risk. In contrast, individual assets do have such risk. Therefore, we obviously must look elsewhere to determine $E[r^i]$ for an individual asset i.

An important concept in portfolio theory is the idea of **diversification**. In a portfolio containing many risky assets, some assets will likely perform poorly due to firm-specific issues. Risk of under-performance due to such issues relative to that which is expected is called **firm-specific risk**, **diversifiable risk**, **idiosyncratic risk** or **fundamental risk**. However, by combining many risky assets into a portfolio, then some assets should perform better than expected in a given period due to firm-specific issues. By the law of large numbers, relative under-performances and over-performances should roughly cancel each other in a portfolio with many assets. So a portfolio with a large number of assets tends to have little residual idiosyncratic risk.

Beyond firm-specific issues, risky assets can also be impacted by common macroeconomic factors, i.e., factors which impact all risky assets to varying degrees. One metric used in finance that attempts to collectively capture these is the return of M, the market portfolio, the hypothetical portfolio of all risky assets, i.e., those whose returns are uncertain.[6] In this context, market return is a so-called **systematic risk factor**, as it impacts returns of essentially all assets whose returns are uncertain. **Systematic risk** is the risk (dispersion) of return of a risky asset *directly* associated with its exposure to a systematic risk factor. In other words, an asset is exposed to systematic risk if its return is influenced by a systematic risk factor.

The sensitivity of asset x's return to that of the market is captured by it's **beta**, where

$$\beta^x = \frac{s^2(r^x, r^m)}{s^2(r^m)} = \rho(r^x, r^m) \frac{s(r^x)}{s(r^m)} \qquad (5.3)$$

is the slope coefficient in a regression of the returns of asset x, r_t^x, on market returns, r_t^m, $t \in \{-T+1, -T+2, ..., 0\}$. The **market model**, which assumes that the sole systematic driver of risky asset return is the market return, is

$$r_t^x = \alpha^x + \beta^x r_t^m + \epsilon_t^x, \qquad (5.4)$$

where error term, ϵ_t^x, is assumed to be normally distributed, $N(0, \sigma^2(\epsilon^x))$, and independent of $r_t^m, \forall t$. An asset with high (low) exposure to market risk, i.e., whose return has high (low) sensitivity to market return, has a large (small) β. An asset's β is also

---

[6]In practice, returns of a diversified index of stocks, such as those of the S&P 500, are used as a proxy for market returns.

a metric for its contribution to the portfolio's market (systematic) risk. Thus, assets with a low (high) β serve to reduce (increase) a portfolio's market (systematic) risk.

As $s(r^x) > 0$ and $s(r^m) > 0$, then per equation (5.3), the sign of β^x is the same as that of $\rho(r^x, r^m)$. Thus, negative asset β^x is possible when the correlation of returns of asset x with those of the market is negative. Such an asset, whose returns generally move in the opposite direction as those of the market, is particularly valuable for diversification purposes. During periods of poor market return, such an asset is likely to perform better than most other assets, which typically have positive β. Summarizing, a well **diversified portfolio** is one with not only a large number of assets to eliminate idiosyncratic risk, but also assets with different exposures to systematic risk.[7]

Once the market model parameters α^x and β^x are determined per regression (5.4), expectation of next period's return for asset x in terms of next period's expected market return can be estimated. Taking expectations of equation (5.4), then

$$E\left[r_1^x\right] = \alpha^x + \beta^x E\left[r_1^m\right], \tag{5.5}$$

as $E[\epsilon_1^x] = 0$. So for any risky asset x, we now have an estimation for the rate of return demanded by investors.

5.3 Security Market Line

The **security market line**, or *SML*, is the graphical equivalent of the **capital asset pricing model**, or *CAPM*. The *CAPM* was developed by Treynor, Sharpe, Lintner and Mossin, and it builds upon Markowitz' work. Figure 5.3 shows the *SML*, where the slope is the **Treynor ratio**, $\frac{E[r^x]-r^f}{\beta^x} = E[r^m] - r^f$. In contrast to the *CML*, whose risk metric is *diversified portfolio* risk $\sigma(r^P)$, the *SML* features the systematic (market) risk metric β^x for *individual asset x*.

For any security x, the **implied rate of return**, IRR^x, is the discount rate that equates its current price to the summation of present values of expected future cash flows, or

$$P_0^x = \sum_{t=1}^{T} \frac{E\left[CF_t\right]}{(1+IRR^x)^t}, \tag{5.6}$$

where T is the investor's anticipated holding period horizon.[8] Again, by definition,

---

[7] For example, combining stocks from a single industry would not be considered a well diversified portfolio, as returns of firms in a single industry are likely to have similar sensitivities to systematic risk.

[8] This may be the security's maturity, its expiration, or the date when the investor plans to sell it.

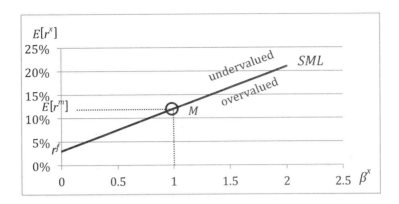

Figure 5.3 Security market line, SML

IRR^x is the rate of return that an investor anticipates to receive when she purchases the asset.

In figure 5.3, we can plot for any asset x not only the point $(\beta^x, E[r^x])$, but also the point (β^x, IRR^x). If $IRR^x > E[r^x]$ for a given β^x, then (β^x, IRR^x) plots above the SML, in which case the investor believes that the asset is undervalued. In contrast, if $IRR^x < E[r^x]$ for a given β^x, then (β^x, IRR^x) plots below the SML, in which case that the investor believes the asset is overvalued.[9]

In what follows, we "develop" the $CAPM$, not in a mathematically rigorous manner, but rather in a way that provides wonderful intuition underlying the $CAPM$.[10] In short, investors in asset x are rewarded (in expectation) *only* for systematic risk that they face, *not* for idiosyncratic risk. As investors can eliminate the latter simply by putting together a portfolio with a large number of risky assets (thanks to the law of large numbers), compensation for such diversifiable risk is unwarranted.

The $CAPM$ implies that the only systematic risk factor driving returns of risky assets is the market return. The market model, an empirical analogue to $CAPM$, implies the same. Thus, we can use the market model to examine asset risk.[11] Specifically, we noted earlier that the CML is absent idiosyncratic risk. Therefore, our strategy is as follows. Using the market model, we develop metrics for total risk, market (systematic) risk and idiosyncratic risk of an individual asset. We show that total risk equals

---

[9]We will have more to say about this in the next chapter.

[10]Our development involves some "hand-waving", as full development is beyond the scope of this discussion.

[11]Again, our approach is not a proof, as we presume a key result, i.e., that the return of the market is the only systematic risk factor. While our key "result" is tautological, our approach drives home the differences in relevant risk metrics between the CML and the SML.

market risk plus idiosyncratic risk. Extracting from this equation the metric for market (systematic) risk of an individual asset, we substitute it into the systematic risk metric of the CML, $\sigma(r^P)$. The result is the $CAPM$.

Using equation (5.4), we calculate the variance of return of asset x as $\sigma^2(r^x) = \sigma^2(\alpha^x + \beta^x r^m + \epsilon^x)$. Adding a constant ($\alpha^x$) to a sum of random variables ($\beta^x r^m + \epsilon^x$) has no impact upon variance, so $\sigma^2(r^x) = \sigma^2(\beta^x r^m + \epsilon^x) = (\beta^x)^2 \sigma^2(r^m) + \sigma^2(\epsilon^x) + 2\beta^x \sigma^2(r^m, \epsilon^x)$. Next, an assumption of an ordinary least squares regression is that an independent variable (r^m) and error term (ϵ^x) are linearly independent, or $\sigma^2(r^m, \epsilon^x) = 0$. Thus,

$$\sigma^2(r^x) = (\beta^x)^2 \sigma^2(r^m) + \sigma^2(\epsilon^x), \tag{5.7}$$

or **total risk = systematic risk + idiosyncratic risk**. Note that an asset's systematic risk per the market model is $(\beta^x)^2 \sigma^2(r^m)$. Having identified the appropriate metric for market (systematic) risk, we substitute it into the CML. Before doing so, note a technical point: the systematic risk metric in CML is $\sigma(r^P)$, having dimensions of rate of return. As $(\beta^x)^2 \sigma^2(r^m)$ has dimensions of the square of rate of return (as β^x is dimensionless), we take the square root of $(\beta^x)^2 \sigma^2(r^m)$, using $\beta^x \sigma(r^m)$ as the appropriate systematic risk metric. Thus, substituting $\beta^x \sigma(r^m)$ for $\sigma(r^P)$ in the CML yields the $CAPM$, or

$$E[r^x] = r^f + \beta^x \left(E[r^m] - r^f \right). \tag{5.8}$$

Let's summarize our journey. We began by finding the efficient portfolio of risky assets via Markowitz' contribution. Adding to this the preferences over risk and expected reward of a rational risk-averse investor via utility function, we identified an individual's optimal risky portfolio. Next, we added a risk-free asset and showed an expanded investment opportunity set. Again using investor preferences, we identified an updated individual optimal portfolio, a convex combination of the risk-free asset and the market portfolio. Afterwards, accepting the market model as given (i.e., that the return of the market is the sole systematic risk factor of an individual asset's return), we decomposed total risk into systematic (market) risk and idiosyncratic risk. Finally, substituting the identified systematic (market) risk metric for an individual asset into the corresponding systematic risk metric in the CML, the $CAPM$ obtains.

5.4 Comparing and Contrasting the CML and the SML

To close this chapter, let's distinguish these two models. The CML is generated via convex combinations of a risk-free asset and the diversified risky-asset market portfolio, both of which lack idiosyncratic risk. Thus, all resulting portfolios on the *CML* are idiosyncratic risk-free; portfolios on the *CML* have only systematic risk. So even though the independent axis is $\sigma(r^P)$, a metric for total risk (which equals systematic risk plus idiosyncratic risk), efficient portfolios on the *CML* have no idiosyncratic risk. Thus, along the *CML*, total risk equals systematic risk.

It is instructive to plot individual assets and portfolios of assets that have idiosyncratic risk on the same graph with the *CML*. Consider figure 5.4, where efficient (and diversified) portfolios *a, d* and *f* have no idiosyncratic risk, as they plot directly onto the *CML*. In stark contrast, *undiversified* assets *b, c* and *e* all have idiosyncratic risk, as their total risk is greater than that of a respective efficient portfolio with the same expected return.

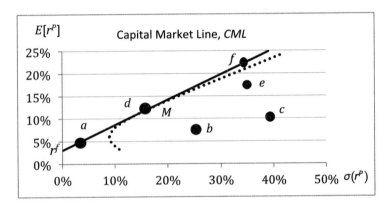

Figure 5.4 Capital market line and various assets

Given the expected return of an asset or portfolio of assets x, $E[r^x]$, total risk equals the horizontal distance of that asset in $(\sigma(r^P), E[r^P])$ space from the dependent axis. Obviously, this equals $\sigma(r^x)$. Given $E[r^x]$, total risk can be decomposed into systematic (market) risk, the horizontal distance from the dependent axis to the *CML*, $\sigma(r^e | E[r^e] = E[r^x])$ for efficient portfolio e on the *CML*, and idiosyncratic risk, the horizontal distance from the *CML* to the asset, $\sigma(r^x) - \sigma(r^e | E[r^e] = E[r^x])$.[12] So assets b, c and e, which have idiosyncratic risk, are plotted "due east" of the *CML*. In each

---

[12]Using $\sigma(\epsilon^x)$ for brevity to represent the the idiosyncratic risk metric $\sigma(r^x) - \sigma(r^e | E[r^e] = E[r^x])$, consider decomposition of total risk, $\sigma(r^x) = \sigma(r^e | E[r^e] = E[r^x]) + \sigma(\epsilon^x)$. In terms of variances and covariances, $\sigma^2(r^x) = \sigma^2(r^e | E[r^e] = E[r^x]) + \sigma^2(\epsilon^x) + 2\rho(\epsilon^x, r^e | E[r^e] = E[r^x])\sigma(r^e | E[r^e] = E[r^x])\sigma(\epsilon^x) = \sigma^2(r^e | E[r^e] = E[r^x]) + \sigma^2(\epsilon^x)$, as $\rho(\epsilon^x, r^e | E[r^e] = E[r^x]) = 0$. From a systematic risk metric previously identified via market model, $(\beta^x \sigma(r^m))^2$, this equals $(\beta^e | (E[r^e] = E[r^x])\sigma(r^m))^2$ per the *SML*. As $\rho(r^e, r^m) = 1, \forall e$, then $(\beta^x \sigma(r^m))^2 = \sigma^2(r^e | E[r^e] = E[r^x])$, consistent with the *CML* systematic risk metric of e, given $E[r^e] = E[r^x]$.

case, this horizontal distance from the *CML* to the asset directly corresponds to its level of idiosyncratic risk.

In contrast to the *CML*, which suggests the appropriate discount rate ($E[r^P]$) given total risk *only for efficient portfolios with no idiosyncratic risk*, the *SML*, shown in figure 5.5, suggests the appropriate rate for *any* asset or portfolio of assets: efficient or not, with idiosyncratic risk or not. The key is that the *relative* risk metric used in the *SML*, β, captures systematic (market) risk, i.e., risk for which an investor is compensated.[13] Thus, *all* assets that are priced correctly plot along the *SML*.

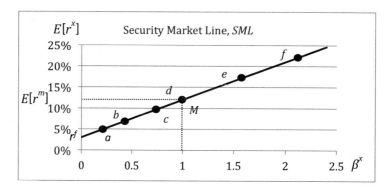

Figure 5.5 Security market line and various assets

Assets with relatively high (low) systematic risk, β, for which investors demand a high (low) expected return per the *SML*, may have low (high) total risk. For example, consider assets c and f. Per the *SML*, figure 5.5, the systematic risk of f ($\beta^f = 2.2$) is much greater than that of c ($\beta^c = 0.8$). Thus, investors demand much greater return for f (23%) than for c (10%). However, per the *CML*, figure 5.4, the total risk of asset f ($\sigma(r^f) = 34\%$) is actually less than that of asset c ($\sigma(r^c) = 39\%$). These differences are reconciled by the fact that asset c has much greater idiosyncratic risk than does asset f, which has none.[14] This drives home the point that investors are compensated for systematic (market) risk, measured by β, and *not* for total risk, which generally includes idiosyncratic risk.

Finally, *CML* and *SML* both display asset return versus systematic (market) risk. However, whereas all correctly priced assets plot along the *SML*, only portfolios with

---

[13]Actually, systematic (market) risk in the *SML* is $\beta\sigma(r^m)$. But as β is the independent axis of *SML*, it is common to state β as the relevant systematic risk metric. No generality is lost in doing so, as $\sigma(r^m)$ is simply an exogenous parameter.

[14]For example, f may be a portfolio of assets from many different industries, each sensitive to the general economy (e.g., luxury goods), whereas c may be the stock of a start-up firm with a new, unproven technology whose fortunes are not strongly tied to the general economy.

no idiosyncratic risk plot along the CML.[15] The SML applies to *all* assets; the CML *only* applies to well-diversified portfolios free of idiosyncratic risk.

Problems

Consider the following parameters for all problems in this chapter. The risk-free rate is $r^f = 4\%$, expected return of the market is $E[r^m] = 8\%$, and volatility of market return is $\sigma(r^m) = 20\%$.

1. What is the market risk premium, in percent (%)?

2. What is the value of the dimensionless market price of risk?

3. Your portfolio x, which includes a well-diversified portfolio of many risky assets and a risk-free asset, has a volatility of $\sigma(r^x) = 14\%$. What is the expected return of your portfolio?

   What is the weight of the risky asset in your portfolio?

4. What is the correlation coefficient, $\rho(r^x, r^m)$, between returns of your portfolio and the market?

5. What is the beta, β^x, of your portfolio?

   What is the expected return of your portfolio?

   What is the systematic risk, $\beta^x \sigma(r^m)$, of your portfolio?

6. If the volatility of return of your friend's portfolio y is $\sigma(r^y) = 28\%$, what is her expected return?

   What is the weight of the risky asset in her portfolio?

   How is this result possible? Specifically, how can the return of a portfolio made of a risk-free asset (of $r^f = 4\%$) and a risky asset, the market, with $E[r^m] = 8\%$, have an expected return greater than 8%?

7. What is the correlation coefficient, $\rho(r^y, r^m)$, between returns of your friend's portfolio and the market?

---

[15] Portfolios with idiosyncratic risk plot "due east" of the CML, as $\sigma(r)$ captures total risk, which includes idiosyncratic risk.

Asset Valuation Theory

8. What is the beta, β^y, of your friend's portfolio?

What is the expected return of your portfolio?

What is the systematic risk, $\beta^y \sigma(r^m)$ of your friend's portfolio?

9. What are the Sharpe ratios of your portfolio x, your friend's portfolio y and the market portfolio M?

10. What are the Treynor ratios of your portfolio x, your friend's portfolio y and the market portfolio M?

11. What is the systematic risk, $\beta^m \sigma(r^m)$ of the market portfolio?

CHAPTER 6 Arbitrage Pricing Theory

In the previous chapter, we examined the *SML* and corresponding capital asset pricing model, *CAPM*, which implies that the return demanded by an investor in a risky asset is related to its exposure to systematic risk. In *CAPM*, the latter is the expected return of the market, $E[r^m]$. The arbitrage pricing theory, *APT*, developed by Ross (1976, 1977), is another model that identifies the appropriate rate of return that an investor demands for holding a risky asset. The *APT* assumes that investors (1) participate in perfectly competitive markets, (2) are rational (more wealth is better, all else equal) and (3) are risk-averse. The *APT* has far fewer assumptions than does the *CAPM*, which additionally assumes (4) the presence of a mean-variance efficient market portfolio, (5) quadratic investor utility functions and (6) that stock returns are normally distributed.[1]

While the *CAPM* very specifically delivers the return of the market portfolio as the sole **systematic risk factor** (SRF), the *APT* presumes that asset returns are driven by a set of (unidentified) SRFs in a linear fashion. In practice, economic reasoning and emprirical testing serve as guidelines in identifying these factors. Both macroeconomic factors (e.g., gross domestic product, unexpected changes in inflation, unexpected changes in bond credit spreads) and microeconomic factors based on firm-specific characteristics have been employed.

An example of a well known **multi-factor model**, that is an empirical application of the *APT*, is the (1993) **Fama and French 3-factor model** (*FF3* model),

$$r^i_t - r^f_t = \alpha^i + \beta^i_m \left(r^m_t - r^f_t \right) + \beta^i_{cap} SMB_t + \beta^i_{bm} HML_t + \epsilon^i_t, \quad (FF3) \qquad (6.1)$$

where ϵ^i captures stock i's idiosyncratic risk, SMB is the difference in returns of two

---

[1] In general, it is desirable that a theory use as few assumptions as possible, as this makes the results more broadly applicable. The trade-off to fewer assumptions is weaker results. In this case, *APT* leaves its systematic risk factors unidentified.

portfolios of stocks segregated by their market capitalizations (small minus big), and HML is the difference in returns of two portfolios of stocks segregated by their ratios of book value to market value (high minus low). These two premia, SMB and HML, are positive in practice, i.e., all else equal, small cap stocks return more than do large cap stocks, and high book-to-market value stocks return more than do low book-to-market value stocks.

The *FF3* model has increased explanatory power beyond that of the market model, the **single factor model** equivalent of the *CAPM*. To the market model, which features the return of the market, the *FF3* model adds two more factors: SMB and HML. Grouping stocks via price-to-earnings ratios (P/E), Fama and French show that returns are better explained by including these two additional factors. Compared to the single factor model, the *FF3* model not only decreases the gap between estimated betas of firms with high and low P/E ratios, but also increases return explanatory power measured by R^2. Additionally, Carhardt (1997) shows further increased explanatory power using a fourth factor, price momentum.[2]

Generally, the *APT*'s linear set of factors can be modeled as $r^i = E[r^i|\delta_k = 0, \forall k] + \sum_{k=1}^{K} \beta_k^i \delta_k + \epsilon^i$, where δ_k is SRF$_k$ with zero mean. Also, β_k^i, asset i's sensitivity or responsiveness to SRF$_k$, is called the **SRF$_k$ beta** or **SRF$_k$ loading**. Again, ϵ^i captures stock i's idiosyncratic risk. Next, $E[r^i|\delta_k = 0, \forall k]$ is asset i's return given no idiosyncratic shock ($\epsilon^i = 0$) and no SRF shocks ($\delta_k = 0$, $\forall k \in \{1, 2, ..., K\}$). Given no shocks in a given period, $r^i = E[r^i|\delta_k = 0, \forall k]$. Finally, given the assumptions above, then with some mathematical manipulations, asset i's expected return is

$$E\left[r^i\right] = \lambda_0 + \sum_{k=1}^{K} \beta_k^i \lambda_k, \quad k \in \{1, 2, ..., K\}, \qquad (6.2)$$

where λ_k is the **risk premium** for SRF$_k$, $k \in \{1, 2, ..., K\}$. Thus, λ_0 is the return of an asset with no exposure to any systematic risk, i.e., an asset for which $\beta_k^i = 0, \forall k \in \{1, 2, ..., K\}$.[3]

Given the assumption of rational risk-averse investors, asset prices are maintained at appropriate levels via *APT* equation (6.2) by **arbitrageurs**. These are investors who seek **arbitrage** opportunities, which by definition, have the following characteristics:

---

[2]Other factors that have been used in multi-factor models include volatility of return, trading activity, earnings growth, capital structure and others.

[3]The market model, which presumes a single systematic risk factor, is a special case of the *APT*, where $K = 1$ and $\lambda_1 = r^m - r^f$. As such, β_1^i in the *APT* corresponds to the *CAPM* β.

(a) cost-free,

(b) idiosyncratic risk-free,

(c) systematic risk-free and

(d) profitable.

Arbitrageurs are vilified at times. However, while they do *not* generally push assets toward theoretically correct prices implied by intrinsic values, they do provide the valuable service of ensuring that asset pricing is consistent.[4] Indeed, existence of an arbitrage opportunity for an indefinite period of time would represent a perversion that should not exist in a well functioning capital market. But in the APT model, arbitrageurs are assumed to do more than simply keep prices consistent; they drive assets prices toward their correct levels implied by equation (6.2).

If an arbitrage opportunity exists, how does an arbitrageur identify and execute the relevant portfolio? Regarding (a), $\sum_{i=1}^{I} w^i = 0$ seems appropriate, where $w^i = \frac{V_0^i}{V_0^P}$ as previously defined. However, for a cost-free portfolio, $V_0^P = 0$, so we need to define w^i differently. Let's define

$$S \equiv \sum_{\text{long } i} V_0^i = -\sum_{\text{long } i} CF_0^i = -\sum_{\text{short } i} V_0^i = \sum_{\text{short } i} CF_0^i > 0, \quad (6.3)$$

where $V_0^i = -CF_0^i, \forall i \in \{1, 2, ..., I\}$. So S is the size (or magnitude of value) of the long half of the arbitrage portfolio. Given a cost-free portfolio, S must also be the magnitude of the short half. Hence, we can now define "cost-free" via

$$\text{(a)} \quad \sum_{i=1}^{I} w^i = 0, \text{ where } w^i = \frac{V_0^i}{S} = -\frac{CF_0^i}{S}. \quad \text{(cost-free)} \quad (6.4)$$

Note that $\sum_{\text{long } i} w^i = -\sum_{\text{short } i} w^i = 1$. So for this chapter on APT, $w^i = \frac{V_0^i}{S}$, where the weight is positive (negative) for each asset in the arbitrage portfolio with a long (short) position, corresponding to positive (negative) value and negative (positive) initial cash flow. In implementing a portfolio per APT, we first calculate weights for assets via an optimization program discussed later. Afterwards, we use the definition of w^i above to calculate the value of each asset, given our selection for portfolio size, S, or $V_0^i = w^i S, \forall i \in \{1, 2, ..., I\}$.

---

[4] "Consistent" in this context has several meanings. For example, a "single" asset (i.e., one of a given quality in a single market at a single point in time) must have only one price. Also, later in our examination of options, we learn that put-call parity establishes a relationship among four different asset prices.

For (b), idiosyncratic risk is eliminated by including many assets such that every single asset's position is "small" relative to the size of the portfolio, S. In short,

$$\text{(b)} \quad w^i = \frac{V_0^i}{S} \approx 0, \quad \forall\, i \in \{1, 2, ..., I\}, \quad \text{(idiosyncratic risk-free)} \quad (6.5)$$

or $w^i = \frac{V_0^i}{S}$ should be "very close to zero" for each asset i, regardless of the sign of w^i. Note that a large number of assets I is necessary but not sufficient to ensuring that (b) is satisfied. By the law of large numbers, positive and negative deviations from expected returns due to firm specific issues should roughly cancel each other in a portfolio with many assets, eliminating idiosyncratic risk, or $\epsilon^P = \sum_{i=1}^{\text{large } I} w^i \epsilon_t^i \approx 0$.

Regarding (c), the return of an arbitrage portfolio P is

$$E[r^P] = \sum_{i=1}^{I} w^i E[r^i] = \sum_{i=1}^{I} w^i \left(\lambda_0 + \sum_{k=1}^{K} \beta_k^i \lambda_k \right)$$

$$= \sum_{i=1}^{I} w^i \lambda_0 + \sum_{i=1}^{I} w^i \sum_{k=1}^{K} \beta_k^i \lambda_k = \lambda_0 \sum_{i=1}^{I} w^i + \sum_{i=1}^{I} \sum_{k=1}^{K} w^i \beta_k^i \lambda_k$$

$$= \sum_{k=1}^{K} \sum_{i=1}^{I} w^i \beta_k^i \lambda_k = \sum_{k=1}^{K} \lambda_k \left(\sum_{i=1}^{I} w^i \beta_k^i \right), \quad (6.6)$$

where $k \in \{1, 2, ..., K\}$, and $i \in \{1, 2, ..., I\}$.[5] Our arbitrage portfolio is systematic risk-free if it has no exposure to the K SRFs. Thus, per the final expression of equation (6.6), we choose weights such that

$$\sum_{i=1}^{I} w^i \beta_k^i = 0, \ \forall k \in \{1, 2, ..., K\}. \quad (6.7)$$

Note that if w^1, w^2, ... and w^I are chosen such that the K equations in expression (6.7) are satisfied, then not only is this cost-free portfolio free of systematic risk, but also it has an expected return of zero, $E[r^P] = 0$, per equation (6.6). So how does an arbitrageur make a profit? She must believe that asset prices are *not* consistent with those implied by equation (6.2). Before we can proceed to item (d), profitability, we must introduce the arbitrageur's beliefs regarding anticipating asset returns. As this

---

[5] As λ_0 is a constant, it can be pulled outside of the summation on the second line. As $\sum_{i=1}^{I} w^i = 0$, then the first summation on the second line simplifies to 0, and thus disappears on the third line. On the second line, as w^i is not a function of index k, then it can be pulled inside the summation over index k. To begin the third line, we switch the order of summation, as $x + y = y + x$. Regarding the finally equality of the third line, as λ_k is not a function of index i, then it can be pulled outside the summation over index i.

critically important topic is a common source of confusion for students, we devote an entire section to it. Afterwards, we return to the question, "how does one profit via arbitrage in the context of *APT*?"

6.1 Demanded, Expected and Implied Rates of Return

Previously we defined the **implied rate of return**, IRR^x, as the discount rate that equates an asset's current price to the summation of present values of expected future cash flows, or

$$P_0^x = \sum_{t=1}^{T} \frac{E[CF_t^x]}{(1+IRR^x)^t}. \tag{6.8}$$

As previously noted, IRR^x is the rate of return that an investor anticipates to receive when she purchases an asset. Also, if $IRR^x > E[r^x]$ ($IRR^x < E[r^x]$), then the investor believes that the asset is under-valued (over-valued). So IRR^x is *not* based directly on any systematic risk metric. It is based solely on an asset's current price and expected cash flows via equation (6.8).

We have shown that $E[r^x]$ can be defined via *CAPM*. In the current chapter, it is defined via *APT*.[6] As $E[r^x]$ is the rate of return demanded by an investor, then we can define the **intrinsic value** of asset x as

$$IV^x = \sum_{t=1}^{T} \frac{E[CF_t^x]}{(1+E[r^x])^t}, \tag{6.9}$$

where $E[r^x]$ is the **demanded** (or **required**) **rate of return** per an asset pricing model, e.g. *CAPM* or *APT*.

Generally speaking, *expected return per any asset pricing model is* NOT *the return that an investor expects.* Possible confusion arises by the term "expected" return in models such as *CAPM* and *APT*. The reason that both models refer to "expected" return is that they are couched in the future, i.e., in terms of expectations. So they generate the appropriate demanded rate of return or required rate of return for investors in a given asset, based on the model's respective metric for systematic risk.

While an "expected" rate of return calculated via asset pricing model is the theoretical return that an investor demands based on the systematic risk of the asset per the model, IRR^x is that which an investor anticipates to earn, based solely on pricing and expected cash flows. Both IRR^x and IV^x are functions of $E[CF_t^x]$, $t \in \{1, 2, ..., T\}$. However, IRR^x is a function of P_0^x, whereas IV^x is a function of $E[r^x]$. In short, these

---
[6]In either case, the conditions defining over-valued and under-valued remain the same.

related concepts are two sides of the same coin when making a decision regarding asset position. One can either compare P_0^x with IV^x or compare $E[r^x]$ with IRR^x. This is because the function $IRR^x(P_0^x)$ is strictly increasing in P_0^x, whereas $IV^x(E[r^x])$ is strictly decreasing in $E[r^x]$.[7] This duality is evident from the first two lines of entries in figure 6.1, which summarizes the general implications of this discussion.[8]

P_0^x **Vs.** IV^x	$P_0^x > IV^x$	$P_0^x < IV^x$	$P_0^x = IV^x$
IRR^x **Vs.** $E[r^x]$	$IRR^x < E[r^x]$	$IRR^x > E[r^x]$	$IRR^x = E[r^x]$
Belief	over-valued	under-valued	fairly valued
Action	short sell	buy	none
Position	liability	asset	none
If asset $P_t^x \uparrow$	Equity $\downarrow$	Equity $\uparrow$	no ΔEquity

Figure 6.1   Summary of price versus intrinsic value

6.2 APT Continued: How to Make a Profit

We now return to answer the question posed earlier, "how does an arbitrageur make a profit?" In general, she expects a portfolio rate of return of

$$IRR^P = \sum_{i=1}^{I} w^i \left(IRR^i \right). \qquad (6.10)$$

Assume that she executes an arbitrage portfolio which is (a) cost-free, satisfying equation (6.4), (b) idiosyncratic risk-free, satisfying the I qualitative restrictions in expression (6.5), and is (c) systematic risk-free, satisfying the K constraints in expression (6.7). Then as previously noted per equation (6.6), $E[r^P] = 0$, so

$$IRR^P = IRR^P - E[r^P] = \sum_{i=1}^{I} w^i \left(IRR^i - E[r^i] \right)$$

$$= \underbrace{\sum w^i \left(IRR^i - E[r^i] \right)}_{\text{long } w^i} + \underbrace{\sum w^i \left(IRR^i - E[r^i] \right)}_{\text{short } w^i}. \qquad (6.11)$$

If all assets are correctly priced, or $E[r^i] = IRR^i, \forall i \in \{1, 2, ..., I\}$, then per equation (6.11), $IRR^P = 0$. This makes sense: if there exists no mis-pricing, then a risk-free

---

[7]Both claims assume **limited liability**, i.e., an investor may never be forced to make an incremental investment in an asset beyond that made voluntarily. Thus, investor cash flows for a long position are all non-negative after the initial asset investment.

[8]In figure 6.1, exceptions may exist to lines 4, 5 and 6 in the context of portfolios, but these relationships are generally true. Line 3 is true by definition of value, given the relations on lines 1 and 2.

portfolio that costs nothing should earn nothing. In short, arbitrage is not possible if all assets are correctly priced.[9]

Let's assume that there exists some mis-pricing. Then $E[r^i] > IRR^i$ exists for over-valued assets, and $E[r^i] < IRR^i$ exists for under-valued assets. In such an environment, consider again a cost-free, risk-free portfolio. Rewriting equation (6.11), then

$$IRR^P = \sum_{\text{long } w^i} w^i \underbrace{\left(IRR^i - E[r^i]\right)}_{\text{typically } > 0} + \sum_{\text{short } w^i} w^i \underbrace{\left(IRR^i - E[r^i]\right)}_{\text{typically } < 0}. \qquad (6.12)$$

Recall that $w^i > 0$ ($w^i < 0$) for long (short) positions. As an investor typically establishes a long (short) position in asset i when $IRR^i > E[r^i]$ ($IRR^i < E[r^i]$) as noted via underbraces in equation (6.12), it follows that $IRR^P > 0$.[10] As such, arbitrage is possible: a cost-free, risk-free, profit. Finally, rearranging $w^i = \frac{V_0^i}{S}$ to $V_0^i = w^i S$, then portfolio profit, π^P, is[11]

$$\pi^P = \sum_{i=1}^{I} V_0^i \left(IRR^i - E[r^i]\right) = S \sum_{i=1}^{I} w^i \left(IRR^i - E[r^i]\right) = S \left(IRR^P\right). \qquad (6.13)$$

In summary, an arbitrageur attempts to assemble I assets in a cost-free, risk-free manner in order to earn a profit. As such, she must satisfy $K+1$ equality constraints: K equations to ensure that the portfolio is systematic risk-free in expression (6.7) plus the one cost-free equation, expression (6.4). She must also satisfy the I qualitative idiosyncratic risk-free conditions, expression (6.5), by ensuring that each asset with idosyncratic risk has a small position. Within these restrictions, she seeks mis-pricing and generally establishes long (short) positions in assets that are under-valued (over-valued).

---

[9]Mis-pricing is a necessary, but not sufficient, condition for arbitrage.

[10]In practice, it is possible that the portfolio may have a long (short) position in an over-valued (under-valued) asset due to its contribution toward elimination of portfolio systematic risk, i.e., due to its particular combination of sensitivities to SRFs. As a simple example, consider two over-valued, well-diversified portfolios with identical systematic risks. The pricing is such that different rates of return are implied, i.e., one is more over-valued than the other. Then an arbitrage portfolio is possible by setting up a long (short) position in the relatively cheaper (more expensive) portfolio, i.e., the one that is less (more) over-valued. Analogously, if both portfolios were under-valued to varying degrees, one would short the lesser under-valued portfolio.

[11]As S is not a function of i, then it can be pulled outside the summation over index i.

6.3 Implementing an Arbitrage Portfolio per *APT*

Let's conclude this chapter with simple examples to illustrate the procedure. Our investor's choice variables are the I arbitrage portfolio weights, $w^A, w^B, ..., w^I$. For an investor modeling $K + 1$ SRFs, she must include at least $I = K + 1$ assets in her *APT* portfolio.[12] If $I = K + 1$, we simply solve our $K + 1$ linear constraints for the I choice variables, $w^A, w^B, ..., w^I$. However, in practice, I will usually be much larger than $K + 1$.[13] If so, then a constrained maximization program ensues, i.e., maximize IRR^P per equation (6.11) subject to the relevant constraints.[14]

As all $K+1$ linear constraints feature an expression equal to zero, then the solution weights are all relative to one another. Recall that we had to define w^i differently in this chapter, i.e., in terms of magnitude of the long side of the portfolio, S, which also equals the magnitude of the short side. An arbitrageur does not execute with "small" S, but rather with the largest S possible, i.e., she increases S until her actions eliminate further opportunity. As she buys an under-valued (sells an over-valued) asset, she exerts upward (downward) pressure on its price; this drives IRR^i down (up) toward $E[r^i]$. Executing her trades in creating the arbitrage portfolio drives asset prices to the point that the profit of incremental portfolio size approaches zero.[15] However, for ease of exposition, our program assumes exogenous, constant pricing.[16] Thus, we will restrict ourselves to an exogenous value of S. We do so by adding another constraint to our maximization program.

Let's assume in this section that $K = 2$, with systematic risk premia, λ_1 and λ_2, respectively. We show an example where the total number of assets $I = K + 1 = 3$ and one where $4 = I > K + 1 = 3$. In each case, at least one asset is mis-priced, per a necessary condition of *APT*. In other words, there exists an $i \in \{A, B, ..., I\}$ such

---

[12]For clarity of exposition, we use letters to denote assets in order to contrast them with numbers, used to denote systematic risk factors.

[13]Typically, $K < 10$. In order to eliminate idiosyncratic risk per expression (6.5), I must be much larger than 10 if individual assets (with idiosyncratic risk) are used. However, I may be small if the assets used as building blocks for the *APT* portfolio are themselves free of idiosyncratic risk, i.e., are well-diversified portfolios.

[14]Maximizing IRR^P is equivalent to maximizing π^P, as S is assumed to be an exogenous parameter. In reality, S is endogenous based on elasticity of asset pricing, and the arbitrageur increases S until the opportunity is eliminated from the capital market.

[15]From $\pi^P = IRR^P S$, then $d\pi^P = IRR^P dS + S dIRR^P$. Ignoring transaction costs, she increases S until $d\pi^P = 0$, or until $dln(S) = -dln(IRR^P)$. Generally, as the opportunity disappears, $dln(S) = -dln(IRR^P) > 0$, if we ignore the price-taking assumption.

[16]If this were true, the arbitrage opportunity would never disappear.

that $IRR^i \neq E[r^i]$. Given individual assets, $I \leqslant 4$ is not nearly enough to eliminate idiosyncratic risk per expressions (6.5). Thus, we skirt this concern by assuming that our assets are not individual assets, but rather well-diversified portfolios, each free of idiosyncratic risk.

6.3.1 Example: Three Assets, Two Systematic Risk Factors

In our first example, where $I = K + 1 = 3$, an investor is not optimizing an arbitrage portfolio *per se*[17], but rather is simply satisfying three simultaneous equations: two to eliminate two systematic risks and one to ensure that the portfolio is cost-free.[18]

$$z^A \beta_1^A + z^B \beta_1^B + z^C \beta_1^C = 0, \quad \text{(eliminate exposure to SRF}_1)$$
$$z^A \beta_2^A + z^B \beta_2^B + z^C \beta_2^C = 0, \quad \text{(eliminate exposure to SRF}_2)$$
$$\text{and} \quad z^A + z^B + z^C = 0, \quad \text{(cost-free)} \tag{6.14}$$

where z^A, z^B and z^C are *relative* asset weights. Let's define $Z \equiv \sum_{\text{long } i} z^i = -\sum_{\text{short } i} z^i > 0$, where the equality is due to the cost-free constraint. Then $w^i = \frac{z^i}{Z}, i \in \{A, B, C\}$. Finally, for each asset i, $V_0^i = w^i S$. Why can't we simply use w^i directly in the three constraints of expression (6.14)? Consider a solution (z^A, z^B, z^C). Then (kz^A, kz^B, kz^C) is also a solution, for any constant k, as the right hand side of the system of equations in expression (6.14) is a vector of zeros. This is related to our earlier discussion, where S must be exogenously bounded, given our "price-taking" assumption. Thus, we start with relative weights and then from these, calculate the actual weights via normalization. So we first calculate the relative weights z^i, then $Z = \sum_{\text{long } i} z^i$, then $w^i = \frac{z^i}{Z}$, $i \in \{A, B, C\}$ and finally, $V_0^i = w^i S, i \in \{A, B, C\}$.

When $I = K+1$, a simple approach to solving the above is to assume that $z^A = 1$, which effectively constrains S. Afterwards, we solve for z^B and z^C. Due to the cost-free constraint, either one asset is short and two are long, or vice versa. Also, the magnitude of the sum of the positive weight(s) equals that of the negative weight(s) equals Z. From the three $w^i = \frac{z^i}{Z}$, then if the resulting $IRR^P = \sum_{i=1}^{I} w^i (IRR^i - E[r^i])$ per equation (6.11) is positive, the correct weights have been identified. If negative, simply reverse the sign of all three weights. This leaves in tact all three equations above but changes the sign of IRR^P from negative to positive.

---

[17]More specifically, two sets of solution weights satisfy our constraints, (w^A, w^B, w^C) and $(-w^A, -w^B, -w^C)$, where $IRR^P(w^A, w^B, w^C) > 0 > IRR^P(-w^A, -w^B, -w^C)$.

[18]In this special case, where we are simply solving $I = K + 1$ simultaneous linear equations, we constrain relative asset weights by initially letting $z^A = 1$, without loss of generality.

In our first example, assume that $\lambda_0 = 5\%$, $\lambda_1 = 2\%$ and $\lambda_2 = 4\%$. Other parameters are as shown in figure 6.2.[19] Arbitrarily letting $z^A = 1$, then the three equations in system (6.14) yield $z^B|(z^A = 1) = -0.5$ and $z^C|(z^A = 1) = -0.5$. Next $z^A = -(z^B + z^C) = Z = 1$, so $w^A = 1$, $w^B = -0.5$ and $w^C = -0.5$. Next, $IRR^P = w^A(IRR^A - E[r^A]) + w^B(IRR^B - E[r^B]) + w^C(IRR^C - E[r^C]) = 1(5\% - 5.25\%) - 0.5(9\% - 8.5\%) - 0.5(3\% - 2\%) = -1.00\% < 0$. As IRR^P is negative given these weights, we simply reverse their signs, or $w^A = -1$, $w^B = +0.5$ and $w^C = +0.5$, resulting in $IRR^P = +1\% > 0$. Let's assume an exogenous value for magnitude of each side (long and short) of the portfolio of $S = \$10,000$. So an investor short sells $\$10,000$ of asset A, and uses this capital to finance purchases of $\$5,000$ each of assets B and C. So $V_0^A = -CF_0^A = -\$10,000$, $V_0^B = V_0^C = -CF_0^B = -CF_0^C = +\$5,000$. Note that consistent with what one expects, the arbitrage portfolio is long in the two assets (B and C) in which $IRR^i > E[r^i]$, and short in asset A, where $IRR^A < E[r^A]$. Finally, $\pi^P = IRR^P S = 1\%(\$10,000) = \$1,000$, per equation (6.13).

	Asset A	Asset B	Asset C
Inputs			
	$\beta_1^A = 0.625$	$\beta_1^B = 0.75$	$\beta_1^C = 0.50$
	$\beta_2^A = -0.25$	$\beta_2^B = 0.50$	$\beta_2^C = -1.00$
	$IRR^A = 5.00\%$	$IRR^B = 9.00\%$	$IRR^C = 3.00\%$
Outputs			
	$E[r^A] = 5.25\%$	$E[r^B] = 8.50\%$	$E[r^C] = 2.00\%$
	$w^A = -100\%$	$w^B = +50\%$	$w^C = +50\%$

Figure 6.2 **APT** example 1: three assets, two systematic risk factors

6.3.2 Example: Four Assets, Two Systematic Risk Factors

Now consider an example where $4 = I > K + 1 = 3$, i.e., where the number of assets exceeds the number of SRFs. Recall that in the previous example ($I = K+1 = 3$), we simply solved three simultaneous linear constraints, resulting in two possible solution weight vectors where $\sum_{\text{long } i} w^i = -\sum_{\text{short } i} w^i = 1$. We chose the one resulting in $IRR^P > 0$. In contrast, now with $I > K + 1$, we have a more challenging optimization program, as there exists an infinite number of vectors solving the $K + 1 = 3$ constraints

---

[19]Note: $E[r^A] = \lambda_0 + \lambda_1 \beta_1^A + \lambda_2 \beta_2^A = 5\% + 2\%(0.625) + 4\%(-0.25) = 5.25\%$. Other expected returns are similarly calculated.

given $\sum_{\text{long } i} w^i = -\sum_{\text{short } i} w^i = 1$. So we constrain each relative weight, z^A, z^B, z^C and z^D, which is related to exogenously constraining S.[20] We arbitrarily bind the relative weights to the interval $[-5, +5]$.[21] The maximization program is

$$\max_{z^A, z^B, z^C, z^D} IRR^P = \sum_{i=A,B,C,D} z^i (IRR^i - E[r^i]), \text{ subject to}$$

$$z^A \beta_1^A + z^B \beta_1^B + z^C \beta_1^C + z^D \beta_1^D = 0, \quad \text{(no SRF 1)}$$

$$z^A \beta_2^A + z^B \beta_2^B + z^C \beta_2^C + z^D \beta_2^D = 0, \quad \text{(no SRF 2)}$$

$$\text{and} \quad z^A + z^B + z^C + z^D = 0, \quad \text{(cost-free)}$$

$$z^i \in [-5, +5], \, i \in \{A, B, C, D\}. \quad \text{(constrain } S\text{)} \quad (6.15)$$

Such a constrained optimization program can be solved via the Lagrangian method.[22]

Assume that $\lambda_0 = 5\%$, $\lambda_1 = 2\%$ and $\lambda_2 = 4\%$. Other parameters are as shown in figure 6.3. The solution consists of relative weights $z^A = +2$, $z^B = -5$, $z^C = +4$ and $z^D = -1$. Normalizing, $Z = 2 + 4 = -(-5 - 1) = 6$, so the portfolio weights are $w^A = \frac{+2}{2+4} = +33.3\%$, $w^B = \frac{-5}{-(-5-1)} = -83.3\%$, $w^C = \frac{+4}{2+4} = +66.7\%$ and $w^D = \frac{-1}{-(-5-1)} = -16.7\%$.[23] Next, $IRR^P = w^A(IRR^A - E[r^A]) + w^B(IRR^B - E[r^B]) + w^C(IRR^C - E[r^C]) + w^D(IRR^D - E[r^D]) = 0.333(12\% - 11\%) - 0.833(12\% - 12.5\%) + 0.667(13\% - 12\%) - 0.167(7\% - 7.5\%) = +1.5\% > 0$. Let's further assume an exogenous value for magnitude of each side (long and short) of the portfolio of $S = \$10,000$. So an investor short sells $\$8,333$ of asset B and $\$1,667$ of asset D. She uses this capital to finance purchases of assets A ($\$3,333$) and C ($\$6,667$). So $V_0^A = -CF_0^A = +\$3,333$, $V_0^B = -CF_0^B = -\$8,333$, $V_0^C = -CF_0^C = +\$6,667$, and $V_0^D = -CF_0^D = -\$1,667$. Note that consistent with what one expects, the arbitrage portfolio is long in the two under-valued assets (A and C) in which $IRR^i > E[r^i]$ and short in the two over-valued

---

[20] Before, we simply assigned $z^A = 1$ and proceeded to solve for z^B and z^C per the three constraints. We chose weights corresponding to $z^A = 1$ or $z^A = -1$, whichever results in $IRR^P > 0$. This time, we explicitly constrain all weights as outlined here. Alternatively, one could again set $z^A = 1$ and proceed to solve for z^B, z^C and z^D which maximize IRR^P subject to the $K+1$ constraints. This would need to be compared to the optimized value of a second maximization program, $(IRR^P | z^A = -1)$, and choose the solution corresponding to the higher IRR^P.

[21] Any interval $[-\alpha, +\alpha]$ works fine, for any $\alpha > 0$.

[22] In Excel, solving such a program is straightforward using the add-in, Solver.

[23] As discussed before, an arbitrageur would increase her positions represented by these weights until the opportunity disappears due to the pressure that she exerts on asset pricing due to her buying (assets A and C) and selling (assets B and D). As she drives the prices of B and D down (A and C up), IRR^B and IRR^D decrease (IRR^A and IRR^C increase) until $IRR^P = 0$. However, our program assumes price-taking.

assets (B and D) in which $IRR^i < E[r^i]$. Finally, $\pi^P = IRR^P S = 1.5\%(\$10,000) = \$1,500$, per equation (6.13).

	Asset A	Asset B	Asset C	Asset D
Inputs				
	$\beta_1^A = 1.00$	$\beta_1^B = 0.75$	$\beta_1^C = 0.50$	$\beta_1^D = 0.25$
	$\beta_2^A = 1.00$	$\beta_2^B = 1.50$	$\beta_2^C = 1.50$	$\beta_2^D = 0.50$
	$IRR^A = 12\%$	$IRR^B = 12\%$	$IRR^C = 13\%$	$IRR^D = 7\%$
Outputs				
	$E[r^A] = 11\%$	$E[r^B] = 12.5\%$	$E[r^C] = 12\%$	$E[r^D] = 7.5\%$
	$w^A = +33.3\%$	$w^B = -83.3\%$	$w^C = +66.7\%$	$w^D = -16.7\%$

Figure 6.3 *APT* example 2: four assets, two systematic risk factors

Problems

Consider the following parameters for problems in this chapter. The risk-free asset has a return of 5%. The premium for holding an asset with systematic risk factor 1 is 2% and the premium for holding an asset with systematic risk factor 2 is 4%, all else equal.

1. Well diversified portfolio x has a systematic risk factor 1 loading of 1.025 and a systematic risk factor 2 loading of 1.25. Well diversified portfolio y has a systematic risk factor 1 loading of 2 and a systematic risk factor 2 loading of 2. Well diversified portfolio z has a systematic risk factor 1 loading of 0.7 and a systematic risk factor 2 loading of 1. You believe that asset x will earn a rate of return of 11% over the coming year, that asset y's rate of return will be 17% and that asset z's rate of return will be 10.4%. In order to create an arbitrage portfolio, what weights of portfolios x, y and z should be held?

Consider a magnitude of $100 invested in portfolio x (i.e., you either invest $100 (a long position) or $-\$100$ (a short position)). Do you invest $100 or $-\$100$ in portfolio x? How much do you invest in portfolio y and portfolio z? Are your positions in y and z long or short?

Per $100 invested long or short in portfolio x, what is your profit?

2. Well diversified portfolio x has a systematic risk factor 1 loading of 0.75 and a sys-

tematic risk factor 2 loading of –0.5. Well diversified portfolio y has a systematic risk factor 1 loading of 1.5 and a systematic risk factor 2 loading of –0.5. Well diversified portfolio z has a systematic risk factor 1 loading of 1 and a systematic risk factor 2 loading of –0.5. You believe that asset x will earn a rate of return of 5% over the coming year, that asset y's rate of return will be 7% and that asset z's rate of return will be 4.5%. In order to create an arbitrage portfolio, what weights of portfolios x, y and z should be held?

Consider a magnitude of $100 invested in portfolio x (i.e., you either invest $100 (a long position) or −$100 (a short position)). Do you invest $100 or −$100 in portfolio x? How much do you invest in portfolio y and portfolio z? Are your positions in y and z long or short?

Per $100 invested long or short in portfolio x, what is your profit?

3. Well diversified portfolio x has a systematic risk factor 1 loading of 2.05 and a systematic risk factor 2 loading of 2.5. Well diversified portfolio y has a systematic risk factor 1 loading of 4 and a systematic risk factor 2 loading of 4. Well diversified portfolio z has a systematic risk factor 1 loading of 1.4 and a systematic risk factor 2 loading of 2. You believe that asset x will earn a rate of return of 18% over the coming year, that asset y's rate of return will be 30% and that asset z's rate of return will be 15.8%. In order to create an arbitrage portfolio, what weights of portfolios x, y and z should be held?

Consider a magnitude of $100 invested in portfolio x (i.e., you either invest $100 (a long position) or −$100 (a short position)). Do you invest $100 or −$100 in portfolio x? How much do you invest in portfolio y and portfolio z? Is your position in y and z long or short?

Per $100 invested long or short in portfolio x, what is your profit?

Now, instead of three portfolios (x, y and z), we add a new, fourth well-diversified portfolio, a, in the following two problems.

4. Well diversified portfolio x has a systematic risk factor 1 loading of 0.25 and a systematic risk factor 2 loading of 0.5. Well diversified portfolio y has a systematic risk factor 1 loading of 0.75 and a systematic risk factor 2 loading of 1.25. Well diversified portfolio z has a systematic risk factor 1 loading of 0.5 and a systematic risk factor

2 loading of –0.5. Well diversified portfolio a has a systematic risk factor 1 loading of –0.25 and a systematic risk factor 2 loading of 0.5. You believe that asset x will earn a rate of return of 7% over the coming year, asset y's rate of return will be 12%, asset z's rate of return will be 5% and that asset a's rate of return will be 7%. In order to create an arbitrage portfolio, what weights of portfolios x, y, z and a should be held?

Consider a magnitude of $100 invested in portfolio x (i.e., you either invest $100 (a long position) or $-$100 (a short position)). Do you invest $100 or $-$100 in portfolio x? How much do you invest in portfolio y, z and a? Is your position in y, z and a long or short?

Per $100 invested long or short in portfolio x, what is your profit?

5. Well diversified portfolio x has a systematic risk factor 1 loading of 0.25 and a systematic risk factor 2 loading of 1. Well diversified portfolio y has a systematic risk factor 1 loading of 0.5 and a systematic risk factor 2 loading of 0.5. Well diversified portfolio z has a systematic risk factor 1 loading of 0.75 and a systematic risk factor 2 loading of 0.25. Well diversified portfolio a has a systematic risk factor 1 loading of 1 and a systematic risk factor 2 loading of 1. You believe that asset x will earn a rate of return of 9% over the coming year, asset y's rate of return will be 9%, asset z's rate of return will be 7% and that asset a's rate of return will be 11%. In order to create an arbitrage portfolio, what weights of portfolios x, y, z and a should be held?

Consider a magnitude of $100 invested in portfolio x (i.e., you either invest $100 (a long position) or $-$100 (a short position)). Do you invest $100 or $-$100 in portfolio x? How much do you invest in portfolio y, z and a? Is your position in y, z and a long or short?

Per $100 invested long or short in portfolio x, what is your profit?

PART III   Equity Valuation

    We have spent the past few chapters exploring how to determine discount rates for cash flows of assets based on their riskiness. Now we shift gears and begin to explore how to value firms and their equities, in both a relative sense as well as an absolute sense. Relative valuation involves comparing relevant metrics of firms with those of comparable firms. Absolute valuation utilizes calculations consistent with those of intrinsic value.

    In chapter 7 we first consider three financial accounting statements: (a) income statement, (b) balance sheet and (c) statement of cash flows. Afterwards in chapter 8 we utilize ratios of entries from these statements in order to analyze the respective firms. Next, we calculate ratios of equity price to various firm specific characteristics. In relative valuation, we compare these ratios across firms in the same industry, i.e., those that face similar risks and opportunities.

    Regarding absolute valuation, in chapter 9 we calculate various types of cash flows from the three financial accounting statements. Discounting these, we determine the intrinsic values of firms and their stock holders' equities.

    In the final chapter of this part, chapter 10, we explore the earnings multiplier model, *EMM*. This is a hybrid of a popular relative valuation metric, the $\frac{price}{earnings}$ ratio, and a popular absolute valuation technique, the dividend discount model.

CHAPTER 7

Review of Financial Accounting Statements

In this chapter, we briefly review three financial accounting statements. The purposes are to be able to calculate: (a) metrics used in financial accounting statement analysis, (b) ratios for use in relative valuation techniques, and (c) various cash flows (section 7.4) for use in absolute valuation.

Of the three statements, the balance sheet is the only one that utilizes **stock variables**, i.e., those whose values do *not* depend on a time duration, i.e., they do *not* depend on a period of time. Balance sheets show values as of a given point in time. For example, given annual time-frames, balance sheets usually show stock variables as of the final day of the year. In contrast, both the income statement and the statement of cash flows utilize **flow variables**, i.e., those whose values depend upon the selected time duration, or period of time, typically one quarter or one year.

Consider a time period of one calendar year, so that the period is bounded by two consecutive year-end dates, year-end$_{t-1}$ and year-end$_t$. In some sense, balance sheet entries corresponding to these two consecutive year-end dates are connected by income statement entries corresponding to year (period) t, which is bounded by the two dates. As financial statements are intended to provide transparency regarding the financial condition of the firm, we can think of them in terms of media. A balance sheet corresponds to a still photograph (i.e., a snapshot in time taken at the end of the year) and the other two statements correspond to videos with a time duration of one calendar year.

7.1 Income Statement

Figure 7.1 is a simple example of an income statement, where the period of time is calendar year $t = 2015$.[1] For the same firm, figure 7.2 shows balance sheets for the

---

[1] In what follows, all figures are in thousands of dollars.

two dates, year-end 2014 and year-end 2015. These two dates serve as "book-ends" corresponding to the income statement's time period, calendar year $t = 2015$.

Income Statement Entry	2015
Net sales (NS)	215,600
Cost of goods sold ($COGS$)	129,364
Gross profit (GP)	86,236
Selling, general and administrative (SGA) expenses	45,722
Advertising	14,258
Depreciation and amortization ($D\&A$)	3,998
Repairs and maintenance	3,015
Operating Profit ($EBIT^*$)	19,243
Other Income (expense)	
Interest income (II)	422
Interest expense (IE)	(2,585)
Earnings before income taxes (EBT^{**})	17,080
Income taxes	7,686
Net earnings, net income (NI)	9,394
Basic earnings per common share	1.96
Diluted earnings per common share	1.93

$^*EBIT$ stands for earnings before interest income (expenses) and taxes.
$^{**}EBT$ stands for earnings before taxes (but *after* interest income (expenses)).
All numbers are in $ thousands.

Figure 7.1   Income statement

From a high level perspective, the **income statement** (IS) calculates a firm's profit as revenues minus costs. Regarding details, cost of goods sold, $COGS$, are manufacturing costs and SGA expenses are non-manufacturing costs. Depreciation and amortization ($D\&A$) are non-cash accounting entries whereby gross property, plant & equipment ($GPPE$) is "written off" over time.[2] Note that $D\&A_{2015}$ on the income statement, $3,998$, ties together accumulated depreciation and amortization (Acc $D\&A$) entries on the two corresponding balance sheets, or Acc $D\&A_{2015}$ − Acc $D\&A_{2014}$ = $\$11,528 - \$7,530 = \$3,998 = D\&A_{2015}$.

Earnings before interest and taxes, $EBIT$, is what remains of revenue after subtracting operating expenses ($COGS$, SGA, Advertising, $D\&A$, repairs and maintenance). So in an accounting sense, $EBIT$ is "available" to pay taxes and to reward contributors of financial capital. From $EBIT$, debt holders are paid first. Afterwards,

---

[2]The firm would reduce its taxable income, EBT, in any year of large investments if it were allowed to expense such purchases of PPE in the corresponding year of purchase. However, tax authorities require the firm to "write off" such purchases over time, in some sense consistent with the relative utilization of asset's useful lifetime capacity.

Balance Sheet Entry	15/12/31	14/12/31
Assets (A)		
Current Assets (CA)		
Cash	4,061	2,382
Marketable securities (MS)	5,272	8,004
Accounts receivable*	8,960	8,350
Inventories	47,041	36,769
Prepaid expenses	512	759
Total current assets	65,846	56,264
Property, Plant & Equipment: PPE		
Land	811	811
Buildings & leasehold improvements	18,273	11,928
Equipment	21,523	13,768
Gross PPE	40,607	26,507
Less accumulated depreciation & amortization	11,528	7,530
Net PPE	29,079	18,977
Other Assets	373	668
Total Assets, TA	95,298	75,909
Liabilities and Stock holders' Equity		
Current Liabilities (CL)		
Accounts payable (AP)	14,294	7,591
Notes payable to banks (NP)	5,614	6,012
Current maturities of LTD (CM)	1,884	1,516
Accrued liabilities	5,669	5,313
Total current liabilities	27,461	20,432
Deferred Incomes Taxes (DIT)	843	635
Long-Term Debt (LTD)	21,059	16,975
Total liabilities	49,363	38,042
Stock holders' Equity		
Common stock, par value of $1**	4,803	4,594
Additional paid-in capital	957	910
Retained earnings (RE)	40,175	32,363
Total Stock holders' Equity	45,935	37,867
Total Liabilities & Stock holders' Equity	95,298	75,909

*This is less allowances for doubtful accounts.
**10,000,000 shares authorized; 4,803,000 shares issued in 2015; 4,594,000 shares issued in 2014;
All numbers are in $ thousands.

Figure 7.2 Balance sheet

tax is calculated and paid to the government. Finally, any residual is claimed by the owners of the firm, the share holders.

Debt holders are paid interest, their return on capital. Only after interest is paid does the firm calculate taxes owed. Thus, by allowing the firm to deduct interest *before* determining its taxable income, tax authorities appropriately recognize interest paid to debt holders as a legitimate business expense. (Interest payments are *not* discretionary;

74   **Asset Valuation Theory**

they represent a legal obligation.[3])

The firm pays cash dividends, d, to equity holders, which in an accounting sense, come from net income. The remainder of net income, $NI_t - d_t = RE_t - RE_{t-1} \equiv \Delta RE_t$, is plowed back into the firm as retained earnings, RE.[4] As we saw earlier regarding $D\&A$ on the income statement and accumulated $D\&A$ entries on corresponding balance sheets, we again see an example of how an income statement item, NI_t via $NI_t - d_t$, ties together a difference of items on two corresponding balance sheets, $RE_t - RE_{t-1}$. In our example, $\Delta RE_{2015} = \$7,812 = RE_{2015} - RE_{2014} = \$40,175 - \$32,363$, which equals $NI_{2015} - d_{2015} = \$9,394 - \$1,582$.

The ratio $b_t \equiv \frac{\Delta RE_t}{NI_t}$, called the **plowback ratio**, is the fraction of equity holders' net income plowed back into the firm on their behalf by the firm's management. In the current example, $b_{2015} = \frac{\Delta RE_{2015}}{NI_{2015}} = \frac{\$7,812}{\$9,394} = 83.2\%$. The complement, $1 - b_{2015} = \frac{d_{2015}}{NI_{2015}} = \frac{1,582}{9,394} = 16.8\%$, is called the **dividend payout ratio**. Finally, note that basic earnings per common share is $\frac{\text{net income}_t}{\text{shares outstanding}_t} = \frac{NI_{2015}}{SO_{2015}} = \frac{\$9,394}{4,803} = 1.96$ earnings per share.

7.2 Balance Sheet

As previously noted, figure 7.2 shows a balance sheet for the two dates, year-end 2014 and year-end 2015. The **balance sheet** (BS) shows the sources and uses of capital. As every dollar of capital raised (i.e., the sources of capital) must be accounted for (i.e., usages of capital), the BS expresses the equality of liabilities plus stock holders' equity (sources) and assets (uses). Hence, this equality suggests the statement's name: balance sheet. The liabilities plus stock holders' equity "side" of the BS can be thought of as the financing side, as it shows from where capital has been raised to support the purchase of assets. The other "side", which shows the firm's present assets, can be thought of as the "capital budgeting" side of the BS, as it shows the cumulative effects of the firm's decisions regarding purchasing and selling of assets. Respective values on the balance sheet are called **book values**.

Current assets, CA **(current liabilities**, CL**)** are those which are expected to be consumed (paid) within one year. **Property, plant and Equipment**, PPE, represents assets *not* to be consumed within a year; they generate the products and

---

[3] After all, failure to pay interest can ultimately lead to bankruptcy and transfer of the firm's control from its owners (stock holders) to debt holders.

[4] Again, any discussion regarding (partial) transfer of net income is done so only in an accounting sense, as NI is *not* a cash flow.

services of the firm. Gross PPE, $GPPE$, is the total historical, cumulative amount spent on existing PPE. Accumulated $D\&A$ is the total historical, cumulative amount of this $GPPE$ that has been written off. Net PPE, $NPPE$, is the difference, or $NPPE = GPPE$ − accumulated $D\&A$. Deferred income taxes (DIT) exist as the firm keeps two sets of accounting books: one for tax authorities and a "public" one for current and potential stakeholders.[5] Finally, **debt** appears in three BS entries: notes payable to banks (NP), current maturities of long-term debt (CM) and long-term debt (LTD).[6] The first two of the three, NP and CM, are current liabilities, whereas long-term debt obviously is not.

Of the four entries under **stock holders' equity**, two (common stock, CS and additional paid-in capital, $APIC$) represent the cumulative historical contributions paid by owners to the firm when it issues new shares of stock.[7] These are "direct" equity contributions in the sense that equity holders pay cash to buy new stock. In contrast, "indirect" equity contributions are made on behalf of owners by the firm's management via increase in retained earnings, RE. As shown before, this is the amount of net income kept within the firm after cash dividends are paid. So RE is the cumulative historical amount of annual NI retained within the firm. Finally, all entries under stock holders' equity are non-decreasing in magnitude from one balance sheet date to the next. This is important to keep in mind when generating future, pro-forma balance sheets.

7.3 Statement of Cash Flows

Continuing our example, figure 7.3 shows the statement of cash flows for our firm, where the period of time is calendar year $t = 2015$, the same as that of the income

---

[5] The firm uses a more aggressive depreciation schedule for tax purposes than it does in its public book. This allows the firm to decrease its current tax liability by deferring some of what it owes to an indeterminate later date. As a result, this creates a liability on its public book.

[6] A firm typically retires a small fraction of its long-term debt each year, before the debt's date of maturity, per restrictive covenants. Such long-term debt to be retired within one year appears as "current maturities of long-term debt", CM. The remainder of long-term debt remains in the account, LTD.

[7] For us, the distinction between these two entries is unimportant. Of each new share issued, so called "par value" is assigned to common stock and the excess collected is assigned to additional paid-in capital.

Though not shown in this example, treasury stock, TS, is a *negative* entry of stock holders' equity. It is the cumulative historical amount paid by a firm to buy back its stock. In doing so, a firm reduces its number of shares outstanding, and it shrinks its total equity value. Consistent with other equity entries, TS is non-decreasing in magnitude over time.

statement in figure 7.1. The purpose of the **statement of cash flows** is to expose the sources and consumers of cash for the year.[8] In short, the general statement is

$$(\text{cash}_t + MS_t) - (\text{cash}_{t-1} + MS_{t-1}) = OCF_t + ICF_t + FiCF_t, \qquad (7.1)$$

where MS denotes marketable securities, and where OCF, ICF and $FiCF$ denote operating, investing and financing cash flows, respectively. Subscript t in balance sheet entries, cash_t and MS_t, indexes date year-end$_t$. In contrast, subscript t of OCF_t, ICF_t and $FiCF_t$ indexes period (year) t, which begins on date year-end$_{t-1}$ and ends on date year-end$_t$.

The statement of cash flows is logical: the change in cash plus MS on the balance sheet in going from year-end$_{t-1}$ to year-end$_t$ equals the net cash generated during year$_t$ by three activities: operating, investing and financing. **Operating cash flow** (OCF) is the most important, as it represents that which is generated by core business activities. In some sense, it's a metric for the ongoing viability of the firm. In broad terms, it equals net income (adjusted for non-cash accounting entries) minus changes in non-cash, non-MS and non-debt net working capital.[9,10] Next, **investing cash flow** (ICF) reflects investing activities, i.e., changes in $GPPE$; buying PPE decreases ICF, whereas selling PPE increases ICF. Finally, **financing cash flow** ($FiCF$) reflects activities related to debt and equity capital. Issuance of a security, which is a claim against future cash flows, generates positive $FiCF$. In contrast, retiring a security, e.g., buying back either outstanding debt or equity, requires cash and thus, reduces $FiCF$. Paying cash dividends to equity holders also requires cash, reducing $FiCF$.

Rewarding an investor a current return on capital requires cash, i.e, is a negative cash flow for the firm. However, note the distinction between legally required interest payments to debt holders and discretionary dividend payments to equity holders. As the former is a legal contractual obligation, it is logically reflected in OCF as a legitimate

---

[8]As marketable securities, MS, are essentially as liquid as cash, then MS is lumped together with the cash account in this reconciliation of "cash", i.e., in the statement of cash flows.

[9]As $D\&A$ represents a non-cash accounting entry, it is reversed in the calculation of OCF, i.e., $D\&A$ is added back to NI in order to offset its subtraction in the income statement. Additionally, DIT is a "non-cash" liability account, as it is generated simply due to keeping two sets of books. As such, relative to the "tax book", the "public book" shows generation (consumption) of current cash for an increase (decrease) in DIT, as explained later.

[10]**Net working capital, NWC** equals current assets minus current liabilities, or $NWC \equiv CA-CL$. Thus, $\Delta NWC = \Delta(CA - CL) = \Delta CA - \Delta CL = (CA_t - CA_{t-1}) - (CL_t - CL_{t-1}) = (CA_t - CL_t) - (CA_{t-1} - CL_{t-1})$. Hence, Δ(non-cash, non-MS, non-debt NWC) *excludes* Δcash, ΔMS, ΔNP and ΔCM, where the latter two are the two Δnon-debt items.

Statement of Cash Flows Entry	2015
Operating Cash Flow Activities	
Net income (NI)	9,394
Non-cash adjustments to reconcile net income	
Depreciation & amortization ($D\&A$)	3,998
Deferred income taxes (DIT)	208
Cash provided (used) by working capital	
Accounts receivable	(610)
Inventories	(10,272)
Prepaid expenses	247
Accounts payable	6,703
Accrued liabilities	356
Operating Cash Flow (OCF)	10,024
Investing Cash Flow Activities	
Additions to property, plant & equipment: PPE	(14,100)
Other investing activities	295
Investing Cash Flow (ICF)	(13,805)
Financing Cash Flow Activities	
Sales of common stock	256
Increase (decrease) in short-term borrowings*	(30)
Additions to long-term borrowings	5,600
Reductions of long-term borrowings	(1,516)
Dividends paid (d)	(1,582)
Financing Cash Flow ($FiCF$)	2,728
Increase (decrease) in cash plus marketable securities	(1,053)
Cash/MS: beginning of year	10,386
Cash/MS: end of year	9,333

*This includes changes in both CM and NP, or $\Delta(CM + NP)$.
All numbers are in $ thousands.

Figure 7.3   Statement of cash flows

business expense. In short, interest payments reduce net income, the core of OCF. In stark contrast, dividends are *not* an obligation; they are simply a discretionary return *of* (not *on*) capital to the firm's owners. Thus, dividends are logically *not* part of OCF, but rather are part of $FiCF$. In summary, as stock holders' dividends are intuitively part of $FiCF$, debt holders' interest payments are *not* considered part of $FiCF$, but rather decrease OCF.

We previously noted the important distinction between BS entries (stock variables) and IS entries (flow variables). The impact of IS entries upon cash flows is intuitive, as both the income statement as well as the statement of cash flows feature flow variables. Logically, on the statement of cash flows, revenues from the IS increase cash flows, whereas expenses from the IS decrease them. However, the impact of BS items is more subtle, as BS items are *not* flow variables. Thus, it's the *change* in BS items that has cash flow implications. Specifically, an increase in an asset account requires cash, while an increase in either a liability account or an equity account generates cash. The first claim is obvious; it takes cash to purchase an asset, i.e., to generate a net increase in an asset account. However, the impact of an increase in a liability account is a bit less obvious. If increased (decreased) from one year to the next, the firm has increased (decreased) the amount it owes the respective "creditor". An increase means that the firm has dug deeper into the pockets of its creditor, i.e., the firm has preserved cash. Analogously, a decrease in magnitude of liability means that the firm owes less to its creditor i.e., the firm has consumed cash by paying down its liability, as it owes less to its creditor than before. In summary, an increase (a decrease) in a liability increases (decreases) cash flow, all else equal.[11]

Digging deeper, as BS items are stock variables and IS items are flow variables, they have different dimensions. As such, we can *not* directly add and subtract items from the two different kinds of financial statements, as their items are "apples and oranges". However, dividing the difference in consecutively dated BS items by the difference in consecutive year-end dates makes the result "look like" a flow variable, i.e., an IS item. In short, $\frac{BS_t - BS_{t-1}}{t-(t-1)} = \frac{\Delta BS_t}{1} = \Delta BS_t$ looks like a flow variable, consistent with an IS item over the same year represented by the difference in two consecutive dates, year-end$_{t-1}$ and year-end$_t$.[12] So all entries in the statement of cash flows are either IS items or *differences* in BS items.

7.4 Free Cash Flows and Free Cash Flows to Equity

One relative valuation metric is $\frac{P}{CF}$, hence, the need for cash flow calculations. In absolute valuation, i.e., that based on intrinsic value, we discount cash flows of a security by the corresponding demanded rate of return based on the riskiness of these

---

[11] Analogously, an increase (a decrease) in an equity account means that the firm has a net injection (outflow) of equity capital, resulting in a positive (negative) cash flow.

[12] We denote $BS_t - BS_{t-1}$ as ΔBS_t. Recall that the index on a BS item refers to date t. But when we take the difference, t in ΔBS_t corresponds to period (year) t, starting at year-end$_{t-1}$, corresponding to BS date $t-1$, and ending at year-end$_t$, corresponding to BS date t.

cash flows. Thus, in both types of valuation, we need metrics for cash flows.

At least two methods of enterprise valuation are based on discounting free cash flows, where **free cash flow, FCF**, is calculated as[13]

$$FCF_t = OCF_t + IE_t\left(1 - T^C\right) \underbrace{-\Delta\left(\text{gross } PPE_t + \text{other assets}_t\right)}_{\equiv ICF_t}$$

$$= OCF_t + IE_t\left(1 - T^C\right) + ICF_t$$

$$= NI_t + IE_t\left(1 - T^C\right) \underbrace{- \Delta(GPPE_t + OA_t)}_{\Delta(GPPE+OA) = -ICF} + \underbrace{D\&A_t + \Delta DIT_t}_{\text{non-cash entries}}$$

$$\underbrace{- \Delta(\text{non-cash, non-}MS\ CA_t - \text{non-debt } CL_t)}_{\Delta \text{ net working capital, excluding: cash, } MS, NP, CM}, \qquad (7.2)$$

where $T^C = \frac{\text{income taxes}_t}{\text{EBT}_t}$ is the corporate tax rate, and $\Delta(GPPE_t + OA_t) \equiv \Delta(\text{gross } PPE_t + \text{other assets}_t) = -ICF$. So per the final expression, at the core of FCF are after-tax income statement entries representing amounts "available" to equity holders and to debt holders, respectively, NI_t and $IE_t(1 - T^C)$.

As noted earlier in discussing ICF, which is a component of FCF, purchases (sales) of $GPPE$ assets consume (generate) cash. Next, in calculating free cash flows, we must offset two types of non-cash accounting entries. First, $D\&A$, which is subtracted in the calculation of NI, must be added back in order to derive cash flow. Second, positive (negative) values of $\Delta DIT_t = DIT_t - DIT_{t-1}$ due to parallel book keeping generates (consumes) cash and must be included in the calculation of FCF. Finally, an increase in current liabilities (assets) generates (consumes) cash.[14]

We will utilize two different interpretations of free cash flows in our study of absolute valuations of equity value and of firm value. To focus our exposition, let's define $\phi_t \equiv -\Delta(\text{gross}PPE_t + \text{other assets}_t) + (D\&A_t + \Delta DIT_t) - \Delta(\text{non-cash}/MSCA_t - \text{non-debt } CL_t)$, which equals the three parts of the final expression of equation (7.2)

---

[13] Again, NP is notes payable to banks and CM is current maturities of long-term debt. So: non-debt $CL_t = CL_t - NP_t - CM_t$.

[14] In the calculation of FCF, we exclude changes in cash, in MS, and in current debt (NP and CM). The latter two are excluded, as ΔNP and ΔCM represent positive contributions to *financing* cash flows, *FiCFs*, *not FCFs* nor *OCFs*.

that have underbraces.[15] Recall that from the IS,[16]

$$NI_t = (EBIT_t - IE_t + II_t)(1 - T^C). \tag{7.3}$$

Thus, using the definition of ϕ_t and equation (7.3), then

$$FCF_t = \underbrace{NI_t + IE_t(1 - T^C)}_{\substack{\text{accounting entries: "available"} \\ \text{to pay all security holders}}} + \phi_t$$

$$= \underbrace{(EBIT_t + II_t)(1 - T^C)}_{\substack{\text{accounting entries: \textbf{hypothetically} "available"} \\ \text{to pay equity holders, if the firm had no debt}}} + \phi_t. \tag{7.4}$$

The two expressions in equation (7.4), both from the firm's perspective, allow us to interpret FCF from two very different perspectives, both of which we will exploit in equity and firm valuation. FCF is the:

- after-tax cash flow which is available to *all* security holders, i.e., to both equity holders and debt holders, and the
- cash flow that would be hypothetically available to equity holders, if the firm had no debt.

The first itemized line interprets the first line of expression (7.4), where FCF equals NI (for equity holders) plus $IE(1 - T^C)$ (for debt holders), adjusted for ϕ. Thus, if we discount such cash flows by the appropriate demanded rate of return that takes into account the "average" riskiness of cash flows available to *all* investors (i.e., to both debt holders and equity holders), then intrinsic value of the enterprise (i.e., firm) obtains.[17]

The second itemized line interprets the second line of expression (7.4), as $EBIT + II$ would equal EBT if the firm had no debt, i.e., if IE were zero. This would be the cash flow hypothetically available to equity holders, if the firm had no debt. Thus, if we discount such cash flows by the corresponding hypothetical discount rate that equity holders would demand if the firm had no debt, the result is the hypothetical

---

[15] Referring to the final expression of equation (7.2), ϕ_t represents the three adjustments of FCF_t to the after-tax amounts "available" in an accounting sense to security holders: NI_t to equity holders and $IE_t(1 - T^C)$ debt holders.

[16] Taxable income is $EBT_t = EBIT_t - IE_t + II_t$, and so $Tax_t = (EBIT_t - IE_t + II_t)T^C$. It follows that $NI_t = EBT_t - Tax_t$. Recall that IE_t is interest expense paid to debt holders, and II_t is interest income received from marketable securities.

[17] Actually, the result is called enterprise value, which we discuss later.

enterprise value for the *unlevered* firm, i.e., that of the firm with no debt. To this hypothetical value, we add the change in value due to debt financing effects to derive actual enterprise (firm) intrinsic value.

Before leaving this discussion on FCF, note that students often fail to recognize that FCF is a single value. Per equations (7.2) and (7.4), the same value of FCF can be derived in several ways, i.e., there is one, single value of FCF. There are *not* two (or more) values of FCF, but rather two interpretations. Furthermore, FCF per the second interpretation is *not* a hypothetical cash flow. It is an actual number with two interpretations, one of which is hypothetical.

To continue our example, FCF_{2015} in our example per the first line of equation (7.2) is $OCF_{2015} + IE_{2015}\left(1 - T^C\right) - \Delta(\text{gross } PPE_{2015} + OA_{2015}) = 10{,}024 + 2{,}585(1 - \frac{7{,}686}{17{,}080}) - [(40{,}607 - 26{,}507) + (373 - 668)] = (\$2{,}359).^{18}$

As FCF can be interpreted as cash flows available to all security holders, then we can interpret cash flows available to equity holders as free cash flows minus those available to debt holders. So in order to disentangle cash flows available to equity holders with those available to debt holders, we introduce **net after-tax cash flow available to debt holders** as $CF_t^D \equiv IE_t(1 - T^C) - \Delta TD_t$, where $\Delta TD_t \equiv TD_t - TD_{t-1}$ is the increase in total debt liability during year t. Digging deeper, given the three debt entries in our balance sheet, then

$$\Delta TD_t \equiv TD_t - TD_{t-1} = \Delta\left(NP_t + CM_t + LTD_t\right), \qquad (7.5)$$

where notes payable (NP) and current maturities of long-term debt (CM) are current liabilities. From $CF_t^D \equiv IE_t(1 - T^C) - \Delta TD_t$, then

$$CF_t^D = IE_t(1 - T^C) - \Delta\left(NP_t + CM_t + LTD_t\right). \qquad (7.6)$$

Continuing our example, per equation (7.5), $\Delta TD_{2015} = (5{,}614 - 6{,}012) + (1{,}884 - 1{,}516) + (21{,}059 - 16{,}975) = \$4{,}054$. Thus from equation (7.6), then $CF_{2015}^D = 2{,}585(1 - \frac{7{,}686}{17{,}080}) - 4{,}054 = (\$2{,}632)$.

Now that we've identified net after-tax cash flow available to debt holders as CF_t^D, then subtracting this from free cash flow yields **free cash flow to equity**

---

[18] So the corporate tax rate in this year is $T^C = \frac{Tax_{2015}}{EBT_{2015}} = \frac{7{,}686}{17{,}080} = 45\%$. To confirm, per the first line of equation (7.4), then $FCF_{2015} = NI_{2015} + IE_{2015}(1 - T^C) + \phi_{2015} = 9{,}394 + 2{,}585(1 - 45\%) + (-13{,}175) = (\$2{,}359)$. Per the second line of equation (7.4), then $(EBIT_{2015} + II_{2015})(1 - T^C) + \phi_{2015} = (19{,}243 + 422)(1 - 45\%) + (-13{,}175) = (\$2{,}359)$.

holders ($FCFE$), or[19]

$$\begin{aligned}
FCFE_t &= \{FCF_t\} - \left[CF_t^D\right] \\
&= \{FCF_t\} - \left[IE_t(1-T^C) - \Delta TD_t\right] \\
&= NI_t + \Delta TD_t + \phi_t \\
&= OCF_t + \Delta TD_t - \Delta(\text{gross } PPE_t + \text{other assets}_t) \\
&= OCF_t + ICF_t + \Delta TD_t.
\end{aligned} \quad (7.7)$$

Continuing our example, per the first line of equation (7.7), then $FCFE_{2015} = FCF_{2015} - CF^D_{2015} = (2,359) - (2,632) = \$273$.[20]

Free cash flow to equity holders is in some sense that which is available to pay the firm's owners. It is calculated from sources of equity cash flow, i.e., from activities that generate this cash flow. This is readily apparent from consideration of equation (7.7), especially the final line. Thus, this should equal that paid to equity holders. In short, sources of equity cash flow must equal its consumption. The cash flow to equity holders can be reconciled as is done in the broader sense for the statement of cash flows. *Roughly* speaking, the consumption of equity cash flow equals the **total equity cash flow, TECF**, where

$$TECF_t = \text{Dividends}_t + EqI_t - EqR_t = \Delta TD_t - FiCF_t, \quad (7.8)$$

where EqI_t (EqR_t) are the total dollars raised via stock issuance (used to repurchase stock, i.e., retired to treasury) in period t. Thus,[21]

$$FCFE_t - TECF_t = \Delta\left(\text{cash}_t + MS_t\right) \quad (7.9)$$

Some practitioners prefer to discount $TECF$s rather than $FCFE$s in determining equity value per discounted cash flow analysis. Finally, recall that the balance sheet shows the cumulative sources (liabilities plus equity) and uses (assets) of capital. In somewhat analogous fashion, $FCFE$ represents the sources of equity cash flow, whereas $TECF$ represents the uses, excluding the net increase in cash plus marketable securities. However, the two differ as balance sheet items are stock variables, so the equivalence between

---

[19] The third line follows from the second as $FCF_t = NI_t + IE_t(1-T^C) + \phi_t$.

[20] Confirming this with subsequent lines of expression (7.7), $FCFE_{2015} = (2,359) - [2,585(1-45\%) - 4,054] = 9,394 + 4,054 + (13,175) = 10,024 + 4,054 - [(40,607 - 26,507) + (373 - 668)] = 10,024 + (13,805) + 4,054$.

[21] As $FCFE_t = OCF_t + ICF_t + \Delta TD_t$, then $FCFE_t - TECF_t = OCF_t + ICF_t + \Delta TD_t - [\Delta TD_t - FiCF_t] = OCF_t + ICF_t + FiCF_t = \Delta(\text{cash}_t + MS_t)$, per the statement of cash flows.

assets and liabilities & stock holders' equity is for cumulative historical values. In contrast, $TECF$ and $FCFE$ are flow variables, whose magnitudes depend on the chosen time frame.

Problems

For this chapter's problem set, consider figures 7.4 and 7.5 found on pages 83 and 84, respectively. **All entries are in $ thousands in both the income statement and the balance sheet.**

1. Fill in the missing numbers of the income statement.

2. Fill in the missing numbers of the balance sheet.

3. What is this firm's plowback ratio for 2015?

4. What is this firm's dividend payout ratio for 2015?

5. Complete a statement of cash flows for this firm for 2015.

Income Statement Entry (in $ thousands)	2015
Net sales (NS)	198,000
Cost of goods sold ($COGS$)	111,000
Gross profit (GP)	xx,xxx
Selling, general and administrative (SGA) expenses	38,000
Advertising	16,500
Depreciation and amortization ($D\&A$)	3,000
Repairs and maintenance	2,000
Operating Profit ($EBIT^*$)	xx,xxx
Other Income (expense)	
Interest income (II)	500
Interest expense (IE)	(2,000)
Earnings before income taxes (EBT^{**})	xx,xxx
Income taxes	6,000
Net earnings, net income (NI)	x,xxx
Basic earnings per common share	z.zz
Diluted earnings per common share	z.zz
$^*EBIT$ stands for earnings before interest income (expenses) and taxes.	
$^{**}EBT$ stands for earnings before taxes (but *after* interest income (expenses)).	
Cash dividends of $3,300 were paid in 2015.	

Figure 7.4 Income statement

6. What is this firm's free cash flow for 2015?

7. What is this firm's free cash flow to equity holders for 2015?

8. What is this firm's total equity cash flow for 2015?

Balance Sheet Entry (in $ thousands)	15/12/31	14/12/31
Assets (A)		
Current Assets (CA)		
Cash	2,500	2,000
Marketable securities (MS)	12,700	8,000
Accounts receivable*	8,000	8,000
Inventories	47,000	36,000
Prepaid expenses	500	700
Total current assets	xx,xxx	xx,xxx
Property, Plant & Equipment: PPE		
Land	800	800
Buildings & leasehold improvements	18,000	11,000
Equipment	21,000	13,000
Gross PPE	xx,xxx	xx,xxx
Less accumulated depreciation & amortization	10,000	7,000
Net PPE	xx,xxx	xx,xxx
Other Assets	800	600
Total Assets, TA	xx,xxx	xx,xxx
Liabilities and Stock holders' Equity		
Current Liabilities (CL)		
Accounts payable (AP)	14,000	7,000
Notes payable to banks (NP)	5,000	6,000
Current maturities of LTD (CM)	2,000	1,000
Accrued liabilities	5,000	6,000
Total current liabilities	xx,xxx	xx,xxx
Deferred Incomes Taxes (DIT)	800	600
Long-Term Debt (LTD)	21,000	16,000
Total liabilities	xx,xxx	xx,xxx
Stock holders' Equity		
Common stock, par value of $1**	4,800	4,500
Additional paid-in capital	900	700
Retained earnings (RE)	52,800	36,100
Less: treasury stock	5,000	4,800
Total Stock holders' Equity	xx,xxx	xx,xxx
Total Liabilities & Stock holders' Equity	xx,xxx	xx,xxx

*This is less allowances for doubtful accounts.

**10,000,000 shares authorized; 4,800,000 shares outstanding in 2015; 4,500,000 shares outstanding in 2014; 4,867,000 diluted shares outstanding in 2015; December 31, 2015 share price equals $10.00 per share.

Figure 7.5 Balance sheet

Chapter 8: Financial Statement Analysis and Relative Valuation

In the previous chapter, we briefly reviewed three financial accounting statements: income statement, balance sheet, and statement of cash flows. Building upon this knowledge, in this chapter we examine ratios used to analyze the health and value of a firm. These ratios focus on different aspects: common-size statements, internal liquidity, operating performance per efficiency and per profitability, financial risk per leverage and per coverage, operational risk and external liquidity. Afterwards, we move to relative valuation via ratio metrics for equity value.

Using ratios to analyze a firm's condition is as much art as science. Calculating more ratios does not necessarily lead to better analysis. The key is to look for outliers. Firms within a single industry face similar risks and opportunities. Thus, all else equal, their financial statements should be proportional to each other, if they are operating optimally. Whether you are a manager, an investor or an analyst, the outliers are what draw your attention. If a firm has a particular ratio that is considerably higher or lower than its competitors, you need to dig deeper to understand why. Often times, an outlier indicates a problem. However, it may also reflect a firm's comparative advantage. What makes your job more challenging is the fact that for most ratios, there exists an interior optimum. If a ratio is unambiguously "better" as it increases (or decreases), then comparing firms against one another on that metric is obvious. However, when an interior optimum exists, outliers are indicative of problems. While this discussion has focused on comparing competitors, ratio analysis of financial statements is also used to compare a firm against itself via time series. This gives a sense of the change in a firm's health or value over time.

8.1 Common Size Financial Accounting Statements

Common size ratios simply convert income statement items and balance sheet items to proportional values so that they can be compared. We can't compare two income statements against one another, if they have different net sales. For example, if firm A has 10 times the sales of firm B, then all entries on A's income statement should be considerably larger than those of B, making direct comparisons impossible. Analogously, if firm A has 10 times the assets that firm B has, then all entries on A's balance sheet should be considerably larger than those of B, making direct comparisons impossible. Thus, to yield a comparison of "apples to apples", we divide each entry of the respective financial accounting statement by its largest value, leaving all entries as fractions no greater than one. So for the income statement (balance sheet), each item is divided by net sales (total assets).

We continue to use the same statements shown in the previous chapter. Consider first the **common size income statement**, shown in figure 8.1.[1] Generally speaking,

Income Statement Entry	2015
Net sales (NS)	100.0
Cost of goods sold ($COGS$)	60.0
Gross profit (GP)	40.0
Selling, general and administrative (SGA) expenses	21.2
Advertising	6.6
Depreciation and amortization ($D\&A$)	1.9
Repairs and maintenance	1.4
Operating Profit ($EBIT^*$)	8.9
Other Income (expense)	
Interest income (II)	0.2
Interest expense (IE)	(1.2)
Earnings before income taxes (EBT^{**})	7.9
Income taxes	3.6
Net earnings, net income (NI)	4.4

$^*EBIT$ stands for earnings before interest income (expenses) and taxes.
$^{**}EBT$ stands for earnings before taxes (and *after* interest income (expenses)).

Figure 8.1 Common size income statement

it would seem that the smaller the $\frac{COGS}{NS}$, the more efficient is the firm's manufacturing process, all else equal. However, consider either a firm with significantly lower $\frac{COGS}{NS}$ than its competitors, or a firm with a sudden drop in time series ratios. In either case,

---

[1] Again, what one can do is compare these figures against those of other firms as well as against its own historical figures.

you would want to understand why. If you gather information consistent with the fact that the firm has superior manufacturing technology than its competitors, resulting in decreased costs, then the low value for this ratio confirms added value. However, the reduced relative manufacturing costs may be the result of cutting corners. If so, one would expect quality concerns to surface.

An elevated $\frac{SGA}{NS}$ ($\frac{\text{advertising}}{NS}$) value may be due to an aggressive selling (advertising) campaign of a new product, which may represent a justifiable investment with satisfactory expected future returns. On the other hand, it may indicate sloppiness in controlling non-manufacturing costs. Next, elevated (suppressed) $\frac{IE}{NS}$ values may be a red flag that the firm has utilized too much (little) debt in its capital structure.

For the same firm, consider the **common size balance sheet**, figure 8.2. Elevated $\frac{\text{cash}}{TA}$ and/or $\frac{MS}{TA}$ may indicate inefficient utilization of capital, as returns from cash and from marketable securities are far less than those generally required by capital contributors, particularly longer-term contributors. In contrast, low levels of $\frac{\text{cash}}{TA}$ and $\frac{MS}{TA}$ may indicate cash flow problems. Next, elevated $\frac{AR}{TA}$, $\frac{Inv}{TA}$ or $\frac{\text{prepaid expenses}}{TA}$ likewise indicate inefficient use of capital, as their presence must be financed. Reduced levels of these three ratios may indicate a problem with the firm's ability to maintain competitive levels of working capital. For example, low $\frac{AR}{TA}$ may suggest that the firm's credit policy is not competitive with its peers. If the firm is demanding its customers pay for products quicker than does its competitors, say in 30 days versus 45 days, then it may be losing customers to its competitors, resulting in a competitive disadvantage. Next, low $\frac{Inv}{TA}$ could lead to longer delivery times, again resulting in a competitive disadvantage relative to its peers. On the other hand, the firm may operate with reduced levels of current assets due to a competitive advantage. For example, a firm might have low $\frac{AR}{TA}$ ratio due to superior negotiating power regarding payment terms.[2] As another example, again due to superior negotiating power, a firm may have low $\frac{Inv}{TA}$ by demanding its suppliers to hold raw materials inventory earmarked for it. Again, your job is to identify outliers and the stories behind them.

For ratios of current liabilities, $\frac{AP}{TA}$ and $\frac{AL}{TA}$, high values may represent cash flow problems (i.e., inability to pay bills on time) or a competitive advantage (e.g., increased creditor financing due to superior negotiating leverage). High long-term debt ratios ($\frac{LTD}{TA}$) may also be a cause for concern due to increased financial risk. However, a firm with superior cash flows may justifiably operate with higher debt levels.

---

[2] A market leader who has superior products is attractive to potential customers. Such a firm may have increased negotiating leverage regarding supply terms relative to its peers.

Balance Sheet Entry	15/12/31	14/12/31
Assets (A)		
Current Assets (CA)		
Cash	4.3	3.1
Marketable securities (MS)	5.5	10.5
Accounts receivable*	9.4	11.0
Inventories	49.4	48.4
Prepaid expenses	0.5	1.0
Total current assets	69.1	74.1
Property, Plant & Equipment: PPE		
Land	0.9	1.1
Buildings & leasehold improvements	19.2	15.7
Equipment	22.6	18.1
Gross PPE	42.6	34.9
Less accumulated Depr. & Amort.	12.1	9.9
Net PPE	30.5	25.0
Other Assets	0.4	0.9
Total Assets (TA)	100.0	100.0
Liabilities and Stock holders' Equity		
Current Liabilities (CL)		
Accounts payable (AP)	15.0	10.0
Notes payable to banks (NP)	5.9	7.9
Current maturities of LTD (CM)	2.0	2.0
Accrued liabilities	5.9	7.0
Total current liabilities	28.8	26.9
Deferred Incomes Taxes (DIT)	0.9	0.8
Long-Term Debt (LTD)	22.1	22.4
Total liabilities	51.8	50.1
Stock holders' Equity		
Common stock, par value of $1**	5.0	6.1
Additional paid-in capital	1.0	1.2
Retained earnings (RE)	42.2	42.6
Total Stock holders' Equity	48.2	49.9
Total Liabilities and Stock holders' Equity	100.0	100.0

*This is less allowances for doubtful accounts.

**10,000,000 shares authorized; 4,803,000 shares issued in 2015; 4,594,000 shares issued in 2014;

Figure 8.2 Common size balance sheet

8.2 Internal Liquidity Ratios

Internal liquidity ratios attempt to provide metrics regarding the firm's ability to pay its bills when they come due. A key concept is **net working capital**, where

$NWC_t \equiv CA_t - CL_t$. The firm needs sufficient NWC to pay its bills on time.[3] Internal liquidity ratios are shown in figure 8.3.

Metric	Statistic	Calculation	Value
Current Ratio	$\frac{CA}{CL}$	$\frac{65,846}{27,461}$	2.40
Quick Ratio*	$\frac{Cash + MS + AR}{CL}$	$\frac{18,293}{27,461}$	0.67
Cash Ratio	$\frac{Cash + MS}{CL}$	$\frac{9,333}{27,461}$	0.34
CF** Liquidity Ratio	$\frac{Cash + MS + OCF}{CL}$	$\frac{19,357}{27,461}$	0.70
$ARTO^{**}$ ($\frac{turns}{year}$)	$\frac{NS}{Avg\ AR}$	$\frac{215,600}{8,655}$	24.9
Inventory TO ($\frac{turns}{year}$)	$\frac{COGS}{Avg\ Inv}$	$\frac{129,364}{41,905}$	3.09
$APTO^{**}$ ($\frac{turns}{year}$)	$\frac{COGS}{Avg\ AP}$	$\frac{129,364}{10,942.5}$	11.8
Days in AR (DAR)	$\frac{365}{ARTO}$	$\frac{365}{24.9}$	14.7
Days in inventory (DI)	$\frac{365}{Inv.\ TO}$	$\frac{365}{3.1}$	118.2
Days in AP (DAP)	$\frac{365}{APTO}$	$\frac{365}{11.8}$	30.9
Cash conversion cycle, CCC	$DAR + DI - DAP$	15+118−31	102.0

*Quick ratio is also called the acid-test ratio.

**CF: cash flow; AR: accounts receivable; TO:Turnover; AP: accounts payable;

Figure 8.3 Internal liquidity ratios

The higher the current ratio, quick ratio or cash ratio, the more easily the firm can pay its current liabilities, CL, as they come due. However, excessively high values indicate inefficient utilization of working capital, as it earns far less than that which investors collectively demand.

All three of these metrics have CL as their denominator. Regarding the respective numerators, the three ratios are in order of increasing conservatism by eliminating lesser liquid assets. The current ratio has *all* current assets, CA, as its numerator. The quick ratio recognizes that generally speaking, prepaid expenses cannot be liquidated to pay off liabilities. It also excludes inventory, as the firm may either need weeks to sell all currently existing inventory at full market value.[4] Further justifying exclusion of inventory, most firms have some fraction of inventory that is of little if any value due to its unacceptable quality, outdated market, etc... Finally, the most conservative of the three metrics, the cash ratio additionally eliminates consideration of accounts

---

[3] As we've seen before when we studied cash flows, excluding cash plus marketable securities, a net increase (decrease) in $\Delta NWC_t = \Delta(CA_t - CL_t) = \Delta CA_t - \Delta CL_t = (CA_t - CL_t) - (CA_{t-1} - CL_{t-1}) = (CA_t - CA_{t-1}) - (CL_t - CL_{t-1})$ consumes (generates) cash flow.

[4] Even if possible to immediately liquidate its inventory, the firm would likely be forced to accept a deep discount, the cost of inventory illiquidity.

receivable, AR. Most firms have some "doubtful" accounts, or credits from customers who ultimately will not pay their account for whatever reason.

A **turnover ratio** indicates how efficiently the firm uses a given BS account. Turnovers are ratios of the form $\frac{IS \text{ item } (\$/\text{year})}{\text{Avg } BS \text{ item } (\$)}$, having units of $\frac{1}{\text{year}}$.[5] This is indicative of a frequency, which is typically quoted in $\frac{\text{cycles}}{\text{year}}$ when the period is in years. Rather than $\frac{\text{cycles}}{\text{year}}$, turnover ratios are quoted in $\frac{\text{turns}}{\text{year}}$, implying that the BS item has "turned-over" this many times per year.[6] Regarding the denominator, taking the average of the two consecutive BS values at the respective period end dates (beginning date and ending date) makes sense, as the IS item corresponds to the period bounded in time by these two dates, end-year$_t$ and end-year$_{t-1}$.

In a comparative static sense, holding fixed the given IS item, the smaller (larger) the BS item, the larger (smaller) the ratio. The larger the turnover ratio, then if the BS item is an asset (a liability), we say that the asset (liability) is more (less) intensely utilized. If an asset, a higher ratio means that the firm more efficiently utilizes the asset. However, an extremely high asset turnover may mean that the firm has an inefficiently small level of this asset, perhaps suggesting issues with respect to cash flow and/or competitiveness.[7] In contrast, a *lower* liability ratio means that the firm more efficiently utilizes the liability. However, an extremely *low* liability turnover may mean that the firm has an inefficiently high level of this liability, perhaps suggesting issues with respect to cash flow and/or competitiveness.[8]

Let's now examine specific internal liquidity turnover ratios. When a firm receives payment corresponding to an AR item, AR is reduced and ultimately, this amount contributes to NS, the revenue entry on the next income statement. Thus, for accounts receivable turnover, we logically divide NS_t by *average* $AR_t = \frac{AR_{t-1}+AR_t}{2}$. In contrast to AR, which is related to revenue, inventory and AP are both related to expenses. When product is sold, the cost of that product is removed from the inventory account,

---

[5] Avg BS item $= \frac{BS \text{ item}_t + BS \text{ item}_{t-1}}{2}$.

[6] For example, an inventory turnover of $\frac{COGS}{Inv} = 12$ means that inventory "turns over" 12 times per year. Relative to annual $COGS$, the average length of time that inventory lasts is $\frac{365}{12} = 30.4$ days. This latter calculation is "days in inventory", discussed later.

[7] For example, due to cash flow problems, a troubled firm may have inefficiently little inventory, leading to longer lead-times for its customers than those offered by its peers. This puts the firm at a competitive disadvantage.

[8] For example, due to cash flow problems, a troubled firm may have a much higher $\frac{AP}{COGS}$ ratio than its peers. This puts the firm at a competitive disadvantage, as it may lead to difficulties with current suppliers and in attracting new suppliers of innovative products.

and this cost contributes to $COGS$ on the next income statement. Analogously, as items in AP are retired, these amounts ultimately contribute to $COGS$ on the next income statement. In short, inventory and AR are asset accounts, while AP is a liability account. So all else equal as previously discussed, marginally larger values for $ARTO$ and inventory TO ($APTO$) may mean that the firm is more (less) efficiently using the respective current asset (liability) account. However, extreme values in these directions raise more questions.

The three "days in" metrics simply give the same information as the three turnovers just discussed, but in a more intuitive manner. Per figure 8.3, on average the firm receives credit extended to its customers in 14.7 days, it sells inventory 118.2 days after receiving it, and it pays its suppliers the credit extended it in 30.9 days. Finally, cash conversion cycle (CCC) measures the length of time that the firm must finance its working capital related to AR and inventory. The smaller the CCC, the more efficiently the firm utilizes its working capital, all else equal.[9] The intuition is as follows. When a firm receives raw materials from its suppliers, two "timelines" simultaneously start, as shown in figure 8.4. The first tracks time as the firm waits to receive payment

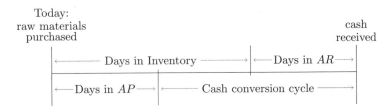

Figure 8.4 Cash conversion cycle: $CCC = DI + DAR - DAP$

against credit that it extends to its customers who buy its product. The second timeline tracks time until the firm must pay its supplier. So the first (second) tracks cash inflow (outflow), i.e., the length of time before the firm receives (pays out) cash. Thus, the difference in the two is the length of time that the firm must finance working capital related to AR and inventory, i.e., the CCC. From when the firm buys raw materials, it must wait $DI + DAR$ days before it receives cash, corresponding to the first timeline. However, the firm has been extended credit and is allowed to wait DAP days before it must pay its suppliers, corresponding to the second timeline.

---

[9] However, an unusually low figure may indicate difficulty with respect to timely payment of bills, i.e., a cash flow problem.

8.3 Operating Performance Ratios

We explore two general types of operating performance ratios. The first type are efficiency ratios. The previous section on internal liquidity includes three efficiency ratios, i.e., the turnover ratios. Whereas the three internal liquidity metrics reference current assets, we now move onto similar types of efficiency ratios regarding fixed assets (i.e., PPE) and equity. The second type of operating performance metrics are profitability ratios. Examples of both types are shown in figure 8.5.

Metric	Statistic	Calculation	Value
Efficiency ratios			
Fixed Asset TO^*	$\frac{NS}{\text{Avg net } PPE}$	$\frac{215{,}600}{24{,}028}$	8.97
Total Asset TO ($TATO$)	$\frac{NS}{\text{Avg TA}}$	$\frac{215{,}600}{85{,}603.5}$	2.52
Gross Fixed Asset TO	$\frac{NS}{\text{Avg gross } PPE}$	$\frac{215{,}600}{33{,}557}$	6.42
Equity TO	$\frac{NS}{\text{Avg equity}}$	$\frac{215{,}600}{41{,}901}$	5.15
Profitability ratios			
GPM^*	$\frac{GP}{NS}$	$\frac{86{,}236}{215{,}600}$	40.0%
OPM^*	$\frac{OP}{NS}$	$\frac{19{,}243}{215{,}600}$	8.9%
NPM^*	$\frac{NI}{NS}$	$\frac{9{,}394}{215{,}600}$	4.4%
Cash Flow Margin	$\frac{OCF}{NS}$	$\frac{10{,}024}{215{,}600}$	4.6%
ROA^*	$\frac{NI}{\text{Avg TA}}$	$\frac{9{,}394}{85{,}603.5}$	11.0%
ROE^*	$\frac{NI}{\text{Avg Equity}}$	$\frac{9{,}394}{41{,}901}$	22.4%
Leverage: $\frac{TA}{Eq}$	$\frac{\text{Avg TA}}{\text{Avg Equity}}$	$\frac{85{,}604}{41{,}901}$	2.04
Dupont ROE	$NPM(TATO)\frac{A.TA}{A.Eq}$	4.36%(2.52)2.04	22.4%
Cash return on assets	$\frac{OCF}{\text{Avg TA}}$	$\frac{10{,}024}{85{,}603.5}$	11.7%
Return on TC^*	$\frac{NI+IE}{\text{Avg }(Eq+D^{**})}$	$\frac{11{,}979}{68{,}431}$	17.5%

*TO:Turnover; GPM, OPM, NPM: gross, operating and net profit margins; ROA: return on (total) assets; ROE: return on equity; TC: total capital;

**D: debt, both long-term + (short-term), i.e., $D = TD = LTD + (STD) = LTD + (NP + CM)$;

Figure 8.5 Operating performance ratios: efficiency and profitability

As noted earlier, most ratio metrics have an interior optimum. Of the broad categories mentioned (common-size statements, internal liquidity, operating performance per efficiency and per profitability, financial risk per leverage and per coverage, operational risk, and external liquidity), only two types are generally monotonic in nature: operating performance and external liquidity. Here we examine the former. In general, firm performance is increasing in both efficiency-related operating performance metrics as well as profitability-related operating performance metrics.[10]

Of the four efficiency metrics shown in figure 8.5, the first three reveal how intensely the firm utilizes the respective assets considered. All else equal, the higher the value, the more efficiently the firm utilizes the respective asset class. For example, consider fixed asset turnover, $FATO$. Holding net sales (NS) fixed, the numerator of $FATO$, then a firm with higher $FATO$ is able to support the given level of sales with less investment in fixed assets, all else equal.[11] Analogously, equity turnover reflects higher sales per dollar of equity employed. Of course, an unusually high value for $FATO$ may be due to extended leverage (i.e., high debt levels), resulting in higher financial risk, which we discuss later.

The first three profitability metrics in figure 8.5, GPM, OPM and NPM, are generally positively correlated with firm value. Higher GPM reflects low relative manufacturing costs, all else equal. But is it high due to superior manufacturing technology or due to cutting corners?[12] OPM reflects, in part, levels of SGA expenses and advertising, both of which are considered in some sense as "discretionary" costs. Given comparable GPMs, a higher OPM may mean either disciplined control over discretionary costs, or it may mean cutting corners, e.g., sub-optimal current advertising expenses, which may cause long-term harm.

Return on equity (ROE) and return on total capital ($ROTC$) are important yield-type metrics, i.e., measures of ROI or return on investment. In all such metrics, be careful to match "investment", the denominator, with the corresponding "return" in the numerator. For example, ROE is the ratio of NI, the accounting entry corresponding to equity holders' return, to their investment, i.e., equity value. Analogously, $ROTC$ normalizes the returns to both equity holders and debt holders, NI plus IE, by their collective investment, Eq plus TD.[13] Regarding these metrics, a higher value is desirable, all else equal. However, extremely large values may be a concern. For example, consider a firm with an extremely high value of ROA relative to its competitors,

---

[10] Again, there is almost never an absolute monotonic relationship between firm performance and respective metric, even for operating performance metrics. An extreme value for any given metric may be cause for concern.

[11] However, too extreme a high value could cause concern. For example, it could mean that the firm is under-capitalized, i.e., it should optimally have a higher level fixed assets.

[12] Generally, cutting corners refers to sacrificing long-term sustainability for short-term gain. Examples include switching to sub-standard raw materials, eliminating preventive maintenance measures, sub-optimal marketing/advertising spending, etc...

[13] Total debt, TD, is long-term debt + short-term debt, or $LTD + NP + CM$.

its peers. The firm may be using too few assets; the firm may be under-capitalized. If we assume that most firms are optimally investing in assets, then the firm in question is under-investing relative to its peers.

The metric ROE is so important that various factor breakdowns have been proposed, e.g., that proposed by the DuPont Corporation as shown in figure 8.5.[14] Except for extreme values, firm performance is increasing in both NPM and $TATO$. The "wild card" is the leverage ratio, $\frac{\text{Avg. }TA}{\text{Avg. }Eq}$, which clearly has an interior optimal as discussed later.

The final two metrics in figure 8.5, cash flow margin and cash return on assets, are comparable to other profitability ratios, where we substitute the cash flow measure OCF for accounting entry NI. Of course, NI forms the core (or basis) of OCF.

8.4 Financial Risk Ratios

Financial risk includes the increased probability of failure by the firm to meet its contractually obligatory payments of interest as it increases its level of debt.[15] Increased debt is a double-edged sword. On the one hand, financial risk increases. On the other hand, given that the firm is profitable, an increase in debt increases the owners' ROE.

Before focusing on the downside of increasing debt, we illustrate the point that increasing the level of debt is desirable, given that the firm remains profitable. Consider figure 8.6, where in each case, firm value equals $225, or $V = D + Eq$. Shown are three cases, corresponding to three levels of leverage: low $D = 100$, or $\frac{D}{Eq} = \frac{100}{125} = 0.80$; medium $D = 150$, or $\frac{D}{Eq} = \frac{150}{75} = 2$; high $D = 200$, or $\frac{D}{Eq} = \frac{200}{25} = 8$. Given that the firm is profitable (i.e., $NI > 0$) and assuming that $ROE > r^D$, then increasing the level of debt increases ROE for the firm's owners. In figure 8.6, increasing leverage per the three cases shown results in increasing ROE from 13.0% to 17.3% to 39.0%, respectively. Finally, to drive home the point that increasing leverage increases ROE if the firm is profitable, we also calculate ROE for these three levels of leverage given

---

[14]Care needs to be taken. In calculating ROE directly, $\frac{NI}{\text{Avg. }Eq}$, then

$$ROE = NPM(TATO)\frac{\text{Avg. }TA}{\text{Avg. }Eq} = \frac{NI}{NS}\left(\frac{NS}{\text{Avg. }TA}\right)\frac{\text{Avg. }TA}{\text{Avg. }Eq}, \tag{8.1}$$

where average equity should be used, as we are dividing an IS item, NI, by an average of BS items. However, in the Dupont decomposition, the final factor is $\frac{\text{Avg. }TA}{\text{Avg. }Eq}$, the ratio of two BS items, where we would normally not use averages.

[15]This increased probability also imposes costs upon the firm, e.g., its ability to negotiate terms with other firms, its cost of capital, etc... This contributes to the expected cost of bankruptcy, which is part of financial risk.

Chapter 8 Financial Statement Analysis and Relative Valuation

IS Entry	Assumption	Low Lev.*	Med. Lev.*	High Lev.*
Net sales		100	100	100
$COGS(VC)$	$VC = 40\%$	40	40	40
$COGS(FC)$	$FC = 10$	10	10	10
SGA expenses	constant 10	10	10	10
$D\&A$	constant 5	5	5	5
$EBIT$		35	35	35
Interest (IE)	$10\%D$	10	15	20
EBT	$EBIT - IE$	25	20	15
Less taxes	$35\%EBT$	8.75	7.00	5.25
NI	$EBT-$ taxes	16.25	13.00	9.75
debt value, D		100	150	200
equity value, Eq		125	75	25
firm value, V	$D + Eq$	225	225	225
ROE	$\frac{NI}{Eq}$	13.0%	17.3%	39.0%

* Lev.: leverage, or extent of debt utilization in the capital structure.
All numbers are in $ thousands.

Figure 8.6 **Leverage can increase ROE, if the firm is profitable**

one more dollar of net sales. The reader can confirm on her own that given net sales of $101, then the ROE increases as follows:

- low leverage: $\Delta ROE = 13.4\% - 13.0\% = 0.4\%$;
- medium leverage: $\Delta ROE = 18.1\% - 17.3\% = 0.8\%$;
- high leverage: $\Delta ROE = 42.3\% - 39.0\% = 3.3\%$.

So for an increase in NS of one dollar, the increase in ROE is increasing in leverage. Again, we stress that all this assumes that both the firm is profitable as well as $ROE > r^D$.

We now turn directly to the negative impact of debt. In figure 8.7, we show the same three scenarios regarding levels of debt and equity for our firm, resulting in constant firm value of $V = 225$. However, rather than $NS = 100$, we show the **break-even level of net sales** for each of three levels of leverage, i.e., that required for a firm to achieve $NI = 0$. All other assumptions regarding calculations in figure 8.7 are the same as those used in figure 8.6. The break-even levels of sales are, respectively, $58.3

IS Entry	Assumption	Low Lev.*	Med. Lev.*	High Lev.*
Net sales		58.3	66.7	75.0
$COGS(VC)$	$VC = 40\%$	23.3	26.7	30.0
$COGS(FC)$	$FC = 10$	10	10	10
SGA expenses	constant 10	10	10	10
$D\&A$	constant 5	5	5	5
$EBIT$		10	15	20
Interest (IE)	$10\%D$	10	15	20
EBT	$EBIT - IE$	0.00	0.00	0.00
Less taxes	$35\%EBT$	0.00	0.00	0.00
NI	$EBT-$ taxes	0.00	0.00	0.00
debt value, D		100	150	200
equity value, Eq		125	75	25
firm value, V	$D + Eq$	225	225	225
ROE	$\frac{NI}{Eq}$	0.00%	0.00%	0%

* Lev.: leverage, or extent of debt utilization in the capital structure. All numbers are in $ thousands.

Figure 8.7 **Increasing leverage increases financial risk**

for low leverage, $66.7 for medium leverage and $75.0 for high leverage. In short, as the firm increases debt, it increases the break-even level of sales. Thus, leverage increases financial risk, i.e., the likelihood that the firm will fail to meet its legally binding debt interest obligations. As sales decrease, the firm with the highest level of debt encounters difficulty in meeting its interest payments before the firm with medium debt does, all else equal. In turn, as sales decrease the latter fails to meet its interest obligations before the firm with the lowest debt level does.

In summary, while increasing leverage increases financial risk (i.e., the likelihood that the firm is unable to pay its creditors), it also increases owners' return, given that the firm meets its financial obligations. The manager's challenge is to correctly navigate this trade-off implied by increasing debt.

The reader should be mindful that no firm knows in advance what its net sales will be in any given year. Thus, a firm should *not* operate at a level of debt consistent with zero net income. Indeed, a firm should operate with a level of debt consistent with interest payments that leave the firm with a significantly positive expectation of NI. For a given level of expected NS, then the greater (lower) the variability of net sales, the lower (higher) the level of debt that the firm should employ, all else equal. In other words, the higher (lower) the level of operational risk, the lower (higher) the level of financial risk that the firm can accept.

Now that we understand the benefits and costs of incremental debt, we are ready to examine metrics related to levels of debt in the firm's capital structure. Figure 8.8 shows two types of financial risk metrics commonly employed: leverage and coverage. For all financial risk metrics, an interior optimal exists, consistent with our previous

Metric	Statistic	Calculation	Value
Leverage ratios			
Debt ratio	$\frac{TL}{TL+Eq}$	$\frac{49{,}363}{95{,}298}$	51.8%
LTD to total Cap*	$\frac{LTD}{LTD+Eq}$	$\frac{21{,}059}{66{,}994}$	31.4%
Debt to equity	$\frac{TL}{Eq}$	$\frac{49{,}363}{45{,}935}$	1.07
Leverage: $\frac{A}{Eq}$ Lev	$\frac{TA}{Eq}$	$\frac{95{,}298}{45{,}935}$	2.07
Debt to assets	$\frac{TD}{TA}$	$\frac{28{,}557}{95{,}298}$	30.0%
Coverage ratios			
Times interest earned	$\frac{EBIT}{IE}$	$\frac{19{,}243}{2{,}585}$	7.44
Cash interest coverage	$\frac{OCF+IE+\text{taxes}}{IE}$	$\frac{20{,}295}{2{,}585}$	7.85
Fixed charge coverage	$\frac{EBIT+\text{Rent Exp}}{IE+\text{Rent Exp}}$		
Cash flow adequacy	$\frac{OCF}{CapEx+IE+Div}$	$\frac{10{,}024}{18{,}267}$	54.9%
Cash flow coverage	$\frac{OCF}{\text{Avg. }TD}$	$\frac{10{,}024}{26{,}530}$	37.8%
Adjusted ROA (for FLI)	$\frac{NI+IE(1-T^C)}{\text{Avg. }TA}$	$\frac{10{,}816}{85{,}603.5}$	12.6%
FLI	$\frac{ROE}{\text{Adj. }ROA}$	$\frac{22.4\%}{12.6\%}$	1.77

*LTD: long-term debt; Cap: capitalization; FLI: financial leverage index; EBIT is also called operating profit, or OP; Rent Exp: rent expense;[16] CapEx: capital expenditures, or $\Delta GPPE$; Div: dividend paid; TL: total liabilities; Eq: equity; TA: total assets; TD: total debt;

Figure 8.8 Financial risk ratios: leverage and coverage

discussion. This implies that some level of financial risk is optimal, as debt payments are tax deductible. The **debt tax shield** is the increase in firm value due to the tax advantage of interest payments.[17] On the other hand, as failure to pay debt interest when due triggers bankruptcy, too much debt increases the probability of this event to unacceptably high levels. So while it is obvious that too much financial risk is sub-

---

[16] In our example, we ignore rental expenses. In actuality, leasing is a very important consideration. Crudely speaking, leasing is a substitute for debt financing. Such consideration is beyond our scope.

[17] Recall that cash dividends to equity holders are *not* tax deductible.

optimal, so is too little. Hence, the presence of an outlier, either an extremely high or low level of any given financial risk metric, requires our attention.

Leverage ratios simply examine capital structure, i.e., how the firm is financed. For all five shown in figure 8.8, the metric is increasing in leverage, i.e., in the use of debt. **Coverage ratios** reflect the firm's ability to "cover" payments related to its debt. In contrast to leverage ratios, coverage ratios are decreasing in leverage, i.e., higher (lower) levels of debt result in lower (higher) coverage ratios. Loosely speaking, the first four coverage metrics shown in figure 8.8 are ratios of a cash flow (plus/or operating profit) "available" to cover interest payments to such payments.[18] Note the inclusion of rental expenses in the fixed charge coverage ratio. In crude terms, leasing an asset is a "substitute" for buying with debt financing. Thus, lease payments are in some sense comparable to interest payments.[19] Cash flow coverage is a bit different than the other four coverage ratios as it features a balance sheet item in the denominator, average total debt. Finally, financial leverage index, FLI, is a metric for how well the firm utilizes debt financing. Generally speaking, effectiveness of leverage is increasing in FLI. In a dichotomous sense, $FLI > 1$ ($FLI < 1$) indicates effective (ineffective) usage of debt.

8.5 Operational Risk Ratios

Before directly examining operational risk metrics, we first need a bit of background information. Specifically, the concept of cost characteristics, i.e., fixed versus variable, underlies operational risk and its metrics. A key idea is the trade-off between fixed costs and variable costs. In broad terms, a firm may be able to decrease variable costs (labor, raw materials, etc...) by increasing fixed costs (fixed asset automation and enhanced flexibility) and vice versa. To this end, we first examine a contribution margin income statement, which explicitly breaks down costs by their nature rather than by the department from which they are borne. Afterwards, we consider a plot of total costs versus production output for firms with varying ratios of fixed costs to variable costs.

Consider the top half of the **contribution margin income statement**, shown in

---

[18] Cash interest coverage includes IE in the numerator. The logic is that IE has been subtracted from NI in calculating OCF, so the numerator of this ratio adds IE back.

[19] The analogy has limitations due to differences in legal and accounting ramifications of the two types of payments.

figure 8.9.[20] Used internally by managers, this statement breaks down costs not via tra-

IS Entry	Value	per Unit	Value	Ratio	Value
Net sales (NS)	215,600	price, P	10.00		100.0%
Variable costs (VC)	65,245	UVC	3.03	VCR	30.3%
CM^*	150,355	UCM	6.97	CMR	69.7%
Fixed costs (FC)	131,112		6.08		60.8%
OM^*	19,243	UOM	0.89	OMR	8.9%

$^*CM$: contribution margin; OM: operating margin = $EBIT$ = operating income;

Figure 8.9 Contribution margin income statement

ditional departments (manufacturing, sales, etc...) as is done in a financial accounting income statement, but rather via cost characteristics. **Variable costs** (**Fixed costs**) are those that (do not) increase in production output. Of the three columns in figure 8.9, consider the first. **Contribution margin** equals $CM = NS - VC = Q(P) - Q(UVC)$, where VC are total variable costs, Q are units of output, P is per-unit price and UVC is variable cost per unit, or $UVC = \frac{VC}{Q}$.[21]

The middle column of figure 8.9 translates values to a "per unit" basis by dividing the first column by the number of units, assumed to be $Q = 21,500$ in this example. The **unit contribution margin**, $UCM = \frac{CM}{Q} = P - UVC$, is an important number. A manager knows that if she sells one more unit of product, then the operating profit will increase by the UCM, $3.03 in this case. Analogously, in the third column, the **contribution margin ratio** (CMR) of 69.7% means that for each incremental dollar of revenue, $0.69 is contributed to the operating profit, where $CMR = \frac{CM}{(Q)P} = \frac{UCM}{P} = \frac{P-UVC}{P} = 1 - \frac{UVC}{P}$.

To further illustrate the trade-off of fixed costs and variable costs, consider a firm trying to decide between two possible manufacturing technologies, **H** (highly automated with **high** **FC**, FC^H, and low UVC, UVC^H) and **L** (labor intensive with **low** **FC**, FC^L, and high UVC, UVC^L), as shown in figure 8.10. Note that superscripts H and L refer to fixed costs, *not* variable costs. As such, technology H (L), with unit variable cost UVC^H (UVC^L) corresponds to low (high) variable costs, i.e., $UVC^H < UVC^L$. In this plot of total costs, TC, versus output, Q, then $TC^i = FC^i + Q^i(UVC^i)$, $i \in \{L, H\}$. So the intercepts are FC^H and FC^L, respectively, where $FC^H > FC^L$. The slopes of these lines are UVC^H and UVC^L, where

---

[20] Only the top half of the contribution margin income statement is shown in figure 8.9, as the bottom half (i.e., beginning with $EBIT$) is the same as that of a traditional income statement.

[21] For simplicity, assume that the firm sells a single product at a single price, P.

$UVC^H < UVC^L$.[22]

One type of **break-even output**, Q^{BE}, is defined by $TC^H(Q^{BE}) \equiv TC^L(Q^{BE})$. So $FC^H + Q^{BE}(UVC^H) = FC^L + Q^{BE}(UVC^L)$. In figure 8.10, $Q^{BE} = 10$ units, represented by the square. So for $Q < (>) Q^{BE}$, then $TC^H > (<) TC^L$.[23] Also shown in figure 8.10 is revenue, or net sales, as a function of output, Q. The triangle (circle) shows a different type of break-even output for L (H), i.e., where the profit is zero. As is intuitive, the break-even output for zero profit is lower for the low FC technology than for the high FC technology.

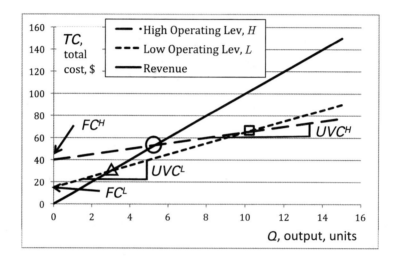

Figure 8.10 Degree of operating leverage

In our previous discussion of financial risk, figure 8.7 shows that the firm with the highest annual interest payments (i.e., the highest levered firm) has greater financial risk than does the firm with the lowest interest payments (i.e., least levered firm), all else equal. This claim follows as the break-even level of sales required to achieve zero profit is higher for the former than for the latter. To repeat, the firm with higher (lower) financial risk requires greater (lesser) net sales just to achieve zero profit.

Analogously, figure 8.10 shows that the firm with higher fixed costs has greater operational risk than does the firm with lower fixed costs, all else equal. This claim follows as the break-even level of sales required to achieve zero profit is higher for the former than for the latter. To repeat, the firm with higher (lower) operational risk

---

[22]Due to the trade-off of fixed costs and variable costs, then we assume that $FC^H > FC^L \Rightarrow UVC^H < UVC^L$.

[23]So if a firm anticipates that its average output will be below (above) Q^{BE}, then it may be more likely to choose L (H).

requires greater (lesser) net sales just to achieve zero profit.[24]

So both high financial risk and high operational risk imply that the firm must eclipse a higher level of sales just to break-even with respect to profitability. As such, for a given level of sales volatility, it is not surprising that firms in industries with inherently high operational risk (i.e., those with high fixed costs) tend to accept lower financial risk, all else equal. In contrast, firms in industries with inherently lower operational risk tend to have higher leveraged capital structures.[25]

We are now in position to directly consider operational risk metrics, as shown in figure 8.11. All metrics shown are increasing in operational risk. The first metric, fixed

Metric	Statistic	Calculation	Value
Fixed cost ratio, FCR	$\frac{FC}{TC}$	$\frac{131{,}112}{196{,}357}$	66.8%
DOL^*	$\frac{NS-VC}{NS-VC-FC}$	$\frac{150{,}355}{19{,}243}$	7.81
DOL	$1 + \frac{FC}{EBIT}$	$1 + \frac{131{,}112}{19{,}243}$	7.81
DOL	$\frac{CMR}{OMR}$	$\frac{69.7\%}{8.9\%}$	7.81
$CV(NS)$	$\frac{\sigma(NS)}{\mu(NS)}$	$\frac{33{,}168}{201{,}020}$	16.5%
Operations Risk	$\frac{CV(EBIT)}{CV(NS)}$	$\frac{123.2\%}{16.5\%}$	7.47

DOL: degree of operating leverage; CV: coefficient of variation;

Figure 8.11 Operational risk ratios

cost ratio, directly captures the importance of fixed costs in determining operational risk. The next, **degree of operating leverage**, is defined by[26]

$$DOL \equiv \frac{\%\Delta EBIT}{\%\Delta NS} = \frac{\left(\frac{\Delta EBIT}{EBIT}\right)}{\left(\frac{\Delta NS}{NS}\right)} = \frac{NS}{EBIT}\frac{\Delta EBIT}{\Delta NS}. \qquad (8.2)$$

---

[24] From another perspective, operational risk is as follows. In a comparative static sense, if a firm sells one fewer unit, it reduces its cost by UVC. Thus, more cost per unit of output is shed, the higher the UVC. So there exists lower operational risk for a technology which utilizes higher UVC, all else equal. As lower UVC is associated with higher FC, then higher fixed costs yield higher operational risk. Analogously, we can think in terms of fixed costs directly. Fixed costs are "sticky", as they are not shed as output wanes. Thus, the higher the fixed costs, the higher the operational risk. We see strong parallels between financial risk and operational risk. Financial risk is directly related to "inescapable" interest payments due to debt financing. Analogously, operational risk is directly proportional to the firm's "inescapable" operational fixed costs.

[25] This effect is somewhat mitigated by the fact that tangible assets often justify higher debt financing, as the assets themselves potentially can be used as collateral.

[26] Recall that $EBIT$ is also called operating income or operating margin, OM.

It is straightforward to show that this also equals

$$DOL = \frac{CM}{EBIT} = \frac{CM}{CM - FC} = 1 + \frac{FC}{EBIT} = \frac{CMR}{OMR}, \quad (8.3)$$

where $OMR = \frac{OM}{NS}$ is the **operations margin ratio**. Note that DOL directly captures the impact of fixed costs upon operational risk, as DOL is increasing in fixed costs, or $\frac{\partial DOL}{\partial FC} = \frac{CM}{EBIT^2} > 0$.

Business risk is captured via coefficient of variation of NS, $CV(NS)$. We assume that $\sigma(NS) = 33,168$ and $\mu(NS) = 201,020$. Then $CV(NS) = 16.5\%$. We further assume that $\sigma(EBIT) = 11,113$ and $\mu(EBIT) = 9,022$. So $CV(EBIT) = \frac{11,113}{9,022} = 123.2\%$. Finally, **operations risk**, $\frac{CV(EBIT)}{CV(NS)} = \frac{123.2\%}{16.5\%} = 7.47$, is closely related to $DOL = 7.81$.

8.6 Sustainable Growth of Equity

Sustainable growth of equity, g, is the *internal* rate of equity growth possible due to the firm's ability to generate cash from its operating activities. By definition of g, external equity financing, i.e., issuing new shares of equity, is excluded. So g depends primarily on the firm's ability to generate (accounting) profit and on its decision regarding plowback ratio. In short,

$$\begin{aligned} g_t &\equiv \frac{\Delta Eq_t}{Eq_{t-1}} = \frac{Eq_t - Eq_{t-1}}{Eq_{t-1}} = \frac{RE_t - RE_{t-1}}{Eq_{t-1}} \\ &= \frac{b_t NI_t}{Eq_{t-1}} = b_t \frac{NI_t}{Eq_{t-1}} = b_t(ROE_t), \end{aligned} \quad (8.4)$$

where $Eq_t = RE_t + (CS_t + APIC_t - TS_t)$ is equity. By definition of g, $CS_t + APIC_t - TS_t$ is held constant, so $\Delta Eq_t = \Delta RE_t$.

For simplicity, we assume that b_t and ROE_t are constant each year, so $g = b(ROE)$ is also constant. We dedicate a later chapter to the earnings multiplier model (EMM), where we assume that the firm's equity grows at constant rate g each year. We examine the EMM to understand implications for other firm parameters, in addition to that of its equity. The sustainable growth rate of equity (g) will feature prominently.

8.7 External Liquidity Ratios

In contrast to prior ratios which give metrics regarding firm performance, external liquidity ratios directly impact investors in the firm's securities. All else equal, *illiquidity* represents a cost to investors. The less traded an asset, the more illiquid (less liquid) it is, all else equal. Illiquidity represents a cost, as selling an illiquid asset relative to a liquid one generally either (a) takes longer for a given desired price, or (b) must be offered at a discount in order to sell it as rapidly as a "comparable" liquid asset.

External liquidity metrics are shown in figure 8.12. A market maker profits via her bid-ask spread. As she is willing to sell a security at a given point in time for a price that is slightly more than that at which she is willing to buy, she executes "buy low and sell high". The more a security is traded, the smaller the bid-ask spread that she is willing to accept, as she is able to offset the smaller bid-ask spread with increased volume of trades. In contrast, the more illiquid an asset, the higher the bid-ask spread that she demands in order to warrant her market making activities.

Metric	Statistic	Calculation	Value
Bid-Ask Spread	Ask P $-$ Bid P	$30.45 - 29.55$	0.90
Trading TO^*	$\frac{\text{Sh. traded/period}}{\text{Avg Sh. Outst.}}$	$\frac{3,784,764}{4,698,500}$	80.6%
Number of owners			
Market Capitalization	$(P)(Sh.Outst.)$	$30(4,803)$	$144,090$
*Sh. Outst.: shares outstanding;			

Figure 8.12   External liquidity ratios

In contrast to the bid-ask spread, trading turnover is *directly* related to liquidity. The higher the trading turnover, the more frequently the asset is bought and sold. Next, the greater the number of owners of a given security, the more liquid is the security, all else equal. Finally, market capitalization also measures liquidity directly via its inclusion of number of shares. All else equal, more shares should imply a wider market, i.e., accessibility to a greater number of market participants.

8.8   Relative Valuation

Valuation can be done in either a relative sense or in an absolute sense. The latter is done via intrinsic value calculations, i.e., discounting cash flows, as shown in a later chapter. Relative valuation considers ratios of equity price to various key metrics, all of which are firm specific characteristics. We will briefly examine four different valuation ratios: price to sales ($\frac{P}{S}$), price to cash flow ($\frac{P}{CF}$), price to book value ($\frac{P}{BV}$) and price to earnings ($\frac{P}{E}$). In short, we consider $\frac{P_0}{\pi_t}$, where $t \in \{0,1\}$ and $\pi \in \{S, CF, BV, E\}$. The higher (lower) the ratio $\frac{P_0}{\pi_t}$, the more (less) expensive is the firm's equity, all else equal, i.e., the more *relatively* over-valued (under-valued) the firm's equity.[27]

Care should be taken *not* to compare ratios of firms in different industries. Competitors within an industry face similar risks and opportunities. As such, if peers execute optimally, in terms of both financing as well as operationally, they should arrive at comparable characteristics. Given that they face similar operational risks, they should tend to congregate around similar capital structures, i.e., around similar financial risks.[28] As such, firms within an industry tend to have similar values for the relative valuation ratios shown in this chapter.

In this section on relative valuation, time $t = 0$ is assumed to be earlier today, and $t = 1$ is one period from today. So π_0 is the realization today of annual S_0 and CF_0 for the past year (i.e., flow variables), whereas BV_0 and Eq_0 are today's values (i.e., stock variables). Analogously, π_1 is today's expectation of annual S_1 and CF_1 for the coming year, whereas BV_1 and Eq_1 are today's expectations for levels of BV and E one year from today. Of course, technically speaking, π_1 is actually $E[\pi_1]$, as it is today's expected value for one year from today.

The choice between $\frac{P_0}{\pi_0}$ and $\frac{P_0}{\pi_1}$ is significant. The former is called a "lagged" $\frac{P}{\pi}$ ratio, while the latter is called a "leading" $\frac{P}{\pi}$ ratio. As P_0 "currently" exists, some prefer the "current" value of π, i.e, the most recent value of π, π_0. In contrast, those who prefer π_1 argue the following two points. Firstly, the market price of a share of equity, P_0, reflects the collective belief of the market regarding the firm's *future* prospects.[29] Thus, π should also be *forward* looking, i.e, π_1 or technically, $E[\pi_1]$. Secondly, π_1 is much less volatile than are possible realizations of π_0.[30] Hence, leading values, $\frac{P_0}{\pi_1}$, or more precisely, $\frac{P_0}{E[\pi_1]}$, are far less volatile than are lagged values, $\frac{P_0}{\pi_0}$.

8.8.1 Price to Sales Ratio

The price to sales ratio ($\frac{P}{S}$) is preferred by some stakeholders as sales lead all

---

[27] All relative valuation metrics can be calculated as ratios of values per share, or $\frac{P}{\pi} = \frac{P/\text{share}}{\pi/\text{share}}$. Equivalently, ratios of total values can be used, or $\frac{P}{\pi} = \frac{\text{market value of } E}{\text{total } \pi} = \frac{(P/\text{share})(\text{shares outstanding})}{(\pi/\text{share})(\text{shares outstanding})}$, e.g., $\frac{P_0}{BV_0} = \frac{\$11.12/sh.}{\$2.56/sh.} = \frac{\$11.12/sh.(10.012 \text{ million shares})}{\$25,588} = 4.35$.

[28] Firms in industries with higher (lower) operations risk tend to accept lower (higher) financial risk, i.e., engage in less (more) leverage, all else equal.

[29] Indeed, per intrinsic value, equity price is the summation of the present value of *future* expected cash flows.

[30] For simplicity, assume that at times $t = 0$ and $t = 1$, π_0 and π_1 are drawn from a common distribution. Then of course realizations of π_0 are more volatile than $E[\pi_1]$, as the latter is a single, well defined value.

else, i.e., increases sales lead to increased profits, cash flows, etc... Indeed, as we see later when we generate future pro-forma income statements and balance sheets, sales lead all other entries on the financial statements, driving home the importance of sales. Additionally, within the bounds of acceptable accounting practices (e.g., GAAP), sales are not easy to manipulate.[31] As a limitation to the $\frac{P}{NS}$ ratio, comparing values across industries is particularly problematic, as net profit margin, a factor influencing $\frac{P}{NS}$, is quite variant across industries. But again, we stress that in general, comparisons of ratios should be restricted to firms in the same industry, i.e., to those which face comparable risks and opportunities.

8.8.2 Price to Cash Flow Ratio

The price to cash flow ratio ($\frac{P}{CF}$) is attractive, for after all, "cash is king". Typical cash flows used are FCFs and OCFs. Sharing an advantage with the price to sales ratio, cash flows, like sales, are difficult to manipulate: either a firm generates cash or it does not. Additionally, price to cash flow is popular, as cash is the basis for absolute valuation via intrinsic value. Crudely speaking, dividing intrinsic value by cash flow results in terms featuring demanded rate of return and growth rate of cash flow, as shown in a later chapter. Thus, $\frac{P}{CF}$ should give a direct metric of relative pricing of equity for competitors who face comparable risks (i.e., comparable demanded rate of return, given similar capital structures) and opportunities (i.e., comparable growth rate of cash flows, g). That said, the primary disadvantage of this ratio is that it can *not* be used for firms that generate negative cash flows, e.g., typically young firms. As such, this ratio should only be used for firms in industries that are mature enough to generate cash flow that is in some sense indicative of what an investor may expect for the foreseeable future, if not in the long run.

8.8.3 Price to Book Value Ratio

The price to book value ratio ($\frac{P}{BV}$) is short for market value of equity to book value of equity, or $\frac{P}{BV} = \frac{P/\text{share}}{BV/\text{share}} = \frac{P*(\text{shs. outst.})}{\text{total BV of E}} = \frac{MV}{BV}$, where $BV = CS + APIC + RE - TS$. One attractive feature of this ratio is that it shows what the market collectively thinks of the firm's management regarding value creation, i.e., $\frac{P}{BV} > 1$ ($\frac{P}{BV} < 1$) means that regarding the firm's current assets, the firm's managers have created (destroyed) value. Also, the reciprocal, $\frac{BV}{MV}$, features prominently in Fama-French's three-factor model,

---

[31] In contrast, NI, which is at the bottom of the income statement, is far more uncertain, as opportunities exist for "interpretations" of all line items along the way before arriving at NI.

as it appears to be a relevant factor in equity valuation. Furthermore, this ratio is attractive as BV of equity is both difficult to manipulate as well as relatively stable from year to year. A weakness for this ratio is that it should be limited to firms in industries that do not have relatively small book values, e.g., consulting firms.

8.8.4 Price to Earnings Ratio

The price to earnings ratio ($\frac{P}{E}$) is widely quoted by the financial press. If for no other reason, this begs our attention to examine it. Another reason why this ratio is interesting is because the inverse is the **earnings yield**, $\frac{E}{P}$, i.e., the *market* equivalent of return on equity, another "return on investment" metric.[32] As such, it is comparable to others yield metrics, such as the coupon yield for bonds, $\frac{\text{coupon}}{\text{price}}$. However, as popular as it is, the $\frac{P}{E}$ ratio does have its drawbacks, as do all ratios. Firstly, as net income (earnings) is the final line item of the income statement, it is subject to potential manipulations of all prior entries. So even within the bounds of acceptable accounting practices, NI can be greatly influenced at the firm's discretion. Next, the $\frac{P}{E}$ ratio is negative for small firms, i.e., small firms that are not yet profitable. Furthermore, as NI is typically quite small and subjected to realizations of several items in the income statement, it is relatively volatile. As NI is far more volatile than NS, $\frac{P}{E}$ is more volatile than $\frac{P}{S}$.

8.9 Relative Valuation Versus Absolute Valuation

As we have seen, relative valuation utilizes ratios to give a sense of comparative value.[33] Thus, one concern of relative valuation is that it is void of any relationship to intrinsic value. As such, care should be taken when attempting to use relative valuation at times when ratios are at extreme values relative to historical levels. Of course, noting the magnitude of such values in historical terms is in itself useful, as we can see how the market currently values equities relative to past levels. In short, relative valuation gives indications regarding values of equities not only relative to each other, but also relative to the past. However, it gives little indication as to whether or not current values are justified. Indeed, currently high (low) values may actually represent undervalued (overvalued) firms in a particularly robust (weak) economy.

---

[32] We say "market" equivalent of ROE as P is market based, whereas BV of Eq is book value. So contrast $\frac{NI}{MV\ Eq}$ with $\frac{NI}{BV\ Eq}$. If not specified, we mean the latter, or $ROE = \frac{NI}{BV\ Eq}$.

[33] Thus, it advisable to restrict comparisons to firms facing comparable risks and opportunities, i.e., competitors in the same industry.

Absolute valuation is attractive, as intrinsic value is fundamental to how we value expected future cash flows.[34] However, as it fails to directly incorporate current pricing, it is somewhat disconnected from valuation by the market. Also, both the long-term growth rate of cash flows as well as the discount rate are critically important factors in determining intrinsic value. This is both a blessing and a curse. Regarding the positive, we see very explicitly how these two factors impact value. However, as intrinsic value is so sensitive to these parameters, it gives pause for concern in any intrinsic value calculation, especially if we lack confidence in the accuracy of our estimates of these values.

Problems

Continue to consider figures 7.4 and 7.5 from the previous chapter's problem set.

1. Complete a common size income statement consistent with that of figure 8.1.

2. Complete a common size balance sheet consistent with that of figure 8.2.

3. Calculate all internal liquidity ratios consistent with those of figure 8.3.

4. Calculate all operating performance ratios consistent with those of figure 8.5.

5. Calculate all financial risk ratios consistent with those of figure 8.8.

6. Complete the top half of a contribution margin income statement consistent with that of figure 8.9.

7. Calculate all operational risk ratios consistent with those of figure 8.11.

8. What is the sustainable growth of equity of this firm, i.e., that which is possible absent external financing?

9. Asssume that the firm's stock is currently trading at $9.00 per share. What is the firm's: (a) price to sales ratio? (b) price to free cash flow ratio? (c) price to book ratio? (d) price to earnings ratio?

---

[34] In the next chapter we will learn multiple cash flow definitions.

CHAPTER 9

Absolute Valuation: Discounting Cash Flows

In the previous chapter, we explored relative valuation of equity via ratios involving the firm's stock price. Now we turn to intrinsic valuation of a firm and its equity by discounting cash flows by the appropriate demanded rate of return.

We begin by analyzing historical income statements and balance sheets in order to understand relevant past relations.[1] Considering ratios of items from both historical income statements (figure 9.2) as well as historical balance sheets (figure 9.4), our objective is to determine relevant relations that allow us to understand how this firm performs. From these, we develop models which allow us to generate five years of future pro-formas for income statements, balance sheets and statements of cash flows. We also calculate additional pro-forma statements of other types of cash flows used in various discounted cash flow (DCF) methods. We then turn to calculations of supplementary inputs such as various types of demanded rates of return including the weighted average cost of capital. Finally, we use five DCF methods to calculate directly either enterprise value or equity value.

One can not perform these calculations in a vacuum. Judgment is always required, and relevant new information, which obviously won't be reflected in historical statements, must be considered in building the future pro-forma statements. For example, if the firm recently released good (bad) information that significantly impacts its future sales, you would increase (decrease) the assumed growth rate, at least in the short term, relative to that implied by recent historical income statements. Consider other such examples. A recent breakthrough in manufacturing technology would decrease future $COGS$ relative to historical values, all else equal. A recent announcement by the CEO that non-manufacturing expenses would be slashed should imply lower SGA

---

[1] For simplicity, we use only three years of historical statements. More commonly, practitioners use either five or 10 years of statements.

expenses going forward. An announcement of a more aggressive long-term advertising campaign would imply higher advertising expenses in the future relative to historical levels, all else equal. Obviously, new information may also impact future balance sheet relations compared to historical values, such as an announcement of a new target capital structure. In summary, all such relevant new information that is not reflected in historical financial statements must be accounted for in building future pro-forma statements.

9.1 Growth Rate Calculations

Before we begin our journey into absolute valuation, we digress for a moment to discuss growth rates. We explore these calculations in order to develop the relationships that we'll need to generate future pro-forma financial accounting statements.

Let's first consider constant *relative* growth rate. By calculating geometric mean growth rate of net sales, we are implicitly assuming that net sales are growing at a constant *relative* rate, or $NS_t = NS_0(1 + g^{GM})^t$. As such, a time series plot of NS_t versus t is increasing ($\frac{dNS_t}{dt} = NS_t \ln[1 + g^{GM}] > 0$) and convex ($\frac{d^2 NS_t}{dt^2} = NS_t[\ln(1 + g^{GM})]^2 > 0$). Thus, given an estimate of g^{GM}, then the model generates future estimates of NS_t via $NS_t | NS_{t-1} = NS_{t-1}(1 + g^{GM})$.

Continuing to assume constant *relative* growth rate, we can use more data points via a time series regression. So regressing $\ln(NS_t)$ on t is appropriate, or $\ln(NS_t) = \alpha + \beta(t) + \epsilon_t$. Thus, given an estimate of β, then this model generates future estimates of NS_t via $NS_t | NS_{t-1} = NS_{t-1}(e^\beta)$.

The above two relative growth rate estimates are closely related. Comparing $NS_t | NS_{t-1} = NS_{t-1}(1 + g^{GM})$ with $NS_t | NS_{t-1} = NS_{t-1}(e^\beta)$, then $g^{GM} \approx e^\beta - 1$ are two estimates of relative growth rates.[2]

Now let's consider constant *absolute* growth rate. Then a plot of NS_t versus t is approximately linear rather than convex, meaning that sales are growing at a constant *absolute* dollar amount each year. As such, regressing NS_t on t is appropriate, or $NS_t = \alpha + \beta^a(t) + \epsilon_t$. Thus, given an estimate of β^a, this model generates future estimates of NS_t via $NS_t | NS_{t-1} = NS_{t-1} + \beta^a$.

---

[2]The reason that they are only approximately equal is that the two data points used to calculate the geometric mean growth rate, NS_{-T} and NS_0, almost certainly do not both fall precisely on the model generated via the regression. In the low probability cases where both points either fall exactly on the regression model or are exactly the same distance above/(below) the regression model, then $g^{GM} = e^\beta - 1$. Otherwise, $g^{GM} \approx e^\beta - 1$.

110   Asset Valuation Theory

In figure 9.1, we graphically depict the differences between constant absolute growth (i.e., constant linear growth) versus constant relative growth. For a time series

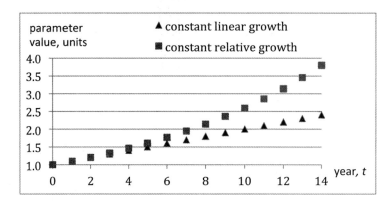

Figure 9.1 Constant linear (absolute) growth versus relative growth

plot of a parameter value over time, constant linear growth appears as a straight line, whereas constant relative growth appears as a convex curve. In figure 9.1, both parameters begin at a value of one in year 1. Furthermore, both "grow" at 10% per year, but constant absolute (linear) growth means that $\pi_{t+1} = \pi_t + g$, whereas constant relative growth means that $\pi_{t+1} = \pi_t(1+g) = \pi_t + \pi_t g$.[3] If a plot of π_t versus t is convex, then plot $\ln(\pi_t)$ versus t; if linear, use the assumption of constant relative growth where $g = (\frac{\pi_0}{\pi_{-T}})^{1/T}$ or $g = \beta$ in a regression of $\ln(\pi_t)$ versus t.

Comparing relative versus absolute growth rates, then constant relative growth means increasing absolute growth. Consider constant relative growth, k^r, or $\frac{d\ln(\pi_t)}{dt} = \frac{1}{\pi_t}\frac{d\pi_t}{dt} = k^r$. So absolute growth is increasing each year, or $\frac{d\pi_t}{dt} = k^r \pi_t$ is increasing, as π_t is increasing. Equivalently, constant absolute growth means decreasing relative growth.[4]

Note that other calculation options exists, such as arithmetic mean growth.

9.2 Historical Relationships: Income Statement

Three historical income statements are shown in figure 9.2. Also shown are cash dividends paid as well as cash raised via stock issuance and cash used to retire out-

---

[3] A plot of $\ln(\pi_t)$ versus time t would be linear for the constant relative growth parameter and concave for the constant absolute one. One should always first plot pi_t versus t. If linear, use the assumption of constant absolute growth where g equals the average of $\pi_t - \pi_{t-1}$, $t = \{-T+1, -T+2, ..., 0\}$.

[4] Given constant absolute growth, k^a, then $\frac{d\pi_t}{dt} = k^a$. So relative growth is decreasing each year, or $\frac{d\ln(\pi_t)}{dt} = \frac{1}{\pi_t}\frac{d\pi_t}{dt} = \frac{k^a}{\pi_t}$ is decreasing, as π_t is increasing.

standing stock. As shown, stock was issued in 2013 ($2,224) and was retired in 2015 ($979).

IS Entry	2015	2014	2013
Net sales (NS)	53,762	51,202	48,304
Cost of goods sold	38,440	36,609	34,537
Gross profit	15,322	14,593	13,767
SGA expenses	4,892	4,659	4,396
Advertising	1,989	1,894	1,787
$D\&A$	439	114	115
Repairs & Maint	847	834	805
$EBIT$	7,155	7,090	6,664
Other Income (Expenses)			
Interest Income	5	8	7
Interest Expenses	(693)	(945)	(1,158)
EBT	6,467	6,153	5,512
Income taxes	2,199	2,092	1,874
NI	4,268	4,061	3,638
cash dividends paid	1,626	1,547	1,386
cash raised: stock issued	0	0	2,224
cash spent: stock repurchased	979	0	0
All numbers are in $ thousands.			

Figure 9.2 Income statement for DCF analysis

Figure 9.3 shows calculations of relevant ratios that will be used to generate future pro-forma income statements. Most future pro-forma income statements are **sales driven**. Net sales are assumed to grow at a certain rate over time, and other income statement items respond to the assumed net sales each year. As such, growth of sales is a critically important assumption. In our example, we simply assume that sales will continue to grow for the next five years at the same relative rate as they did in the most recent three years.[5] We calculate a geometric mean growth rate of net sales 5.5%, as shown in figure 9.3.

We now turn to our analysis of relevant relations for use in our future pro-forma

---

[5] We calculate $g^{sales} = 5.5\%$. We later assume that respective calculated cash flows grow at this same rate in perpetuity. In reality, the long-term growth probably should be no greater than about $2\% - 3\%$, even for a firm with the brightest of outlooks. The maximum long-term growth of cash flow cannot exceed that of the overall economy.

We don't dwell on the assumed future perpetual growth rate of cash flows because we do a scenario analysis at the end of our example where we consider an entire range of values for this estimate. You should always perform such a scenario analysis, examined in detail later.

IS Entry	Key relationship	Statistic	Calculation	Value
Net sales (NS)	geometric mean Gr.	$\left(\frac{NS_{2015}}{NS_{2013}}\right)^{\frac{1}{3}} - 1$	$\left(\frac{53{,}762}{48{,}304}\right)^{\frac{1}{3}} - 1$	5.5%
Cost of goods sold	mean $\frac{COGS_t}{NS_t}$	$\frac{1}{3}\left[\frac{COGS_{15}}{NS_{15}} + \frac{COGS_{14}}{NS_{14}} + \frac{COGS_{13}}{NS_{13}}\right]$	$\frac{1}{3}\left[\frac{38{,}440}{53{,}762} + \frac{36{,}609}{51{,}202} + \frac{34{,}537}{48{,}304}\right]$	71.5%
Gross profit: $GP = NS - COGS$				
SGA expenses	mean $\frac{SGA\ \text{Expenses}_t}{NS_t}$	$\frac{1}{3}\left[\frac{SGA_{15}}{NS_{15}} + \frac{SGA_{14}}{NS_{14}} + \frac{SGA_{13}}{NS_{13}}\right]$	$\frac{1}{3}\left[\frac{4{,}892}{53{,}762} + \frac{4{,}659}{51{,}202} + \frac{4{,}396}{48{,}304}\right]$	9.1%
Advertising	mean $\frac{Adv_t}{NS_t}$	$\frac{1}{3}\left[\frac{Adv_{15}}{NS_{15}} + \frac{Adv_{14}}{NS_{14}} + \frac{Adv_{13}}{NS_{13}}\right]$	$\frac{1}{3}\left[\frac{1{,}989}{53{,}762} + \frac{1{,}894}{51{,}202} + \frac{1{,}787}{48{,}304}\right]$	3.7%
D&A	mean $\frac{D\&A_t}{GPPE_{t-1}}$	$\frac{1}{3}\left[\frac{D\&A_{15}}{GPPE_{14}} + \frac{D\&A_{14}}{GPPE_{13}} + \frac{D\&A_{13}}{GPPE_{12}}\right]$	$\frac{1}{3}\left[\frac{439}{19{,}287} + \frac{114}{18{,}907} + \frac{115}{18{,}210}\right]$	1.2%
Repairs & Maint.	mean $\frac{R\&M_t}{NPPE_{t-1}}$	$\frac{1}{3}\left[\frac{R\&M_{15}}{NPPE_{14}} + \frac{R\&M_{14}}{NPPE_{13}} + \frac{R\&M_{13}}{NPPE_{12}}\right]$	$\frac{1}{3}\left[\frac{847}{16{,}949} + \frac{834}{16{,}683} + \frac{805}{16{,}101}\right]$	5.0%
$EBIT$: $EBIT = GP - $ advertising $- D\&A - $ repairs & maintenance				
Interest Income	mean $\frac{II_t}{\left(\frac{MS_t + MS_{t-1}}{2}\right)}$	$\frac{1}{3}\left[\frac{II_{15}}{\left(\frac{MS_{15}+MS_{14}}{2}\right)} + \frac{II_{14}}{\left(\frac{MS_{14}+MS_{13}}{2}\right)} + \frac{II_{13}}{\left(\frac{MS_{13}+MS_{14}}{2}\right)}\right]$	$\frac{1}{3}\left[\frac{5}{\left(\frac{526}{2}\right)} + \frac{8}{\left(\frac{750}{2}\right)} + \frac{7}{\left(\frac{656}{2}\right)}\right]$	2.0%
Interest Expense	mean $\frac{IE_t}{\left(\frac{TD_t+TD_{t-1}}{2}\right)}$	$\frac{1}{3}\left[\frac{IE_{15}}{\left(\frac{TD_{15}+TD_{14}}{2}\right)} + \frac{IE_{14}}{\left(\frac{TD_{14}+TD_{13}}{2}\right)} + \frac{IE_{13}}{\left(\frac{TD_{13}+TD_{12}}{2}\right)}\right]$	$\frac{1}{3}\left[\frac{693}{8{,}659} + \frac{945}{11{,}813} + \frac{1{,}158}{14{,}479}\right]$	8.0%
$TD_{15} = 3{,}733 + 1{,}880 + 722 = \$6{,}335$; $TD_{14} = 2{,}779 + 1{,}713 + 6{,}490 = \$10{,}982$; $TD_{13} = 2{,}666 + 1{,}677 + 8{,}301 = \$12{,}644$; $TD_{12} = 2{,}535 + 1{,}588 + 12{,}191 = \$16{,}314$;				
EBT: $EBT = EBIT + $ interest income $- $ interest expense; Income taxes $= EBT\,(T^C)$				
Income tax rate, T^C	mean $\frac{\text{taxes}}{EBT}$	$\frac{1}{3}\left[\frac{\text{taxes}_{15}}{EBT_{15}} + \frac{\text{taxes}_{14}}{EBT_{14}} + \frac{\text{taxes}_{13}}{EBT_{13}}\right]$	$\frac{1}{3}\left[\frac{2{,}199}{6{,}467} + \frac{2{,}092}{6{,}153} + \frac{1{,}874}{5{,}512}\right]$	34.0%
$NI = EBT - $ income taxes				

Figure 9.3 Relevant ratios from income statements for *DCF* analysis

income statements. Manufacturing costs, $COGS$, are directly related to output produced, which in turn is directly related to sales, all else equal. Thus going forward, we hold constant the ratio $\frac{COGS}{NS}$, equal to the historical mean. In our model, we assume that SGA expenses and advertising expenses also increase proportionately with net sales. These expenses are not as directly tied to NS as are $COGS$ in most firms, so the assumptions of constant $\frac{SGA \text{ expenses}}{NS}$ and $\frac{\text{advertising}}{NS}$ are a bit tenuous.[6]

As depreciation and amortization, $D\&A$, is the "writing-off" of gross PPE, we assume that the ratio $\frac{D\&A_t}{GPPE_{t-1}}$ is constant each year. Note the year lag, as $D\&A_t$ for year t is assumed to be calculated from $GPPE_{t-1}$ existing on the books at date $t-1$, the beginning of year t. Next, repairs and maintenance ($R\&M$) should be proportional to assets still "usable", i.e., net PPE. So we assume that $\frac{R\&M_t}{NPPE_{t-1}}$ is constant each year. Again, note the lag in year due to causality: $NPPE_{t-1}$ existing at date year-end$_{t-1}$, which begins year t, drive $R\&M_t$ expenses in year t. Regarding interest income, it is generated by marketable securities, so we assume constant $\frac{II_t}{\text{average } MS_t}$, where $average$ $MS_t = \frac{MS_t + MS_{t-1}}{2}$. Next, as interest expense is payment based on the level of debt, we assume that $\frac{IE_t}{\text{average } TD_t}$ is constant going forward, where $average$ $TD_t = \frac{TD_t + TD_{t-1}}{2}$, and where $TD_t = NP_t + CM_t + LTD_t$. Also, we calculate the historical arithmetic mean $\frac{\text{taxes}_t}{EBT_t}$ as 34% and use this figure in our future pro-forma income statements.

Of course, we respect all income statement relations as follows:

- $GP = NS - COGS$;
- $EBIT = GP - SGA$ expenses $-$ advertising $-D\&A-$ repairs & Maint;
- $EBT = EBIT + II - IE$;
- income taxes $= EBT(T^C)$;
- $NI = EBT - $ income taxes.

9.3 Historical Relationships: Balance Sheet

We now move on to determining relevant relations for our future pro-forma balance sheets. Our historical balance sheets are shown in figure 9.4. Relative to those of the previous chapter, there is only one additional entry, treasury stock, TS, which is the cumulative cash spent by the firm to retire some of its outstanding shares of stock. It represents a *negative* equity account, so that total stock holders' equity $= CS + APIC + RE - TS$. Note that all four equity accounts, including treasury stock, are non-decreasing in magnitude. So in generating future pro-forma statements, care

---

[6]An alternative would be to assume constant relative or absolute growth rate of each.

must be taken to ensure that none decrease in magnitude from one year to the next.

BS Entry	2015	2014	2013	2012
Assets (A)				
Current Assets (CA)				
Cash	255	920	910	890
Marketable securities	111	415	335	321
Accounts receivables	2,183	4,126	4,002	3,997
Inventories	10,336	12,528	12,323	12,111
Prepaid Expenses	391	422	411	402
Total CA	13,276	18,411	17,981	17,721
Property, Plant & Equipment				
Land	21	18	17	16
Buildings & improvements	4,636	3,809	3,888	3,607
Equipment	16,453	15,460	15,002	14,587
Gross PPE	21,111	19,287	18,907	18,210
Less accumulated D&A	2,777	2,338	2,224	2,109
Net PPE	18,334	16,949	16,683	16,101
Other Assets	1,603	477	472	460
Total Assets	33,213	35,837	35,136	34,282
Liabilities & Stock holders' Equity				
Current Liabilities (CL)				
Accounts payable (AP)	879	567	709	698
Notes payable to banks	3,733	2,779	2,666	2,535
Current maturities of LTD	1,880	1,713	1,677	1,588
Accrued liabilities	252	222	237	213
Total Current Liabilities	6,744	5,281	5,289	5,034
Deferred Incomes Taxes	158	141	135	122
Long-Term Debt (LTD)	722	6,490	8,301	12,191
Total Liabilities	7,625	11,912	13,725	17,347
Stock holders' Equity				
Common stock, $1 par*	12,080	12,080	12,080	11,180
Additional paid-in capital	4,400	4,400	4,400	2,376
Retained earnings (RE)	10,641	7,999	5,485	3,233
Less treasury stock (TS)	1,533	554	554	554
Total Stock holders' Equity	25,588	23,925	21,411	16,935
Total Liabilities & Stock holders' Equity	33,213	35,837	35,136	34,282
Shares outstanding*	10,012	10,100	10,100	9,900
*50,000 shares authorized;				
All numbers are in $ thousands.				

Figure 9.4   Historical balance sheets for *DCF* analysis

Figure 9.5 shows relevant historical assets relations. (We split the balance sheet into two halves for ease of exposition. Next, we review figure 9.6, which shows relevant historical relations for liabilities plus stock holders' equity.)

Chapter 9 Absolute Valuation: Discounting Cash Flows 115

BS asset entry	Key relationship	Statistic	Calculation	Value
Cash	mean $\frac{cash}{TA}$	$\frac{1}{3}\left[\frac{cash_{15}}{TA_{15}} + \frac{cash_{14}}{TA_{14}} + \frac{cash_{13}}{TA_{13}}\right]$	$\frac{1}{3}\left[\frac{255}{33,213} + \frac{920}{35,837} + \frac{910}{35,136}\right]$	1.97%
Marketable Securities	mean $\frac{MS}{TA}$	$\frac{1}{3}\left[\frac{MS_{15}}{TA_{15}} + \frac{MS_{14}}{TA_{14}} + \frac{MS_{13}}{TA_{13}}\right]$	$\frac{1}{3}\left[\frac{111}{33,213} + \frac{415}{35,837} + \frac{335}{35,136}\right]$	0.82%
Accounts Receivable	mean $\frac{\text{Avg } AR}{NS}$	$\frac{1}{3}\left[\frac{\frac{AR_{15}+AR_{14}}{2}}{NS_{15}} + \frac{\frac{AR_{14}+AR_{13}}{2}}{NS_{14}} + \frac{\frac{AR_{13}+AR_{12}}{2}}{NS_{13}}\right]$	$\frac{1}{3}\left[\frac{\frac{2,183+4,126}{2}}{53,762} + \frac{\frac{4,126+4,002}{2}}{51,202} + \frac{\frac{4,002+3,997}{2}}{48,304}\right]$	7.36%
Inventories	mean $\frac{\text{Avg } Inv}{COGS}$	$\frac{1}{3}\left[\frac{\frac{Inv_{15}+Inv_{14}}{2}}{COGS_{15}} + \frac{\frac{Inv_{14}+Inv_{13}}{2}}{COGS_{14}} + \frac{\frac{Inv_{13}+Inv_{12}}{2}}{COGS_{13}}\right]$	$\frac{1}{3}\left[\frac{\frac{10,336+12,528}{2}}{38,440} + \frac{\frac{12,528+12,323}{2}}{36,609} + \frac{\frac{12,323+12,111}{2}}{34,537}\right]$	33.0%
Prepaid Expenses	mean $\frac{PExp}{TA}$	$\frac{1}{3}\left[\frac{PExp_{15}}{TA_{15}} + \frac{PExp_{14}}{TA_{14}} + \frac{PExp_{13}}{TA_{13}}\right]$	$\frac{1}{3}\left[\frac{391}{33,213} + \frac{422}{35,837} + \frac{411}{35,136}\right]$	1.17%

Total CA = cash $+ MS + AR +$ inventories $+$ prepaid expenses

Land	mean $\frac{land}{grossPPE}$	$\frac{1}{3}\left[\frac{land_{15}}{GPPE_{15}} + \frac{land_{14}}{GPPE_{14}} + \frac{land_{13}}{GPPE_{13}}\right]$	$\frac{1}{3}\left[\frac{21}{21,111} + \frac{18}{19,287} + \frac{17}{18,907}\right]$	0.1%
Buildings/ Improvements	mean $\frac{Bld}{grossPPE}$	$\frac{1}{3}\left[\frac{Bld_{15}}{GPPE_{15}} + \frac{Bld_{14}}{GPPE_{14}} + \frac{Bld_{13}}{GPPE_{13}}\right]$	$\frac{1}{3}\left[\frac{4,636}{21,111} + \frac{3,809}{19,287} + \frac{3,888}{18,907}\right]$	20.8%
Equipment	mean $\frac{Equ}{grossPPE}$	$\frac{1}{3}\left[\frac{Equ_{15}}{GPPE_{15}} + \frac{Equ_{14}}{GPPE_{14}} + \frac{Equ_{13}}{GPPE_{13}}\right]$	$\frac{1}{3}\left[\frac{16,453}{21,111} + \frac{15,460}{19,287} + \frac{15,002}{18,907}\right]$	79.1%

Gross PPE_t = net PPE_t + accumulated $D\&A_t$. (This follows from Gross PPE = land + buildings & improvements + equipment.)
accumulated $D\&A_t$ = accumulated $D\&A_{t-1} + D\&A_t$

Net PPE_t	mean $\frac{\text{Avg } NPPE}{NS}$	$\frac{1}{3}\left[\frac{\frac{NPPE_{15}+NPPE_{14}}{2}}{NS_{15}} + \frac{\frac{NPPE_{14}+NPPE_{13}}{2}}{NS_{14}} + \frac{\frac{NPPE_{13}+NPPE_{12}}{2}}{NS_{13}}\right]$	$\frac{1}{3}\left[\frac{\frac{18,334+16,949}{2}}{53,762} + \frac{\frac{16,949+16,683}{2}}{51,202} + \frac{\frac{16,683+16,101}{2}}{48,304}\right]$	33.2%
Other Assets	mean $\frac{OA}{TA}$	$\frac{1}{3}\left[\frac{OA_{15}}{TA_{15}} + \frac{OA_{14}}{TA_{14}} + \frac{OA_{13}}{TA_{13}}\right]$	$\frac{1}{3}\left[\frac{1,603}{33,213} + \frac{477}{35,837} + \frac{472}{35,136}\right]$	2.50%

Total Assets = totalCA + netPPE + other assets

Figure 9.5   Relevant ratios from balance sheets for DCF analysis: assets

As shown, cash, marketable securities, prepaid expenses and other assets are all assumed to represent a constant fraction of total assets.[7] As accounts receivable (AR) are directly related to the level of sales, the historical arithmetic mean $\frac{\text{average } AR_t}{NS_t}$ is assumed to hold constant in future pro-forma statements, where $\text{average } AR_t = \frac{AR_t + AR_{t-1}}{2}$. Analogously, as inventories (Inv) are directly related to $COGS$, the historical arithmetic mean $\frac{\text{average } Inv_t}{COGS_t}$ is assumed to hold constant in future pro-forma statements, where $\text{average } Inv_t = \frac{Inv_t + Inv_{t-1}}{2}$.

Land, building & improvements and equipment, the three components of gross fixed assets ($GPPE$), are assumed to remain at relative levels such that their fractions of $GPPE$ each year continue to be the same as their respective historical arithmetic means. Regarding the total value of $GPPE$ itself each year on the future pro-forma balance sheets, we back into it as follows. We first calculate the level of net PPE. As net PPE represents, in crude terms, the remaining "usable" assets, we argue that they are what support the firm's sales via manufacturing the firms products. Thus, $\frac{\text{average net } PPE_t}{NS_t}$ is held constant each year, where $\text{average net } PPE_t = \frac{\text{net } PPE_t + \text{net } PPE_{t-1}}{2}$. Finally, as accumulated $D\&A_t = $ accumulated $D\&A_{t-1} + D\&A_t$, then we back into $GPPE_t$ as follows. Respecting $NPPE_t = GPPE_t - $ accumulated $D\&A_t$, then $GPPE_t = NPPE_t + $ accumulated $D\&A_t$.

Other balance sheet asset relations are respected as follows:

- total $CA = $ cash $+ MS + AR + $ inventories $+$ prepaid expenses;
- $GPPE = $ land $+$ property & improvements $+$ equipment;
- total assets $= $ total $CA + $ net $PPE + $ other assets.

Having completed the assets half of the balance sheet, we now proceed to the second half. Figure 9.6 shows relevant historical relations for liabilities and stock holders' equity. As shown, both $\frac{\text{average } AP_t}{COGS_t}$ and $\frac{\text{average } AL_t}{COGS_t}$ are assumed to be held constant each year and are equal to their respective historical arithmetic mean values, where $\text{average } AP_t = \frac{AP_t + AP_{t-1}}{2}$ and $\text{average } AL_t = \frac{AL_t + AL_{t-1}}{2}$. Both assumptions are logical, as expenses of these two accounts ultimately move to the income statement as $COGS$ in the year that respective product is sold. Both notes payable (NP) and current maturities of long-term debt (CM) are assumed to be constant fractions of total assets. We further assume that deferred income taxes (DIT), common stock (CS), additional

---

[7]Other possibilities include assuming that these four (a) are fixed each year at their most recent value, i.e., as of December 31, 2015, or (b) grow at the same relative rate as their respective historical geometric mean.

BS Liabilities & Equity	Key relationship	Statistic	Calculation	Value
Accounts payable	mean $\frac{\text{Avg } AP}{COGS}$	$\frac{1}{3}\left[\frac{\left(\frac{AP_{15}+AP_{14}}{2}\right)}{COGS_{15}} + \frac{\left(\frac{AP_{14}+AP_{13}}{2}\right)}{COGS_{14}} + \frac{\left(\frac{AP_{13}+AP_{12}}{2}\right)}{COGS_{13}}\right]$	$\frac{1}{3}\left[\frac{\left(\frac{879+567}{2}\right)}{38,440} + \frac{\left(\frac{567+709}{2}\right)}{36,609} + \frac{\left(\frac{709+698}{2}\right)}{34,537}\right]$	1.89%
Notes payable	mean $\frac{NP}{TA}$	$\frac{1}{3}\left[\frac{NP_{15}}{TA_{15}} + \frac{NP_{14}}{TA_{14}} + \frac{NP_{13}}{TA_{13}}\right]$	$\frac{1}{3}\left[\frac{3,733}{33,213} + \frac{2,779}{35,837} + \frac{2,666}{35,136}\right]$	8.86%
CM of LTD	mean $\frac{CM}{TA}$	$\frac{1}{3}\left[\frac{CM_{15}}{TA_{15}} + \frac{CM_{14}}{TA_{14}} + \frac{CM_{13}}{TA_{13}}\right]$	$\frac{1}{3}\left[\frac{1,880}{33,213} + \frac{1,713}{35,837} + \frac{1,677}{35,136}\right]$	5.07%
Accrued liabilities	mean $\frac{\text{Avg } AL}{COGS}$	$\frac{1}{3}\left[\frac{\left(\frac{AL_{15}+AL_{14}}{2}\right)}{COGS_{15}} + \frac{\left(\frac{AL_{14}+AL_{13}}{2}\right)}{COGS_{14}} + \frac{\left(\frac{AL_{13}+AL_{12}}{2}\right)}{COGS_{13}}\right]$	$\frac{1}{3}\left[\frac{\left(\frac{252+222}{2}\right)}{38,440} + \frac{\left(\frac{222+237}{2}\right)}{36,609} + \frac{\left(\frac{237+213}{2}\right)}{34,537}\right]$	0.63%

Total current liabilities = accounts payable + notes payable + current maturities of LTD + accrued liabilities

Deferred incomes taxes are assumed to be held constant each year.

Plug: Long-term debt (LTD) = total assets − (total current liabilities + deferred incomes taxes + total stock holders' equity)

Total liabilities = total current liabilities + deferred incomes taxes + long-term debt

Common stock is assumed to be held constant each year.

Additional paid-in capital is assumed to be held constant each year.

Retained earnings$_t$ (RE_t) = NI_t − cash dividend paid$_t$

Treasury stock is assumed to be held constant each year.

Total stock holders' equity = common stock + additional paid-in capital + retained earnings − treasury stock

Total liabilities & stock holders' equity = total liabilities + total stock holders' equity

Figure 9.6 Relevant ratios from balance sheets for *DCF* analysis: liabilities & stock holders' equity

paid-in capital ($APIC$) and treasury stock (TS) are held constant each year.

As the name implies, the balance sheet "balances", i.e, $TA = TL + TE$. As such this equation represents one degree of freedom that must be accounted for. Thus, in our future pro-forma balance sheets, one entry is specifically calculated per this equation. This item is called **the plug**, as its value is "plugged in" to ensure that the balance sheet balances. For simplicity, we use long-term debt, LTD, as the plug in our model. Respecting $TA = (TL) + TE = (CL + DIT + LTD) + TE$ per the balance sheet, then LTD is calculated as $LTD = TA - CL - DIT - TE$. As such, an increase (a decrease) in debt from one year to the next implies issuance (retirement) of this much debt.

Other balance sheet liabilities & stock holders' relations are respected as follows:

- total $CL = AP + NP + CM + AL$;
- total liabilities = total $CL + DIT + LTD$;
- Δretained earnings (ΔRE) = $NI-$ cash dividends paid;
- total stock holders' equity = $CS + APIC + RE - TS$;
- total stock holders' equity & liabilities = total liabilities + total stock holders' equity.

9.4 Future Pro-forma Statements for DCF Analysis

With relevant ratios in hand, we can now generate future pro-forma income statements (figure 9.7) and balance sheets (figure 9.8). From these, we generate future pro-forma statements of cash flows (figure 9.9) as well as additional future cash flows needed for our various DCF calculations (figure 9.10). In generating all future pro-forma statements (figures 9.7, 9.8, 9.9 and 9.10), we incorporate all relations previously shown, including the income statement relations itemized on page 113, the balance sheet asset relations itemized on page 116 and balance sheet liabilities & stock holders' equity relations itemized on page 118. Of course, all relations derived in figures 9.3, 9.5 and 9.6 are likewise incorporated into all future pro-forma statements.

As noted before, net sales for the next five years (2016 − 2020 in figure 9.7) are calculated via assumption that the rate of relative growth is the same as that calculated via historical geometric mean over the past three years, equal to 5.5%. Given this firm's historical profitability (i.e., $NI_t > 0$ for each of the past three years) and the assumed positive growth rate of sales each year of 5.5%, then predictably both the $EBIT$ and the NI are positive and increase each year.

Future pro-forma balance sheets are shown in figure 9.8. Recall that we assume

IS Entry	2016	2017	2018	2019	2020
Net sales (NS)	56,718	59,837	63,127	66,599	70,261
Cost of goods sold	40,554	42,784	45,136	47,618	50,236
Gross profit	16,165	17,054	17,991	18,981	20,024
SGA expenses	5,161	5,445	5,745	6,060	6,394
Advertising	2,099	2,214	2,336	2,464	2,600
$D\&A$	746	807	872	941	1,015
Repairs & Maint	2,764	2,916	3,076	3,246	3,424
$EBIT$	5,395	5,672	5,963	6,269	6,592
Other Income (Expenses)					
Interest Income	4	6	7	7	8
Interest Expenses	(651)	(798)	(803)	(809)	(814)
EBT	4,749	4,880	5,166	5,467	5,785
Income taxes	1,615	1,659	1,756	1,859	1,967
NI	3,134	3,221	3,410	3,608	3,818

All numbers are in $ thousands.

Figure 9.7 Future pro-forma income statements for DCF analysis

fixed values for three of the four equity accounts (CS, $APIC$ and TS). Due to the firm's calculated positive future profitability ($NI > 0$ each of the five future years), then $RE_t = RE_{t-1} + NI_t(b)$ increases each year.[8] As such, the firm's need for borrowing decreases each year, as LTD, our plug, decreases each year. This implies that the firm will generate excess cash each year (from 2016 to 2020) and will use it to retire some of its outstanding long-term debt in each of these years.

With future pro-forma income statements and balance sheets in hand, it is straightforward to generate corresponding statements of cash flows, shown in figure 9.9. Lastly, we perform other future pro-forma calculations per various definitions of cash flows. Shown in figure 9.10, these are later used in multiple DCF analyses.

9.5 Costs of Capital: *WACC* and Others

With cash flows in hand, we now turn our attention to demanded rates of return needed to discount these cash flows. The firm's **weighted average cost of capital**, $WACC$, is calculated as

$$WACC = \frac{D}{D+Eq} r^D \left(1 - T^C\right) + \frac{Eq}{D+Eq} r^E, \qquad (9.1)$$

where D and Eq are market values of debt and equity, respectively, and $r^E(r^D)$ is the rate of return demanded by investors in the firm's equity (debt). Note that the $WACC$

---

[8] Recall that all four equity accounts, including RE, are non-decreasing in magnitude. So if NI were negative one year, then b would have to be zero in the year.

BS Entry	2016	2017	2018	2019	2020
Assets, A					
Current Assets, *CA*					
Cash	764	806	850	897	946
MS	315	333	351	370	391
Accounts Receivable	3,858	4,070	4,293	4,530	4,779
Inventories	13,084	13,803	14,562	15,363	16,208
Prepaid Expenses	454	479	506	534	563
Total *CA*	18,475	19,491	20,563	21,693	22,886
PPE					
Land	21	23	25	27	29
Buildings	4,724	5,111	5,524	5,964	6,432
Equipment	18,012	19,488	21,062	22,738	24,525
GPPE	22,758	24,622	26,610	28,729	30,986
Less: accumulated depreciation & amortization	3,522	4,329	5,201	6,143	7,158
Net *PPE*	19,235	20,293	21,409	22,586	23,828
Other Assets	967	1,020	1,076	1,136	1,198
Total Assets	38,677	40,804	43,048	45,415	47,912
Liabilities & Stock holders' Equity					
Current Liabilities, *CL*					
Accounts Payable	796	840	886	934	986
Notes Payable	3,427	3,616	3,814	4,024	4,246
CM	1,961	2,069	2,183	2,303	2,430
Accrued Liabilities	264	278	293	309	326
Total *CL*	6,448	6,803	7,177	7,571	7,988
DIT	158	158	158	158	158
LTD	4,543	4,322	4,081	3,820	3,537
Total Liabilities	11,149	11,282	11,416	11,549	11,683
Stock holders' Equity, *SE*					
CS, $1 par	12,080	12,080	12,080	12,080	12,080
APIC	4,400	4,400	4,400	4,400	4,400
RE	12,581	14,574	16,685	18,919	21,282
Less *TS*	1,533	1,533	1,533	1,533	1,533
Total SE	27,528	29,522	31,632	33,866	36,229
Total Liabilities & SE	38,677	40,804	43,048	45,415	47,912

All numbers are in $ thousands.

Figure 9.8 Future pro-forma balance sheets for *DCF* analysis

recognizes the tax advantage of debt-based interest payments.[9]

As the weighted average cost of capital is a function of both equity holders' de-

---

[9]Interest payments to debt holders are safer than equity holders' residual claim, as interest payments are (a) paid first and (b) less volatile, given that they are well defined, if not constant, per the debt's covenants. Thus, $r^D < r^E$. So debt (equity) holders pay more (less) per dollar of expected payoff, or $\frac{E[\$1\ \text{Int.}]}{1+r^D} = \text{``}P_0^{D\text{''}} > \text{``}P_0^{Eq\text{''}} = \frac{E[\$1\ \text{Div.}]}{1+r^E}$. As such, per the *WACC* calculation (equation (9.1)), one might think that 100% debt would minimize the *WACC*. However, this fails to recognize the ever increasing rate of return demanded by equity holders as leverage increases, as Miller and Modigliani's proposition II teaches us, via equation (9.2).

SCFs Entry	2016	2017	2018	2019	2020
Operating CF Activities					
Net income (NI)	3,134	3,221	3,410	3,608	3,818
Non-cash adjustments					
D&A	746	807	872	941	1,015
DIT	0	0	0	0	0
Cash provided (used) by WC					
Accounts Receivable	(1,675)	(212)	(224)	(236)	(249)
Inventories	(2,748)	(719)	(759)	(801)	(845)
Prepaid Expenses	(63)	(25)	(26)	(28)	(29)
Accounts Payable	(83)	44	46	49	51
Accrued Liabilities	11	14	15	16	17
Operating CF (OCF)	(678)	3,130	3,334	3,550	3,779
Investing CF Activities					
Additions PPE	(1,647)	(1,865)	(1,988)	(2,119)	(2,257)
Other Investments	636	(53)	(56)	(59)	(62)
Investing CF (ICF)	(1,011)	(1,918)	(2,044)	(2,178)	(2,320)
Financing CF Activities					
Sales of CS	0	0	0	0	0
Purchases CS	(0)	(0)	(0)	(0)	(0)
Inc (Decr) STD	(225)	296	313	330	348
Additions to LTD	3,821	0	0	0	0
Decreases to LTD	0	222	241	261	282
Dividends paid	1,194	1,227	1,299	1,375	1,455
Financial CF ($FiCF$)	2,402	(1,153)	(1,227)	(1,306)	(1,389)
Incremental cash $+MS$	713	59	63	66	70
Cash+MS_{t-1}	366	1,079	1,138	1,201	1,267
Cash+MS_t	1,079	1,138	1,201	1,267	1,337
BS C+MS_t	1,079	1,138	1,201	1,267	1,337

All numbers are in $ thousands.

Figure 9.9 Future pro-forma statements of CFs for DCF analysis

manded rate of return, r^E, as well as debt holders' demanded rate of return, r^D, we need to address their calculations. Also, we need estimates for T^C, D and Eq before we move on to calculate the $WACC$.

We can calculate r^E from multiple models. We have seen the market model, which implies a single systematic risk factor, the return of the market, consistent with the underlying concept of the $CAPM$. In figure 9.11 we show 61 pairs of monthly closing price data for both the equity of our firm as well as a well diversified index, which serves as our proxy for the market.[10] First, continuously compounded rates of return

---
[10] An example of a stock index used as a proxy for the market is the $S\&P$ 500.

Asset Valuation Theory

CF Entry	2016	2017	2018	2019	2020
Operating CF	(678)	3,130	3,334	3,550	3,779
Investing CF	(1,011)	(1,918)	(2,044)	(2,178)	(2,320)
Financing CF	2,402	(1,153)	(1,227)	(1,306)	(1,389)
$IE(1-T^C)$	429	526	530	534	537
ΔLTD	3,821	(222)	(241)	(261)	(282)
ΔSTD	(225)	296	313	330	348
ΔDebt, ΔTD	3,596	75	72	69	66
After-tax CF^D	(3,167)	452	458	465	472
FCFE	1,907	1,287	1,362	1,441	1,524
FCF	(1,259)	1,738	1,820	1,906	1,996
Cash dividends	1,194	1,227	1,299	1,375	1,455
TECF	1,194	1,227	1,299	1,375	1,455
Δ(Cash+MS)	713	59	63	66	70
FCFE	1,907	1,287	1,362	1,441	1,524

ΔDebt = $\Delta TD = \Delta LTD + \Delta STD$; After-tax $CF^D = IE(1-T^C) - \Delta$Debt;
$FCFE = OCF + ICF + \Delta TD$; $FCF = FCFE +$ after-tax CF^D;
cash dividends = (plowback ratio)$(NI) = b(NI)$;
$TECF$ = cash dividends + cash raised from stock issuances $-$ cash used for stock repurchase; Also, $FCFE = TECF + \Delta$(Cash+MS);
All numbers are in $ thousands.

Figure 9.10 Future pro-forma calculations of CFs for DCF analysis

are calculated from $r_t^i = \ln\left(\frac{P_t^i}{P_{t-1}^i}\right)$, $t \in \{1, 2, ..., 60\}$, $i \in \{E, m\}$, which are also shown in figure 9.11. Next, the market model regression, $r_t^E = \alpha^E + \beta^E r_t^m + \epsilon_t^E$, $t \in \{1, 2, ..., 60\}$, yields $\beta^E = 1.42$. As this β^E can be used in the $CAPM$, then we assume that next period's risk-free rate of return and expected market return are 3% and 8%, respectively. Then per the $CAPM$, $E[r^E] = r^f + \beta^E(E[r^m] - r^f) = 3\% + 1.42(8\% - 3\%) = 10.10\%$.

Miller and Modigliani's (MM) proposition II is another model that can be used to calculate r^E. In a world free of frictions, MM show that the rate of return demanded by equity holders is directly related to the firm's debt to equity ratio, or[11]

$$r^E = r^0 + \frac{D}{Eq}\left(r^0 - r^D\right)\left(1 - T^C\right), \tag{9.2}$$

where r^0 is the hypothetical rate of return demanded by equity holders, if the firm had no debt.

---

[11]Setting $D = 0$, then $r^E = r^0$ per the definition of r^0.

Mo.	P^E	P^m	r^E	r^m	Mo.	P^E	P^m	r^E	r^m
0	1.26	4.41							
1	1.31	4.53	0.036	0.026	31	2.21	5.68	0.035	0.025
2	1.41	4.74	0.076	0.046	32	2.34	5.93	0.059	0.044
3	1.45	4.82	0.031	0.018	33	2.43	6.11	0.039	0.029
4	1.49	4.88	0.023	0.011	34	2.36	5.92	-0.030	-0.032
5	1.36	4.60	-0.091	-0.058	35	2.32	5.83	-0.019	-0.015
6	1.27	4.41	-0.067	-0.043	36	2.40	5.98	0.034	0.025
7	1.36	4.62	0.071	0.047	37	2.62	6.23	0.086	0.042
8	1.42	4.77	0.041	0.032	38	2.50	5.99	-0.044	-0.039
9	1.50	4.94	0.056	0.035	39	2.44	5.89	-0.024	-0.017
10	1.50	4.86	-0.002	-0.016	40	2.50	5.95	0.023	0.009
11	1.51	4.86	0.009	0.000	41	2.53	5.95	0.010	0.002
12	1.54	4.88	0.015	0.003	42	2.63	6.15	0.039	0.033
13	1.55	4.90	0.012	0.005	43	2.72	6.30	0.036	0.024
14	1.59	4.94	0.022	0.008	44	2.61	6.11	-0.043	-0.031
15	1.62	4.97	0.018	0.008	45	2.80	6.33	0.070	0.036
16	1.70	5.12	0.047	0.030	46	2.78	6.21	-0.006	-0.021
17	1.71	5.11	0.006	-0.003	47	2.93	6.35	0.053	0.023
18	1.68	4.96	-0.016	-0.029	48	3.00	6.47	0.024	0.019
19	1.75	5.11	0.043	0.030	49	3.03	6.46	0.008	-0.001
20	1.78	5.12	0.013	0.002	50	3.11	6.52	0.026	0.010
21	1.69	4.94	-0.047	-0.036	51	3.20	6.59	0.027	0.011
22	1.74	4.99	0.026	0.010	52	3.25	6.67	0.018	0.011
23	1.68	4.86	-0.034	-0.026	53	3.39	6.79	0.040	0.019
24	1.72	4.92	0.026	0.012	54	3.36	6.66	-0.008	-0.020
25	1.74	4.92	0.009	0.000	55	3.39	6.66	0.009	0.000
26	1.84	5.04	0.055	0.024	56	3.42	6.66	0.009	0.000
27	1.89	5.14	0.028	0.020	57	3.40	6.60	-0.008	-0.010
28	2.01	5.41	0.061	0.052	58	3.48	6.74	0.024	0.021
29	2.10	5.51	0.043	0.018	59	3.53	6.78	0.014	0.006
30	2.13	5.54	0.015	0.004	60	3.19	6.40	-0.100	-0.057

$Mo.$: month; P^E: equity share price; P^m: market index value;
r^E: monthly continuously compounded equity rate of return;
r^m: monthly continuously compounded market index rate of return;
Of course, $r_t^E = ln\left(\frac{P_t^E}{P_{t-1}^E}\right)$ and $r_t^m = ln\left(\frac{P_t^m}{P_{t-1}^m}\right)$, $t \in \{1, 2, ..., 60\}$.
Price data is rounded to two decimal places, resulting in round-off error for some of the return calculations.
Per market model, $r_t^E = \alpha^E + \beta^E r_t^m + \epsilon_t^E$, $t \in \{1, 2, ..., 60\}$.
In this regression with 60 pairs of monthly returns, $\beta^E = 1.42$.
This $\beta^E = 1.42$ is subsequently used in $CAPM$ to calculate r^E.

Figure 9.11 Price data for stock and for market index

In what follows, we will use $r^E = 10.10\%$ per $CAPM$.[12] Later we utilize equation (9.2) to calculate r^0.

We need the **cost of debt**, r^D, in order to calculate $WACC$. It can be calculated in a number of ways, including the following two manners.[13]

$$r^D = \text{mean } \frac{IE}{\text{Average } TD}, \quad \text{or} \quad r^D = \text{mean } \frac{IE - II}{\text{Average } (TD - MS)}, \quad (9.3)$$

where IE is interest expense, TD (total debt) $= LTD + STD = LTD + NP + CM$, and II is interest income earned from marketable securities, MS.[14] From our example, we calculate $r^D = 8.00\%$ from the first equation in expression (9.3) and $r^D = 8.17\%$ from the second equation. As firms pay debt holders a higher interest rate than what they earn from marketable securities, the second equation in expression (9.3) yields a higher value for r^D than does the first.

The $WACC$ is a function of T^C, D and Eq. The average corporate tax rate was earlier calculated as 34% via historical arithmetic mean. Next, the market value of debt equals the number of bonds times their price. In our example, we assume that this is the same as the current book value of debt, or $TD_{2015} = NP_{2015} + CM_{2015} + LTD_{2015} = 3,733 + 1,880 + 722 = \$6,336$. Lastly, for Eq, given an assumed number of shares outstanding of 10,012 and a share price of \$11.12, the market value of equity is $10,012(\$11.12) = \$111,333$.

We are finally equipped to calculate the $WACC$ per equation (9.1) as $WACC = \frac{6,336}{6,366+111,333} 8.00\%(1 - 34\%) + \frac{111,333}{6,366+111,333} 10.10\% = 9.84\%$.

9.6 Hypothetical Demanded Rate of Return: No Debt

In the adjusted present value method discussed later, we will need the hypothetical rate of return demanded by equity holders, if the firm had no debt, r^0. Rearranging

---

[12] Other models for r^E include Fama and French's (FF) 3-factor model, or $r_t^i = \alpha^i + \beta^m r_t^m + \beta^{HML} RP_t^{HML} + \beta^{SMB} RP_t^{SMB}$, where RP^{HML} and RP^{SMB} are premia related to the ratio of the firm's $\frac{BV}{MV}$ (high minus low) and to the firm's size (small minus big), respectively. To the FF model, Carhart adds a fourth factor, momentum of stock return. A fifth factor, liquidity, has also been modeled.

[13] Another method to calculate r^D is to regress yield-to-maturity (y) on time-to-maturity (ttm), ttm^2 and ttm^3, i.e, a third-order polynomial regression, for a collection of bonds of the same credit rating. This builds a model for any bond of that rating. Then one may proxy r^D with y. This is conservative, as $y > r^D$ for risky bonds because promised cash flows, used to calculate y, are greater than expected cash flows, used to calculate r^D. For high grade bonds, $y - r^D > 0$ is small, so this proxy is reasonable. Care must be taken, however, for low grade bonds, as $y - r^D > 0$ is not so small. Thus, you may want to estimate r^D using a number a bit smaller than y.

[14] For example, mean $\frac{IE}{\text{Avg. } TD} = \frac{1}{3}(\frac{IE_{15}}{(TD_{15}+TD_{14})/2} + \frac{IE_{14}}{(TD_{14}+TD_{13})/2} + \frac{IE_{13}}{(TD_{13}+TD_{12})/2})$.

equation (9.2), then

$$r^0 = \frac{D(1-T^C)}{D(1-T^C)+Eq}r^D + \frac{Eq}{D(1-T^C)+Eq}r^E. \quad (9.4)$$

For our example, $r^0 = 10.02\%$ per equation (9.4).

Comparing equations (9.1) and (9.4), then $r^0 \geqslant WACC$, where the inequality is strict as long as both $D > 0$ and $T^C > 0$, noting that $r^0 > r^D$. So the difference $r^0 - WACC$ is due to the tax advantage of debt interest payments. The similarities between the calculations of $WACC$ and r^0 are obvious: $WACC$ has weights of D and Eq, whereas r^0 has weights of $D(1 - T^C)$ and Eq. Additionally, both $WACC$ and r^0 place weight on r^E. However, $WACC$ also places weight on $r^D(1-T^C)$, i.e., after-tax r^D, whereas r^0 places weight on r^D.[15]

9.7 Discounted Cash Flow (DCF) Techniques

We now have inputs needed to use DCF techniques. The most common DCF method is the **weighted average cost of capital ($WACC$) method**, which discounts free cash flows by the $WACC$. The logic is obvious. One interpretation of free cash flows is that which is available to pay all security holders, i.e., both equity holders and debt holders. Also, the $WACC$ is the firm's overall cost of capital; it considers all security holders' demanded rates of return with weights assigned to their relative investment in the firm. Thus, discounting free cash flows by the $WACC$ yields **enterprise value, EV**, or firm value, as follows.

$$EV = \sum_{t=1}^{\infty} \frac{FCF_t}{(1+WACC)^t}$$

$$= \sum_{t=1}^{T} \frac{FCF_t}{(1+WACC)^t} + \frac{FCF_T(1+g^{FCF})}{(WACC - g^{FCF})(1+WACC)^T}, \quad (9.5)$$

where g^{FCF} is the assumed growth rate in perpetuity of FCF_t beyond date T.[16] The first line in expression (9.5) is general, whereas the second reflects implementation of this concept. Specifically, T years of future pro-forma statements generate estimates of FCFs for the next T years, where T is typically five or 10 years. The contributions

---

[15] An alternative to calculating r^0 via Miller-Modigliani's proposition II is to use **unlevered beta**. A regression of r_t^E on r_t^m, generates levered beta, β^E. Next, unlevered beta, i.e., that which corresponds to the hypothetical firm with no debt, is calculated as $\beta_u^E = \frac{\beta^E}{1+\frac{D}{E}(1-T^C)} \leqslant \beta^E$, where the weak inequality is strict as long as both $D > 0$ and $T^C > 0$. Finally, we can use $r^0 = r^f + \beta_u^E(E[r^m] - r^f)$.

[16] We assume that $g^{FCF} < WACC$ so that the second line of expression (9.5) is valid.

to EV of free cash flows for the first T years are calculated directly via the explicit summation. To this is added the final term of the second line, the present value of a growing perpetuity which begins at date $T+1$. The first cash flow of this growing perpetuity is the numerator, $FCF_{T+1} = FCF_T(1+g^{FCF})$. It's value at date T is $\frac{FCF_{T+1}}{WACC-g^{FCF}}$. Discounting this by $(1+WACC)^T$ yields its present value, at time $t=0$.

Equity value (Eq) is calculated from enterprise value (EV) as

$$Eq = EV - [\text{liabilities} - (\text{cash} + MS)] = EV - \Gamma, \qquad (9.6)$$

where $\Gamma = \text{liabilities} - (\text{cash} + MS)$ is the firm's liabilities, adjusted for cash plus marketable securities.[17]

Another DCF technique is the **flows to equity method, FTE**, where free cash flows to equity holders ($FCFE$) are discounted by the rate of return demanded by equity holders, r^E. Thus, this intrinsic value calculation directly generates equity value.[18] Explicitly, the FTE method calculates

$$\begin{aligned} Eq &= \sum_{t=1}^{\infty} \frac{FCFE_t}{(1+r^E)^t} \\ &= \sum_{t=1}^{T} \frac{FCFE_t}{(1+r^E)^t} + \frac{FCFE_T(1+g^{FCFE})}{(r^E - g^{FCFE})(1+r^E)^T}, \end{aligned} \qquad (9.7)$$

where g^{FCFE} is the assumed growth rate in perpetuity of $FCFE_t$ beyond date T.[19] The first line in expression (9.7) is general, whereas the second reflects implementation of this concept. The logic of this expression for the FTE method is analogous to that discussed following expression (9.5) for the $WACC$ method.

Two DCF methods, **total equity cash flows model ($TECFM$)** and **dividend discount model (DDM)**, are parallel to the FTE method just discussed. The only difference is definition of equity cash flow. The total equity cash flows model discounts $TECF$s (per equation (7.8)), whereas the dividend discount model discounts dividends.[20]

---

[17] One way to think of cash plus marketable securities is as *negative* debt. Indeed, excess cash plus MS can be used to retire debt.

[18] To this, we can add Γ to derive enterprise value, $EV = Eq + \Gamma$.

[19] We assume that $g^{FCFE} < r^E$ so that the second line of expression (9.7) is valid.

[20] Of course, g refers to the growth rate of $TECF_t$ (d_t) beyond date T in the $TECFM$ (DDM); also, $g < r^E$ in both models by assumption.

In our example, these two models ($TECFM$ and DDM) result in the same equity value, as we hold fixed the shares of equity; we use debt as the plug. If we had used either $CS + APIC$ or TS as the plug, holding $\frac{D}{A}$ fixed, then the two models would have generated two distinct equity values.

A special case of the DDM is the **Gordon constant growth DDM**, or $P_0^E = \frac{d_1}{r^E - g^d}$, where d_1 is the expected dividend payment one year from now, and g^d is the growth rate of dividends in perpetuity. This model is an application of the constant growth perpetuity formula from chapter 1.

We cannot assume constant growth of dividends for firms that are not mature and/or are not in mature industries. **Multi-stage DDMs** exist for such cases. For example, consider a firm with forecasted initial high dividend growth of g^h for t^h years before it settles down to lower dividend growth of g^l in perpetuity thereafter. Further assume that the firm paid a dividend yesterday of d_0, yielding an expected dividend one year from today of $d_0(1 + g^h)$. Then equity value given this **two-stage constant growth DDM** is[21]

$$Eq = \sum_{t=1}^{t^h} \frac{d_0(1+g^h)^t}{(1+r^E)^t} + \frac{d_0(1+g^h)^{t^h}(1+g^l)}{(1+r^E)^{t^h}(r^E-g^l)}. \tag{9.8}$$

For a young firm, limiting the number of growth stages to two is restrictive. Consider a **three-stage constant growth DDM** for a firm with forecasted initial high dividend growth of g^h for t^h years, medium dividend growth of g^m for the subsequent t^m years followed by low dividend growth of g^l in perpetuity thereafter. Then equity value is

$$Eq = \sum_{t=1}^{t^h} \frac{d_0(1+g^h)^t}{(1+r^E)^t} + \sum_{t=t^h+1}^{t^h+t^m} \frac{d_0(1+g^h)^{t^h}(1+g^m)^{(t-t^h)}}{(1+r^E)^t}$$
$$+ \frac{d_0(1+g^h)^{t^h}(1+g^m)^{t^m}(1+g^l)}{(1+r^E)^{t^h+t^m}(r^E-g^l)}. \tag{9.9}$$

Other models, including a four-stage model, a five-stage model, etc... are possible.

Rather than assuming abrupt step changes of growth rates at points in time as is assumed in equations (9.8) and (9.9), we can assume linearly decreasing growth rates over particular time frames. An example is the following schedule of assumed growth rates: {11%, 11%, 11%, 11%, 10%, 9%, 8%, 7%, 6%, 5%, 4%, 3%}, followed by 3% in perpetuity. Conceptually, the calculation of equity per the DDM given this growth schedule is no different than that for any other growth schedule: $Eq = \sum_{t=1}^{\infty} \frac{d_t}{(1+r^E)^t}$.

Figure 9.12 shows two examples of three-stage constant growth DDMs. The series of squares show annual growth rates consistent with the example of the previous

---

[21] For the final term, $d_0(1+g^h)^{t^h}$ is d_{t^h} and $d_{t^h}(1+g^l)$ is d_{t^h+1}. Dividing this by $r^E - g^l$ gives the growing perpetuity value as of date t^h. Finally, dividing by $(1+r^E)^{t^h}$ yields today's value of the growing perpetuity which begins with d_{t^h+1}.

paragraph. The series of diamonds has the following growth schedule: $\{12\%, 12\%, 12\%, 12\%, 12\%, 6.5\%, 6.5\%, 6.5\%, 6.5\%, 6.5\%, 3\%\}$, followed by 3% in perpetuity.

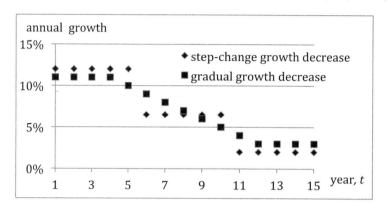

Figure 9.12 Examples of three-stage DDM annual growth rates

The DDM can be used to provide an estimate for r^E. Rearranging the Gordon model, $P_0^E = \frac{d_1}{r^E - g^d} = \frac{d_0(1+g^d)}{r^E - g^d}$, then $r^E = g^d + \frac{d_1}{P_0^E}$, where the second term, $\frac{d_1}{P_0^E}$, is the dividend yield. So in the market, participants adjust the price until the rate of return demanded by equity holders equals the growth rate plus the dividend yield. More generally, one can use multi-stage expressions like equations (9.8) or (9.9) to calculate r^E implicitly.[22]

The **adjusted present value method** is a two-step method. In the first step, we discount free cash flows, as does the $WACC$ method. However, in stark contrast to the $WACC$ method, where the interpretation of FCFs is that which is available to all security holders, the interpretation of FCFs in the APV method is the hypothetical cash flow that would be available to equity holders, if the firm had no debt. Given this interpretation of FCFs, we discount them by the corresponding rate of return, r^0. Hence, the resulting intrinsic value calculated is the hypothetical enterprise value, if the firm had no debt. We designate this as $EV^U = EV|(D=0)$, the hypothetical **value of the unlevered firm**, EV^U, or

$$EV^U = EV|(D=0) = \sum_{t=1}^{\infty} \frac{FCF_t}{(1+r^0)^t}$$

$$= \sum_{t=1}^{T} \frac{FCF_t}{(1+r^0)^t} + \frac{FCF_T(1+g^{FCF})}{(r^0 - g^{FCF})(1+r^0)^T}, \quad (9.10)$$

where g^{FCF}, assumed to be less than r^0, is the rate of growth of free cash flows in perpetuity beyond year T.

---

[22] For such cases where an explicit solution doesn't exist, Goal Seek in Excel can be used.

In the second step of the APV method, we recognize that the firm does have debt in its capital structure. So to the hypothetical no-debt enterprise value, EV^U, we add various debt financing effects, $NPVF^k, k \in \{1, 2, ..., K\}$. Thus, the actual (levered) enterprise value or **levered firm value**, EV^L, is

$$EV = EV^L = EV^U + \sum_{k=1}^{K} NPVF^k. \tag{9.11}$$

We focus on the most important of these financing effects, the **debt tax shield** (DTS).[23] The DTS is the increase in firm value due to tax savings associated with interest payments, or[24]

$$DTS \equiv \sum_{t=1}^{\infty} \frac{IE_t T^C}{\left(1+r_t^D\right)^t} = T^C \sum_{t=1}^{\infty} \frac{D_t \left(r_t^C\right)}{\left(1+r_t^D\right)^t}, \tag{9.12}$$

where $IE_t = D_t(r_t^C)$, as r_t^C is the coupon rate. In calculating the DTS, annual tax savings, $IE_t T^C$, are discounted by the rate of return demanded by debt holders, as the riskiness of these tax savings is the same as the riskiness of the interest payments themselves.

If we assume that the coupon rate is fixed, or $r_t^C = r^C$, and that the level of debt is held constant, or $D_t = D$, then equation (9.12) becomes $DTS = T^C D r^C \sum_{t=1}^{\infty} \frac{1}{(1+r_t^D)^t}$. Also, if we assume that $r_t^D = r^D$ is constant over time, then the summation in the previous sentence becomes a perpetuity of $1, resulting in $DTS = T^C D r^C \frac{1}{r^D}$. Finally, if we further assume par debt, or $r^C = r^D$, then[25]

$$DTS \,|\, (r^D = r^C \text{ are constant}; T^C \text{ and } D \text{ are constant}) \; = T^C D. \tag{9.13}$$

Completing the second step of the APV method,[26]

$$EV = EV^L \approx EV^U + DTS$$
$$\approx \sum_{t=1}^{T} \frac{FCF_t}{(1+r^0)^t} + \frac{FCF_T(1+g^{FCF})}{(r^0 - g^{FCF})(1+r^0)^T} + T^C D. \tag{9.14}$$

---

[23] All debt financing effects should be included, such as cost of issuing debt, municipal bond financing, etc... For simplicity, we focus on the all important debt tax shield.

[24] We assume that T^C is constant over time.

[25] By developing expression (9.13) as a special case of the general DTS, equation (9.12), we see the strong assumptions implied when we use this common expression, $DTS = T^C D$. Though there are several assumptions, making the exact value implied by equation (9.13) unlikely, deviations from these assumptions should not be extreme for most firms. Thus, $T^C D$ is usually a reasonable estimate for the DTS.

[26] The first approximation in equation (9.14) is because we exclude potential debt financing effects other than the DTS, and the second recognizes that generally speaking, $DTS \approx T^C D$, per equation (9.13).

As before, equity is calculated from $Eq = EV - \Gamma$, where $\Gamma = \text{liabilities} - (\text{cash} + MS)$.

Results of these five DCF methods are summarized in figure 9.13.[27] Numerical values pertaining to our ongoing example are shown in figure 9.14.

In summary, the various DCF analyses yield different results. Enterprise value and equity value per the various techniques differ. Your job is to determine representative values for EV and Eq, based on various values calculated from the different models.

9.8 Scenario Analyses: *WACC* and Growth of *FCF*s Impact Enterprise Value

Critical assumptions in any DCF analysis include values of both the $WACC$ as well as the growth rate of cash flows in perpetuity, g^{FCF}. Any complete DCF analysis includes a two-dimensional table of scenarios of the impacts of these two inputs upon enterprise value and upon equity value. As an example, figure 9.15 shows enterprise value per the $WACC$ method as a function of $WACC$ and of g^{FCF}. Obviously, enterprise value, EV, is decreasing in discount rate, $WACC$, evident from traveling from left to right across any row. In contrast, EV is increasing in growth rate of terminal free cash flows, g^{FCF}, as seen in traveling down any column.

As noted before, $g^{FCF} < WACC$ is necessary; hence, values in the lower left portion of the table, where $g^{FCF} \geq WACC$, do not exist.

The impacts of both $WACC$ and g^{FCF} upon EV are striking. Indeed, the ratio of highest value to lowest value in the table exceeds 10.[28] On the one hand, such a table shows the high sensitivity of enterprise value to these two inputs. On the other hand, it gives pause for concern in using DCF methods, particularly if one is not confident in the accuracy of estimates for $WACC$ and for g^{FCF}.

---

[27]Other DCF methods are possible. For example, OCFs discounted by the $WACC$ gives another estimate of enterprise value, $EV = \sum_{t=1}^{\infty} \frac{OCT_t}{(1+WACC)^t}$. From this, $Eq = EV - \Gamma$, as usual.

[28]Specifically, $\frac{155,572}{13,807} = 11.3$. Of course, greater ranges of g^{FCF} and of $WACC$ would produce even greater ranges of EV, all else equal.

Chapter 9 Absolute Valuation: Discounting Cash Flows   131

DCF method	Cash flow	Discount rate	Intrinsic value, IV	IV equals:	Enterprise value, EV	Equity value, Eq
WACC	FCF	$WACC$	$\left[\sum_{t=1}^{T}\frac{FCF_t}{(1+WACC)^t}\right] + \frac{FCF_T(1+g)}{(1+WACC)^T}\left[\frac{1}{WACC-g}\right]$	EV	IV	$EV - \Gamma$
FTE	$FCFE$	r^E	$\left[\sum_{t=1}^{T}\frac{FCFE_t}{(1+r^E)^t}\right] + \frac{FCFE_T(1+g)}{(1+r^E)^T}\left[\frac{1}{r^E-g}\right]$	Eq	$IV + \Gamma$	IV
TECFM	$TECF$	r^E	$\left[\sum_{t=1}^{T}\frac{TECF_t}{(1+r^E)^t}\right] + \frac{TECF_T(1+g)}{(1+r^E)^T}\left[\frac{1}{r^E-g}\right]$	Eq	$IV + \Gamma$	IV
DDM	d	r^E	$\left[\sum_{t=1}^{T}\frac{d_t}{(1+r^E)^t}\right] + \frac{d_T(1+g)}{(1+r^E)^T}\left[\frac{1}{r^E-g}\right]$	Eq	$IV + \Gamma$	IV
APV	FCF	r^0	$\left[\sum_{t=1}^{T}\frac{FCF_t}{(1+r^0)^t}\right] + \frac{FCF_T(1+g)}{(1+r^0)^T}\left[\frac{1}{r^0-g}\right]$	$EV\|(D=0)$	$IV + \sum_{k=1}^{K} NPVF^k$	$EV - \Gamma$
				EV^U	$EV^L = EV^U + \sum_{k=1}^{K} NPVF^k$	$EV^L - \Gamma$

EV^U: unlevered enterprise value; EV^L: levered enterprise value; $NPVF_k$: k^{th} net present value financing factor; In our example, we consider only one factor, $NPVF = DTS \approx T^C(D)$, the debt tax shield.
In the intrinsic value (IV) calculations of all methods, g is the perpetual growth rate of respective cash flow beginning in year $T+1$.
The difference between enterprise value and equity value is Γ = total liabilities $-($cash$+MS) = EV - Eq$.

DCF methods: $WACC$: weighted average cost of capital; FTE: flows to equity; $TECFM$: total equity cash flows method; DDM: dividend discount model; APV: adjusted present value;

Figure 9.13 *DCF* **techniques**

DCF method	Cash flow	Discount rate	Intrinsic value, IV	IV equals:	Enterprise value, EV	Equity value, Eq
$WACC$	FCF	9.84%	$4,226 + 30,338 = 34,564$	$EV = 34,564$	$34,564$	$34,564 - 7,259 = 27,305$
FTE	$FCFE$	10.10%	$5,737 + 21,603 = 27,340$	$Eq = 27,340$	$27,340 + 7,259 = 34,599$	$27,340$
$TECFM$	$TECF$	10.10%	$4,905 + 20,616 = 25,521$	$Eq = 25,521$	$25,521 + 7,259 = 32,780$	$25,521$
DDM	d	10.10%	$4,905 + 20,616 = 25,521$	$Eq = 25,521$	$25,521 + 7,259 = 32,780$	$25,521$
APV	FCF	10.02%	$4,197 + 28,866 = 33,063$	$EV\|(D=0)$ $= EV^U = 33,063$	$EV^L = EV^U + T^C(D_0)$ $33,063 + 34\%(6,336) = 35,217$	$35,217 - 7,259 = 27,958$

Figure 9.14 *DCF results*

g^{FCF}	weighted average cost of capital, $WACC$						
	7%	8%	9%	10%	11%	12%	13%
2%	33,739	27,625	23,266	20,004	17,474	15,455	13,807
3%	41,354	32,516	26,633	22,439	19,300	16,864	14,920
4%	54,045	39,852	31,347	25,685	21,648	18,626	16,281
5%	79,427	52,080	38,418	30,230	24,779	20,892	17,981
6%	155,572	76,534	50,203	37,047	29,162	23,912	20,168
7%		149,899	73,772	48,409	35,737	28,141	23,083
8%			144,481	71,133	46,695	34,484	27,164
9%				139,306	68,611	45,056	33,285

Figure 9.15 Impact of $WACC$ and g^{FCF} upon EV per $WACC$ method

Problems

Use the following information for problems 1 – 4 of this chapter. You estimate that a firm's cost of debt is 9%, cost of equity is 16% and corporate tax rate is 30%. The firm has a capital structure of 40% debt and 60% equity.

1. What is this firm's weighted average cost of capital?

2. For this firm, assume that free cash flows of the next seven years are estimated to be $10, $18, $26, $34, $40, $46 and $52, respectively. The long term growth rate of free cash flows is estimated to be 4%. What is the enterprise value of this firm?

3. For this firm, assume that free cash flows to equity holders of the next four years are estimated to be $7, $13, $18 and $23, respectively. The long term growth rate of free cash flows to equity holders is estimated to be 4%. What is the equity value of this firm?

4. For this firm, assume that dividends of the next six years are estimated to be $6, $12, $17, $22, $26 and $29, respectively. The long term growth rate of dividends is estimated to be 4%. What is the equity value of this firm?

5. For a given firm with an estimated cost of equity of 12%, assume that yesterday's dividend per share was $2.00. The next five years' growth rate of dividends is estimated to be 8% per year, followed by a long term annual growth rate of 3%. What is the equity value of this firm?

6. For a given firm with an estimated cost of equity of 10%, assume that yesterday's dividend per share was $3.00. The next four years' growth rate of dividends is estimated to be 9% per year, followed by an annual growth rate of 6% for three years, followed

by a long term annual growth rate of 4%. What is the equity value of this firm?

7. For a given firm with an estimated cost of equity of 11%, assume that yesterday's dividend per share was $1.00. The next four years' growth rate of dividends is estimated to be 15% per year, followed by annual growth rates of 12%, 9%, 7%, 5% and 4%, respectively, in years 5 through 9. Beginning in year 10 and beyond, the estimated long term annual growth rate is 2%. What is the equity value of this firm?

CHAPTER 10

Earnings Multiplier Model

The **earnings multiplier model** (*EMM*) is a hybrid model, combining both relative valuation via price to earnings ratio and absolute valuation via constant growth dividend discount model. We explore the model in detail, including its implications for changes in the firm's characteristics over time. Lastly, we perform comparative statics analyses.

10.1 Developing the Model

As a reminder, the **Gordon constant growth dividend discount model** is $P_0 = \frac{d_1}{r^E - g^d}$, where d_1 is the cash dividend paid a year henceforth, r^E is the rate of return demanded by equity holders and g^d is the growth rate of cash dividends in perpetuity.[1] We assume that g^d also pertains to year 1, so $d_0 = \frac{d_1}{1+g^d}$. Thus, $P_0 = \frac{d_0(1+g^d)}{r^E - g^d}$.

As before, the **sustainable growth rate of equity** is $g_t^{Eq} = b_t ROE_t$.[2] For this chapter, we assume constant plowback ratio ($b_t = b$) and constant $ROE_t = ROE$, $\forall t \in \{1, 2, 3, \dots\}$. So $g_t^{Eq} = b[ROE] = g^{Eq}$ is also constant. Again, g^{Eq} is the rate of growth possible when external financing is excluded, i.e., that due to the firm's ability to generate earnings. So $Eq_t = Eq_{t-1}(1 + g^{Eq}) = Eq_{t-1}(1 + b[ROE])$, or using this iteratively,

$$Eq_t = Eq_0 \left(1 + b[ROE]\right)^t, \tag{10.1}$$

where Eq_0 is the exogenous, current level of the firm's equity.

As $ROE = \frac{NI_t}{Eq_{t-1}}$ by definition, then $NI_t = Eq_{t-1}ROE$, where the earnings in year t depend on ROE and the equity at the beginning of the period, i.e., at date $t-1$. Thus,

$$NI_t = (ROE) Eq_0 \left(1 + b[ROE]\right)^{t-1}. \tag{10.2}$$

---

[1] Of course, we assume that $r^E > g$ throughout this chapter.

[2] Recall that $g_t^{Eq} = \frac{\Delta Eq}{Eq} = \frac{Eq_t - Eq_{t-1}}{Eq_{t-1}} = \frac{NI_t - d_t}{Eq_t} = \frac{NI_t - NI_t(1-b_t)}{Eq_t} = b_t \frac{NI_t}{Eq_t} = b_t ROE_t$.

As b is assumed to be constant, then so is the **dividend payout ratio**, $1-b = \frac{d_t}{NI_t}$. From $d_t = (1-b)NI_t$, then

$$d_t = (1-b)(ROE)Eq_0(1+b[ROE])^{t-1}. \tag{10.3}$$

Per equation (10.3), d_t is a function of t via the factor $(1+b[ROE])^{t-1}$. In short, d_t grows each year at a rate of $g^{Eq} = b[ROE]$ in perpetuity. However, per the Gordon model, dividends grow in perpetuity at g^d. Thus, it must be true that $g^d = g^{Eq}$. In what follows, we sometimes designate $g^d = g^{Eq}$ simply as g.

As $d_{t+1} = d_t(1+g) = d_t(1+b[ROE])$, then from $P_t = \frac{d_{t+1}}{r^E - g} = \frac{d_{t+1}}{r^E - b[ROE]}$,

$$P_t = \frac{(1-b)(ROE)Eq_0(1+b[ROE])^t}{r^E - b[ROE]}. \tag{10.4}$$

Finally, the leading price to earnings ratio is $\frac{P_t}{NI_{t+1}}$, where we choose to use the leading ratio (versus lagged) as it is more stable and is completely forward looking. From $P_t = \frac{d_{t+1}}{r^e - g} = \frac{NI_{t+1}(1-b)}{r^E - b[ROE]}$, then $\frac{P_t}{NI_{t+1}}$ becomes

$$\frac{P_t}{NI_{t+1}} = \frac{1-b}{r^E - b[ROE]}. \tag{10.5}$$

In reviewing equations (10.1) through (10.4), we see that the only impact of variable t (or $t-1$) is as an exponent of the term $(1+b[ROE]) = 1+g$. In short, all four variables (equity, earnings, dividends and price) grow at the same constant relative rate, g. Digging deeper, Eq_t and P_t are of the form $\pi_t = \lambda^\pi(1+g)^t$, and NI_t and d_t are of the form $\pi_t = \lambda^\pi(1+g)^{t-1}$, where each λ^π are *not* functions of t, but rather are simply functions of exogenous parameters: Eq_0, ROE, b and r^E. So for all four variables ($\pi_t \in \{Eq_t, NI_t, d_t, P_t\}$), $\frac{d\pi_t}{dt} = \pi_t \ln(1+g) > 0$.[3] We have confirmed that all four grow over time. Repeating the process, $\frac{d^2\pi_t}{dt^2} = \pi_t[\ln(1+g)]^2 > 0$. So all four variables increase at an increasing rate over time. Combining these two results for the *EMM*, figure 10.1 shows that in time series plots of equity, earnings, dividends and price, all are increasing and convex. (Also shown is the price to earnings ratio, $\frac{P_t}{NI_{t+1}} = \frac{P_t}{E_{t+1}}$, discussed next.)

Per equation (10.5), the ratio $\frac{P_t}{NI_{t+1}}$ is *not* a function of time, t. As both price and earnings grow at relative rate g, it is logical that their ratio remains unchanged over time.

We can also consider the time series of $\ln(\pi_t)$, $\pi_t \in \{Eq_t, NI_t, d_t, P_t\}$. We know that a plot of $\ln(\pi_t)$ versus t is linear, as all four variables grow at constant *relative*

---

[3]Recall that $\frac{d\lambda a^{f(x)}}{dx} = \lambda a^{f(x)} \ln(a) \frac{df(x)}{dx}$.

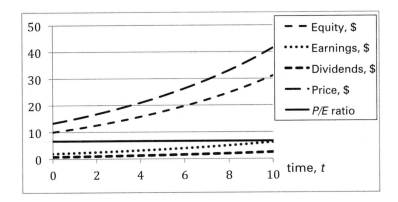

Figure 10.1 Time series of *EMM* variables

growth rate. To confirm this, $\pi_t = \lambda^\pi (1+g)^t$ for Eq_t and P_t, while $\pi_t = \lambda^\pi (1+g)^{t-1}$ for NI_t and d_t. Thus, $\ln(\pi_t) = \ln(\lambda^\pi) + t[\ln(1+g)]$ for Eq_t and P_t, while $\ln(\pi_t) = \ln(\lambda^\pi) + (t-1)\ln(1+g)$ for NI_t and d_t. So for all four, a time series plot of the log of the variable is linear with slope of $\ln(1+g)$, as shown in figure 10.2. (Of course, as the price to earnings ratio is constant over time, so is its log, $\ln(\frac{P_t}{NI_{t+1}}) = \ln(\frac{P_t}{E_{t+1}})$.)

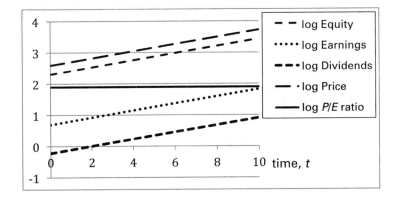

Figure 10.2 Time series of log of *EMM* variables

10.2 Comparative Statics

With time series expressions in hand for equity (Eq_t), earnings (NI_t), cash dividends (d_t), price (P_t) and price to earnings ratio ($\frac{P_t}{NI_{t+1}}$), we now turn to the impact of our five exogenous parameters on these five variables of our *EMM* model. The five exogenous parameters include initial equity (Eq_0), return on equity (ROE), plowback ratio (b), rate of return demanded by equity holders (r^E), and time (t). (Obviously, we have previously examined how our five variables change over time, so we now consider the impact of the other four exogenous parameters upon our five *EMM* variables.)

We assume that at time $t = 0$, the firm "announces" it parametric change. One second earlier, the firm realized earnings NI_0 and it paid its current cash dividend, d_0. (Obviously, in reality there is a time lag between when net income is earned and when it is calculated. There is another time lag to when cash dividends are declared, and yet another to when they are paid. But for simplification, we assume that both NI_0 and d_0 were realized one second ago, which corresponds to the end of the previous period, i.e., the previous year.) Thus, NI_0 and d_0 *cannot* be impacted by any parametric change that we consider.[4]

10.2.1 Impact of Initial Equity, Eq_0

Four of the five variables, Eq_t, NI_t, d_t and P_t, are obviously increasing in Eq_0, evidenced by equations (10.1) through (10.4). These four results are not surprising. The larger the firm's equity initially, the larger the firm's equity at all future dates, holding fixed ROE and b. Hence, the larger the firm's equity at any point in time, the greater its earnings, holding ROE fixed. Obviously, greater earnings at each point in time implies larger cash dividends, holding b fixed. Next, the larger the dividends at any point in time, then the larger the price of equity, holding fixed b and r^E. Finally, regarding the timing, an increase in Eq_0 (i.e., at time $t = 0$, one second after NI_0 and d_0 are realized) increases P_0. However, an increase in Eq_0 first impacts earnings and dividends one year later, i.e., NI_1 and d_1, respectively.

As $\frac{P_t}{NI_{t+1}}$ per equation (10.5) does not feature Eq_0, it is not impacted by an increase in Eq_0. This is logical, as we showed earlier that the price to earnings ratio is invariant over time. As the firm's equity grows over time, then this ratio is not dependent upon equity size. From a second perspective, as both P_t as well as NI_{t+1} are directly proportional to Eq_0, then it makes sense that as Eq_0 increases, the ratio is invariant.

10.2.2 Impact of Equity Holders' Demanded Rate of Return, r^E

Of our five EMM variables, three (Eq_t, NI_t and d_t) are *not* functions of r^E. This makes sense, as r^E is market driven, whereas Eq_t, NI_t and d_t are not. (For a given initial equity, then Eq_t, NI_t and d_t are only functions of b and ROE.) Regarding the other two, both P_t per equation (10.4) as well as $\frac{P_t}{NI_{t+1}}$ per equation (10.5) feature r^E. Specifically, both are intuitively decreasing in r^E, as the price of a security is decreasing

---

[4] Even an increase in Eq_0 in a comparative static sense has no impact on NI_0 and d_0. However, as we will see, P_0 and $\frac{P_0}{NI_1}$ are impacted by changes in all four parameters: Eq_0, b, ROE and r^E.

in the demanded rate of return of its cash flows. Finally, regarding the timing, if the market suddenly applies greater r^E to the firm's equity cash flows, (i.e., at time $t = 0$, one second after NI_0 and d_0 are realized) then both P_0 and $\frac{P_0}{NI_1}$ decrease *immediately*.

10.2.3 Impact of Equity Holders' ROE

Inspection of equations (10.1) – (10.5) reveals that all five variables (Eq_t, NI_t, d_t, P_t and $\frac{P_t}{NI_{t+1}}$) are impacted by ROE. It is obvious that the first three, Eq_t, NI_t and d_t, are all increasing in ROE. These results are intuitive. Given Eq_0, then the greater the ROE that the firm realizes, the faster the equity grows, i.e., the greater the equity (Eq_t) at each future point in time, holding b fixed. (Recall that $g = b[ROE]$.) Hence, the greater that Eq_t and ROE are at each point in time, the greater NI_t is. All else equal, holding b fixed, the greater the NI_t, then the greater is d_t.

Via equation (10.5), $\frac{d(\frac{P_t}{NI_{t+1}})}{dROE} = \frac{b(1-b)}{(r^E - g)^2} > 0$. This result is intuitive. The $\frac{P_t}{NI_{t+1}}$ ratio is the price that an equity investor is willing to pay per dollar of expected earnings. As higher ROE implies higher future earnings, then it makes sense that each dollar of expected earnings becomes more valuable, all else equal.

The other EMM variable, price (P_t), also increases in ROE. Though ROE features three times in P_t per equation (10.4), resulting in a challenging partial derivative $\frac{dP_t}{dROE}$, simple inspection is enough to determine that P_t increases in ROE.[5] The result in intuitive, as a credible announcement of increased future ROE would be well received by market participants.

In summary, all five variables increase in ROE, all else equal.

Regarding the timing, an increase in ROE (i.e., at time $t = 0$, one second after NI_0 and d_0 are realized) first impacts each of our EMM variables at these respective times: Eq_1, NI_1, d_1, P_0 and $\frac{P_0}{NI_1}$. Intuitively, the market reacts *immediately* to the increase in ROE via increase in P_0 and $\frac{P_0}{NI_1}$. In contrast, an immediate increase in ROE going forward first impacts next period's earnings, NI_1. In turn, this increases d_1, given fixed b. Finally, this also increases the magnitude of earnings plowed back into the firm, so Eq_1 increases.

10.2.4 Impact of Plowback Ratio, b

The fifth and final exogenous parameter, plowback ratio b, has the most interesting comparative statics results. Two variables, Eq_t and NI_t, are obviously increasing in b,

---

[5]Specifically, both occurrences of ROE in the numerator obviously increase P_t, while the occurrence in the denominator has a negative sign in front of it. Thus, it also has a direct relationship with P_t.

per inspections of equations (10.1) and (10.2), respectively. Both make sense; as the manager plows a higher fraction of earnings back into the firm each year, equity will grow faster. Holding ROE constant, then earnings will also grow faster.

Regarding timing, an announcement of increased plowback ratio today impacts Eq_t and NI_t as follows. Given Eq_0 and fixed ROE, then $NI_1 = Eq_0[ROE]$ is *not* impacted. However, increased plowback ratio means that $Eq_1 = Eq_0 + NI_1(b)$ will be increased, holding Eq_0 constant. Given ROE, then as Eq_1 is increased, so is $NI_2 = Eq_1[ROE]$. In summary, an increase in b impacts Eq_t and NI_t for the first time, respectively at Eq_1 and NI_2.

Inspection of equations (10.3) – (10.5), corresponding to d_t, P_t and $\frac{P_t}{NI_t}$, respectively, reveals that the impact of plowback ratio upon future cash dividends, price and price to earnings ratio are ambiguous.

Consider first cash dividends, d_t.[6] Then

$$\frac{\partial d_t}{\partial b} < 0 \Leftrightarrow t < t^* \equiv 1 + \frac{1 + b[ROE]}{ROE(1-b)}, \text{ where } t^* > 1, \text{ and}$$
$$\frac{\partial d_t}{\partial b} > 0 \Leftrightarrow t > t^* > 1. \quad (10.6)$$

We note that $t^* > 1$, which means that the next dividend is smaller than if the plowback ratio had *not* been increased, i.e., $d_1|b_1 < d_1|b_0$, where $b_1 > b_0$. This makes sense. If at time $t = 0$ a firm announces that it will increase its plowback ratio (b), i.e., decrease its dividend payout ratio $(1-b)$, then the next dividend, d_1, must be smaller, all else equal. However, as the firm increases plowback ratio, b, then the growth rate of equity, $g = (b)ROE$, obviously increases, all else equal. Thus, the firm grows faster, i.e., Eq_t is greater for all future times $t \in \{1, 2, 3, \ldots\}$. So at some point in time in the future, the firm must also pay a greater dividend, despite its movement to lower dividend payout ratio, $1 - b$ (i.e., higher plowback ratio b). In summary, when the firm announces an increase in plowback ratio, its next few dividends will be smaller (i.e., as long as $t < t^*$), as its dividend payout ratio is decreased. However, given the firm's increased growth rate of equity, then at some point in the future (i.e., when $t > t^*$), the firm's dividends will be greater than they otherwise would have been had the firm not increased its plowback ratio.

Now consider P_t via equation (10.4). Taking its partial derivative with respect to

---

[6]Taking the partial derivative of equation (10.3) with respect to d_t, then $\frac{\partial d_t}{\partial b} = Eq_0 ROE(1 + g)^{t-2}[(1-b)ROE(t-1) - (1+g)]$. Solving for t results in expressions (10.6).

plowback ratio, b, then[7]

$$\frac{\partial P_t}{\partial b} > 0 \Leftrightarrow t > t^{**} \equiv (r^E - ROE)\frac{1 + b[ROE]}{ROE(1-b)(r^E - b[ROE])}, \text{ and}$$

$$\frac{\partial P_t}{\partial b} < 0 \Leftrightarrow t < t^{**} \equiv (r^E - ROE)\frac{1 + b[ROE]}{ROE(1-b)(r^E - b[ROE])}. \qquad (10.7)$$

Obviously, the sign of $\frac{\partial P_t}{\partial b}$ depends on the sign of $r^E - ROE$, as $1 - b > 0$, and $r^E - b[ROE] = r^E - g > 0$ by assumption. The result is intuitive. The firm creates (destroys) equity value if $ROE > r^E$ ($ROE < r^E$). Thus, holding ROE and r^E fixed, then if the firm creates (destroys) equity value, an announcement of increased plowback ratio is good (bad) news for equity holders; they do (not) welcome the announcement; hence, the announcement is met with an equity price increase (decrease). As market participants react instantaneously to the announcement of increased b, current price P_0 is impacted.

Finally, consider the $\frac{P_t}{NI_{t+1}}$ ratio per equation (10.5). Taking its partial derivative with respect to plowback ratio, b, then

$$\frac{\partial \left(\frac{P_t}{NI_{t+1}}\right)}{\partial b} = \frac{ROE - r^E}{(r^E - b[ROE])^2}. \qquad (10.8)$$

So as is the case with the sign of $\frac{\partial P_t}{\partial b}$, the sign of $\frac{\partial \left(\frac{P_t}{NI_{t+1}}\right)}{\partial b}$ also depends on the sign of $r^E - ROE$. If the firm creates (destroys) equity value, then market participants immediately react to an announcement of increased plowback ratio by paying more (less) for a dollar of earnings, i.e., $\frac{P_0}{NI_1}$ increases (decreases). So even though the $\frac{P_t}{NI_{t+1}}$ ratio is invariant over time, a change in plowback ratio changes the $\frac{P_t}{NI_{t+1}}$ ratio immediately to a new value, where it remains invariant over time.

Problems

For problems in this chapter, use the following parameters. The annual dividend payout ratio is 60%, net income for the year that ended yesterday was $0.24 per share, book value of equity is $2.00 per share and the firm has 10 shares outstanding. Equity holders demand an annual rate of return of 9%.

---

[7]From equation (10.4), then $\frac{dP_t}{db} = Eq_0 ROE^2(1+g)^{t-1}(1-b)(r^E - g)[t - \frac{(1+g)(r^E - ROE)}{(r^E - g)(1-b)ROE}]$, which yields expressions (10.7).

1. What is this firm's ROE?

2. What is this firm's plowback ratio?

3. What is this firm's annual sustainable growth rate?

4. What dividend per share did this firm pay yesterday? (For this problem, assume that the annual dividend is paid on the final day of the year, which is the same day that earnings are calculated.)

5. What is the book value of the firm's total equity?

6. What is this firm's share price?

7. Which is greater: share price or book value per share? Explain what this relationship means.

8. What is this firm's price to earnings ratio?

9. Five years from yesterday, what will be the values of: (a) dividend per share? (b) book value of equity per share? (c) share price? (d) price to earnings ratio?

What are each of these values 10 years from yesterday?

10. Assume that the firm's equity holders suddenly require a rate of return of 15%. What are the new values for: (a) share price? (b) price to earnings ratio?

Which is greater: share price or book value per share? What does this mean?

11. Return to the original assumption that equity holder demand a rate of return of 9%, but let's now assume that the firm suddenly announces that it is immediately increasing its plowback ratio to 70%. What are the new values for: (a) annual sustainable growth rate? (b) book value of equity? (c) share price? (d) price to earnings ratio?

Compared to the answer in problem 6, did the share price increase or decrease as plowback ratio is increased? Explain.

PART IV   Bond Theory

We now turn to bonds, whose market is many times larger than the equity market. We begin in chapter 11 by valuing bonds and understanding how their prices vary with changes in yield. We consider sources of bond returns, discuss various yield metrics based on promised cash flows and introduce the price-yield curve.

In chapter 12 we examine comparative statics of fixed coupon bonds, leaning heavily on the work of Malkiel. We then seek price-yield approximations in chapter 13. These can be useful when exact relations are challenging, e.g., when considering large complex portfolios of fixed income securities. Important metrics such as duration and convexity are introduced.

We address the concept of valuing bonds between coupon dates in chapter 14. This topic is important as this is by far the most common scenario. Finally, in chapter 15 we examine a number of important yield and rate concepts, such as spot rates, forward rates, realized holding per yields, and others.

CHAPTER 11

Introduction to Bonds

The bond market typically works in a world with semi-annual compounding. **Effective annual rate of return, EAr**, is the "actual" annual rate. In contrast, an **annual percentage rate, APr**, is a nominal rate used for simplicity. In general, the two are *not* equal.[1] The relation between the two is

$$1 + EAr = \left(1 + \frac{APr}{m}\right)^m, \qquad (11.1)$$

where m is the number of compounding periods per year, and $\frac{APr}{m}$ is the **effective periodic rate**. Hence, at the end of one period, \$100 grows to $\$100(1+\frac{APr}{m})$, regardless of the length of the time period. So $\frac{APr}{m}$ is the effective periodic rate of the compounding period. For example, $\frac{APr}{2}$ ($\frac{APr}{4}$) is the actual or effective rate for one half-year (one quarter).

One must use an *effective* period rate, not an APr, in doing calculations. For example, with half-year (quarterly) compounding, the effective periodic rate is $\frac{APr}{2}$ ($\frac{APr}{4}$), where the number of periods equals $\frac{2}{\text{year}}$ ($\frac{4}{\text{year}}$) if an APr is quoted on a half-year (quarterly) basis. One can never use an APr in doing calculations. Annual percentage rates are nominal rates used for simplicity in quoting rates. The relation between nominal APr and effective periodic rate is simply, $APr = \frac{APr}{m}m$.

Perhaps an example is the easiest way to illustrate the relation between EAr and APr, per equation (11.1). Assume that three banks all offer its depositers an APr of 10%. However, bank A offers annual compounding (i.e., once per year, $m = 1$), bank B offers semi-annual compounding (two times per year, $m = 2$) and bank C offers quarterly compounding (four times per year, $m = 4$). In actuality, this corresponds to the following periodic rates:

- bank A offers $\frac{10\%}{1} = 10\%$ once per year, at the end of each year,

---

[1] They are equal if there is only one compounding period per year, i.e., $m = 1$ in equation (11.1).

- bank B offers $\frac{10\%}{2} = 5\%$ twice per year, at the end of each half-year,
- bank C offers $\frac{10\%}{4} = 2.5\%$ four times per year, at the end of each quarter.

So at the end of one year, a $100 deposit in bank A yields $100(1 + \frac{10\%}{1})^1 = \$110.00$. Regarding bank B, $100 grows to $100(1 + \frac{10\%}{2})^2 = \$110.25 > \$100.00$, and $100 deposited in bank C grows to $100(1 + \frac{10\%}{4})^4 = \$110.38$ in one year. In summary, even though all three banks offer the same APr of 10%, the amount that an investor earns is different, as all three offer different compounding frequencies. The greater the number of compounding periods per year (i.e., $4 > 2 > 1$), then the greater the increase in value (respectively, $110.38 > \$110.25 > \$110.00$). Equivalently per equation (11.1), the higher the frequency of compounding periods, the greater the EAr: $10.38\% > 10.25\% > 10.00\%$.

As is obvious from the previous example, an APr *must* be quoted with the corresponding compounding frequency; otherwise, as the previous example shows, the EAr is ambiguous. In contrast, an EAr or effective periodic rate is unambiguous.

Consistent with the previous example, it is possible to show mathematically that $\frac{dEAr}{dm} > 0$.[2] To drive home this point, we provide a plot of a numerical example. In figure 11.1, we show the value of EAr versus compounding period (m), for an APr of 15%. As previously claimed, the function $EAr(m)$ is everywhere increasing, $\forall m \in \{1, 2, 3, ...\}$. As noted in the figure, as $m \to \infty$, then from equation (11.1), $1 + EAr(m) \to e^{APr}$. So in the limit as $m \to \infty$, then $EAr(m) \to e^{APr} - 1$.

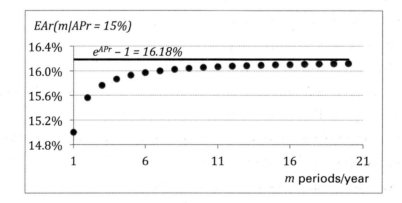

Figure 11.1 Effective annual rate as function of compounding periods

---

[2]Taking logs of both sides of equation (11.1), then $\frac{dEAr}{dm} = (1 + EAr)[\ln(1 + \frac{APr}{m}) - \frac{APr}{APr+m}]$. As $EAr > 0$, then we just need to show that $f(APr, m) \equiv \ln(1 + \frac{APr}{m}) - \frac{APr}{APr+m} > 0$. In the limit as $m \to \infty$, then $f(APr, m) \to 0$. Next, $\frac{df(APr,m)}{dm} = -\frac{1}{m}(\frac{APr}{APr+m})^2 < 0$. Thus, as $f(APr, m)$ is decreasing and approaches zero as $m \to \infty$, then $f(APr, m)$ must be positive, for all positive integers m.

The bond market quotes prices as $APrs$, compounded semi-annually, or $m = 2$. Unless otherwise noted, all rates and yields in this book are $APrs$, compounded semi-annually. Thus, all calculations are done on a semi-annual basis. So any quoted rate (APr), for example a coupon rate, must first be divided by two, resulting in an effective semi-annual rate of $\frac{APr}{2}$. Also, periods are half-years, the number of which equals $2 \times T$, where T is the years to maturity. Then after an effective 6-month rate or yield is determined, an APr is quoted, where $APr = \frac{APr}{2} 2$. (Again, $\frac{APr}{2}$ is an effective semi-annual rate and $EAr = (1 + \frac{APr}{2})^2 - 1$ is the corresponding effective annual rate.)

While this all may seem a bit confusing, it is really quite simple: do all calculations on a semi-annual basis. So for any quoted rate of return (or yield), simply divide it by two, and do all calculations on a semi-annual basis. This means using six-month periods (or twice the number of years) and their corresponding cash flows. After all calculations, any rates are again quoted on an APr basis compounded semi-annually, quite simply by multiplying by two any effective six-month rate.

11.1 Time-lines and Basics

Having addressed the semi-annual timing of the bond market, we now review a few basic concepts. As shown in figure 11.2, at time $t = 0$, a bond is bought for P_0^B, a negative cash flow to the buyer. Its owner is subsequently entitled to interest payments, called **coupons**, C_t, paid every six months. The amount equals $F \frac{r_t^C}{2}$, where r_t^C is the **coupon rate**, an APr compounded semi-annually, so $\frac{r_t^C}{2}$ is the effective half-year coupon rate. Next, F is the **face value** of the bond. The final payment, made when the bond matures (i.e., its **maturity date**, $t = T$), equals the final coupon, C_T, plus F, or $CF_T = F(1 + \frac{r_T^C}{2})$.

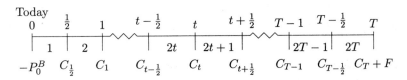

Figure 11.2 Bond cash flows

Index t generally refers to a period, whose duration is six months, or one half year. (In figure 11.2, periods are shown immediately below the time-line and in between dates.) Subscripts on cash flows, $\frac{t}{2}$, refer to dates, in years, corresponding to the vertical hash marks of the time-line. So $CF_{t/2}$ occurs at date $\frac{t}{2}$ years, e.g., $CF_{1/2}$ arrives $\frac{1}{2}$ year (i.e., 6 months) from today, CF_1 arrives 1 year from today, etc...

We previously discussed the intimate relations between $P_0(IRR)$ and $IV_0(r^D)$. Regarding the latter for a bond,

$$IV_0^B\left(r^D\right) \equiv \sum_{t=1}^{2T} \frac{E\left[CF_{\frac{t}{2}}\left(L_{\frac{t}{2}}\right)\right]}{\left(1+\frac{r^D}{2}\right)^t}$$

$$= \sum_{t=1}^{2T-1} \frac{E\left[CF_{\frac{t}{2}}\left(L_{\frac{t}{2}}\right)\right]}{\left(1+\frac{r^D}{2}\right)^t} + \frac{E\left[C_T\left(L_T\right)\right]+F}{\left(1+\frac{r^D}{2}\right)^{2T}}, \qquad (11.2)$$

where r^D is the demanded rate of return of debt holders as an APr compounded semi-annually, $CF_{t/2} = C_{t/2}$, $\forall t < 2T$, is the coupon prior to maturity, and $CF_T = C_T + F$ is the cash flow at maturity.[3] As noted in equation (11.2), coupon payments $PC_{t/2}(L_{t/2})$ may be tied to a rate determined by the market, a **reference rate** $L_{t/2}$ i.e., $\frac{dCF_{t/2}(L)}{dL} \neq 0$.[4]

Regarding the definition of IRR, then

$$P_0 \equiv \sum_{t=1}^{2T} \frac{E\left[CF_{\frac{t}{2}}\left(L_{\frac{t}{2}}\right)\right]}{(1+\frac{IRR}{2})^t}, \qquad (11.3)$$

where $\frac{IRR}{2}$ is the effective six-month implied rate of return. In this case, IRR is an APr, compounded semi-annually ($m=2$).

11.2 Sources of Bond Return

There are three potential sources of a bond's return: interest coupon payments, returns from reinvestment of these coupon payments and capital gain/(loss). For the

---

[3]So the *effective* six-month rate of return demanded by debt holders equals $\frac{r^D}{2}$. Hence this is equivalent to $(1+\frac{r^D}{2})^2 - 1 = EAr$ on an effective annual basis, where $EAr > r^D$.

[4]If coupons are not "fixed", i.e., if they depend on a reference rate $L_{t/2}$, the rate is usually a well known one, such as $LIBOR$, London interbank offer rate, the short-term rate at which highly rated banks lend to others. Generally when $\frac{dCF_{t/2}(L)}{dL} \neq 0$, then $\frac{dCF_{t/2}(L)}{dL} > 0$, or cash flow increases (decreases) when the reference rate, L, increases (decreases). Such a bond is called a **floating rate bond**, or **floater**. Floating rate bonds help mitigate **interest rate risk**: the magnitude of decrease in bond value for a given interest rates change. Regarding floating rate bonds, as market rates increase (meaning y generally increases, all else equal, as typically $\frac{dL}{dy} > 0$), coupons increase. So the decrease in value due to increased discount rates is mitigated by the increase in coupons, all else equal. For **inverse floaters**, $\frac{dCF_{t/2}(L)}{dL} < 0$, so these are particularly sensitive to interest rate changes, i.e., they have high interest rate risk.

We subscript L with $\frac{t}{2}$ to show its time dependence. But in reality, there typically is a lag, often one period, between when the market rate L is observed and the date $\frac{t}{2}$ when the corresponding coupon, $C_{t/2}$, is paid.

moment, let's assume that the bond is held to maturity, date T. The **total of interest coupon payments** is simply $\sum_{t=1}^{2T} C_{t/2} \geqslant 0$, where it is positive unless the bond is a zero-coupon bond, i.e., a pure discount bond. Returns from their reinvestment at an assumed rate of rr, an APr compounded semi-annually, is the difference between the future value of these coupon payments minus the total amount of the coupon interest payments. This **reinvestment of coupons**, also called **interest-on-interest**, equals $\sum_{t=1}^{2T} C_{t/2}[(1+\frac{rr}{2})^{2T-t} - 1] \geqslant 0$, where it is positive unless the bond is a zero-coupon bond. The third and final component of bond return is **capital gain/(loss)** $= F - P_0^B$, which may be positive or negative.

Summing the three sources of **total bond return** gives the difference between cash outlays and cash receipts, including reinvestment of coupons, or

$$\text{bond return} = F + \sum_{t=1}^{2T} C_{\frac{t}{2}} \left(1 + \frac{rr}{2}\right)^{2T-t} - P_0^B. \tag{11.4}$$

A bond may also be sold prior to maturity, at horizon date $H < T$. In such a case, total interest coupon payments is $\sum_{t=1}^{2H} C_{t/2} > 0$. Reinvestment of coupons, or interest-on-interest, equals $\sum_{t=1}^{2H} C_{t/2}[(1+\frac{rr}{2})^{2H-t} - 1] > 0$. The capital gain/(loss) $= P_H^B - P_0^B$, which may be positive or negative, where P_H^B is the price for which the bond is sold at date H. Finally, total bond return, the difference between cash outlays and cash receipts, equals

$$\text{bond return} = P_H^B + \sum_{t=1}^{2H} C_{\frac{t}{2}} \left(1 + \frac{rr}{2}\right)^{2H-t} - P_0^B. \tag{11.5}$$

11.3 Promised Cash Flows Versus Expected Cash Flows

Bond cash flows are defined by a contract. Thus, we can speak of *promised* cash flows, and we can substitute these for expected cash flows in a formula similar to equation (11.3).[5] Indeed, using **promised cash flows**, PC_t, rather than expected cash flows is the normal convention in the bond world. Regarding the two different types of cash flows, expected cash flows are less than (equal to) promised cash flows for risky (risk-free) bonds. For simplicity, we can model expected cash flows via

$$E[CF_t] = PC_t * p(PC_t) + E[CF_t|CF_t < PC_t] * p(CF_t < PC_t), \tag{11.6}$$

where PC_t is the time t promised cash flow, $p(PC_t)$ is the probability that PC_t is paid at time t, $E[CF_t|CF_t < PC_t]$ is the expected cash flow given that it is less than that which

---

[5] As dividend payments to equity holders are at the discretion of the firm, there is no contract *per se*, so there are no promised cash flows.

is promised, and $p(CF_t < PC_t)$ is the probability that the cash flow is less than the promised amount.[6] So $PC_t - E[CF_t] = \{PC_t - E[CF_t|CF_t < PC_t]\}p(CF_t < PC_t) > 0$.

In summary, for risky bonds $PC_t > E[CF_t]$, and for risk-free bonds $PC_t = E[CF_t]$, $\forall t \in \{0.5, 1, 1.5, ..., T - 0.5, T\}$.

11.4 Yield to Maturity, Nominal Yield, Current Yield

Now that we understand the relation between expected and promised cash flows, we move to the convention of the bond world, i.e., discounting of *promised* cash flows. Unless otherwise noted, we use promised cash flows, PC_t, for now on. As such, we can define the **yield to maturity, y** as the discount rate that equates the bond's price (P_0^B) to the summation of its *promised* cash flows (PC_t), or

$$P_0^B \equiv \sum_{t=1}^{2T} \frac{PC_{\frac{t}{2}}\left(L_{\frac{t}{2}}\right)}{\left(1 + \frac{y}{2}\right)^t} = \sum_{t=1}^{2T-1} \frac{C_{\frac{t}{2}}\left(L_{\frac{t}{2}}\right)}{\left(1 + \frac{y}{2}\right)^t} + \frac{C_T(L_T) + F}{\left(1 + \frac{y}{2}\right)^{2T}}, \quad (11.7)$$

where $C_{t/2}(L_{t/2})$ is the promised coupon payment at date $\frac{t}{2}$ in years, $t \in \{1, 2, ..., 2T\}$. Even though cash flows may depend on a reference rate of interest, $(L_{t/2})$, they are still "promised" as they are well defined by contract, i.e., the calculation of $C_{t/2}(L_{t/2})$ is defined per contract, though $L_{t/2}$ is not known in advance.

It is obvious from equation (11.7) that the calculation of yield to maturity assumes that not only must promised cash flows be realized, but also the investor will hold the bond until it matures. Another assumption which is not so obvious is that the reinvestment rate of coupons must equal the calculated yield to maturity in order for this rate of return to be realized.[7]

We pause for an important issue. In much of what follows in our study of bonds, we "treat" price as a function of yield to maturity. We have discussions consistent with price as the dependent variable and yield to maturity as the independent variable. Indeed, per convention, the price-yield curve plots $P^B(y)$, not $y(P^B)$. However, always keep in mind that the market determines bond price as a function of the riskiness and expectation of cash flows as well as the rate of return demanded by debt holders based on perceived cash flow riskiness. Then, from this market-determined price, we can calculate yield to maturity. In sum, price is *not* a function of yield to maturity, but rather the latter is a function of the former.

---

[6] For risky bonds, $PC_t > E[CF_t|CF_t < PC_t]$ and $p(CF_t < PC_t) > 0$, so $p(PC_t) < 1$. (For risk-free bonds, $PC_t = E[CF_t|CF_t < PC_t]$ and $p(CF_t < PC_t) = 0$, i.e., $p(PC_t) = 1$.)

[7] We later prove this assumption after we introduce realized holding period yield.

Before continuing we can order yield to maturity y and debt holders' demanded rate of return r^D for a fairly priced bond (i.e., where $IV_0^P = P_0^B$). As just shown for a risky bond, $PC_{t/2} > E[CF_{t/2}]$, $\forall t \in \{1, 2, ..., 2T\}$. Thus, in comparing equations (11.2) and (11.7), then for a fairly price bond, $y > r^D$. Analysts often use y as an estimate for r^D. So the higher rated the bond, the smaller the difference $PC_{t/2} - E[CF_{t/2}] > 0$, so the smaller the difference $y - r^D > 0$, all else equal. In summary, using y as an estimate for r^D makes more sense, the safer the bond is and the more fairly priced it is, all else equal.

Investors also consider simpler yield metrics. The **nominal yield** is simply the coupon rate, r^C. Obviously, the nominal yield ignores several relevant factors in determining a bond's rate of return, including the bond's current price. All else equal, the greater the bond's price, the smaller (greater) is the potential for a capital gain (loss). The **current yield** = $\frac{C}{P_0^B}$ takes into consideration the current price of the bond, given fixed coupon payment, C. Thus, for a premium (discount) bond, the current yield is less (greater) than the nominal yield.

11.5 Price-yield Curve

With equation (11.7), we can now proceed to the all important **price-yield curve**, i.e, the plot of bond price as a function of yield to maturity. In general, from equation (11.7), then

$$\frac{\partial P_0^B}{\partial y} = \sum_{t=1}^{2T} \left[\frac{\frac{\partial PC_{\frac{t}{2}}(L)}{\partial L} \frac{dL}{dy}}{\left(1 + \frac{y}{2}\right)^t} - \frac{t}{2} \frac{PC_{\frac{t}{2}}\left(L_{\frac{t}{2}}\right)}{\left(1 + \frac{y}{2}\right)^{t+1}} \right]. \tag{11.8}$$

Of the two sets of terms in equation (11.8), the summation of the second set of terms is unambiguously less than zero due to the negative sign. However, the sign of the summation of the first set of terms depends on the signs of the $\frac{\partial PC_{\frac{t}{2}}(L)}{\partial L}$ terms in the numerators.[8] So the sign of this first summation is ambiguous due to the $\frac{\partial PC_{\frac{t}{2}}(L)}{\partial L}$ terms, which may be positive, negative or zero. Hence the sign of $\frac{\partial P_0^B}{\partial y}$ is generally ambiguous. Specifically, note that for floaters, where $\frac{\partial PC_{\frac{t}{2}}(L)}{\partial L} > 0$, then it is possible that $\frac{\partial P_0^B}{\partial y} > 0$.

Given our limited scope for bonds compared to that of a textbook on fixed income securities, we assume that cash flows are *not* a function of a reference rate. In short, we restrict ourselves to "fixed" cash flows in this book. Hence, we examine **fixed**

---

[8]The denominator terms $\left(1 + \frac{y}{2}\right)^t$ are positive. Also, generally, $\frac{dL}{dy} > 0$.

coupon payments: coupons that are *not* a function of a reference rate of interest, i.e., $\frac{\partial PC_{\frac{t}{2}}(L)}{\partial L} = 0, \forall t$.[9] So equation (11.8) becomes

$$\frac{\partial P_0^B}{\partial y} = -\sum_{t=1}^{2T} \left(\frac{t}{2}\right) \frac{PC_{\frac{t}{2}}}{\left(1+\frac{y}{2}\right)^{t+1}} < 0, \tag{11.9}$$

implying that the price-yield curve for a fixed coupon bond is downward sloping. Next, taking the partial derivative of equation (11.9) with respect to yield to maturity, then[10]

$$\frac{\partial^2 P_0^B}{\partial y^2} = +\sum_{t=1}^{2T} \frac{t}{2}\left(\frac{t+1}{2}\right) \frac{PC_{\frac{t}{2}}}{\left(1+\frac{y}{2}\right)^{t+2}} > 0, \tag{11.10}$$

i.e., the price-yield curve is convex. Thus, combining these two results, the price-yield curve for a fixed coupon bond is both downward sloping ($\frac{\partial P_0^B}{\partial y} < 0$) as well as convex ($\frac{\partial^2 P_0^B}{\partial y^2} > 0$).

For a fixed coupon bond, the coupons are an example of an annuity stream of cash flows, as seen in chapter 1. As the bond also includes payment of the final face value at maturity, then

$$P_0^B = \frac{F}{\left(1+\frac{y}{2}\right)^{2T}} + \sum_{t=1}^{2T} \frac{C_{\frac{t}{2}}}{\left(1+\frac{y}{2}\right)^t}$$

$$= \frac{F}{\left(1+\frac{y}{2}\right)^{2T}} + \frac{\frac{r^C F}{2}}{\frac{y}{2}}\left[1 - \left(\frac{1}{1+\frac{y}{2}}\right)^{2T}\right]$$

$$= F\left\{\frac{r^C}{y} + \left(\frac{1}{1+\frac{y}{2}}\right)^{2T}\left(1 - \frac{r^C}{y}\right)\right\}, \tag{11.11}$$

where r^C is the coupon rate on an *APr* basis with semi-annual compounding. Per equation (11.11), when $r^C = y$, then $P_0^B = F$, or so-called **par value**. Such a bond is called a **par bond**: $P_0^B = F \Leftrightarrow r^C = y$.

An example of a fixed coupon bond is shown in figure 11.3, where the fixed coupon rate is 3%, $T = 50$ years, face value $F = \$1000$ and compounding periods per year equals $m = 2$.[11]

---

[9] Indeed, a very large number of bonds issued around the world are of this nature.

[10] In the general case, the second derivative is ambiguous as is the first derivative, or $\frac{\partial^2 P_0^B}{\partial y^2} = \sum_{t=1}^{2T} A_t + B_t + C_t$, where $A_t = \frac{t}{2}(\frac{t+1}{2})\frac{PC_{t/2}(L_{t/2})}{(1+y/2)^{t+2}} > 0$, $B_t = -2\frac{t}{2}\frac{PC'_{t/2}(L_{t/2})}{(1+y/2)^{t+1}}\frac{dL}{dy}$, and $C_t = \frac{PC''_{t/2}(L_{t/2})(\frac{dL}{dy})^2 + PC'_{t/2}(L_{t/2})\frac{d^2L}{dy^2}}{(1+y/2)^t}$. So the signs of both B_t terms and C_t terms are ambiguous. Of course, for fixed coupon bonds, $B_t = C_t = 0, \forall t$, as $PC'_{t/2}(L_{t/2}) = PC''_{t/2}(L_{t/2}) = 0$, so $\frac{\partial^2 P_0^B}{\partial y^2} = \sum_{t=1}^{2T} A_t > 0$, consistent with equation (11.10).

[11] Unless otherwise noted in this book, $F = \$1000$ and $\frac{\text{compounding periods}}{\text{year}} = m = 2$.

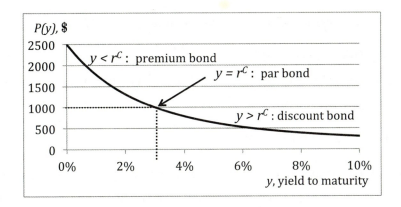

Figure 11.3 Price-yield curve

We previously showed per equation (11.9) that $\frac{\partial P_0^B}{\partial y} < 0$ for a fixed coupon bond. Thus, given this and the fact that $P_0^B = F$ when $r^C = y$, then $y > r^C \Leftrightarrow P_0^B < F$ corresponds to a so-called **discount bond**: one whose price is at a "discount" relative to par value (i.e., face value), F. Consistent with this math, figure 11.3 shows that when $y > r^C = 3\%$, then $P_0^B < F = \$1000$. Finally, figure 11.3 also confirms that when $y < r^C$, then $P_0^B > F$, corresponding to a **premium bond**: one whose price is at a "premium" relative to par value, F.

Problems

1. You hear on the radio that a bank pays an annual percentage rate on a checking account of 12%. However, you didn't hear the number of compounding periods per year. You construct a table of effective annual rates as a function of compounding periods per year. For assumed given numbers of compounding periods per year of: 1, 2, 4, 6, 12, 24, 52 and 365, what are the respective effective annual rates? Also calculate the effective annual rate assuming continuous compounding.

2. A semi-annual fixed coupon bond has a face value of $1000, coupon rate of 8%, yield to maturity of 9% and time to maturity of 7 years. What is this bond's price? Is this a premium bond, par bond or discount bond?

3. For the bond in problem 2, what is its current yield? What is its nominal yield?

4. A semi-annual fixed coupon bond has a face value of $1000, coupon rate of 8%, price of $1112.22 and time to maturity of 11 years. What is this bond's yield to maturity? Is this a premium bond, par bond or discount bond?

What is this bond's current yield? What is its nominal yield?

5. A semi-annual fixed coupon bond has a face value of $1000, coupon rate of 8%, yield to maturity of 6% and time to maturity of 14 years. What is this bond's price? Is this a premium bond, par bond or discount bond?

What is this bond's current yield? What is its nominal yield?

6. A semi-annual fixed coupon bond has a face value of $1000, coupon rate of 8%, price of $912.22 and time to maturity of 11 years. What is this bond's yield to maturity? Is this a premium bond, par bond or discount bond?

What is this bond's current yield? What is its nominal yield?

CHAPTER 12

March to Maturity and Malkiel Results

In deriving the price-yield curve in the previous chapter, we explored the bond's price sensitivity to changing interest rates. The purpose of this chapter is to further examine price sensitivities to various bond parameters.

We remind the reader of an important issue. The market determines bond price as a function of the riskiness and expectation of cash flows as well as the rate of return demanded by debt holders based on perceived cash flow riskiness. Then, from this market-determined price, we can calculate yield to maturity. Thus, price is *not* a function of yield to maturity, but rather the latter is a function of the former. Keep this in mind, as we "treat" price as a function of yield throughout this chapter.

12.1 March to Maturity

As previously shown for par bonds, $P_0^B = F \Leftrightarrow y = r^C$, whereas for premium (discount) bonds, $P_0^B > F \Leftrightarrow y < r^C$ ($P_0^B < F \Leftrightarrow y > r^C$). Now we consider the differences $P_0^B(T) - F > 0$ for premium bonds and $F - P_0^B(T) > 0$ for discount bonds as functions of time to maturity, T.

From before, we showed that $P_0^B = F\{\frac{r^C}{y} + (1+\frac{y}{2})^{-2T}(1-\frac{r^C}{y})\}$ in equation (11.11) for a fixed coupon bond. Hence[1]

$$\frac{\partial P_0^B}{\partial T} = -2F\left(1+\frac{y}{2}\right)^{-2T}\left(1-\frac{r^C}{y}\right)\ln\left(1+\frac{y}{2}\right) > 0, \text{ if } y < r^C;$$

---

[1]Does it make you uncomfortable that we calculate $\frac{\partial P_0^B}{\partial T}$, where T is treated as a continuous parameter, even though by definition of an annuity of coupon payments, T must be discrete? Consider a discrete equivalent to the derivative in expression (12.1), or $\frac{\Delta P}{\Delta T} = \frac{P_T - P_{T-0.5}}{T - (T-0.5)} = \frac{F\{(1+\frac{y}{2})^{-2T} - (1+\frac{y}{2})^{-2T+1}\}(1-\frac{r^C}{y})}{0.5} = F(r^C - y)(1+\frac{y}{2})^{-2T}$. Using the first order Taylor series approximation for $\ln(1+\frac{y}{2}) \approx \frac{y}{2}$ for "small" $\frac{y}{2}$, then from equation (12.1), $\frac{\partial P_0^B}{\partial T} \approx -2F(1+\frac{y}{2})^{-2T}(1-\frac{r^C}{y})\frac{y}{2} = F(r^C - y)(1+\frac{y}{2})^{-2T}$, the same as the discrete result.

$$\frac{\partial P_0^B}{\partial T} < 0, \text{ if } y > r^C; \quad \text{and} \quad \frac{\partial P_0^B}{\partial T} = 0, \text{ if } y = r^C. \tag{12.1}$$

Regarding the second derivative,

$$\frac{\partial^2 P_0^B}{\partial T^2} = \frac{4F}{y}\left(1+\frac{y}{2}\right)^{-2T}(y-r^C)\left[\ln\left(1+\frac{y}{2}\right)\right]^2 < 0, \text{ if } y < r^C;$$

$$\frac{\partial^2 P_0^B}{\partial T^2} > 0, \text{ if } y > r^C; \quad \text{and} \quad \frac{\partial^2 P_0^B}{\partial T^2} = 0, \text{ if } y = r^C. \tag{12.2}$$

For a par bond, $P_0^B = F$, $\forall T$, $T \in \{1, 2, 3, \dots\}$, as $y = r^C$. So holding coupon rate fixed, if the yield to maturity remains equal to the coupon rate, the price equals par value, invariant to maturity, T. However, for a premium (discount) bond, where $y < r^C$ ($y > r^C$), the first derivative in T is positive (negative) and the second derivative is of the opposite sign, i.e., negative (positive). So holding fixed yield to maturity (and coupon rate) for a series of premium bonds of increasing maturity, then the pricing $P_0^B(T) > F$ is increasing, but at an ever decreasing rate. Analogously, holding fixed y (and r^C) for a series of discount bonds of increasing T, then $F < P_0^B(T)$ is increasing, but at an ever slowing rate.

To graphically illustrate the previous results, consider figure 12.1, where $r^C = 8\%$ and $F = \$1000$. Shown are three cases: 31 premium bonds (where for each, $2\% = y < r^C = 8\%$), 31 par bonds (where for each, $8\% = y = r^C$) and 31 discount bonds (where for each, $16\% = y > r^C$). In each of the three cases, the 31 bonds correspond to maturities of $T = \{0, 2, 3, \dots, 30\}$ years, respectively, where the case $T = 0$ is for a bond that matures later today. Consistent with the math, the prices of the series of par bonds is always par, $\$1000$. In contrast, the prices of the series of premium (discount) bonds are increasing and concave (decreasing and convex) in maturity, T. In summary, the greater the bond's time to maturity, the greater the deviation of the bond's price from par: the greater the differences $P_0^B - F$ for a premium bond and $F - P_0^B$ for a discount bond, all else equal.

In figure 12.1, the independent axis represents time to maturity, T, in years. In some sense, this is the negative of time. Hence reversing this axis represents the passage of time. In doing so, we can see how the price of a bond evolves over time, holding fixed the bond's yield to maturity (and coupon rate). In figure 12.2, $r^C = 8\%$ and $F = \$1000$, the same parameter values as in figure 12.1. Consistent with the three different cases of yield to maturity ($y = 2\%$, 8% and 16%) shown in figure 12.1, figure 12.2 includes 31 different points in time for a premium bond (where for each point in time shown, $2\% = y < r^C = 8\%$), 31 different points in time for a par bond (where for each point

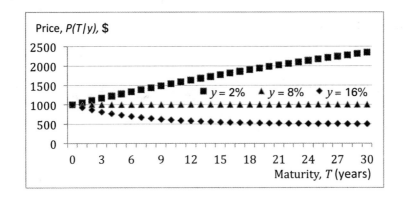

Figure 12.1 Impact of maturity on price

in time, $8\% = y = r^C$) and 31 different points in time for a discount bond (where $16\% = y > r^C$). In each of the three cases, the 31 prices correspond to maturities of $T = \{30, 29, 28, ..., 0\}$ years, respectively, where the case $T = 0$ is for a bond that matures later today. So for each of the three bonds, they are issued with maturities of $T = 30$ years, corresponding to the first data point in each of the three time series of figure 12.2. For each bond, we additionally see the price one year later (when $T = 29$), two years later ($T = 28$), etc...

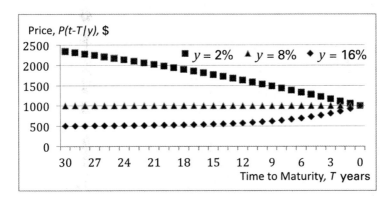

Figure 12.2 March to maturity

To summarize, we see in figure 12.2 that as the bond's time to maturity decreases over time, so does the deviation of the bond's price from par: the smaller the differences $P_0^B(T) - F > 0$ for a premium bond and $F - P_0^B(T) > 0$ for a discount bond, all else equal. Convergence of the bond's price toward par value (or face value, F) as it approaches maturity, *regardless* of whether $y < r^C$ or $y > r^C$, is called **march to maturity**. In short, over the passage of time, a bond's price converges to par, all else equal.

12.2 Malkiel Results

In an important paper, Malkiel derived several results for fixed coupon bonds. We offer them here without proof.[2]

12.2.1 Impact of Yield to Maturity, y

In generating the price-yield curve, we have already derived two of his results, equations (11.9) ($\frac{\partial P_0^B}{\partial y} < 0$) and (11.10) ($\frac{\partial^2 P_0^B}{\partial y^2} > 0$).

Malkiel employs a *relative* interest rate risk metric, $\frac{\partial \ln(P_0^B)}{\partial y} = \frac{1}{P_0^B} \frac{\partial P_0^B}{\partial y} = \frac{\partial P_0^B / P_0^B}{\partial y}$.[3] For a given absolute increase in yield (∂y), this risk metric considers *relative* change in price ($\frac{\partial P_0^B}{P_0^B}$), versus *absolute* change in price (∂P_0^B). A *relative* interest rate risk metric is more relevant than an absolute metric, as it removes the impact of magnitude of value of the bond (or bonds) under consideration.

Recall that for a fixed coupon bond, $\frac{\partial P_0^B}{\partial y} < 0$. Consider two bonds, x and z, such that initially, $P_0^x = P_0^z$ and $y_0^x = y_0^z$. Further assume that for a given equal increase in yields of $y_1^x - y_0^x \equiv \Delta y^x = \Delta y^z \equiv y_1^z - y_0^z > 0$, the price changes in x and z are such that $P_1^x - P_0^x \equiv \Delta P^x < \Delta P^z \equiv P_1^z - P_0^z < 0$. This implies that $P_1^x < P_1^z$, i.e., x has lost more value than has z, where both bonds have decreased in value. So $\frac{\partial P^x}{\partial y} < \frac{\partial P^z}{\partial y} < 0$.[4] As $P_0^x = P_0^z > 0$, then $\frac{1}{P_0^x} \frac{\partial P^x}{\partial y} < \frac{1}{P_0^z} \frac{\partial P^z}{\partial y} < 0$.

In the previous example, clearly x has greater interest rate risk than z, as the *magnitude* of x's *relative* change in price per absolute change in yield is greater than that of z. Again, $\frac{\partial \ln(P^x)}{\partial y} < \frac{\partial \ln(P^z)}{\partial y} < 0$, i.e., both are negative. So for fixed coupon bonds, the larger (smaller) the value of $\frac{\partial \ln(P_0^B)}{\partial y}$, then the lesser (greater) is this bond's interest rate risk, i.e., $\frac{\partial \ln(P_0^B)}{\partial y}$ is closer to (farther from) zero. So in what follows, for a given parameter π, if $\frac{\partial}{\partial \pi}(\frac{\partial \ln(P_0^B)}{\partial y})$ is positive (negative), then this bond's interest rate risk decreases (increases) in π, $\pi \in \{y, T, r^C\}$. The key takeaway is that our relative interest rate risk metric, $\frac{\partial \ln(P_0^B)}{\partial y} < 0$, actually *decreases* in interest rate sensitivity: the closer to zero, the less the interest rate risk, all else equal. So in some sense, our metric captures *non*-interest rate risk. The more (less) *negative* that $\frac{\partial \ln(P_0^B)}{\partial y} < 0$ is, the greater (smaller) is this bond's price sensitivity to changes in yield for a given change

---

[2]One can find the details in Malkiel (1962).

[3]Later we study modified duration, MD, which is the negative of this metric, or $MD = -\frac{\partial \ln(P_0^B)}{\partial y}$. For fixed coupon bonds, as $\frac{\partial P_0^B}{\partial y} < 0$, then $MD > 0$.

[4]For simplicity, we assume that the signs of discrete changes (Δ) and infinitesimal changes (∂) are the same.

in π, all else equal.

Consider the following simple numerical example. Two bonds, x and z, both decrease in value by \$100 when their respective yields increase by 1%. So for both, the *absolute* change in value per change in yield is $\frac{-\$100}{1\%}$. Next, assume that x's (z's) initial value is $P_0^x = \$1000$ ($P_0^z = \$500$). Then the *relative* change in value is $\Delta P_0^x = \frac{-100}{1000}$ ($\Delta P_0^z = \frac{-100}{500}$). As the *absolute* change in value is the same for both, then the one with the smaller (larger) initial value has the greater (smaller) change in *relative* value, $z(x)$ in this example.[5] So $0 > \frac{\Delta P^x}{\Delta y^x} > \frac{\Delta P^z}{\Delta y^z}$, meaning that in this example, x's price sensitivity for a given change in yield is less than that of z.

To summarize, in comparing bond price sensitivities, it is important that we use *relative* metrics so that we compare bonds and portfolios of bonds on an "apples to apples" basis. In short, we cannot compare absolute changes in values when initial values are not equal. However, by normalization (i.e., dividing by initial values), we are able to compare bonds and bond portfolios *regardless* of the magnitude of their initial values, all else equal.

With our relative interest rate risk metric in hand, consider

$$\frac{\partial}{\partial y}\left(\frac{1}{P_0^B}\frac{\partial P_0^B}{\partial y}\right) = \frac{1}{P_0^B}\left[\frac{\partial^2 P_0^B}{\partial y^2} - \frac{1}{P_0^B}\left(\frac{\partial P_0^B}{\partial y}\right)^2\right] > 0, \qquad (12.3)$$

where Malkiel proves the result that this expression is positive. So per our previous discussion, the positive sign in expression (12.3) means that as the yield to maturity increases, the bond's relative price sensitivity to changes in absolute yield *decreases*, all else equal.[6] This seems intuitive, as there is obviously a lower bound on the bond's price. Furthermore, inspection of the price-yield curve for a fixed coupon bond per figure 11.3 seems to be consistent with decreasing magnitude of relative slope as the yield increases.

Note that expression (12.3) is an *even stronger* result than $\frac{\partial^2 P_0^B}{\partial y^2} > 0$, which we previously proved. Per Malkiel, expression (12.3) implies that $\frac{\partial^2 P_0^B}{\partial y^2} > \frac{1}{P_0^B}(\frac{\partial P_0^B}{\partial y})^2$, where $\frac{1}{P_0^B}(\frac{\partial P_0^B}{\partial y})^2 > 0$. In short, Malkiel shows that the second derivative, $\frac{\partial^2 P_0^B}{\partial y^2}$, is not just positive, but is greater than another term which itself is positive, $\frac{1}{P_0^B}\left(\frac{\partial P_0^B}{\partial y}\right)^2 > 0$.

---

[5]As a more extreme example, in comparing interest rate risk for two bond portfolios, we can't compare absolute changes in values, as their magnitudes can be even more significantly different.

[6]Equivalently, as y increases, the "increase" in relative price per increase in absolute yield is increasing. In other words, the decrease in relative price per increase in absolute yield is diminishing in yield.

As previously discussed, the relative interest rate risk metric $\frac{\partial \ln(P_0^B)}{\partial y}$ considers relative change in value per *absolute* change in yield. Malkiel also considers another metric, the relative change in price per *relative* change in yield, or $\frac{\partial \ln(P_0^B)}{\partial \ln(y)} = \frac{\partial P_0^B / P_0^B}{\partial y / y} = \frac{y}{P_0^B}\frac{\partial P_0^B}{\partial y}$. For a fixed coupon bond, Malkiel proves that this decreases in yield, or

$$\frac{\partial}{\partial y}\left(\frac{\partial \ln\left(P_0^B\right)}{\partial \ln(y)}\right) = \frac{y}{P_0^B}\left[\frac{\partial^2 P_0^B}{\partial y^2} - \frac{1}{P_0^B}\left(\frac{\partial P_0^B}{\partial y}\right)^2 + \frac{1}{y}\frac{\partial P_0^B}{\partial y}\right] < 0. \qquad (12.4)$$

So while the relative price decrease per absolute yield change is diminishing in yield (i.e., becomes less negative per expression (12.3)), the relative price decrease per *relative* increase in yield is increasing in yield (i.e., becomes more negative per expression 12.4).[7] As $\frac{y}{P_0^B} > 0$, then $\frac{\partial^2 P_0^B}{\partial y^2} < \frac{1}{P_0^B}\left(\frac{\partial P_0^B}{\partial y}\right)^2 - \frac{1}{y}\frac{\partial P_0^B}{\partial y}$ per expression (12.4).

Combining two previous results, equations (12.3) and (12.4), yields a strong result (i.e., a small window) regarding the convexity of the price-yield curve.

$$\frac{\partial^2 P_0^B}{\partial y^2} - \frac{1}{P_0^B}\left(\frac{\partial P_0^B}{\partial y}\right)^2 \in \left\{0, -\frac{1}{y}\frac{\partial P_0^B}{\partial y}\right\}. \qquad (12.5)$$

Obviously, $-\frac{1}{y}\frac{\partial P_0^B}{\partial y} > 0$, as $\frac{\partial P_0^B}{\partial y} < 0$.

To further illustrate these results, consider the following discrete analysis per figure 12.3. First consider the discrete approximation of $\frac{\partial}{\partial y}(\frac{1}{P}\frac{\partial P}{\partial y}) > 0$, or $\frac{\Delta}{\Delta y^*}(\frac{1}{P}\frac{\Delta P}{\Delta y}) = \frac{\frac{1}{P^\alpha}\frac{\Delta P^\alpha}{\Delta y^\alpha} - \frac{1}{P^\beta}\frac{\Delta P^\beta}{\Delta y^\beta}}{y^\alpha - y^\beta}$, or

$$\frac{\Delta}{\Delta y^*}\left(\frac{1}{P}\frac{\Delta P}{\Delta y}\right) = \frac{\frac{1}{P^\alpha}\frac{P_+^\alpha - P_-^\alpha}{y_+^\alpha - y_-^\alpha} - \frac{1}{P^\beta}\frac{P_+^\beta - P_-^\beta}{y_+^\beta - y_-^\beta}}{y^\alpha - y^\beta} > 0, \qquad (12.6)$$

where $\Delta y^* \equiv y^\alpha - y^\beta > 0$ for two chosen yields y^α and y^β; $\Delta y \equiv y_+^\alpha - y^\alpha = y^\alpha - y_-^\alpha > 0$; $P^\alpha \equiv P(y^\alpha)$, $P_+^\alpha \equiv P(y_+^\alpha)$ and $P_-^\alpha \equiv P(y_-^\alpha)$.[8] In a later chapter, we will explore discrete approximations further when we discuss effective price-yield metrics. In such calculations, Δy^* and Δy should both be quite small, e.g., 0.01% each. In this chapter, we use much larger values for ease of illustration of concepts.

As an example from figure 12.3, consider two different arbitrary starting points,

---

[7] The negative sign in expression (12.4) means that as the yield to maturity increases, the bond's relative price sensitivity to changes in relative yield *increases*, all else equal. Equivalently, as y increases, the "increase" in relative price per increase in relative yield is decreasing.

[8] Analogously, $\Delta y = y_+^\beta - y^\beta = y^\beta - y_-^\beta > 0$, $P^\beta \equiv P(y^\beta)$, $P_+^\beta \equiv P(y_+^\beta)$ and $P_-^\beta \equiv P(y_-^\beta)$.

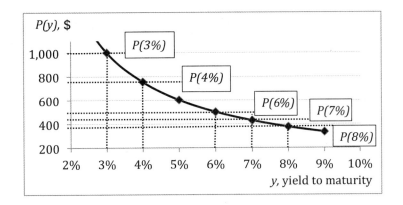

Figure 12.3 Impact of yield on price-yield curve

3% and 6%, respectively. Then $\frac{\Delta(\frac{1}{P}\frac{\Delta P}{\Delta y})}{\Delta y^*} = \frac{\frac{1}{P^6}(\frac{P^7-P^6}{7\%-6\%}) - \frac{1}{P^3}(\frac{P^4-P^3}{4\%-3\%})}{6\%-3\%} > 0$, per Malkiel.[9] This simplifies to $0 < \frac{P^4}{P^3} < \frac{P^7}{P^6} < 1$, consistent with the appearance in figure 12.3. In short, for given $\Delta y^\alpha = \Delta y^\beta$ (= 7% − 6% = 4% − 3% = 1%), then $\frac{\Delta P}{P} < 0$ at higher yields is greater than (i.e., less negative than) $\frac{\Delta P}{P} < 0$ at lower yields, all else equal. So as the yield increases, the bond's relative price is less sensitive to changes in yield, all else equal.

Next consider the discrete approximation of $\frac{\partial}{\partial y}(\frac{\partial \ln(P)}{\partial \ln(y)}) = \frac{\partial}{\partial y}(\frac{y}{P}\frac{\partial P}{\partial y}) < 0$, or $\frac{\Delta}{\Delta y^*}(\frac{y}{P}\frac{\Delta P}{\Delta y}) = \frac{\frac{y^\alpha}{P^\alpha}\frac{\Delta P^\alpha}{\Delta y^\alpha} - \frac{y^\beta}{P^\beta}\frac{\Delta P^\beta}{\Delta y^\beta}}{y^\alpha - y^\beta}$, or

$$\frac{\Delta}{\Delta y^*}\left(\frac{y}{P}\frac{\Delta P}{\Delta y}\right) = \frac{\frac{y^\alpha}{P^\alpha}\frac{P_+^\alpha - P_-^\alpha}{y_+^\alpha - y_-^\alpha} - \frac{y^\beta}{P^\beta}\frac{P_+^\beta - P_-^\beta}{y_+^\beta - y_-^\beta}}{y^\alpha - y^\beta} < 0. \quad (12.7)$$

As an example from figure 12.3, consider two different starting points, 3% and 6%, respectively. Then $\frac{\Delta(\frac{y}{P}\frac{\Delta P}{\Delta y})}{\Delta y^*} = \frac{\frac{6\%}{P^6}(\frac{P^8-P^6}{8\%-6\%}) - \frac{3\%}{P^3}(\frac{P^4-P^3}{4\%-3\%})}{6\%-3\%} < 0$ per Malkiel. Note that in contrast to the previous two cases, where we used $\Delta y^\alpha = \Delta y^\beta$, in this case we use $\Delta y^\alpha = 8\% - 6\% > 4\% - 3\% = \Delta y^\beta$. The reason we do this is because $\Delta \ln(y^\alpha) \approx \frac{\Delta y^\alpha}{y^\alpha} = \frac{8\%-6\%}{6\%} = \frac{1}{3} = \frac{4\%-3\%}{3\%} = \frac{\Delta y^\beta}{y^\beta} \approx \Delta \ln(y^\beta)$.[10] Simplifying previous inequalities, then $0 < \frac{P^8}{P^6} < \frac{P^4}{P^3} < 1$, consistent with the appearance in figure 12.3.

Let's simultaneously consider two previous results, $\frac{\Delta}{\Delta y^*}\left(\frac{y}{P}\frac{\Delta P}{\Delta y}\right) < 0 \Rightarrow 0 < \frac{P^8}{P^6} <$

---

[9] For ease of exposition, we use $\frac{\Delta}{\Delta y^*}(\frac{1}{P}\frac{\Delta P}{\Delta y}) = \frac{\frac{1}{P^\alpha}\frac{P_+^\alpha - P_-^\alpha}{y_+^\alpha - y_-^\alpha} - \frac{1}{P^\beta}\frac{P_+^\beta - P_-^\beta}{y_+^\beta - y_-^\beta}}{y^\alpha - y^\beta}$. In the limit as $\Delta y \to 0$, this expression results in the same value as expression (12.6). Also, in this case we use $\Delta y^* = y^\alpha - y^\beta = 3\%$, and $\Delta y = y_+^\alpha - y^\alpha = y_+^\beta - y^\beta = 1\%$.

[10] From $\Delta \ln(y) = \ln(y^+) - \ln(y) = \ln(\frac{y^+}{y}) = \ln(\frac{y+y^+-y}{y}) = \ln(1 + \frac{\Delta y}{y})$, and using the first order Taylor series approximation for $\ln(1+x) \approx x$ for small x, then $\Delta \ln(y) \approx \frac{\Delta y}{y}$.

$\frac{P4}{P3} < 1$ and $\frac{\Delta}{\Delta y^*}\left(\frac{1}{P}\frac{\Delta P}{\Delta y}\right) > 0 \Rightarrow 0 < \frac{P4}{P3} < \frac{P7}{P6} < 1$. Combining these, then $0 < \frac{P8}{P6} < \frac{P4}{P3} < \frac{P7}{P6} < 1$. The first inequality ($\frac{P8}{P6} < \frac{P4}{P3}$) follows from the fact that for a given absolute increase in yield, the magnitude of relative price sensitivity per *relative* increase in yield increases, all else equal. However, per the second inequality, ($\frac{P4}{P3} < \frac{P7}{P6}$), for a given absolute increase in yield, the magnitude of relative price sensitivity per *absolute* increase in yield decreases, all else equal.

12.2.2 Impact of Coupon Rate

With a good understanding of how the price of a bond varies with yield, we now move on to another parameter, coupon rate r^C. Obviously, differentiating P_0^B per equation (11.11) with respect to r^C yields $\frac{F}{y}[1 - (1 + \frac{y}{2})^{-2T}] > 0$. Intuitively, larger coupon rates imply larger cash flows; thus, the more valuable the bond.

Next, Malkiel proves the following positive result.

$$\frac{\partial}{\partial r^C}\left(\frac{\partial \ln\left(P_0^B\right)}{\partial y}\right) > 0. \tag{12.8}$$

The positive sign in expression (12.8) means that as the coupon rate increases, the bond's relative price sensitivity to changes in yield *decreases*, all else equal. The result is intuitive. As coupons increase, they represent a greater fraction of the bond's value relative the the face value, F, which remains unchanged. As coupons (except for the final one) are received prior to when the face value is received, their present values are less impacted by a change in yield than is the present value of F.[11] In short, as coupons increase, greater fractions of the bond's present value are received at earlier periods, where cash flows are less impacted by changes in yield, all else equal. The final payment, whose present value is the most sensitive to an increase in yield, represents a smaller fraction of the bond's present value. Thus, the bond's relative price sensitivity to a change in yield decreases as coupon rate increases, all else equal.

To illustrate the previous result, consider figure 12.4, where $F = \$1000$, $T = 30$ years and $m = 2$. Obviously, as the coupon rate increases, so does $P_0^B(y)$, $\forall y \geq 0$. Interestingly, it can be shown that $\frac{\partial^2 P_0^B}{\partial y \partial r^C} = \frac{\partial}{\partial y}\frac{\partial P_0^B}{\partial r^C} = \frac{\partial}{\partial r^C}\frac{\partial P_0^B}{\partial y} < 0$.[12] So for a fixed coupon bond, as the coupon rate increases, the bond's *absolute* price sensitivity to yield increases, i.e., the price sensitivity $\frac{\partial P_0^B}{\partial y} < 0$ becomes even more negative. This is

---

[11] This follows as $(1 + \frac{y_1}{2})^t - (1 + \frac{y_0}{2})^t < (1 + \frac{y_1}{2})^{2T} - (1 + \frac{y_0}{2})^{2T}$, $\forall y_1 > y_0$, $\forall t \in \{1, 2, ..., 2T - 1\}$.

[12] From $\frac{\partial P_0^B}{\partial r^C} = F\{(1 + \frac{y}{2})^{-0.5} + (1 + \frac{y}{2})^{-1} + (1 + \frac{y}{2})^{-1.5} + ... + (1 + \frac{y}{2})^{-2T}\}$, which is obviously decreasing in yield, then $\frac{\partial^2 P_0^B}{\partial r^C \partial y} < 0$.

consistent with the appearance of figure 12.4. For a given yield, e.g., 2%, then as the coupon rate increases (i.e., in observing ever higher price-yield curves in figure 12.4), the *magnitude* of the slope increases, i.e., $\frac{\partial P_0^B}{\partial y} < 0$ decreases; the slope becomes more negative. So all else equal, the *absolute* price sensitivity to an absolute change in yield increases in coupon rate. However, what Malkiel's expression (12.8) tells us is that the *relative* price sensitivity to an absolute change in yield *decreases* in coupon rate. The difference in the two results is that the relative metric divides by P_0^B. Thus the larger the coupon rate, the larger the price, which decreases the magnitude of sensitivity, $\frac{1}{P_0^B} \frac{\partial P_0^B}{\partial y}$, all else equal.

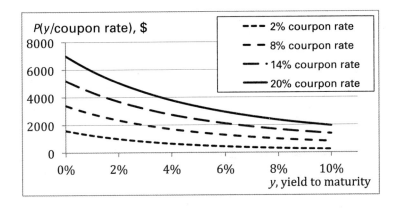

Figure 12.4 **Impact of coupon rate on price-yield curve**

12.2.3 Impact of Time to Maturity, T

Via equations (12.1) and (12.2), we already have a good start on understanding how time to maturity, T, impacts bond price. We previously showed that as time to maturity increases, then the magnitude of difference between P_0^B and F increases, i.e., $P_0^B(T) - F$ increases for a premium bond and $F - P_0^B(T)$ increases for a discount bond.

Now we want to investigate how T impacts our relative interest rate risk metric, $\frac{\partial \ln(P_0^B)}{\partial y}$. Per Malkiel,

$$\frac{\partial}{\partial T}\left(\frac{\partial \ln(P_0^B)}{\partial y}\right) < 0, \quad \text{and} \quad \frac{\partial^2}{\partial T^2}\left(\frac{\partial \ln(P_0^B)}{\partial y}\right) > 0. \tag{12.9}$$

The negative sign in the first derivative, $\frac{\partial}{\partial T}(\frac{\partial \ln(P_0^B)}{\partial y}) < 0$, means that as the time to maturity increases, the bond's relative price sensitivity to absolute changes in yield *increases*, all else equal. In other words, as T increases, the bond's relative price sensitivity to a change in yield increases. This is intuitive; one would expect that a bond that matures in one year has less relative interest rate risk than one that matures in 30 years.[13]

The positive sign of the second derivative, $\frac{\partial^2}{\partial T^2}(\frac{\partial \ln(P_0^B)}{\partial y}) > 0$, means that the rate of increasing sensitivity of the bond's relative price for a given absolute yield change as time to maturity increases is decreasing in time to maturity.

As all this is a bit of a "mouthful", let's show a numerical example, figure 12.5, where $F = \$1000$ and $r^C = 10\%$. Let's consider the first inequality of expression (12.9). Via inspection of figure 12.5, note the slopes, $\frac{\partial P_0^B}{\partial y}$, of the four curves when $y = r^C = 10\%$ (i.e., when $P_0^B = F$). It is apparent that the slope becomes *more negative* (i.e., greater in magnitude) as T increases, consistent with $\frac{\partial}{\partial T}(\frac{\partial \ln(P_0^B)}{\partial y}) < 0$. (This ordering of slopes is even more noticeable at lower yields, e.g., at $y = 5\%$.)

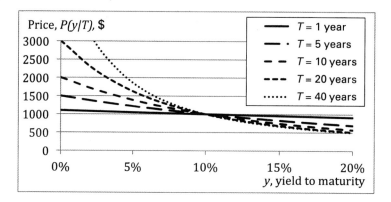

Figure 12.5 Impact of time to maturity on price-yield curve

To interpret the second inequality of expression (12.9), note the difference in vertical spaces between price-yield curves at any chosen yield other than $y = r^C = 10\%$. For example, consider $y = 15\%$. The positive distances between the price-yield curves monotonically decrease, as T increases. In other words, in going from $T = 1$ to $T = 5$ to $T = 10$ to $T = 20$ to $T = 40$, the differences in prices between consecutive maturities at $y = 15\%$ is decreasing in time to maturity.[14]

We summarize the key Malkiel results.

---

[13] Furthermore, if rates increase, then a bond that matures in one year can be reinvested at the resulting higher rates in one year, all else equal, than one that matures in 30 years. However, this story is distinct from the current result, i.e, it does *not* explain why $\frac{\partial}{\partial T}(\frac{\partial \ln(P_0^B)}{\partial y}) < 0$.

[14] The result $\frac{\partial}{\partial T}(\frac{\partial \ln(P_0^B)}{\partial y}) < 0$ is even stronger than this exposition, given that ΔT is decreasing in these four differences, i.e. $5 - 1 < 10 - 5 < 20 - 10 < 40 - 20$. In other words, if ΔT were consistent between these five $P - y$ curves, then the decreasing nature of differences between curves would be even more obvious.

- $$\frac{\partial\left(\frac{\partial \ln(P_0^B)}{\partial y}\right)}{\partial y} > 0, \qquad \frac{\partial\left(\frac{\partial \ln(P_0^B)}{\partial \ln(y)}\right)}{\partial y} < 0, \qquad \frac{\partial\left(\frac{\partial \ln(P_0^B)}{\partial y}\right)}{\partial r^C} > 0,$$
- $$\frac{\partial\left(\frac{\partial \ln(P_0^B)}{\partial y}\right)}{\partial T} < 0, \qquad \frac{\partial^2\left(\frac{\partial \ln(P_0^B)}{\partial y}\right)}{\partial T^2} > 0.$$

Problems

1. A semi-annual fixed coupon bond has a face value of $1000, coupon rate of 8%, yield to maturity of 4% and time to maturity of 14 years. What is this bond's price? Is this a premium bond, par bond or discount bond?

2. For the same bond in problem 1 except for a time to maturity of 20 years, what is its price? Is the price greater or smaller than that of problem 1? Explain this relationship in terms of march to maturity.

3. A semi-annual fixed coupon bond has a face value of $1000, coupon rate of 8%, yield to maturity of 12% and time to maturity of 14 years. What is this bond's price? Is this a premium bond, par bond or discount bond?

4. For the same bond in problem 3 except for a time to maturity of 20 years, what is its price? Is the price greater or smaller than that of problem 1? Explain this relationship in terms of march to maturity.

5. The bonds in problems 1 (yield to maturity of 4%) and 3 (yield to maturity of 12%) have the same parameters except for yield to maturity. Which one has the higher price? Explain why this is so.

6. A semi-annual fixed coupon bond has a face value of $1000, coupon rate of 15%, yield to maturity of 4% and time to maturity of 14 years. What is this bond's price? Is this a premium bond, par bond or discount bond?

7. The bonds in problems 1 (coupon rate of 8%) and 6 (coupon rate of 15%) have the same parameters except for coupon rate. Which one has the higher price? Explain why this is so.

CHAPTER 13

Approximations to Price-yield Relations

In the previous chapter, we explored in detail the price sensitivities of fixed coupon bonds to all relevant parameters. In this chapter, we delve deeper into the impact of yield upon the price-yield curve. Our purpose is to develop useful approximations of the price-yield curve. Managers find these useful when quick price-yield relations are needed and when larger portfolios of complex securities make exact relations difficult.

We once again remind the reader that price is *not* a function of yield to maturity, but rather the latter is a function of the former. We repeat this here as we "treat" price as a function of yield throughout this chapter. Obviously, yields are related to market-determined interest rates, making the analysis relevant.

13.1 Macaulay Duration and Modified Duration

We begin with **Macaulay duration, *MaD*,** developed by Frederick Macaulay and used as a metric for interest rate risk. It is also sometimes called effective maturity. By definition, for a semi-annual bond

$$MaD \equiv \frac{1}{P_0^B} \sum_{t=1}^{2T} \frac{t}{2} \frac{CF_{\frac{t}{2}}}{\left(1+\frac{y}{2}\right)^t} = \frac{1}{\sum_{n=1}^{2T} \frac{CF_{\frac{n}{2}}}{\left(1+\frac{y}{2}\right)^n}} \sum_{t=1}^{2T} \frac{t}{2} \frac{CF_{\frac{t}{2}}}{\left(1+\frac{y}{2}\right)^t}$$

$$= \sum_{t=1}^{2T} \frac{t}{2} \underbrace{\left(\frac{PV\left(CF_{\frac{t}{2}}\right)}{\sum_{n=1}^{2T} PV\left(CF_{\frac{n}{2}}\right)}\right)}_{\equiv w_{\frac{t}{2}}} = \sum_{t=1}^{2T} \frac{t}{2} w_{\frac{t}{2}}, \qquad (13.1)$$

where the "present value" of a cash flow is $PV(CF_{t/2}) = \frac{CF_{t/2}}{(1+\frac{y}{2})^t}$, and weight $w_{\frac{t}{2}}$ is the fraction of the bond's "present value" represented by the corresponding cash flow received at date $\frac{t}{2}$, $CF_{t/2}$.[1] So Macaulay duration is a weighted average time of cash flow receipt (i.e., date, $\frac{t}{2}$), where weights correspond to fractional present value of the bond.

Figure 13.1 graphically depicts Macaulay duration for a bond with maturity $T = 4$ years, face value $F = \$1000$, yield to maturity $y = 10\%$, coupon rate $r^C = 14\%$, compounding periods per year are $m = 2$ and the bond's price is $P_0^B = \$1129.30$. Doing the calculation, $MaD = 3.248$ years. So firstly, the height of the eight columns in figure 13.1 equals the bonds price, \$1129.30. Secondly, for a zero coupon bond, the entire "weight" occurs at a single date, maturity T. Given a weight of one on T, then for a zero coupon bond, $MaD = T$. Next, for fixed coupon bonds, where positive weights are placed on dates prior to maturity, i.e., $t < T$, then $MaD < T$.[2]

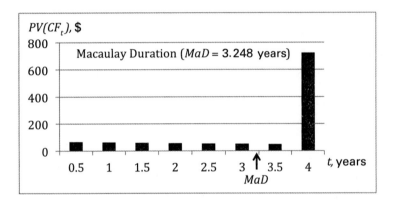

Figure 13.1 Macaulay duration

Macaulay duration is a metric for interest rate risk, though it may not be readily apparent. So let's examine an obvious metric and see the relation between the two. Consider a relative interest rate risk metric, **modified duration**, $MD = -\frac{1}{P_0^B}\frac{\partial P_0^B}{\partial y}$. Note the negative sign. In this text we live in a world of fixed coupon bonds, so $MD > 0$, as $\frac{\partial P_0^B}{\partial y} < 0$. Hence for a fixed coupon bond, its relative price sensitivity increases (decreases) as MD increases (decreases).

What is the relation between Macaulay duration, MaD, and modified duration,

---

[1] By definition of yield, the bond's price is the summation of "present value" of cash flows, or $P_0^B = \sum_{t=1}^{2T} \frac{CF_{t/2}}{(1+\frac{y}{2})^t}$. So each weight is one of these terms in the sum divided by the sum. We place "present value" in quotes as yield is not a discount rate, per se, like rate of return demanded by debt holers. Yield to maturity is calculated by setting bond price equal to the summation of discounted cash flows.

[2] For some bonds with embedded options, $Mac > T$ is possible. These bonds are beyond the scope of this book.

MD? As $w_{\frac{t}{2}} = \frac{PV(CF_{t/2})}{P_0^B}$, then for a fixed coupon bond, $\frac{\partial P_0^B}{\partial y} = -\sum_{t=1}^{2T} \frac{t}{2} \frac{CF_{t/2}}{(1+y/2)^{t+1}} = -\frac{P_0^B}{P_0^B} \sum_{t=1}^{2T} \frac{t}{2} \frac{PV(CF_{t/2})}{(1+y/2)^1} = -\frac{P_0^B}{1+\frac{y}{2}} \sum_{t=1}^{2T} \frac{t}{2}(w_{\frac{t}{2}})$.[3] So $MD = -\frac{1}{P_0^B}\frac{\partial P_0^B}{\partial y} = -\frac{1}{P_0^B}(-\frac{P_0^B}{1+\frac{y}{2}} \cdot \sum_{t=1}^{2T} \frac{t}{2}(w_{\frac{t}{2}})) = \frac{+1}{1+\frac{y}{2}} \sum_{t=1}^{2T} \frac{t}{2}(w_{\frac{t}{2}})$. Comparing this final expression with equation (13.1), then for a fixed coupon bond,

$$MD = \frac{MaD}{1+\frac{y}{2}}, \quad \text{or} \quad MaD = MD\left(1+\frac{y}{2}\right) \qquad (13.2)$$

Expression (13.2) makes it clear that Macaulay duration captures interest rate risk, as we've already seen how modified duration does so. Intuitively, we saw in a previous chapter that a bond's interest rate risk is generally increasing in its maturity, all else equal. The further into the future that a cash flow is received, the greater is the sensitivity of its present value to changes in yield. As Macaulay duration is a weighted average time of when cash flows are received, then the greater it is, the more sensitive is the bond's price to changes in yield.

Lastly, we offer comparative statics regarding modified duration, MD, without proof.

$$\frac{\partial MD}{\partial r^C} < 0, \quad \text{and} \quad \frac{\partial MD}{\partial y} < 0. \qquad (13.3)$$

Both are logical. The greater the coupon rate, then the larger is the fraction of the bond's value represented by the coupon payments relative to the face value. Moving a greater fraction of a bond to earlier periods (and away from the maturity date) reduces the bond's relative price sensitivity to changes in yield. Also, regarding the second result of expression (13.3), we have seen that the bond's relative price sensitivity per change in absolute yield is decreasing in yield. Finally, regarding the impact of time to maturity on modified duration, $\frac{\partial MD}{\partial T}$, it is generally positive, though there are exceptions. The generally positive result is intuitive, as we have seen that a bond's relative price sensitivity to an increase in absolute yield is increasing in time to maturity, T.

13.2 Convexity

Regarding the price-yield curve, duration captures the slope, as modified duration equals $MD = -\frac{1}{P_0^B}\frac{\partial P_0^B}{\partial y}$ for fixed coupon bonds, and Macaulay duration equals $MaD = MD(1+\frac{y}{2})$. We now turn our attention to the second derivative which captures the curvature of the price-yield curve.

---

[3] As neither P_0^B nor $1+\frac{y}{2}$ is not a function of index t, they may be passed through the summation over t.

As a reminder, a convex function is one whose second derivative is positive. As previously shown, the price-yield curve for a fixed coupon bond is convex. Consistent with duration, where we divide slope by initial price to capture relative price sensitivity, **convexity** is defined by $Conv \equiv \frac{1}{P_0^B}\frac{\partial^2 P_0^B}{\partial y^2}$. For a fixed coupon bond, this is obviously positive, as we have shown that $\frac{\partial^2 P_0^B}{\partial y^2} > 0$. It is straightforward to show that

$$\frac{\partial^2 P_0^B}{\partial y^2} = \frac{P_0^B}{(1+\frac{y}{2})^2}\sum_{t=1}^{2T}\frac{t}{2}\left(\frac{t+1}{2}\right)w_{\frac{t}{2}}. \tag{13.4}$$

Hence

$$Conv \equiv \frac{1}{P_0^B}\frac{\partial^2 P_0^B}{\partial y^2} = \frac{1}{(1+\frac{y}{2})^2}\sum_{t=1}^{2T}\frac{t}{2}\left(\frac{t+1}{2}\right)w_{\frac{t}{2}}. \tag{13.5}$$

In general, convexity may be desired by an investor. Consider figure 13.2. Two bonds have been chosen whereby their price-yield curves touch, but other than at this one point (5%, $1000), the price of bond A is everywhere greater than that of bond B. Bond A has parameters $F = \$353.27$, $T = 50$ years, $r^C = 15\%$ and $m = 2$. Bond B has $F = \$2303.64$, $T = 16.90$ years, $r^C = 0\%$ and $m = 2$. Note that both bonds have a price of $1000 when $y = 5\%$. However, at any other yield to maturity, $y^A \neq y^B \Leftrightarrow P^A > P^B$. Consider $y^A = y^B = 5\%$ as the starting point. Then if market rates decrease, driving both bonds' yields downward, then A's price increases more than does B's. Also, if market rates increase, driving both bonds' yields upward, then A's price decreases less than does B's.

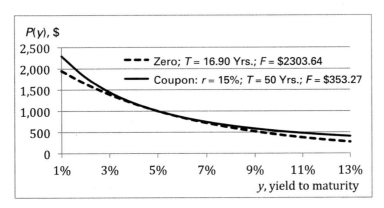

Figure 13.2 Convexity is desirable

The above paragraph might lead one to wonder why an investor would purchase B versus A. Consider the case where $y^A = y^B = 13\%$. In such case, if rates were to decrease such that both yields decreased to 12%, then bond B's price would increase more than that of A's price. Analogously, starting at $y^A = y^B = 1\%$, then for an increase in rates resulting in $y^A = y^B = 2\%$, bond A's price would fall more than would B's price. Summarizing, if yields of the two bonds are moving away from their point of commonality ($y = 5\%$ in the case of figure 13.2), then A's price change is favorable compared to that of B. However, as yields move toward this point of commonality, A's price change is the less favorable of the two.[4]

Lastly, we offer without proof the following comparative statics regarding convexity, $Conv$.

$$\frac{\partial Conv}{\partial r^C} < 0, \quad \frac{\partial Conv}{\partial y} < 0, \quad \text{and} \quad \frac{\partial Conv}{\partial T} > 0. \tag{13.6}$$

The first two results are identical to the respective comparative statics with respect to modified duration. Regarding the third, recall that MD is generally increasing in T, whereas $Conv$ is strictly increasing. Thus, these two results with respect to time to maturity are generally similar. In short, bonds with high (low) duration tend to also have high (low) convexity.

13.3 Price-yield Approximations

Consider a Taylor series expansion of $P^B(y)$ about initial yield, y_0.[5]

$$\begin{aligned}
P^B(y_1) &= \sum_{n=0}^{\infty} \frac{1}{n!} (\Delta y)^n \frac{\partial^n P^B(y_0)}{\partial y^n} \\
&= P^B(y_0) + \frac{1}{1!} (\Delta y)^1 \frac{\partial P^B(y_0)}{\partial y} + \frac{1}{2!} (\Delta y)^2 \frac{\partial^2 P^B(y_0)}{\partial y^2} \\
&\quad + \sum_{n=3}^{\infty} \frac{1}{n!} (\Delta y)^n \frac{\partial^n P^B(y_0)}{\partial y^n},
\end{aligned} \tag{13.7}$$

where y_0 is the current yield to maturity, y_1 is a yield to maturity "close to" y_0 where an estimate of P^B is desired, $\Delta y \equiv y_1 - y_0$, $P^B(y_0)$ is $P^B(y)$ evaluated at y_0, and $P^B(y_1)$ is $P^B(y)$ evaluated at y_1.[6]

For small Δy, terms become progressively smaller due to the $(\Delta y)^n$ factors. Indeed, for sufficiently small Δy, terms beyond the second order are so small that they

---

[4] Parameters other than convexity may make bond B more attractive than bond A for some investors. These include maturity, coupon rate, timing of cash flows, etc... all of which may factor into portfolio decisions.

[5] We define $0! = 1$ and $\frac{\partial^0 P^B(y_0)}{\partial y^0} = P^B(y_0)$.

[6] Analogously, $\frac{\partial P^B(y_0)}{\partial y}$ is $\frac{\partial P^B(y)}{\partial y}$ evaluated at y_0, $\frac{\partial P^B(y_1)}{\partial y}$ is $\frac{\partial P^B(y)}{\partial y}$ evaluated at y_1, and higher order derivatives are analogously interpreted. Also, $n! = 1 \times 2 \times 3 \times ... \times n$.

may be ignored in practice. Thus, we can approximate expression (13.7) via[7]

$$P^B(y_1) \approx P^B(y_0) + \Delta y \frac{\partial P^B(y_0)}{\partial y} + \frac{(\Delta y)^2}{2} \frac{\partial^2 P^B(y_0)}{\partial y^2}$$
$$= P^B(y_0)\left[1 - (MD)\Delta y + (Conv)\frac{(\Delta y)^2}{2}\right]. \qquad (13.8)$$

We call expression (13.8) our **second order estimate** of the price-yield curve.

We can also consider a simpler **first order estimate**, expression (13.9),

$$P^B(y_1) \approx P^B(y_0)\left[1 - (MD)\Delta y\right]. \qquad (13.9)$$

Consider figure 13.3, where we show an actual price-yield curve, a first order estimate per expression (13.9) and a second order estimate per expression (13.8). For this bond, $T = 100$ years, $F = \$1000$, $r^C = 3\%$ and $m = 2$. Obviously, the first order estimate is linear (i.e., constant slope) and the second order estimate has positive convexity (positive second derivative). By design, both estimates match the price-yield curve exactly at the current pair of ordinates, $(y_0, P^B(y_0))$, assumed to be $(3\%, \$1000)$. Not only do both estimates match $P^B(y_0)$, but both match $\frac{\partial P^B(y_0)}{\partial y}$. As the slopes of both estimates match that of the price-yield curve at y_0, then for small changes in yield, both estimates deviate very little from the actual curve, as desired. Additionally, the second order estimate matches the convexity of the actual price-yield curve at y_0, $\frac{1}{P^B}\frac{\partial^2 P^B(y_0)}{\partial y^2}$. Hence, the second order estimate, which matches *both* the slope and convexity of the actual curve at y_0, deviates less from the actual curve than does the first order estimate, which *only* matches the slope of the actual curve at y_0. For examples, at $y = 2\%$ and at $y = 4\%$, i.e, $\Delta y = -1\%$ and $+1\%$, respectively, the second order estimate is visibly much closer to the actual price-yield curve than is the first order estimate.

Adding more Taylor series terms (third order, fourth order, etc...) to the price-yield curve approximation decreases the magnitude of the estimate's error, i.e., the magnitude of difference between actual curve and estimate. However, practitioners often find the second order estimate sufficiently accurate, especially for cases of relatively small magnitude of Δy. Also note that the first order estimate always underestimates the price $P^B(y_1)$, $\forall y_1 \neq y_0$, *regardless* of the sign of $\Delta y = y_1 - y_0$. Regarding the error

---
[7]The first line can be rewritten as

$$P^B(y_1) \approx P^B(y_0)\left[1 - \left(-\frac{1}{P^B(y_0)}\frac{\partial P^B(y_0)}{\partial y}\right)\Delta y + \left(\frac{1}{P^B(y_0)}\frac{\partial^2 P^B(y_0)}{\partial y^2}\right)\frac{(\Delta y)^2}{2}\right].$$

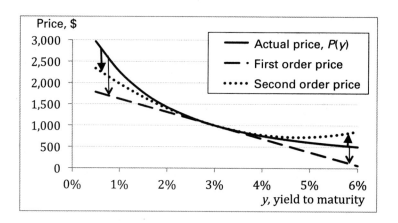

Figure 13.3 Price-yield curve approximations

of the second order estimate, that shown in figure 13.3 is typical; for small $\Delta y < 0$ ($\Delta y > 0$), the estimate is slightly below (above) the actual price-yield curve.

13.4 Effective Duration and Effective Convexity

In utilizing expression (13.8), one needs modified duration, MD, and convexity, $Conv$. For some some bonds, these may be difficult to calculate, e.g., bonds with embedded options. For bonds whose cash flows are variable (i.e., not fixed), one cannot use expressions (13.2) and (13.5) for modified duration and convexity, respectively. Thus, one may resort to discrete approximations, similar (but different) to those used in the previous chapter.

First consider a discrete approximation of modified duration ($MD = -\frac{1}{P}\frac{\partial P}{\partial y}$), called **effective duration, ED**, where

$$ED = -\frac{1}{P^B(y_0)}\frac{\Delta P^B(y)}{\Delta y} = -\frac{1}{P^B(y_0)}\frac{P^B(y_0 + \Delta y) - P^B(y_0 - \Delta y)}{(y_0 + \Delta y) - (y_0 - \Delta y)}$$
$$= \frac{1}{P^B(y_0)}\frac{P^B(y_0 - \Delta y) - P^B(y_0 + \Delta y)}{2\Delta y}, \qquad (13.10)$$

where $\Delta y > 0$ is "small" relative to the current yield to maturity, y_0, e.g., $\Delta y = 0.01\%$. Of course, for a fixed coupon bond, $ED > 0$.

Figure 13.4 shows a graphical interpretation of effective duration.[8] Consider the solid line segment connecting points $(y_0 + \Delta y, P(y_0 + \Delta y))$ and $(y_0 - \Delta y, P(y_0 - \Delta y))$. The negative of the slope of this line divided by $P(y_0)$ equals the effective duration. Also note the similarly negatively sloped dashed line segment that runs through the point $(y_0, P(y_0))$. The negative of the slope of this dashed line segment divided by $P(y_0)$

---

[8] In parts of this chapter, including figure 13.4, we suppress superscript B for notational ease.

equals modified duration, i.e., that which we attempt to replicate via our discrete approximation, effective duration. In figure 13.4, the careful observer will note that the slope of the dashed line segment is slightly greater (i.e., less negative) than the slope of the solid line segment. This is due to the fact that the convexity of the price-yield curve is decreasing in yield. However, as one can visualize, in the limit as $\Delta y \to 0$, then the limit of the slope of the solid line segment is that of the dashed line segment. In short, the limit of effective duration as $\Delta y \to 0$ is modified duration. Hence one should use very small Δy in calculating effective duration.

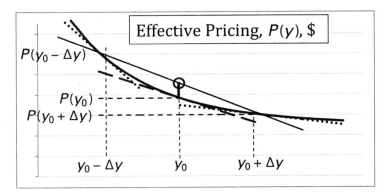

Figure 13.4 Effective duration and effective convexity

Now consider a discrete approximation of convexity ($Conv = \frac{1}{P}\frac{\partial^2 P}{\partial y^2}$), called **effective convexity, EC**, where

$$
\begin{aligned}
EC &= \frac{1}{P^B(y_0)} \frac{\Delta}{\Delta y}\left(\frac{\Delta P^B(y)}{\Delta y}\right) \\
&= \frac{1}{P^B(y_0)} \frac{\frac{P^B(y_0+\Delta y)-P^B(y_0)}{(y_0+\Delta y)-y_0} - \frac{P^B(y_0)-P^B(y_0-\Delta y)}{y_0-(y_0-\Delta y)}}{\Delta y} \\
&= \frac{1}{P^B(y_0)} \frac{P^B(y_0+\Delta y)+P^B(y_0-\Delta y)-2P^B(y_0)}{(\Delta y)^2} \\
&= \frac{2}{P^B(y_0)(\Delta y)^2}\left[\frac{P^B(y_0+\Delta y)+P^B(y_0-\Delta y)}{2} - P^B(y_0)\right]. \quad (13.11)
\end{aligned}
$$

The first two lines of expression (13.11) show that effective convexity is the difference in slopes of the price-yield curve at two points that frame the initial price-yield point, $(y_0, P^B(y_0))$, divided by the initial price and by one half the difference in the two framing yields, $\frac{2\Delta y}{2} = \Delta y$. The third line of the expression is perhaps the simplest to use in performing the calculation of EC. However, we add the fourth and final line of expression (13.11) as it has a nice graphical interpretation. In figure 13.4, note the short vertical line segment with a circle surrounding the top of it. This distance is precisely that captured by the terms in square brackets in the fourth line of expression (13.11), $\frac{P^B(y_0+\Delta y)+P^B(y_0-\Delta y)}{2} - P^B(y_0)$. The average of $P^B(y_0 + \Delta y)$ and $P^B(y_0 - \Delta y)$ is the top of the vertical line segment, whereas $P^B(y_0)$ is the bottom. It is obvious that the greater the curvature of the price-yield curve, the greater is this difference, i.e., the greater is the effective convexity, all else equal.[9]

With our estimates for effective duration and effective convexity, we can use them in our price-yield approximations, replacing modified duration and convexity, respectively. Hence, using expression (13.8), our second order approximation becomes

$$P^B(y_1) \approx P^B(y_0) \left[1 - (ED)\Delta y + (EC)\frac{(\Delta y)^2}{2}\right]. \quad (13.12)$$

Next, using expression (13.9), our first order approximation of the price-yield curve becomes

$$P^B(y_1) \approx P^B(y_0) \left[1 - (ED)\Delta y\right]. \quad (13.13)$$

13.5 Empirical Duration

For a particularly complex portfolio, one may find it difficult to calculate not only modified duration and convexity but also their respective effective equivalents, effective duration and effective convexity. Thus, one may resort to an empirical approach.

Consider a first order approximation to the price-yield curve, expression (13.9). Hence we need an estimate for $MD = -\frac{1}{P^B}\frac{\partial P^B}{\partial y} = -\frac{\partial \ln(P^B)}{\partial y}$. Consider a regression of the log of historical prices on yields, or

$$\ln P_t^B = \alpha^B + \beta^B y_t + \epsilon_t. \quad (13.14)$$

We interpret the slope coefficient as $\beta^B = \frac{\partial \ln(P^B)}{\partial y}$. Hence comparing this to $MD = -\frac{\partial \ln(P^B)}{\partial y}$, then **empirical duration**, EmD, equals $-\beta^B$, the negative of the slope coefficient in regression (13.14).

Substituting this for MD into the first order approximation, expression (13.9) becomes

$$P^B(y_1) \approx P^B(y_0) \left[1 - (EmD)\Delta y\right]. \quad (13.15)$$

---

[9]Indeed, consider a special case. If the curve were a straight line, then $\frac{P^B(y_0+\Delta y)+P^B(y_0-\Delta y)}{2} - P^B(y_0)$ would equal zero.

13.6 Other Price-yield Metrics

Before leaving this chapter, we offer some common definitions used in the bond world to address bond price elasticity. First, with respect to yield, a **basis point** equals 0.0001, or 0.01%. The **price value of a basis point, PVBP**, also called the **dollar value of an 01, DV01**, is the negative of the change in value given a one basis point increase in yield. **Dollar duration** is the negative of the change in value for a quoted increase in yield. Hence $PVBP = DV01$ are special cases of dollar duration where $\Delta y = 1$ basis point. Note that these metrics are all measured in dollars, as they are metrics of absolute changes in value, $\Delta V = -[V(y_0 + 0.01\%) - V(y_0)]$. These are in contrast to the dimensionless modified duration, which measures a relative change in value, $\frac{\Delta V}{V} = \frac{-[V(y_0+0.01\%)-V(y_0)]}{V(y_0)}$.

Problems

1. A semi-annual fixed coupon bond has a face value of $1000, coupon rate of 8%, yield to maturity of 4% and time to maturity of 3 years. What is this bond's price?

2. Calculate the price of this bond for a yield of 3.99%, and calculate the price of this bond for a yield of 4.01%.

3. Continuing, what is the difference in prices for the 0.01% decrease in yield, i.e., what is the difference $P(3.99\%) - P(4\%)$? Is it positive or negative?

What is the difference in prices for the 0.01% increase in yield, i.e., what is the difference $P(4.01\%) - P(4\%)$? Is it positive or negative?

Of these two differences, which has the greater magnitude, the yield increase or the yield decrease? Explain the result.

4. For the bond in problem 1, what is this bond's Macaulay duration, in years? Interpret this result.

5. What is the modified duration of the bond in problem 1?

6. What is the convexity of the bond in problem 1?

7. Using a first-order approximation of the price-yield curve for the bond in problem 1, what is the new price when the yield changes: (a) to 3.99%? (b) to 4.01%?

8. Compare the results of problems 2 and 7. Specifically, which is greater: the first-order price approximation or the actual price, given a change in yield: (a) to 3.99%? (b) to 4.01%? Explain these results.

9. Using a second-order approximation of the price-yield curve, what is the new price when the yield changes: (a) to 3.99%? (b) to 4.01%?

For a yield of 3.99%, which magnitude of error, $|P^{estimate} - P^{actual}|$, is smaller: the first order error or the second order error?

For a yield of 4.01%, which magnitude of error, $|P^{estimate} - P^{actual}|$, is smaller: the first order error or the second order error?

Chapter 14: Pricing Bonds Between Coupon Dates

Referring back to the third line of expression (11.11), a fixed coupon bond may be considered as a security which entitles the owner to a single cash flow of face value F paid at maturity, date T, plus an annuity of coupon payments, the last of which is paid at date T. However, by definition of an annuity, each cash flow must arrive at the end of its respective period. Hence as semi-annual bonds pay coupons twice per year, the final line in expression (11.11) is only valid two days per year.[1] We *cannot* use the expression for the other 363 days per year. Our goal in this chapter is to understand a bond's price path between coupon dates. Furthermore, we examine how the bond market attempts to remove the impact of a bond's coupon cycle upon its price so that investors may compare prices of different bonds, regardless of differences in timing of cash flows.

The astute reader may have noticed that in figure 12.2 we used discrete points (squares, traingles, diamonds) rather than continuous lines in showing the bonds' march to maturity. The reason is because these points correspond to anniversary dates where future coupons are exactly whole periods away. The reason we did not, and *cannot*, simply connect these points with a continuous line is because the price path, perhaps counter-intuitively, is *not* a smooth interpolation of these points, despite holding fixed the yield to maturity.

14.1 A New Time-line

We introduce a variable that represents the fraction of the current semi-annual period that has passed, $f \in [0, 1)$, as illustrated in figure 14.1. As always, dates (in

---

[1] Once again, price is *not* a function of yield to maturity, but rather the latter is a function of the former. Indeed, we hold yield to maturity fixed in this chapter, focusing instead on the passage of time, i.e., on dates between coupon payments.

years), denoted via vertical hash marks, are labeled on the top of the time-line. Periods 1, 2, ..., $2T$ are noted below the time-line. Cash flows are subscripted via date of occurrence. As drawn in figure 14.1, 40% of the first period has passed, so $f = 0.4$ and $1 - f = 0.6$. Hence the first coupon will be received $1 - f$ periods from now, equal to $\frac{1-f}{2}$ years from now, i.e., in approximately $\frac{0.6}{2}(365) = 110$ days.[2] Analogously, subsequent coupons will be paid $2 - f$, $3 - f$, etc... periods from now. Finally, the final coupon plus face value will be received $2T - f$ periods (half-years) from now.

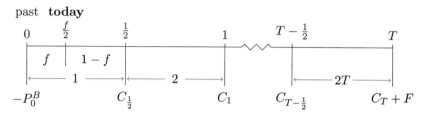

Figure 14.1 A bond between coupon dates

Throughout this text, we have defined date $t = 0$ as now, the current time. Only for this chapter of the book do we deviate from this convention. We presently define date $t = 0$ as the date of issuance of the bond.[3] Thus, fraction f of the current period has passed, so today is date $t = \frac{f}{2} \geqslant 0$. So while the bond still matures at date T, it is currently $2(T - \frac{f}{2}) = 2T - f$ periods from now.[4]

14.2 Dirty Price

Modifying the first line of expression (11.11) to account for the passage of fraction f of the current period, then[5]

$$P^B(f) = \frac{F}{\left(1+\frac{y}{2}\right)^{2T-f}} + \sum_{t=1}^{2T} \frac{C_{\frac{t}{2}}}{\left(1+\frac{y}{2}\right)^{t-f}} = \sum_{t=1}^{2T} \frac{CF_{\frac{t}{2}}}{\left(1+\frac{y}{2}\right)^{t-f}}$$

$$= \left(1+\frac{y}{2}\right)^f \sum_{t=1}^{2T} \frac{CF_{\frac{t}{2}}}{\left(1+\frac{y}{2}\right)^t}, \qquad (14.1)$$

where $CF_{t/2} = C_{t/2}$ at the end of periods $t \in \{1, 2, ..., 2T - 1\}$, and $CF_T = C_T + F$. Equation (14.1) gives us the bond's **dirty price** or **invoice price** as a function of f,

---

[2] So bond issuance was $f = 0.4$ half-years ago $\approx \frac{0.4}{2}(365) = 73$ days ago.
[3] Or once a coupon is paid, date $t = 0$ continually updates and becomes the date of the most recently paid coupon.
[4] Consistent with our updating of $t = 0$ as coupons are paid, $2T$ updates and equals the number of remaining periods until maturity, including the current one regardless if it is whole or partial. In other words, updated $T = \frac{1}{2}$(remaining periods, including the current (partial) one).
[5] As $(1 + \frac{y}{2})^f$ is not a function of index t, it can be pulled out of the summation over index t.

i.e., as a function of time between coupon dates.[6]

When the bond is issued, $f = 0$, so $P^B(0) = \sum_{t=1}^{2T} \frac{CF_{t/2}}{(1+\frac{y}{2})^t}$, consistent with equation (11.11). Thus, equation (14.1) simplifies to

$$P^B(f) = \left(1 + \frac{y}{2}\right)^f P^B(0), \quad f \in [0, 1). \tag{14.2}$$

As $\frac{da^{f(x)}}{dx} = a^{f(x)} \ln(a) \frac{df(x)}{dx}$, then from equation (14.2),

$$\frac{\partial P^B(f)}{\partial f} = \ln\left(1 + \frac{y}{2}\right) P^B(f) > 0, \quad \text{and}$$

$$\frac{\partial^2 P^B(f)}{\partial f^2} = \left[\ln\left(1 + \frac{y}{2}\right)\right]^2 P^B(f) > 0. \tag{14.3}$$

Within a semi-annual period bounded by coupon dates, as time passes (i.e., as $f \in [0,1)$ increases), then the bond's dirty price is increasing ($\frac{\partial P^B(f)}{\partial f} > 0$) and convex ($\frac{\partial^2 P^B(f)}{\partial f^2} > 0$).

Now let's consider the bond's dirty price path around the coupon payment. One second before the first coupon is paid, the price is

$$P^B = C_{\frac{1}{2}} + \frac{C_1}{\left(1+\frac{y}{2}\right)^1} + \frac{C_{\frac{3}{2}}}{\left(1+\frac{y}{2}\right)^2} + \ldots + \frac{C_T + F}{\left(1+\frac{y}{2}\right)^{2T-1}}, \tag{14.4}$$

where we have obviously ignored the impact of discounting of cash flows over the next second of time.[7] Two seconds later, i.e., one second after $C_{1/2}$ is paid, then ignoring the impact of discounting of cash flows over the one second of time since the payment of the first coupon, then

$$P^B = \frac{C_1}{\left(1+\frac{y}{2}\right)^1} + \frac{C_{\frac{3}{2}}}{\left(1+\frac{y}{2}\right)^2} + \ldots + \frac{C_T + F}{\left(1+\frac{y}{2}\right)^{2T-1}}. \tag{14.5}$$

Comparing equations (14.4) and (14.5), the bond's price drops by the value of the coupon when it is paid. This discontinuity is comparable to the price drop of a share of stock once a cash dividend is paid.[8]

Let's summarize. Between coupon dates, the bond's dirty price increases at an ever increasing rate (i.e., is increasing and convex in time). Then, the instant when a coupon is paid, the bond's price drops by the amount of the coupon. Our variable

---
[6] As a reminder, price is determined by the market. Equation (14.1) then defines $y(P^B, f, CF_{\frac{t}{2}})$.
[7] We are also ignoring the time delay between when a coupon is "paid" (and thus no longer included as a claim to a new buyer of the bond) and when "received".
[8] The stock's price drop actually takes into account the average personal tax rate and happens on the ex-dividend date, but the concept is the same.

$f \in [0,1)$, which captures the passage of time, approaches one just before the coupon is paid, and then returns to zero as the coupon is paid, with the process starting over again.

In figure 14.2, we show the price path for three different bonds: a premium bond, a par bond and a discount bond. For each of the three, holding fixed the bond's yield to maturity, we show the dirty price path over the final three years, i.e., each matures at time $t = 3$ years in figure 14.2. For all three, $F = \$1000$, $r^C = 8\%$ and $m = 2$. The yields to maturity, held constant over these three years for all three bonds, are respectively, 2% for the premium bond, 8% for the par bond and 16% for the discount bond. These three bonds are the same three used in figure 12.2, where we illustrated march to maturity. While figure 12.2 shows the final 30 years of the three bonds, figure 14.2 shows the final 3 years. For each bond, we see a discontinuity of dirty price at each of the coupon dates, i.e., each half year. While it is obvious that the dirty price always increases between coupon dates, it is challenging to see convexity in figure 14.2. But indeed, the continuous segments are convex, i.e., have increasing slope. The three dotted curves shown are smooth interpolations of the two prices per year that exist one second after a coupon is paid.[9] Finally, note that regardless of yield, the dirty price converges to $C_T + F$ as the bond matures, or \$1040 in these examples, as this equals the final cash flow.

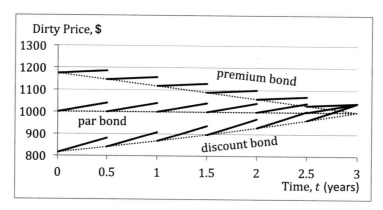

Figure 14.2 Dirty price path over time

14.3 Accrued Interest and Clean Price

Returning to figure 14.2 for a moment, the dirty price paths over time obviously

---

[9]The smooth dotted curves are generated by treating discrete variable T in the second and third lines of expression (11.11) as a continuous variable.

exhibits large negative jumps, each one equal to the amount of the coupons, when they are paid.[10] As bonds are issued throughout the year, it creates a challenge in comparing value of different bonds by simply observing their prices. Hence the bond world seeks a method to put bonds on an "apples to apples" basis by removing the impact of the cycling of prices as bonds pass through their coupon periods. This is the purpose of quoting a bond's clean price, discussed now.

In contrast to discontinuous dirty prices, we illustrated three smoothed dotted curves in figure 14.2 which interpolate the bond's prices immediately after coupons are paid, i.e., as f cycles back to zero from (slightly less than) one. Again, these three lines were calculated simply by treating time to maturity T as a continuous variable in the final line of expression (11.11). However, recall that this expression derives from the annuity formula, where by definition, T is the number of whole periods until maturity and each coupon must be received at the end of the corresponding period. Nonetheless, even though such a procedure smooths the coupon cycles, this is *not* used by the bond world.

In an attempt to mitigate the strong dependence of the bond's dirty price upon the value of f in the current coupon cycle, the bond world calculates **accrued interest**, **AI**, where

$$AI(f) = fC, \tag{14.6}$$

and where C is the next coupon to be paid. As $f \in [0,1)$, then $AI(f) \in [0,C)$. Quite simply, accrued interest uses a linear assignment of the current period's coupon. With AI in hand, the **clean price** or **quoted price** of the bond is

$$CP(f) = P^B(f) - AI(f) = P^B(f) - fC, \tag{14.7}$$

where $P^B(f)$ is the dirty price of the bond. So by quoting the clean price, the bond world attempts to remove the impact of the bond's current partial period upon its price. In other words, the clean price attempts to price the bond "as if" the coupon payments were full periods from today.

What does a bond's clean price path look like, and how well does it correspond to a smoothed interpolation comparable to the three dotted curves illustrated in figure 14.2?

First note that $AI(f) = fC$, $f \in [0,1)$, increases linearly over time, whereas the dirty price path is convex. So AI cannot possibly remove the impact of time passage

---

[10]It is obviously necessary that one know the coupon dates to calculate a bond's yield.

upon invoice price exactly. (As we'll see, accrued interest is in some sense an "oversimplification".) Next, at $f = 0$, then $AI(0) = 0$ means that $CP(0) = P^B(0)$, per equation (14.7). So the clean price and dirty price are equal at the bond's issuance and immediately after all coupon payments. Next, immediately before a coupon payment, as $f \to 1_-$, then $AI = C$ means that $CP(1_-) = P^B(1_-) - C$. But as we previously saw, one second prior to coupon payment, the bond's dirty price is C greater than it is two seconds later, i.e., after the coupon is paid. Hence just prior to coupon payment, the clean price approaches the dirty price that the bond will have a moment later. As this is also the clean price just after the coupon payment ($CP(0) = P^B(0)$), then the clean price path must be a continuous function. As such, accrued interest helps "smooth" the discontinuities of the dirty price path, which is desirable characteristic for a quoted price path.

Next, differentiating equation (14.7), then

$$\frac{\partial CP(f)}{\partial f} = \frac{\partial P^B(f)}{\partial f} - C \quad \text{and} \quad \frac{\partial^2 CP(f)}{\partial f^2} = \frac{\partial^2 P^B(f)}{\partial f^2} > 0, \quad (14.8)$$

$f \in (0, 1)$. So between coupon payments, the clean price is convex.

For simplicity, let's assume a par bond, or $y = r^C$. Hence when coupons are whole periods away, then $f = 0$, so $P^B(0) = CP(0) = F$. As we argued that the clean price path is convex between coupon dates, and as it returns to F each coupon date, then it must begin each period with a negative slope, reach a minimum at roughly mid-period, and then begin increasing to arrive back at F on the next coupon date. In figure 14.3, we show the clean price path for a par bond, where $y = r^C = 8\%$, for each day over the final three years of the bond until it matures. (In order to highlight the nature of the price path, we use a narrow range of prices in figure 14.3.) So for this par bond the maximum difference between face value F and clean price CP is only about

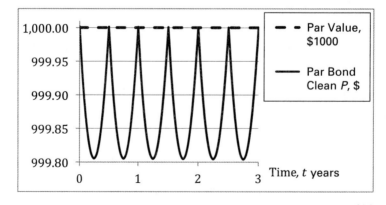

Figure 14.3 Clean price path for a par bond over time

$0.20.[11] Hence for a par bond, $CP(f) < F$, $\forall f \in (0,1)$. The clean price of a par bond is less than the face value for 363 days per year. In short, the simple calculation for accrued interest, $AI(f) = fC$, slightly *overstates* the difference between a bond's dirty price and a smoothed interpolation of prices that exist on anniversary coupon dates, comparable to the three dotted curves shown in figure 14.2. Thus, the clean price dips slightly below these smoothed interpolations between coupon dates.

Analogously, the clean price paths for both premium and discount bonds are continuous. Likewise, they are also convex in between coupon dates, i.e., $\forall f \in (0,1)$. Thus, though not shown in figure 14.2, the clean price paths for both premium and discount bonds touch the corresponding dotted smooth curves in figure 14.2 on coupon dates. In between coupon dates, the clean price paths dip slightly below the corresponding smooth curves, which are smoothed interpolations of prices that exist on anniversary coupon dates.[12]

It has been asserted that the difference between face value and clean price for a par bond between coupon dates is due to "the difference between the accrued interest and the present value of the accrued interest".[13] This is not correct. The difference is due to the difference between componded growth interest, used in determining the bond's dirty price, and simple growth interest, used to calculate accrued interest.

In figure 14.4, we consider the final coupon period of a par bond whose face value is $F = \$1000$ and whose yield to maturity equals the coupon rate of $y = r^C = 8\%$. The x−axis captures the fraction of final coupon period that has passed, f. The dotted curve shows the actual amount by which the clean price dips below the face value. (The maximum drop of approximately \$0.20 at about $f = 0.5$ is consistent with that shown in figure 14.3.) In contrast, the solid curve shows the difference between accrued interest and its present value. For the entire coupon period, the latter overstates the former by a factor of about two.

Clearly, the dip in clean price of a par bond below face value between coupon dates is not due to the difference between accrued interest and its present value. The dip is due to the difference between compounded growth interest and simple growth interest

---

[11]This is the same par bond as that shown in figure 14.2.

[12]As in the case of a par bond, the smoothed interpolations for premium and discount bonds are generated by treating time to maturity, T, as a continuous variable in the pricing formula of a fixed coupon bond where coupons are treated as an annuity of cash flows (second and third lines of expression (11.11)).

[13]*Introduction to Fixed Income Analytics*, Fabozzi, Frank J. and Steven V. Mann, 2001, Frank J. Fabozzi Associates.

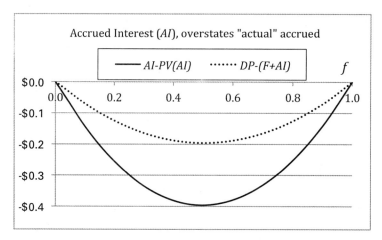

Figure 14.4 Explanation of deviation of par bond's clean price from face value

as follows. For a par bond, where $y = r^C$, equation (14.2) becomes $P^B(f) = F(1+\frac{y}{2})^f$, $f \in [0,1)$, as $P^B(0) = F$. Next, from equation (14.7), then $CP(f) = F(1+\frac{y}{2})^f - f(F\frac{r^C}{2})$. Hence, the difference between clean price and face value for a par bond is

$$CP(f) - F = \underbrace{F\left(1+\frac{y}{2}\right)^f}_{compounded} - \underbrace{F\left(1+f\frac{y}{2}\right)}_{simple} < 0, \forall f \in (0,1), \qquad (14.9)$$

assuming $y > 0$.[14] As compounded growth interest is less than simple growth interest for any positive duration of time of less than one full (6-month) period, i.e., for $f \in (0,1)$, then the par bond's clean price dips below the face value between coupon dates. It is this difference in interest growth calculations that accounts for the par bond's clean price dip between coupon dates, not negligence with respect to discounting. To drive this home, contrast the difference between a par bond's clean price and face value with that of accrued interest and it present value. The former is $CP(f) - F = F\{(1+\frac{y}{2})^f - (1+f\frac{y}{2})\}$, while the latter is $Ff\frac{y}{2}\{1 - (1+\frac{y}{2})^{-(1-f)}\}$. Clearly these two expressions differ.

Interestingly, we *generally* think of compounded growth interest, which considers "interest on interest", as being greater than simple growth interest, which only pays interest on the principle. Indeed, $(1+\frac{y}{2})^t - (1+t\frac{y}{2}) > 0, \forall t > 1$.[15] Of course, this expression equals zero for $t = 0$ and $t = 1$, corresponding to coupon dates. However, for a fractional period, $t \in (0,1)$, then this difference is *negative*, consistent with the dipping of the par bond's clean price below face value between coupon dates. Finally,

---

[14] The expression denoted "compounded" ("simple") in equation (14.9) equals compounded (simple) interest plus face value, F.

[15] This is simplified from $\{(1+\frac{y}{2})^t - 1\} - \{(1+t\frac{y}{2}) - 1\}$.

at any given point in time between coupon dates, while the actual difference between clean price and face value for a par bond is only roughly half of the difference between accrued interest and its present value, the magnitudes of differences discussed here are relatively small.

14.4 Theoretical Accrued Interest

Accrued interest, $AI(f) = fC$, serves the useful purpose of (imperfectly) removing the impact of coupon cycle upon quoted bond price. If the bond world wanted to *perfectly* account for the coupon cycle, then clean price or quoted price should be the diference between dirty price and the smoothed curve connecting the bond's price on coupon dates. We denote this difference as the **theoretical accrued interest**, *TAI*, where

$$TAI \equiv \sum_{t=1}^{2T} \frac{CF_{\frac{t}{2}}}{\left(1+\frac{y}{2}\right)^{t-f}} - F\left[\frac{1}{\left(1+\frac{y}{2}\right)^{2T-f}} + \frac{rC}{y}\left(1 - \frac{1}{\left(1+\frac{y}{2}\right)^{2T-f}}\right)\right], \quad (14.10)$$

$\forall f \in [0,1)$, where $CF_{\frac{t}{2}} = C_{\frac{t}{2}}$, $\forall t \in \{1, 2, ..., 2T-1\}$, and where $CF_T = F + C_T$. *TAI* perfectly removes the impact of coupon cycle upon clean price. The use of *TAI* would result in a smoothed clean price path, regardless of whether a bond is a par bond, a discount bond, or a premium bond, as illustrated in figure 14.5. Though the curvature is only slight, the clean price path using *TAI* is concave (convex) for a premium (discount) bond. Obviously, it has a constant value of F for a par bond, by design.

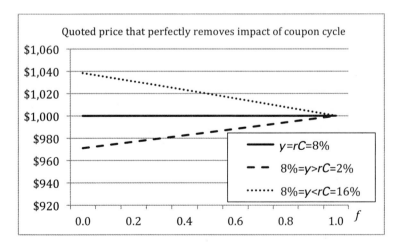

Figure 14.5 **Clean price path for bonds using theoretical accrued interest**

Computation of accrued interest, $AI(f) = fC$, is simpler than that of theoretical accrued interest, $TAI(f)$, given by expression (14.10). Considering the small magnitude of "error" in calculating accrued interest versus TAI, it is not surprising that the bond world chose the former. Nonetheless, in this age of computational power and speed, one wonders if movement to TAI might be advantageous, as it perfectly removes the impact of coupon cycle upon clean price. In summary, TAI is superior to AI in satisfying the intended goal of smoothing the bond's quoted price path.

Problems

1. A semi-annual fixed coupon bond has a face value of $1000, coupon rate of 8%, yield to maturity of 4% and time to maturity of 14 years. What is this bond's price? Is this a premium bond, par bond or discount bond?

2. Now assume the same bond in problem 1, but 3 months have passed. So now the time to maturity is 13.75 years. What is the bond's dirty price? What is its accrued interest? What is its clean price?

3. A semi-annual fixed coupon bond has a face value of $1000, coupon rate of 8%, yield to maturity of 12% and time to maturity of 14 years. What is this bond's price? Is this a premium bond, par bond or discount bond?

4. Now assume the same bond in problem 3, but 3 months have passed. So now the time to maturity is 13.75 years. What is the bond's dirty price? What is its accrued interest? What is its clean price?

5. A semi-annual fixed coupon bond has a face value of $1000, coupon rate of 8%, yield to maturity of 8% and time to maturity of 14 years. What is this bond's price? Is this a premium bond, par bond or discount bond?

6. Now assume the same bond in problem 5, but 3 months have passed. So now the time to maturity is 13.75 years. What is the bond's dirty price? What is its accrued interest? What is its clean price?

7. Regarding the bond in problem 6 (i.e., that of problem 5, but 3 months later, so time to maturity is 13.75 years), is the clean price greater than or less than or equal to the face value?

Given that it's a par bond, why does the clean price not equal the face value? More specifically, why is the clean price less than par, i.e, why is the clean price less than the face value of the bond?

Chapter 15. Rate and Yield Metrics

While yield to maturity is a useful metric of investor rate of return driven by the market, it is by definition an overall average return that depends on the bond's price, all cash flows, their amounts and timings. What we seek now are market-determined rates of return for *individual* cash flows received at specific points in time. From these so-called spot rates, we also calculate forward rates, those implied for future periods of time. Forward rates can be calculated for any future single period or multiple periods, beginning at any chosen time in the future. Afterwards, we return to other yield metrics, extending the concept of yield to maturity.

15.1 Spot Rates

Inspection of the definition of yield to maturity, equation (11.7), reveals that it is an overall average return that depends on a bond's price, all cash flows, their amounts and timings. Yield to maturity is a function of price, not the other way around; we don't use yield to discount cash flows. In order to calculate the intrinsic value of a security, we need appropriate discount rates. Specifically, we seek to develop a set of appropriate spot rates, one for each time duration from today corresponding to receipt of a cash flow at the end of the respective period. In short, we seek to derive discount factors, one for each individual cash flow depending upon the date of its receipt. We invoke a process called bootstrapping. Our inputs are parameters of U.S. Treasury securities, our proxies for risk-free securities. These inputs include prices, cash flows and their timings. To these spot rates, we can add appropriate premia to reflect the perceived level of cash flow riskiness.

Bootstrapping begins with calculation of the six-month spot rate and continues by calculating spot rates for ever increasing durations, one at a time. A US Treasury bill (T-bill) that matures in six months is a zero coupon bond. So its return to the investor is that which is implied by its price, $P_0^{0.5}$, which is discounted from the face value, $F_{0.5}$. The subscript on $P_0^{0.5}$ indicates that the price is as of today (i.e., the current price) and the superscript denotes the maturity date of the security, in 0.5 years. So

$$P_0^{0.5} = \frac{F_{0.5}}{1 + \frac{y_{0.5}}{2}}, \quad \text{and} \quad P_0^{0.5} = \frac{F_{0.5}}{1 + \frac{SR_{0.5}}{2}}, \tag{15.1}$$

where the first equality defines yield to maturity of the six-month T-bill, $y_{0.5}$, and the second defines the six-month spot rate, $SR_{0.5}$. Comparing these two equalities, then $SR_{0.5} = y_{0.5} = 2[\frac{F_{0.5}}{P_0^{0.5}} - 1]$. Note that the subscript on the spot rate indexes the date of receipt of the corresponding cash flow, in years.[1]

Analogously, a one-year T-bill is also a zero coupon bond (i.e., pure discount bond), so

$$P_0^1 = \frac{F_1}{\left(1 + \frac{y_1}{2}\right)^2}, \quad \text{and} \quad P_0^1 = \frac{F_1}{\left(1 + \frac{SR_1}{2}\right)^2}. \tag{15.2}$$

Comparing these two equalities, then $SR_1 = y_1 = 2[(\frac{F_1}{P_0^1})^{1/2} - 1]$. Before continuing, note that we have shown the calculations for $y_{0.5}$ and y_1 in equations (15.1) and (15.2), respectively. We do this to simply make the point that for the six-month and one-year zero coupon US T-securities, $y_{0.5} = SR_{0.5}$ and $y_1 = SR_1$. However, we stress that spot rates are *not* functions of yields to maturity.

Moving on to determining $SR_{1.5}$, we use an 18-month T-note, which pays fixed coupons. So while the first two spot rates, based on zero coupon T-bills, were trivially calculated as $SR_{0.5} = y_{0.5}$ and $SR_1 = y_1$, respectively, the calculations of longer term spot rates, which are based on coupon-paying treasury securities, are a bit more complex. Hence,

$$\begin{aligned}
P_0^{1.5} &= \sum_{t=1}^{3} \frac{CF_{\frac{t}{2}}}{\left(1 + \frac{y_{1.5}}{2}\right)^t} = \frac{C_{0.5}^{1.5}}{\left(1 + \frac{y_{1.5}}{2}\right)^1} + \frac{C_1^{1.5}}{\left(1 + \frac{y_{1.5}}{2}\right)^2} + \frac{C_{1.5}^{1.5} + F_{1.5}}{\left(1 + \frac{y_{1.5}}{2}\right)^3}, \\
&= \sum_{t=1}^{3} \frac{CF_{\frac{t}{2}}}{\left(1 + \frac{SR_{\frac{t}{2}}}{2}\right)^t} \\
&= \frac{C_{0.5}^{1.5}}{\left(1 + \frac{SR_{0.5}}{2}\right)^1} + \frac{C_1^{1.5}}{\left(1 + \frac{SR_1}{2}\right)^2} + \frac{C_{1.5}^{1.5} + F_{1.5}}{\left(1 + \frac{SR_{1.5}}{2}\right)^3},
\end{aligned} \tag{15.3}$$

where $C_{t/2}^T$ is the fixed coupon associated with the US Treasury security that matures at date T ($T = 1.5$ years in this case) and is paid at date $\frac{t}{2}$. Note that the first line of expression (15.3) is unnecessary in calculating $SR_{1.5}$, as we do not calculate spot rates

---

[1] Consistent with other rates and yields in the bond world, spot rates are quoted as *APrs*, compounded semi-annually.

from yields to maturity. However, we want to drive home the point that there exists a single yield for a security, $y_{1.5}$ for this 18-month Treasury note. In contrast, spots rates correspond to a specific time of receipt of a cash flow; thus, they are indexed with date $\frac{t}{2}$ per the final two lines of expression (15.3). In summary, a yield to maturity corresponds *only* to the specific bond from which it is calculated. In contrast, a spot rate corresponds to *any* (risk-free) cash flow received at the point in time for which it is calculated.

Let's continue with our calculation of the 18-month spot rate, $SR_{1.5}$. As $SR_{0.5}$ and SR_1 have been previously calculated, then we can rearrange the final line of expression (15.3) to solve for the next spot rate, where

$$SR_{1.5} = 2\left(\left[\frac{C_{1.5}^{1.5} + F_{1.5}}{P_0^{1.5} - \left(\frac{C_{0.5}^{1.5}}{\left(1+\frac{SR_{0.5}}{2}\right)^1} + \frac{C_1^{1.5}}{\left(1+\frac{SR_1}{2}\right)^2}\right)}\right]^{\frac{1}{3}} - 1\right). \quad (15.4)$$

Generalizing, one can calculate the **spot rate**, SR_T, for all times to receipt of cash flow $T \in \{0.5, 1, 1.5, 2, ...\}$, used to discount any single risk-free cash flow (CF_T) received T years from today, or $2T$ six-month periods from today. For the general case of spot rate SR_T, from[2]

$$P_0^T = \sum_{t=1}^{2T} \frac{CF_{\frac{t}{2}}}{\left(1+\frac{SR_{\frac{t}{2}}}{2}\right)^t} = \sum_{t=1}^{2T-1} \frac{C_{t/2}^T}{\left(1+\frac{SR_{\frac{t}{2}}}{2}\right)^t} + \frac{C_T^T + F_T}{\left(1+\frac{SR_T}{2}\right)^{2T}}, \quad (15.5)$$

we can rearrange it to calculate

$$SR_T = 2\left(\left[\frac{C_T^T + F_T}{P_0^T - \left(\sum_{t=1}^{2T-1} \frac{C_{t/2}^T}{\left(1+\frac{SR_{\frac{t}{2}}}{2}\right)^t}\right)}\right]^{\frac{1}{2T}} - 1\right). \quad (15.6)$$

As the first $2T - 1$ spot rates have been calculated at this point in the bootstrapping process, we can solve explicitly for the value of SR_T. Continuing the bootstrapping

---

[2] Again note that $P_0^T = \sum_{t=1}^{2T} \frac{CF_{t/2}}{(1+\frac{y_T}{2})^t}$ has only one "discount" rate, y_T, by definition of yield. In contrast, there exists $2T$ spot rates, one for each date corresponding to the end of each period, i.e., $SR_{0.5}$, SR_1, ..., SR_T.

process in this manner, we can calculate spot rates as far into the future as the date corresponding to the existing fixed coupon US Treasury bond with the longest time to maturity.

Equation (15.6) makes it obvious that a spot rate is a type of geometric mean rate, as it has the structure $\frac{SR_T}{2} = [\frac{V_T}{V_0}]^{\frac{1}{2T}} - 1$, consistent with a geometric mean. Translated, the number of periods is $2T$, and the final value V_T is the final cash flow, $F_T + C_T^T$. The initial value is the initial price, adjusted for the summation of the present value of interim cash flows received before date T, i.e., $V_0 = P_0^T - \sum_{t=1}^{2T-1} \frac{C_{t/2}^T}{(1+\frac{SR_{t/2}}{2})^t}$.

In summary, we can discount any given risk-free cash flow by the appropriate risk-free spot rate. These can be converted to the appropriate risky spot rates by adding risk premia, or $SR_{t/2}^r = SR_{t/2} + \sum_{n=1}^{N} \beta^n (RP^n)$, $n \in \{1, 2, ..., N\}$, for N risk factors. Thus, for *any* given security, it may be valued via

$$IV^f = \sum_{t=1}^{2T} \frac{CF_{t/2}^f}{\left(1+\frac{SR_{t/2}}{2}\right)^t}, \quad \text{and} \quad IV^r = \sum_{t=1}^{2T} \frac{CF_{t/2}^r}{\left(1+\frac{SR_{t/2}^r}{2}\right)^t}, \quad (15.7)$$

where the first corresponds to risk-free securities and the second to risky securities.

15.2 Forward Rates

From previously calculated spot rates, we now turn to forward rates, those implied for future periods of time. We can calculate such rates for both any future single six-month period as well as any future multi-period duration of time.

15.2.1 Single Period Forward Rates

We denote a single six-month period forward rate as $_{t-0.5}f_t$, expressed as an APr compounded semi-annually, where the leading subscript $t-0.5$ (lagging subscript t) refers to the beginning (ending) date of the period, expressed in years. So the effective six-month forward rate is $\frac{_{t-0.5}f_t}{2}$.

Consider the first period. A cash flow received six months from now is discounted to today via division by $(1+\frac{SR_{0.5}}{2})^1$, or, by definition of the first period forward rate, by $(1+\frac{_0f_{0.5}}{2})^1$. So comparing these two expressions, $_0f_{0.5} = SR_{0.5}$.[3]

Now consider the forward rate for the second six-month period, $_{0.5}f_1$. A cash flow received one year from now is discounted to today via division by $(1+\frac{SR_1}{2})^2$. Equivalently, we can discount it over the second period by $(1+\frac{_{0.5}f_1}{2})^1$ and over the

---
[3] One can think of spot rates having a leading superscript of 0, as spot rates always correspond to a duration of time that begins today, from $t=0$.

first period by $(1+\frac{SR_{0.5}}{2})^1$. Specifically, $_{0.5}f_1$ is defined by determining $(1+\frac{_{0.5}f_1}{2})^1$, the appropriate discount factor over the second period implied by spot rates. So this latter strategy discounts CF_1 to today by dividing by $(1+\frac{SR_{0.5}}{2})(1+\frac{_{0.5}f_1}{2})$. Equating the two expressions used discount CF_1 two periods backward in time to today,

$$\left(1+\frac{SR_1}{2}\right)^2 = \left(1+\frac{SR_{0.5}}{2}\right)\left(1+\frac{_{0.5}f_1}{2}\right). \tag{15.8}$$

Rearranging equation (15.8), then

$$_{0.5}f_1 = 2\left(\frac{\left(1+\frac{SR_1}{2}\right)^2}{\left(1+\frac{SR_{0.5}}{2}\right)^1}-1\right). \tag{15.9}$$

Generalizing, consider a cash flow received at date t, which is $2t$ six-month periods from now. Its present value may be calculated by dividing by

$$\left(1+\frac{SR_t}{2}\right)^{2t} = \left(1+\frac{SR_{t-0.5}}{2}\right)^{2t-1}\left(1+\frac{_{t-0.5}f_t}{2}\right). \tag{15.10}$$

Rearranging equation (15.10), then the **single six-month period forward rate**, which begins at date $t-0.5$ (in years) and ends at date t (in years), is calculated via

$$_{t-0.5}f_t = 2\left(\frac{\left(1+\frac{SR_t}{2}\right)^{2t}}{\left(1+\frac{SR_{t-0.5}}{2}\right)^{2t-1}}-1\right), \tag{15.11}$$

where $_{t-0.5}f_t$ is expressed as an APr, compounded semi-annually. So $\frac{_{t-0.5}f_t}{2}$ is an effective six-month period forward rate beginning at date $t-0.5$ years from today.

For a US Treasury security of any given maturity, we know how to calculate its yield to maturity. Thus, plotting calculated yields to maturity versus times to maturity for T-securities over a wide range of maturities results in the so-called **yield curve**. For these same T-securities, we can also calculate spot rates and from these, forward rates. Most of the time, the US Treasury yield curve is upward sloping; in other words, the longer the maturity, the greater the yield.

Figure 15.1 shows an upward sloping yield curve, denoted by triangles. Additionally, we have plotted spot rates (squares) and single period forward rates (diamonds). (We have also interpolated all three sets of yields, of which there are two per year for each set, with smooth curves.)

Generally speaking, for an increasing yield curve, then spots rates and forward rates are also increasing in time to maturity. Regarding forward rates and spot rates,

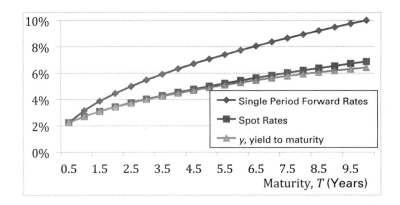

Figure 15.1 Increasing yield curve; corresponding spots and forwards

if $_{t-0.5}f_t > SR_{t-0.5}$, then $_{t-0.5}f_t > SR_t > SR_{t-0.5}$ per equation (15.10). So if $_{t-0.5}f_t > SR_{t-0.5}$, $\forall t \in \{1, 2, 3, \ldots\}$, then the spot rate curve is monotonically increasing, but always beneath the forward rate curve.[4] Lastly, if the single period forward rate curve is strictly increasing, then so is the spot rate curve, or $_{t-0.5}f_t > {}_{t-1}f_{t-0.5}$, $\forall t \in \{1, 2, 3, \ldots\} \Rightarrow {}_{t-0.5}f_t > SR_t$ and $SR_t > SR_{t-0.5}$, $\forall t \in \{1, 2, 3, \ldots\}$.[5]

The input parameters for figure 15.1 are shown in the first three columns of figure 15.2. In the final three columns we show calculated rates: y_T, SR_T and $_{T-0.5}f_T$, which are plotted in figure 15.1.

15.2.2 Multi-period Forward Rates

We now turn to multi-period forward rates. Figure 15.3 graphically depicts appropriate discount factors over not only single six-month periods but also multi-period durations of time. Discount factors are shown in terms of both spot rates as well as forward rates.[6]

Consider the two-period forward rate which begins six months from now and ends 18 months from now, $_{0.5}f_{1.5}$. Thus, this rate corresponds to a time duration of one year, beginning six months from now. It is the appropriate discount rate used to discount $CF_{1.5}$, received at date 1.5 (in years), back one year to date 0.5 (in years). Once again using our strategy of equating appropriate discount factors, consider that which is used

---

[4]In this case, the forward rate curve may or may not be monotonically increasing.

[5]Analogous comments apply to a downward sloping yield curve, e.g., $_{t-0.5}f_t < SR_{t-0.5} \Rightarrow {}_{t-0.5}f_t < SR_t < SR_{t-0.5}$. However, such a curve is rare. Humped curves are also possible, where the slope of the yield curve is initally positive (at low maturities) and negative at higher maturities.

[6]From figure 15.3, we see that $_0f_{0.5} = SR_{0.5}$, as previously noted. Other previous results can likewise be observed.

Chapter 15 Rate and Yield Metrics   193

Input parameters			Calculated yield or rates		
Maturity, T	Price, P_0^B	Coupon rate, r^C	Yield, y_T	Spot rate, SR_T	Forward rate, $_{T-0.5}f_T$
0.5	98.89	0.0%	2.2%	2.2%	2.2%
1.0	97.36	0.0%	2.7%	2.7%	3.2%
1.5	97.69	1.5%	3.1%	3.1%	3.9%
2.0	98.23	2.5%	3.4%	3.4%	4.5%
2.5	98.28	3.0%	3.7%	3.7%	5.0%
3.0	98.60	3.5%	4.0%	4.0%	5.5%
3.5	99.18	4.0%	4.3%	4.3%	5.9%
4.0	99.32	4.3%	4.5%	4.6%	6.3%
4.5	99.57	4.6%	4.7%	4.8%	6.7%
5.0	99.94	4.9%	4.9%	5.0%	7.1%
5.5	99.96	5.1%	5.1%	5.2%	7.4%
6.0	100.57	5.4%	5.3%	5.4%	7.7%
6.5	100.20	5.5%	5.5%	5.6%	8.1%
7.0	100.41	5.7%	5.6%	5.8%	8.4%
7.5	100.71	5.9%	5.8%	6.0%	8.7%
8.0	101.08	6.1%	5.9%	6.2%	8.9%
8.5	102.21	6.4%	6.1%	6.4%	9.2%
9.0	103.47	6.7%	6.2%	6.6%	9.5%
9.5	104.86	7.0%	6.3%	6.7%	9.7%
10.0	106.38	7.3%	6.4%	6.9%	10.0%

T: time to maturity, in years; P_0^B: US Treasury bond price, in dollars;
r^C: annualized coupon rate; y_T: annualized yield to maturity;
SR_T: annualized spot rate; $_{T-0.5}f_T$: annualized forward rate;
All rates (r^C, y_T, SR_T and $_{T-0.5}f_T$) are expressed as annual percentage rates, compounded semi-annually, or $m = 2$.

Figure 15.2   US Treasury data and calculations of rates

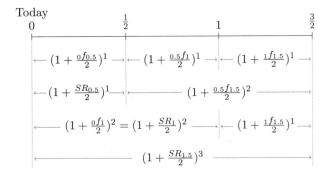

Figure 15.3   Spot rates and forward rates

to discount a cash flow received at date $t = 1.5$ back to *today*, $t = 0$, *not* just back to date $t = 0.5$. Using figure 15.3 as a visual aid, then

$$\left(1 + \frac{SR_{1.5}}{2}\right)^3 = \left(1 + \frac{SR_{0.5}}{2}\right)^1 \left(1 + \frac{_{0.5}f_{1.5}}{2}\right)^2. \tag{15.12}$$

Rearranging,

$$_{0.5}f_{1.5} = 2\left(\left[\frac{\left(1+\frac{SR_{1.5}}{2}\right)^3}{\left(1+\frac{SR_{0.5}}{2}\right)^1}\right]^{\frac{1}{2}} - 1\right). \tag{15.13}$$

Generalizing, consider a cash flow received at date t_2 (in years), which is to be discounted to date t_1 (in years), where $0 < t_1 < t_2$. The appropriate discount factor can be calculated from[7]

$$\left(1+\frac{SR_{t_2}}{2}\right)^{2t_2} = \left(1+\frac{SR_{t_1}}{2}\right)^{2t_1}\left(1+\frac{{}_{t_1}f_{t_2}}{2}\right)^{2(t_2-t_1)}. \tag{15.14}$$

Rearranging equation (15.14), then the **multi-period forward rate**, ${}_{t_1}f_{t_2}$, that begins at date t_1 (in years) and ends at date t_2 (in years), where $t_1 < t_2$, is calculated via

$$_{t_1}f_{t_2} = 2\left(\left[\frac{\left(1+\frac{SR_{t_2}}{2}\right)^{2t_2}}{\left(1+\frac{SR_{t_1}}{2}\right)^{2t_1}}\right]^{\frac{1}{2(t_2-t_1)}} - 1\right), \tag{15.15}$$

where ${}_{t_1}f_{t_2}$ is expressed as an APr, compounded semi-annually. So $\frac{{}_{t_1}f_{t_2}}{2}$ is an *average* effective six-month period forward rate corresponding to the multiple six-month periods (of which there are $2(t_2 - t_1)$) between dates t_1 and t_2, both expressed in years.

15.3 Realized Holding Period Yield

As previously discussed, two strong assumptions of yield to maturity are that the investor not only holds the bond until maturity, but also reinvests coupons at the calculated yield to maturity.[8] We now introduce another metric used by investors to calculate the return that they can expect from purchasing a bond. However, it has the flexibility of relaxing the assumptions implicit in the calculation of yield to maturity. The cost of this flexibility is increased calculation complexity.

Consider a bond whose initial price is P_0^B and whose maturity T is beyond that of the investor's expected holding period, HP, measured in years. As such, the investor anticipates receiving $2(HP)$ semi-annual coupons, the final one on her horizon date HP. Immediately after receiving that coupon, she sells the bond and receives the selling price SP_{HP} which exists in the market on date HP immediately after that coupon is paid. Figure 15.4 shows her anticipated cash flows. So for an investment of P_0^B, she receives

---

[7]There are $2(t_2 - t_1)$ periods, each of six-month duration, between dates t_1 and t_2.
[8]Yield to maturity also assumes that the bond is "risk-free" in the sense that it uses promised cash flows, *not* expected cash flows.

$2(HP)$ semi-annual coupon payments, interest earned due to reinvestment of these coupons at an assumed reinvestment rate of rr (expressed as an APr compounded semi-annually) and the price that she can retrieve by selling the bond on date HP.

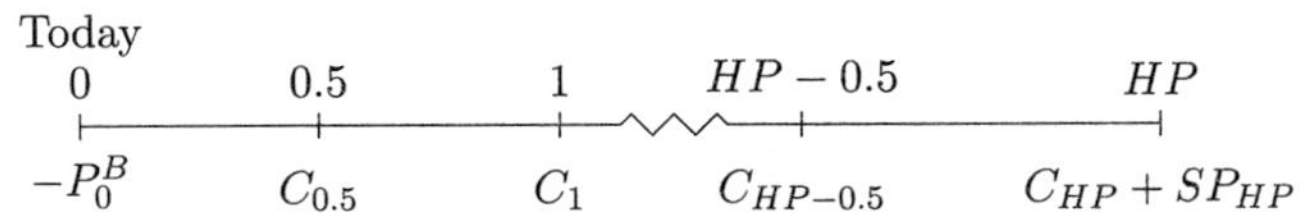
Today
0
0.5
1
$HP - 0.5$
HP
$-P_0^B$
$C_{0.5}$
C_1
$C_{HP-0.5}$
$C_{HP} + SP_{HP}$

Figure 15.4 Cash flows for realized holding period yield

Our first task is to calculate the future value of the received and reinvested coupons at the investor's horizon date, HP, as shown in figure 15.5. As the first $2(HP)$ coupons received represent an annuity of cash flows, we can determine their value as of date HP via future value of an annuity, or

$$FV_{HP}^{C}(rr) = \sum_{t=1}^{2HP} C\left(1+\frac{rr}{2}\right)^{2HP-t} = \frac{C}{\left(\frac{rr}{2}\right)}\left[\left(1+\frac{rr}{2}\right)^{2HP} - 1\right], \tag{15.16}$$

where $C = F(\frac{r^C}{2})$ is the semi-annual coupon payment. We explicitly write the future value as a function of assumed reinvestment rate, rr, to stress this enhanced flexibility of realized holding period yield, contrasted with the yield to maturity.

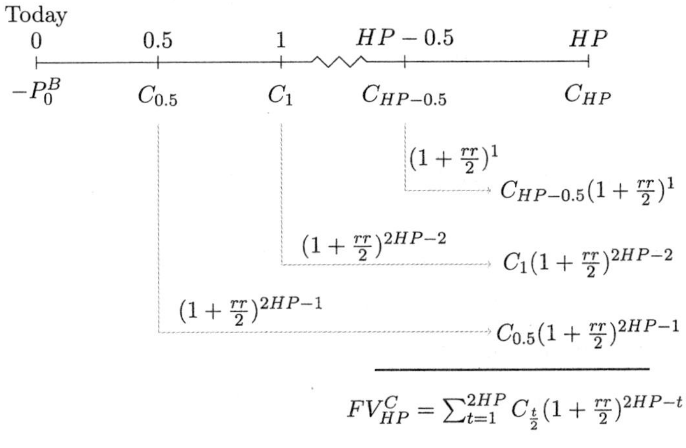
Today
0
0.5
1
$HP - 0.5$
HP
$-P_0^B$
$C_{0.5}$
C_1
$C_{HP-0.5}$
C_{HP}
$(1+\frac{rr}{2})^1$
$C_{HP-0.5}(1+\frac{rr}{2})^1$
$(1+\frac{rr}{2})^{2HP-2}$
$C_1(1+\frac{rr}{2})^{2HP-2}$
$(1+\frac{rr}{2})^{2HP-1}$
$C_{0.5}(1+\frac{rr}{2})^{2HP-1}$
$FV_{HP}^{C} = \sum_{t=1}^{2HP} C_{\frac{t}{2}}(1+\frac{rr}{2})^{2HP-t}$

Figure 15.5 Realized holding period yield: reinvested coupons

Our next task is to estimate the selling price that the investor will realize on date HP, SP_{HP}. The investor has the flexibility to introduce her beliefs regarding future interest rates via assumption of the bond's remaining yield to maturity on date HP, denoted ys. Figure 15.6 illustrates this calculation. This is a straightforward intrinsic value calculation. Specifically, for a fixed coupon bond, the selling price is simply the present value of an annuity of remaining semi-annual coupon payments plus that of the face value. Hence,

$$SP_{HP} = \sum_{t=2HP+1}^{2T} \frac{CF_{\frac{t}{2}}}{(1+\frac{ys}{2})^{t-2HP}}$$

$$= \frac{F}{\left(1+\frac{ys}{2}\right)^{2(T-HP)}} + \frac{C}{\left(\frac{ys}{2}\right)}\left[1 - \frac{1}{\left(1+\frac{ys}{2}\right)^{2(T-HP)}}\right]. \quad (15.17)$$

Not only does this calculation allow the investor the flexibility to assume that her horizon is shorter than the maturity, $HP < T$, but she may also introduce her beliefs regarding future interest rates via ys.[9]

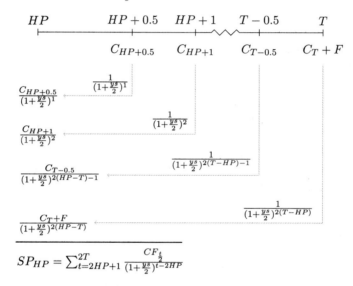

Figure 15.6 Realized holding period yield: selling price

For an investment at date $t = 0$ of P_0^B, the investor has a total value at date HP of the future value of reinvested coupons, FV_{HP}^C, plus the price for which she can sell the bond on that date, SP_{HP}. Thus, the investor's estimate for **realized holding period yield**, $rhpy$, expressed as an APr compounded semi-annually, is implicitly given by

$$P_0^B \left(1 + \frac{rhpy}{2}\right)^{2(HP)} = FV_{HP}^C + SP_{HP}. \quad (15.18)$$

Solving this explicitly for the realized holding period yield, then

$$rhpy = 2\left(\left[\frac{FV_{HP}^C + SP_{HP}}{P_0^B}\right]^{\frac{1}{2(HP)}} - 1\right). \quad (15.19)$$

---

[9] We are treating price, SP_{HP}, as a function of ys. In reality, ys is a function of SP_{HP}, by definition of yield to maturity.

Equation (15.19) makes it obvious that the realized holding period yield is a type of geometric mean rate, as it has the structure $\frac{rhpy}{2} = [\frac{V_{HP}}{V_0}]^{\frac{1}{2HP}} - 1$, consistent with a geometric mean. Translated, the number of periods in the investor's investment horizon is $2(HP)$, and the final value V_{HP} is the total terminal value at date HP, $FV_{HP}^C + SP_{HP}$. The initial value is the purchase price, $V_0 = P_0^B$.

Let's review the increased flexibility of this calculation versus that of yield to maturity. Firstly, the investor can assume a holding period shorter than the maturity of the bond. Secondly, she can assume whatever reinvestment rate of coupons that she believes is reasonable. Thirdly, she can further introduce her beliefs regarding future interest rates that will exist beyond her holding period via her assumption of the future yield.[10] Finally, she can introduce her beliefs regarding cash flow riskiness via cash flow assumptions. Specifically, she can use expected cash flows versus promised cash flows.[11]

Before leaving this topic, we are now in position to prove that the calculation of yield to maturity assumes that coupons must be reinvested at a rate equal to the yield in order for this rate of return to be realized. Consider a modification to equation (15.18), given that the bond is held to maturity, or

$$P_0^B \left(1 + \frac{rhpy}{2}\right)^{2T} = FV_T = \sum_{t=1}^{2T} CF_{\frac{t}{2}} \left(1 + \frac{rr}{2}\right)^{2T-t}, \qquad (15.20)$$

where $CF_{\frac{t}{2}} = C$, $\forall t \in \{1, 2, ..., 2T-1\}$, and $CF_T = F + C$. Dividing equation (15.20) by $P_0^B = \sum_{t=1}^{2T} CF_{\frac{t}{2}} (1 + \frac{y}{2})^{-t}$, followed by multiplying and dividing the right hand side by $(1 + \frac{y}{2})^{2T}$, then

$$\left(1 + \frac{rhpy}{2}\right)^{2T} = \left(1 + \frac{y}{2}\right)^{2T} \left[\frac{\sum_{t=1}^{2T} CF_{\frac{t}{2}} \left(1 + \frac{rr}{2}\right)^{2T-t}}{\sum_{t=1}^{2T} CF_{\frac{t}{2}} \left(1 + \frac{y}{2}\right)^{2T-t}}\right]. \qquad (15.21)$$

When $rr = y$, then the ratio in square brackets in equation (15.21) equals one, so $rr = y \Rightarrow rhpy = y$. Next, the right hand side of equation (15.21) is increasing in rr. Hence, combining these two results, $rr > y \Rightarrow rhpy > y$, and $rr < y \Rightarrow rhpy < y$. As claimed, the reinvestment rate of coupon payments (rr) must equal the yield to maturity (y) in order for the investor to realize a rate of return equal to y. Otherwise, $rr > y$ ($rr < y$) means that the investor's realized return will be greater (less) than the calculated yield to maturity.

---

[10]Of course, this directly impacts her selling price at date HP, SP_{HP}. Equivalently, an assumption regarding SP_{HP} can be made directly, which implies a value for ys.

[11]For simplicity, we have used promised cash flows in this section, which are greater than expected cash flows, as previously discussed.

15.4 Yield to Worst

We have focused on fixed coupon bonds in this book. Nonetheless, we take a moment to introduce various yield metrics based on the uncertainty of cash flows from bonds with embedded options, as the concept behind these metrics parallels that of yield to maturity.

Recall that yield to maturity (y), by definition, is the discount rate that equates price to summation of present value of promised cash flows. As equation (11.7) confirms, y is a function of price and promised cash flows, where cash flows depend on time to maturity. We can write this succinctly as $y(P_0^B, PC_{\frac{t}{2}}, T, F)$. Analogously, other yield metrics used for bonds with embedded options equate price to summation of present value of "promised" cash flows. However, for bonds with embedded options, there exists uncertainty regarding the size and timing of promised cash flows.

Consider a callable fixed coupon bond, which is a security consisting of a long position of a fixed bond and a short position of a call, or

$$\text{investor: long callable bond} = \text{long bond} + \text{short call}, \quad \text{and}$$
$$\text{issuer: short callable bond} = \text{short bond} + \text{long call}. \quad (15.22)$$

So if the issuer, who is long the call, exercises this option, then the issuer forces the investor to deliver the bond (i.e., return it to the issuer) for a price, the strike price, paid by the issuer to the investor. For callable bonds, there exists a schedule defining how the strike price changes over time, and the first date at which the issuer may call the bond, the first call date, is usually years after it is issued.[12] As such, we can calculate **yield to first call**, $yt1c(P_0^B, PC_{t/2}, t_1, X_{t_1})$, as

$$P_0^B \equiv \sum_{t=1}^{2t_1} \frac{PC_{\frac{t}{2}}\left(L_{\frac{t}{2}}\right)}{\left(1+\frac{yt1c}{2}\right)^t} = \sum_{t=1}^{2t_1-1} \frac{C_{\frac{t}{2}}\left(L_{\frac{t}{2}}\right)}{\left(1+\frac{yt1c}{2}\right)^t} + \frac{C_{t_1}\left(L_T\right) + X_{t_1}}{\left(1+\frac{yt1c}{2}\right)^{2t_1}}, \quad (15.23)$$

where $C_{t/2}(L_{t/2})$ is the promised coupon payment at date $\frac{t}{2}$ in years, $t \in \{1, 2, ..., 2T\}$, t_1 is the date in years when the issuer can first call the bond, C_{t_1} is the final coupon payment (paid on date t_1), and X_{t_1} is the strike price per call schedule on date t_1. So compared to yield to maturity $y(P_0^B, PC_{t/2}, T, F)$, then yield to first call $yt1c(P_0^B, PC_{t/2}, t_1, X_{t_1})$ simply replaces time to maturity, T, with date of first call, t_1, and it replaces face value, F, with the first strike price, X_{t_1}.

---

[12] Per the schedule, these strike prices are greater than the face value (F) and are usually decreasing over time.

Analogously, **yield to second call**, $yt2c(P_0^B, PC_{t/2}, t_2, X_{t_2})$, is defined by

$$P_0^B \equiv \sum_{t=1}^{2t_2} \frac{PC_{\frac{t}{2}}\left(L_{\frac{t}{2}}\right)}{\left(1+\frac{yt2c}{2}\right)^t} = \sum_{t=1}^{2t_2-1} \frac{C_{\frac{t}{2}}\left(L_{\frac{t}{2}}\right)}{\left(1+\frac{yt2c}{2}\right)^t} + \frac{C_{t_2}(L_T) + X_{t_2}}{\left(1+\frac{yt2c}{2}\right)^{2t_2}}, \tag{15.24}$$

where t_2 is the date in years when the issuer can call the bond at the second strike price of the call schedule, X_{t_2}, and C_{t_2} is the final coupon payment, paid on date t_2.

Likewise, we can calculate yield to third call ($yt3c$), yield to fourth call ($yt4c$), etc... Finally, for conservatism, an investor can calculate the smallest of all comparable yield metrics, the **yield to worst**, or $ytw = \min(y, yt1c, yt2c,...)$.

Fixed income securities may have an embedded put option. In such a case, the investor is long the option, and the issuer is short, or

investor: long putable bond = long bond + long put, and

issuer: short putable bond = short bond + short put. (15.25)

So if the investor, who is long the put, exercises the option, then the investor forces the issuer to pay her the strike price in exchange for delivering the bond to the issuer. Given the defined schedule of strike prices, yields comparable to those for a callable bond may be calculated. Hence, after calculating yield to first put, $yt1p$, yield to second put, $yt2p$, etc..., then an investor may determine the conservative yield to worst, $ytw = \min(y, yt1p, yt2p,...)$.

15.5 Other Yield Metrics

One commonly used metric is **yield spread**, the difference between calculated yield to maturity for a risky bond and that of a risk-free bond (e.g., US Treasury security) of the same maturity, or

$$\text{yield spread} = y^r - y^f. \tag{15.26}$$

We highlight the fact that yield spread is for a specific risky bond relative to a specific risk-free benchmark bond. It has relevance *neither* for any other risky bond *nor* for any other risk-free benchmark bond. Hence, yield spread is a remarkably specific metric, though is it very widely quoted.

The riskier the bond, the lower is a bond's price due to higher rates of return demanded by bond holders. This implies a higher yield. So yield spread increases in riskiness, all else equal.

Recall our discussion of spot rates. For a given risk-free security of maturity T in years, then via bootstrapping,

$$P_0^f = \sum_{t=1}^{2T} \frac{CF_{t/2}^f}{\left(1 + \frac{SR_{\frac{t}{2}}}{2}\right)^t}. \qquad (15.27)$$

As investors demand to be compensated for risk, then discount rates are higher for risky bonds than for risk-free bonds. As we saw earlier, we determine spot rates for risky cash flows from risk-free spot rates via $SR_{t/2}^r = SR_{t/2} + \sum_{n=1}^{N} \beta^n (RP^n)$, $n \in \{1, 2, ..., N\}$, for N risk factors. Rather than this framework, consider a risk-free bond and a risky fixed coupon bond of the same maturity, then $P_0^r < P_0^f = \sum_{t=1}^{2T} \frac{CF_{t/2}}{(1+\frac{SR_{t/2}}{2})^t}$. So for a given risky bond with identical cash flows, it is possible to add to all risk-free spot rates a single spread metric that equates the risky bond price to the summation of discounted risky cash flows. This particular single yield metric is called the **zero volatility spread**, or **z-spread**, z^T, defined by

$$P_0^r \equiv \sum_{t=1}^{2T} \frac{CF_{t/2}}{\left(1 + \frac{SR_{\frac{t}{2}} + z^T}{2}\right)^t}, \qquad (15.28)$$

where z^T is expressed as an APr, compounded semi-annually.

So like yield spread, zero volatility spread is calculated for a particular risky bond relative to a chosen risk-free benchmark. Both yield spread and z-spread are single values specific to a given bond and a given risk-free benchmark, usually US Treasuries. Both are increasing in bond riskiness, all else equal.

Among their differences, yield spread compares a single risky bond to a single risk-free benchmark bond of the same maturity. In contrast, for a given risky bond of maturity T, as zero volatility spread depends upon all spots rates of all maturities less than or equal to T, then z^T depends upon all risk-free benchmark securities of equal or lesser maturity.[13]

---

[13] Modeling future interest rates via a multi-period binomial tree is beyond the scope of this text. However, for a given binomial tree calibrated to a set of risk-free benchmark securities, then **option adjusted spread** is the single value added to all values of interest rates in the tree that equates risky bond price to the summation of its present values. The reason that it is called option adjusted is because this model accommodates the dependence of future cash flows upon future interest rate scenarios.

Problems

Assume the following US Treasuries exist.

maturity (years)	0.5	1	1.5	2	2.5	3	5
price($)	98.02	95.50	101.01	102.31	100.34	99.34	100.07
coupon	0	0	6%	9%	8%	8.5%	9.5%

1. Calculate the following spot rates: $SR_{0.5}$, SR_1, $SR_{1.5}$, SR_2, $SR_{2.5}$, SR_3 and SR_5.

2. Calculate the following single-period (6-month) forward rates: $_0f_{0.5}$, $_{0.5}f_1$, $_1f_{1.5}$, $_{1.5}f_2$, $_2f_{2.5}$ and $_{2.5}f_3$.

3. Calculate the following multi-period (1-year) forward rates: $_0f_1$, $_{0.5}f_{1.5}$, $_1f_2$, $_{1.5}f_{2.5}$ and $_2f_3$.

4. Calculate the following multi-period (1.5-year) forward rates: $_0f_{1.5}$, $_{0.5}f_2$, $_1f_{2.5}$ and $_{1.5}f_3$.

5. Calculate the following multi-period (2-year) forward rates: $_0f_2$, $_{0.5}f_{2.5}$, $_1f_3$ and $_3f_5$.

6. You buy a semi-annual fixed coupon bond that has a face value of $1000, coupon rate of 12%, price of $1114.56 and time to maturity of 30 years. You intend to sell the bond in 20 years to help pay for your child's college. You estimate that the yield to maturity for the final 10 years will be 10%. You believe that you can reinvest coupons over the next 20 years at 7%. What do you estimate that your realized holding period yield will be?

PART V Options

Options are securities that involve two parties. The writer sells the security to the buyer for a price, the option premium. At expiration of the option, the non-negative payoff from the option's seller to its buyer depends upon the future price behavior of a particular risky asset.

In chapter 16 we introduce the basics of option mechanics. We investigate the payoffs and profits of both calls and puts, showing these from the perspectives of both the long and short positions. Afterwards, we investigate these same concepts for portfolios involving positions in options. Finally, we develop the all important put-call spot parity relation via a no-arbitrage argument.

In chapter 17 we examine lower and upper bounds for American options via no-arbitrage arguments. Afterwards we introduce a single period binomial stock price model, which is subsequently used to value options. We first value an option via delta hedge. By creating a portfolio of an option and its underlying asset such that its payoff is certain regardless of expiration date stock price, we are able to argue that its rate of return is risk-free, which ultimately allows us to value the option. Equivalently, we construct a portfolio of the underlying asset of an option and a risk-free bond that replicates the payoffs of a call option, regardless of expiration stock price. We can thus assign the value of this replicating portfolio to that of the corresponding option. A third related method of option valuation employed in this chapter is risk-neutral valuation, based on implied probabilities from the other two methods. Lastly, we perform comparative statics on option values.

In chapter 18 we expand the single period binomial model to include multiple periods. For a given time to maturity, then adding more periods reduces the duration of each period. We first develop a two-period model and afterwards a generalized multi-period model.

In chapter 19 we demonstrate how to value American options in a multi-period binomial model. Afterwards we develop a detailed example for an American put. We see the increase in value compared to an equivalent European put, i.e., the flexibility to exercise early generally adds value. We also calculate the cumulative probability of exercising early the American put as time passes.

In chapter 20, we present the Black-Scholes model, a valuation method for European options. We perform comparative statics analyses, showing comparable results to those derived from the binomial model.

Chapter 16

Expiration Date Option Payoffs and Profits

In our exploration of options, we first examine their payoffs when they expire. After reviewing payoffs and profits of both long and short positions of simple options, we do the same for portfolios containing options and other securities. From one such portfolio, a collar, we derive the important pricing relation among four different securities called put-call spot parity. Development of this relation is via an argument based on the no-arbitrage principle, a cornerstone of well functioning capital markets.

16.1 Option Basics

As the name implies, an **option** is a security that affords its owner a valuable right to choose between two alternatives. One alternative involves a transaction that is precisely defined by the option contract. The second alternative affords the option's owner the opportunity to simply "walk away" from the first alternative, i.e., to cancel the transaction. As such, the owner *never* has to accept the first alternative defined by the contract; she has the right to render the contract null and void per the second alternative. Thus, the option's **owner**, who is the **buyer** and is thus, **long** the option, has an advantageous position compared to the **seller**, who has **written** the option and thus, has the **short** position. The seller's position is disadvantageous as she must accept whichever of the two alternatives that the owner chooses. Hence, when the contract is traded at time $t = 0$, the buyer pays the seller the **option premium**, the cost of the option, to appropriately compensate the seller for her relatively unfavorable payoff position.

The option **contract** details the first alternative, i.e. that which involves fulfillment of a future transaction. Included are the **underlying asset** to be exchanged and the corresponding price, the **strike price**. Also specified is the final date that the transaction may occur, the **expiration date** or expiry. A **European** option permits the owner to **exercise** the option, i.e., to choose the transaction alternative, *only* on the expiration date, and not before. In contrast, an **American** option permits exercising the option not only at expiration, but also prior to expiry. If the owner chooses the second alternative, i.e., to not exercise the option, then the option is said to **expire worthless**.

A **call option** gives the buyer the right to buy the underlying asset by paying to the seller the strike price. If exercised, the seller is said to **deliver** (or to make delivery of) the underlying asset while the owner **takes delivery**.

In contrast to a call option, a **put option** gives the buyer the right to sell (or to deliver) the underlying asset to the seller, who in turn pays to the buyer the strike price. Don't be confused by this nomenclature. The terms "buyer/owner" versus "seller" refer to the initial contract transaction, *not* the subsequent transaction at expiration if the option is exercised. For a call option, it's perhaps convenient that the buyer of the option subsequently buys (or takes delivery) of the underlying asset at expiration. However, students sometimes get confused for a put option, where the contract buyer subsequently sells (delivers) the underlying asset if exercised.

16.2 Long Call Payoff and Profit at Expiration

Let's begin with the payoff function of a long position in a call. Though the strike price, K, is well defined by the call option contract, the future value of the underlying asset is uncertain. Let's assume that a European option, which expires on date $t = T$, has an underlying asset of one share of a firm's stock with value S_t at date t, where $t \in [0, T]$.[1] So if exercised, the net payoff is the value of the share received at expiration, S_T, minus the paid strike price, K.[2] Otherwise, no transaction happens, so the payoff is obviously zero. Hence, as the owner seeks to maximize wealth, she chooses the greater of the two payoffs: $S_T - K$ if exercised or 0 if not. Thus the long position of a call has

---

[1] In reality, if the underlying asset is a firm's equity, the number of shares is 100, not one. We use one for ease of exposition. So the non-zero slopes in our subsequent figures of payoffs and profits are either 1 or -1. In reality, the non-zero slopes are actually either 100 or -100.

[2] Regarding the underlying asset, the share is one that is currently outstanding; the firm does *not* issue a new one to satisfy the call contract. Indeed, the contract and its execution have no direct impact on the firm. The contract is simply an agreement between buyer and seller. This leads to options being "zero-sum games", discussed later. In contrast, a warrant is a type of call option where new shares *are* issued by the firm upon exercise. Warrants are beyond the scope of this textbook.

Also, it is not a problem if the seller does not own a share of stock at expiration when the call is exercised. She simply buys one in the market for S_T and delivers it to the owner in exchange for the strike price, K.

a payoff of $\max(0, S_T - K)$, which is non-negative: either zero or positive. Finally, the decision rule of the owner is obvious. If $S_T - K > 0$, then exercise. Otherwise, do not.

Consistent with previous concepts, three definitions are used to describe the status of a call option at any time during its life, $t \in [0, T]$.

$$S_t < K : \text{call is } \textbf{out-of-the-money}$$
$$S_t = K : \text{call is } \textbf{at-the-money}$$
$$S_t > K : \text{call is } \textbf{in-the-money} \qquad (16.1)$$

So at expiration, when $t = T$, the buyer exercises the option if it is in-the-money; otherwise, she lets it expire worthless.

As the buyer must pay the call premium, c_0, to the seller at date $t = 0$, then her profit, π^c, is her payoff minus the premium.[3] Summarizing,

$$\text{payoff} : c_T = \max(0, S_T - K) \geq 0, \quad \text{and} \quad \text{profit} : \pi^c = c_T - c_0 \geq -c_0. \qquad (16.2)$$

The smallest "profit" that the long position can realize is the loss of the call premium, $-c_0 < 0$, consistent with the option expiring worthless. Otherwise, she exercises her option, and her profit is greater than $-c_0$. Indeed, her profit potential is unlimited, as her payoff conditionally increases dollar for dollar in expiration stock price given that the option is in-the-money.

Figure 16.1 shows the long call's payoff, $c_T(S_T)$, and profit, $\pi^c(S_T)$, as functions of expiration stock price, S_T.[4] In figure 16.1, the call premium is $c_0 = \$3.53$, so $c_T - \pi^c = \$3.53, \forall S_T$. The strike price is at the kink point, $K = \$40$.[5] So for $S_T < \$40$, then $S_T - K < 0$, and the option expires worthless; this would leave the owner with a payoff of zero and a profit of $-\$3.53 < 0$ due to her initial premium payment. In contrast, for $S_T > \$40$, then $S_T - K > 0$, so the option is exercised with a positive payoff of $S_T - K = S_T - 40$. Despite positive payoff, the profit is still negative for $S_T < K + c_0 = \$40 + \$3.53 = \$43.53$. So for $S_T \in (\$40, \$43.53)$, the profit is negative, though the payoff is positive. Finally, for $S_T > K + c_0 = \$43.53$, both payoff and profit are positive.

---
[3]We use small letters (c and p) in reference to European calls and puts and capital letters (C and P) to denote American calls and puts.

[4]From $S_0 = \$40, K = \$40, r^f = 4\%, T = 0.5$ years, $\sigma = 30\%$ and $k = 2\%$, then per Black-Scholes discussed later, $c_0 = \$3.53$ and $p_0 = \$3.14$.

[5]In reality, with an underlying asset of 100 shares, the actual premium would be $100c_0$, or $\$353$ for a quoted premium of $\$3.53$.

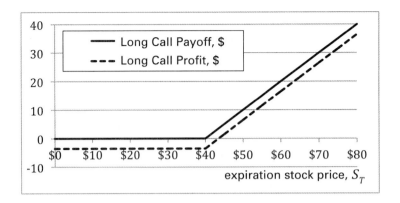

Figure 16.1 Payoff and profit of long call

The 45 degree kinks in the payoff and profit functions are what the owner "pays for", i.e., it's why she buys the option. If she had to fulfill the transaction at expiration regardless of expiration stock price, then her payoff function would continue downward at ever decreasing expiration stock prices less than the strike price. In other words, for out-of-the-money cases, the payoff would decrease dollar for dollar as the expiration stock price decreases.[6] The fact that she can let the option expire worthless changes her payoff to zero for all expiration stock prices less than the strike price, i.e., when the call is out-of-the-money at expiration.

16.3 Short Call Payoff and Profit at Expiration

Now let's consider the payoff and profit functions of the short call position. If the buyer/owner does not exercise, the seller's payoff is zero. However, if the buyer exercises at expiration date T, then the seller must deliver a share of stock valued at S_T and in return receives K from the buyer. Hence, her payoff is the difference $K - S_T$. From before, we argued that the buyer would only exercise if $S_T - K > 0$. Thus, if exercised the seller suffers a negative payoff, $K - S_T < 0$. So the payoff of the short call position

---

[6]This dollar for dollar payoff corresponds to the payoff of a **forward** contract, where the long (short) position has a slope *everywhere* of $+1$ (-1). Furthermore, forwards have a payoff of zero when $S_T = P^f$, the forward price P^f, which corresponds to the strike price K of an option. However, the payoff for the long (short) forward position is $S_T - P^f$ ($P^f - S_T$), i.e., there is no choice for either position, long or short; there are simply obligations. Beyond this, forwards are beyond the scope of this textbook. That said, the difference in payoffs between an option and corresponding forward (i.e., a forward with the same time to maturity, underlying asset and one whose forward price equals the option's strike price, or $P^f = K$) represents the incremental value of the option relative to the forward contract, i.e., its premium. Specifically, the difference in value is a direct metric of the incremental value represented by an option in letting it expire worthless.

is non-positive: either zero or negative. Combining these two scenarios, the short call payoff equals $\min(0, K - S_T) = -\max(0, S_T - K)$, as $\min(0, a) = -\max(0, -a)$. From before, the long call payoff is $c_T = \max(0, S_T - K)$. Hence, the short call payoff, equal to $-\max(0, S_T - K)$, is simply the negative of the long call payoff. So we denote the short call payoff by $-c_T \leqslant 0$.

The previous result is an important concept underlying options. As options are simply a "side-bet" between two parties (buyer and seller), then they represent a zero-sum game. In short, what the long position "gains" at expiration, the seller "loses", where the gain and loss are zero if the option expires worthless. Otherwise, the positive payoff to the buyer exactly equals the magnitude of the negative payoff to the seller.[7] So the sum of the payoffs of the long position and the short position always equals zero. Analogously, the sum of their profits also equals zero.

As the seller receives the call premium, c_0, from the buyer at date $t = 0$, then her profit equals $c_0 - c_T$, the negative of the profit of the long position. Hence we designate it by $-\pi^c$. We again see the concept of a zero sum game between buyer and seller. Summarizing,

$$\text{payoff}: -c_T = \min(0, K - S_T) = -\max(0, S_T - K) \leqslant 0, \quad \text{and}$$
$$\text{profit}: -\pi^c = c_0 - c_T \leqslant c_0. \tag{16.3}$$

The largest profit that the short position can realize is the call premium, c_0, consistent with the option expiring worthless. Otherwise, the buyer exercises the call and the seller's profit is reduced. Indeed, the magnitude of potential loss is unlimited, as her payoff conditionally decreases one dollar per each dollar increase in expiration stock price given that the option is in-the-money.

Figure 16.2 shows the short call's payoff, $-c_T(S_T)$, and profit, $-\pi^c(S_T)$, as functions of expiration stock price, S_T. Whereas the long call payoff function is above the profit function by the premium (c_0) for all expiration stock prices, the short payoff function is below the profit function by $c_0 = \$3.53$.

We have previously noted that options are a zero sum game. Thus, the short payoff (profit) function in figure 16.2 can be obtained by flipping about the x-axis the long payoff (profit) function in figure 16.1. Furthermore, adding the two payoff (profit)

---

[7] Another example of a zero-sum game is a poker game among friends. At the end of the night, some players win, and some lose. Yet the total dollars that enter the room to begin the game exactly equal the total dollars which leave the room as the game ends. No net economic wealth is created, but rather there is simply a transfer of existing wealth among players.

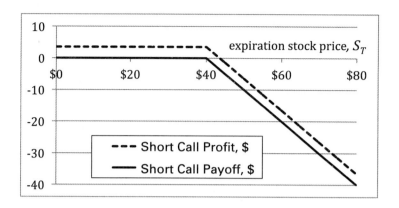

Figure 16.2 Payoff and profit of short call

functions in figures 16.1 and 16.2 results in a value of zero, for all expiration stock prices, S_T.

16.4 Long Put Payoff and Profit at Expiration

We now consider a long position in a European put option that expires on date $t = T$ with an underlying asset of one share of stock. So if exercised, the buyer's net payoff is the value of the strike price received, K, minus the value of the share that she must deliver at expiration, S_T. Otherwise, no transaction happens, so the buyer's payoff is zero. As the buyer/owner seeks to maximize wealth, she chooses the higher of the two payoffs: $K - S_T$ if exercised, or 0 if not. Thus the long position of a put has a payoff of $\max(0, K - S_T)$. Analogous to a call option, the payoff of a long put position is non-negative. Finally, the decision rule of the owner is obvious. If $K - S_T > 0$, then exercise; otherwise, do not.

Consistent with previous concepts, three definitions are used to describe the status of a put option at any time during its life, $t \in [0, T]$.

$$S_t < K : \text{put is } \textbf{in-the-money}$$
$$S_t = K : \text{put is } \textbf{at-the-money}$$
$$S_t > K : \text{put is } \textbf{out-the-money} \qquad (16.4)$$

So at expiration, when $t = T$, the buyer exercises the option if it is in-the-money; otherwise, she lets it expire worthless. This last sentence also applies to a call option. However, the definitions for in-the-money and out-of-the-money for a put are opposite to those for a call.

As the buyer must pay the put premium, p_0, to the seller when the contract is traded at date $t = 0$, then her profit, π^p, is her payoff minus the premium. Summarizing,

$$\text{payoff}: p_T = \max(0, K - S_T) \geq 0, \quad \text{and}$$
$$\text{profit}: \pi^p = p_T - p_0 \geq -p_0. \qquad (16.5)$$

The smallest "profit" that the long position can realize is her loss of the put premium, $-p_0 < 0$, consistent with the option expiring worthless. Otherwise, she exercises the put option resulting in a profit greater than $-p_0$. Her maximum payoff (profit) is limited to K $(K - p_0)$, corresponding to $S_T = 0$.[8]

Figure 16.3 shows the long put's payoff, $p_T(S_T)$, and profit, $\pi^p(S_T)$, as functions of expiration stock price, S_T. The put premium is \$3.14, so $p_T - \pi^p = \$3.14$, $\forall S_T$. The strike price is at the kink point, $K = \$40$. So for $S_T > \$40$, then $K - S_T < 0$ means that the option expires worthless, leaving the owner with a payoff of zero. Her profit is $-\$3.14 < 0$ due to her premium payment when she purchased the put. In contrast, for $S_T < \$40$, then $K - S_T > 0$, so the option is exercised with positive payoff. Despite positive payoff, the profit is still negative for $S_T > K - p_0 = \$40 - \$3.14 = \$36.86$. So for $S_T \in (\$36.86, \$40)$, profit is negative, though payoff is positive. Finally, for $S_T < K - p_0 = \$36.86$, both payoff and profit are positive.

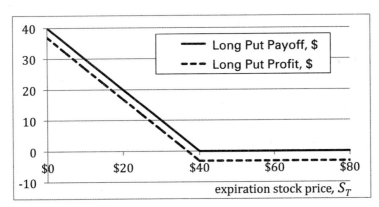

Figure 16.3   Payoff and profit of long put

Again we see the value to the buyer of the 45 degree kink in the payoff and profit functions. If the put buyer had to fulfill the transaction at expiration regardless of expiration stock price, her payoff would continue downward at a slope of negative one at ever increasing expiration stock prices greater than the strike price, i.e., when the put option expires out-of-the-money. The fact that she can let the option expire worthless changes her payoff to zero for all expiration stock prices greater than the strike price.

---

[8]This contrasts with the long call payoff and profit, which are potentially unlimited.

16.5 Short Put Payoff and Profit at Expiration

Now let's consider the payoff and profit of the short put position. If the buyer does not exercise, the seller's payoff is zero. However, if the buyer exercises at expiration date T, then the buyer delivers to the seller a share of stock valued at S_T, and seller in return must pay K to the buyer. Hence, the short put payoff is $S_T - K$, if exercised. From before, we argued that the owner would only exercise if $K - S_T > 0$. Thus, if exercised, the short put position suffers a negative payoff, $S_T - K < 0$. So the short put payoff equals $\min(0, S_T - K) = -\max(0, K - S_T)$. Analogous to a short position of a call option, the payoff of the short put position is non-positive.

As the long put payoff is $p_T = \max(0, K - S_T)$, then the short put payoff, equal to $-\max(0, K - S_T)$, is simply the negative of the long put payoff. Hence we simply denote the short put payoff by $-p_T$. Again we see that options represent a zero-sum game. In short, what the long position "gains" at expiration, the seller "loses", where the gain and loss are zero if the option expires worthless. Otherwise, the positive payoff to the buyer exactly equals the magnitude of the negative payoff to the seller.

As the seller receives the put premium, p_0, from the buyer when the option is traded at date $t = 0$, then her profit equals $p_0 - p_T$, the negative of the profit of the long position. Hence we designate it by $-\pi^p$. We again see the concept of a zero sum game between owner and seller. Summarizing,

$$\text{payoff} : -p_T = \min(0, S_T - K) = -\max(0, K - S_T) \leqslant 0, \quad \text{and}$$
$$\text{profit} : -\pi^p = p_0 - p_T \leqslant p_0. \tag{16.6}$$

The largest profit that the short position can realize is the put premium, p_0, consistent with the option expiring worthless. Otherwise, the buyer exercises the put, so the seller's profit is less than p_0 and may be negative. However, in contrast to the unlimited loss potential for a short call position, the magnitude of potential loss for a short put position is limited to $K - p_0$.

Figure 16.4 shows the short put's payoff, $-p_T(S_T)$, and profit, $-\pi^p(S_T)$, as functions of expiration stock price, S_T. Whereas the long put payoff function is above the profit function by the premium (p_0) for all expiration stock prices, the short put payoff function is below the profit function by $p_0 = \$3.14$.

We have previously noted that options are a zero sum game. Thus, the short put payoff (profit) function in figure 16.4 can be obtained by flipping about the x-axis the long put payoff (profit) function in figure 16.3. Furthermore, adding the two payoff

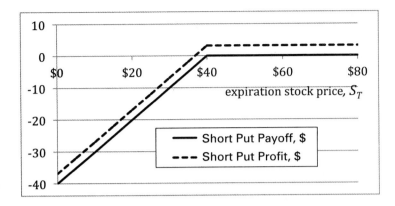

Figure 16.4 Payoff and profit of short put

(profit) functions in figures 16.3 and 16.4 results in a value of zero, for all expiration stock prices, S_T.

We have seen that payoffs and profits of both calls and puts can be illustrated via mathematical formulas (expressions (16.2), (16.3), (16.5) and (16.6)) as well as graphically, e.g., figures 16.1, 16.2, 16.3 and 16.4. Option payoffs and profits can also be depicted via tabular form, as shown in figure 16.5. The call (put) premium is assumed to be $c_0 = \$3.53$ ($p_0 = \$3.14$). For both call and put, the strike price is $K = \$40$.[9]

| | European call option | | | | European put option | | | |
| | long position | | short position | | long position | | short position | |
price S_T	payoff c_T	profit π^c	payoff $-c_T$	profit $-\pi^c$	payoff p_T	profit π^p	payoff $-p_T$	profit $-\pi^p$
0	0	-3.53	0	3.53	40	36.86	-40	-36.86
5	0	-3.53	0	3.53	35	31.86	-35	-31.86
10	0	-3.53	0	3.53	30	26.86	-30	-26.86
15	0	-3.53	0	3.53	25	21.86	-25	-21.86
20	0	-3.53	0	3.53	20	16.86	-20	-16.86
25	0	-3.53	0	3.53	15	11.86	-15	-11.86
30	0	-3.53	0	3.53	10	6.86	-10	-6.86
35	0	-3.53	0	3.53	5	1.86	-5	-1.86
40	0	-3.53	0	3.53	0	-3.14	0	3.14
45	5	1.47	-5	-1.47	0	-3.14	0	3.14
50	10	6.47	-10	-6.47	0	-3.14	0	3.14
55	15	11.47	-15	-11.47	0	-3.14	0	3.14
60	20	16.47	-20	-16.47	0	-3.14	0	3.14
65	25	21.47	-25	-21.47	0	-3.14	0	3.14
70	30	26.47	-30	-26.47	0	-3.14	0	3.14
75	35	31.47	-35	-31.47	0	-3.14	0	3.14
80	40	36.47	-40	-36.47	0	-3.14	0	3.14

Figure 16.5 Tabular payoffs and profits for a call and put

---

[9]Going forward, we will typically show payoffs and profits graphically and/or via mathematical formula, but exhibition via tabular payoff and profit functions are always possible.

16.6 Expiration Payoffs of Portfolios Containing Options

With payoffs and profits for calls and puts in hand as building blocks, we now consider portfolios involving options.

16.6.1 Protective Put

We begin with a **protective put**, which combines one long put option and one long share of stock, corresponding to the underlying asset.[10] The payoff of the stock at expiration is simply S_T, and that of the put is $p_T = \max(0, K - S_T)$. Hence, the payoff is simply the sum of the two, $S_T + \max(0, K - S_T) = \max(S_T + 0, S_T + K - S_T) = \max(S_T, K)$. Note that the minimum possible payoff is K. This explains the term "protective" in the portfolio's name. Compared to the payoff of a share of stock alone (i.e., a share of stock in isolation, minus the put option), which has minimum possible payoff of zero, adding the put places a lower bound of the payoff of $K > 0$. For this reason, a put is also sometimes called **insurance**.

Generalizing, when one buys insurance, one buys a put option. For example, car insurance is a put option, where the premium is paid up front, the expiration date is when the insurance coverage lapses, the underlying asset is the car, and the strike price is the amount that the insurance company pays in exchange for the car. Generally, this American put option is out-of-the-money as long as the car is not damaged, so it is not exercised; the car's owner rationally chooses to *not* deliver an undamaged car whose value is greater than the strike price offered in return by the insurance company. However, if the car is severely damaged, then its value drops below the strike price offered by the insurance company. If so, the insurance (i.e., the American put) is in-the-money and thus, is exercised, i.e., the buyer (car owner) delivers the damaged car to the seller (insurance company) in exchange for the strike price. So combining the put option (insurance) with the underlying asset (car), the minimum payoff is K (amount paid by the insurance company for the car), providing insurance to owning the underlying asset.

Regarding a protective put, pp, the setup cost, pp_0, that an investor must pay is $pp_0 = S_0 + p_0$. Hence,

$$\text{payoff}: pp_T = \max(S_T, K) \geq K, \quad \text{and}$$
$$\text{profit}: \pi^{pp} = \max(S_T, K) - pp_0 = \max(S_T, K) - (S_0 + p_0). \qquad (16.7)$$

---

[10] We continue to assume that the underlying asset is one share of stock. In reality, for an underlying asset of 100 shares, a protective put combines one put and 100 shares of stock.

Figure 16.6 shows the protective put's payoff, $pp_T(S_T)$, and profit, $\pi^{pp}(S_T)$, as functions of expiration stock price, S_T. In figure 16.6, we assume that the put's premium is \$3.14 and its strike price is $K = \$40$. Furthermore we assume that the initial stock price is $S_0 = \$40$, so the put option is issued at-the-money. The difference between payoff and profit is $S_0 + p_0 = \$43.14, \forall S_T$. The strike price of both functions is at the kink point, $K = \$40$.

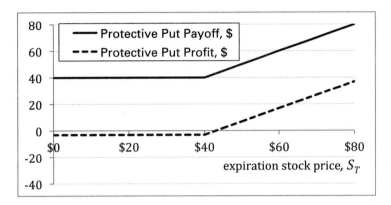

Figure 16.6 Payoff and profit of protective put

16.6.2 Covered Call

A **covered call** combines a short position in one call option and a long position in one share of stock that is the underlying asset of the call.[11] The payoff of the stock at expiration is simply S_T, and that of the short call is $-c_T = -\max(0, S_T - K) = \min(0, K - S_T)$. Hence, the payoff of a covered call is the sum of the two, $cc_T = S_T - c_T = S_T + \min(0, K - S_T) = \min(S_T + 0, S_T + K - S_T) = \min(S_T, K)$. So whereas the protective put has payoff $pp_T = \max(S_T, K)$, the covered call has payoff $cc_T = \min(S_T, K)$.

Regarding the portfolio's setup cost, the investor pays S_0 for the stock and receives c_0 for the call that she writes. Hence,

$$\text{payoff}: cc_T = \min(S_T, K) \leqslant K, \quad \text{and}$$
$$\text{profit}: \pi^{cc} = \min(S_T, K) - (S_0 - c_0) \leqslant K - (S_0 - c_0). \tag{16.8}$$

Figure 16.7 shows the covered call's payoff, $cc_T(S_T)$, and profit, $\pi^{cc}(S_T)$, as functions of expiration stock price, S_T. In the figure we assume that the call premium

---

[11] We continue to assume that the underlying asset is one share of stock. In reality, for an underlying asset of 100 shares, a covered call combines one short call and 100 long shares of stock.

is $3.53 and that its strike price is $K = \$40$. Furthermore we assume that the initial stock price is $S_0 = \$40$, so the call option is issued at-the-money. Hence the difference between payoff and profit is $S_0 - c_0 = \$40 - \$3.53 = \$36.47, \forall S_T$. The strike price of both functions is at the kink point, $K = \$40$.

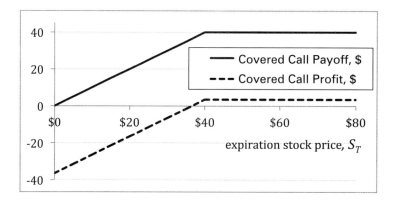

Figure 16.7 Payoff and profit of covered call

Why would an investor set up a covered call? Often times the investor initially owns the stock. If she believes that the stock will not experience an increase in the near future, she can supplement her current income by receiving the call premium when she writes the call. However, the potential downside of writing the call is obvious from inspection of figure 16.7. If the stock price rises sharply, she fails to profit from her long stock position due to her short call position. In short, an investor sets up a covered call position in order to receive current income via the call premium in exchange for sacrificing upside potential of the stock.[12]

16.6.3 Long Straddle

A **long straddle**, ls, combines a long call and a long put, both with the same strike price, same expiration date and same underlying asset. The payoff of the long call (put) at expiration is $c_T = \max(0, S_T - K)$ ($p_T = \max(0, K - S_T)$). Hence, the payoff is the sum of the two. Regarding the portfolio's setup cost, the investor pays $c_0 + p_0$ for the long positions in the call and put. Thus,

$$\text{payoff}: ls_T = \max(0, S_T - K) + \max(0, K - S_T) \geq 0, \quad \text{and} \quad (16.9)$$
$$\text{profit}: \pi^{ls} = ls_T - (c_0 + p_0) \geq -(c_0 + p_0).$$

---

[12]In contrast to a covered call, a "naked" call is simply a short call position, i.e, without being long the underlying asset.

An example of a long straddle is illustrated in figure 16.8, as it shows the long straddle's payoff, $ls_T(S_T)$, and profit, $\pi^{ls}(S_T)$, as functions of expiration stock price, S_T. In this figure, both strike prices equal \$40. Furthermore, $c_0 = \$3.53$ and $p_0 = \$3.14$. So the difference between payoff and profit is $p_0 + c_0 = \$3.53 + \$3.14 = \$6.67$, $\forall S_T$. The kink point of both functions is at the strike prices, $K = \$40$.

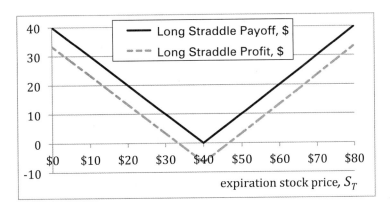

Figure 16.8 Payoff and profit of long straddle

Why would an investor set up a long straddle? Inspection of figure 16.8 makes it obvious that this portfolio generates a profit if the difference between the expiration stock price and strike price is large. For example, assume that a firm has gambled on a single product that is to be released in 60 days. If successful, the stock price will soar to \$100; if a failure, the price will drop to \$10. The market collectively believes that each outcome is equally likely. Hence the current stock price is $\$\frac{100+10}{2}e^{-12\%(60/365)} = \$53.93$, assuming that $r^E = 12\%$, expressed an APr, continuously compounded. So in 60 days, the price will be either \$10 or \$100, all else equal. A long straddle with this firm's stock as the underlying asset would be ideal in such a case.[13]

16.6.4 Short Straddle

A **short straddle**, ss, combines a short call and a short put, both of the same strike price, same expiration date and same underlying asset. The payoff of the short call (put) at expiration is $-c_T = \min(0, K - S_T)$ ($-p_T = \min(0, S_T - K)$). Hence, the payoff is the sum of the two. Regarding the portfolio's setup "cost", the investor

---

[13] As another example, consider a firm being sued where the pending decision is expected soon. For a large potential award, the difference in subsequent prices between the firm winning the suit versus losing could be substantial. Though uncertain of the outcome of the legal suit, an investor in a long straddle enjoys a profit via extreme movement in stock price, either upward or downward.

receives $c_0 + p_0$ for the short positions in the call and put. Hence,

$$\text{payoff}: -ss_T = \min(0, S_T - K) + \min(0, K - S_T) \leq 0, \quad \text{and}$$
$$\text{profit}: -\pi^{ss} = (c_0 + p_0) - ss_T \leq (c_0 + p_0). \tag{16.10}$$

An example of a short straddle is illustrated in figure 16.9, as it shows the short straddle's payoff, $ss_T(S_T)$, and profit, $\pi^{ss}(S_T)$, as functions of expiration stock price, S_T. In this figure, both strike prices equal \$40. Furthermore, $p_0 = \$3.14$ and $c_0 = \$3.53$. So the difference between profit and payoff is $p_0 + c_0 = \$6.67$, $\forall S_T$. The kink point of both functions is at the strike prices, $K = \$40$.

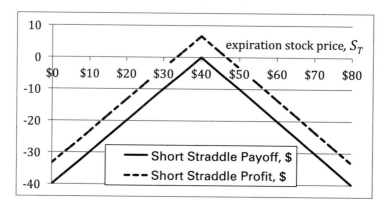

Figure 16.9 Payoff and profit of short straddle

Why would an investor set up a short straddle? Inspection of figure 16.9 makes it obvious that this portfolio will make a profit if the difference between the expiration stock price and strike price is small. So the equity in a firm whose stock price is believed to move sideways for the foreseeable future might be an ideal candidate as the underlying asset for a short straddle.

16.6.5 Collar

A **collar** combines a long share of stock, a short call and a long put, where the strike price of the call is greater than that of the put, $K_p < K_c$. The call and put have the same expiration date and same underlying asset. The respective expiration payoffs are S_T, $-c_T = \min(0, K_c - S_T)$, and $p_T = \max(0, K_p - S_T)$. Hence, the payoff is the sum of the three,

$$co_T = S_T - c_T + p_T = S_T + \min(0, K_c - S_T) + \max(0, K_p - S_T), \quad \text{and}$$
$$\pi^{co} = co_T - (S_0 + p_0 - c_0). \tag{16.11}$$

To understand these payoff and profit schedules, consider figure 16.10, where $K_p = \$30$, $K_c = \$50$, $S_0 = \$40$, $T = 5$ years, the risk free rate of return, an APr continuously compounded, is $r^f = 5\%$, and the underlying asset is assumed to pay a continuous dividend stream of 2%. Using Black-Scholes' European option pricing model reviewed later, $p_0 = \$3.39$ and $c_0 = \$7.92$. So the initial cost of this collar is $S_0 - c_0 + p_0 = \$40 - \$7.92 + \$3.39 = \$35.47$.

price	payoffs			profit
S_T	p_T	$-c_T$	co_T	π^{co}
0	30	0	30	-5.47
5	25	0	30	-5.47
10	20	0	30	-5.47
15	15	0	30	-5.47
20	10	0	30	-5.47
25	5	0	30	-5.47
30	0	0	30	-5.47
35	0	0	35	-0.47
40	0	0	40	4.53
45	0	0	45	9.53
50	0	0	50	14.53
55	0	-5	50	14.53
60	0	-10	50	14.53
65	0	-15	50	14.53
70	0	-20	50	14.53
75	0	-25	50	14.53
80	0	-30	50	14.53

Figure 16.10 Tabular payoffs and profits for a collar

In figure 16.11, we summarize succinctly via formulas the payoff and profit schedules shown in figure 16.10. These same payoff and profit functions for the collar, $co_T(S_T)$ and $\pi^{co}(S_T)$, in figures 16.10 and 16.11 are illustrated graphically in figure 16.12. In this latter figure, the payoff (profit) begins flat at $30 (-\$5.47)$ in the region $0 < S_T < \$30$ exactly for the same reason that a protective put does. As expiration stock price increases from zero in a comparative statics sense, the increasing stock price is exactly offset by the decreasing put value. The call expires worthless over this range of expiration stock price. Next, in the expiration stock price range of $\$30 < S_T < \$50$, the transitions from flat payoff and profit to positive slopes of one happen when the put becomes out-of-the-money. The call continues to remain out-of-the-money, so only the share of stock has value. Thus, the slope is one. Finally, in the third region, $\$50 < S_T$, the call finishes in-the-money as the put is worthless. As the position in the call is short, its increasing loss as the stock price increases exactly offsets the rise in stock value, mimicking the flat portions of the covered call payoff and profit at higher stock prices.

price	payoffs			payoff
S_T	S_T	p_T	$-c_T$	co_T
0 – 30	S_T	$K_p - S_T$	0	K_p
30 – 50	S_T	0	0	S_T
50 – 80	S_T	0	$K_c - S_T$	K_c

Figure 16.11 Tabular payoffs and profits for a collar

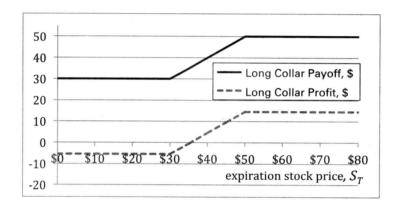

Figure 16.12 Payoff and profit of long collar

As noted before, the cost of the collar is $S_0 + p_0 - c_0$. Often times, investors choose a put and call (both with the same expiration date and underlying asset) of the same price, so $p_0 = c_0$. In such a case, the cost of the collar is simply the share of stock. An investor may set up a collar to put bounds on the payoff compared to that of just the stock itself. In doing so, she limits her downside risk, due to decreasing stock price, by sacrificing upside potential, due to increasing stock price.

16.7 Put-Call Spot Parity

We develop an important relation for security pricing, put-call spot parity. We do so by building upon previous results for a collar. We also use the critically important concept of no-arbitrage, a key feature of any well functioning capital market.

Recall the collar's payoff, $co_T = S_T + \min(0, K_c - S_T) + \max(0, K_p - S_T)$. Now consider a special case where $K_p = K_c$, denoted by K. Then $co_T|(K_p = K_c) = S_T + \min(0, K - S_T) + \max(0, K - S_T) = K$, as $\min(a,b) + \max(a,b) = a + b$. This is an interesting result. Combining three risky assets (long stock, long put and short call), all whose prices are functions of expiration stock price, S_T, in just the right combination results in a constant payoff of K. As such this particular combination of three risky assets results in a risk-free portfolio, as its payoff is *not* a function of S_T. Hence, $co_T|(K_p = K_c) = S_T + p_T - c_T = K$. In words, investing in long positions of one share of stock and one put plus a short position in one call has a certain (i.e., risk-free) payoff of K.[14]

As we discussed in an earlier chapter, arbitrage is characterized by a cost-free, risk-free profit. Such an opportunity should not exist. Hence, the payoff of a collar exactly equals K with certainty, or $S_T + p_T - c_T = K$. So its cost today must equal the present value of K, discounted at the risk-free rate of return, or $co_0 = PV(S_T + p_T - c_T) = \frac{K}{(1+r^f)^T}$. As $PV(S_T + p_T - c_T) = S_0 + p_0 - c_0$, then **put-call spot parity** obtains, or

$$S_0 + p_0 = c_0 + \frac{K}{(1+r^f)^T}. \qquad (16.12)$$

The astute reader may recognize the left hand side of equation (16.12) as a protective put, with payoff of $\max(S_T, K)$ as shown before. The right hand side has an expiration payoff of $c_T + K = \max(S_T - K, 0) + K = \max(S_T, K)$, confirming the equivalent payoffs. Again, their equivalent payoffs regardless of stock price implies equivalent present values today.

Put-call spot parity is an important pricing relation of these three risky assets. For a moment, assume that $S_0 + p_0 > c_0 + \frac{K}{(1+r^f)^T}$, violating put-call spot parity. Consider an investor setting up a portfolio that is long in one call, long a risk-free zero-coupon bond that pays K on date T (i.e., has a face value of K), short one share of stock and short one put option.[15] This portfolio costs $c_0 + \frac{K}{(1+r^f)^T} - S_0 - p_0 < 0$, i.e., the investor would generate positive cash flow today (date $t = 0$) of $S_0 + p_0 - c_0 - \frac{K}{(1+r^f)^T} > 0$.[16] At expiration, her payoff is $c_T + K - S_T - p_T = 0$ per put-call spot parity.

Summarizing the previous example, the investor has positive cash flow at time $t = 0$ and neutral cash flow at time $t = T$, all at no risk. In a well functioning capital market, this cannot last indefinitely. As long as this arbitrage opportunity presents

---

[14]Of course, the call and put must have the same expiration date, and they must have the corresponding stock as their underlying asset.

[15]In practice, one could buy multiple US T-bills expiring on date T, buy multiple calls, sell multiple shares of stock and sell multiple puts such that the ratio of expenditures is c_0 on calls and $\frac{K}{(1+r^f)^T}$ on US T-bills, while the revenues from short selling shares of stock and puts analogously are proportional to S_0 for the stock and c_0 for the call.

[16]Throughout this book, we ignore transaction costs. However, by including them, put-call spot parity no longer relates asset prices via specific values but rather via ranges of values. But the basic concept still holds.

itself, an investor would continue this strategy of buying proportional amounts of calls and risk-free bonds while selling proportional amounts of puts and shares of stock. In doing so, non-stop buying drives upward the prices of the call and the risk-free bond, $c_0 + K$, and non-stop selling drives downward $p_0 + S_0$. An investor would continue this buying and selling until put-call spot parity is restored.[17]

Problems

1. A call option has a strike price of $30, expires in 6 months and has a premium of $1.89. The underlying asset is a share of stock that has a current price of $29. Complete a table of expiration payoffs and profits for the long call position, using stock price increments of $5 over a range of [$0, $70]. Plot the payoff and profit functions of stock price over a range of [$0, $70].

At what expiration stock price is the profit equal to zero?

2. For the call option in problem 1, complete a table of expiration payoffs and profits for the short call position, using stock price increments of $5 over a range of [$0, $70]. Plot the payoff and profit functions of stock price over a range of [$0, $70].

3. A put option has a strike price of $30, expires in 6 months and has a premium of $1.43. The underlying asset is a share of the same stock as that for the call in problem 1. Complete a table of expiration payoffs and profits for the long put position, using stock price increments of $5 over a range of [$0, $70]. Plot the payoff and profit functions of stock price over a range of [$0, $70].

At what expiration stock price is the profit equal to zero?

4. For the put option in problem 3, complete a table of expiration payoffs and profits for the short put position, using stock price increments of $5 over a range of [$0, $70]. Plot the payoff and profit functions of stock price over a range of [$0, $70].

5. Consider the put option in problem 3. Create a protective put portfolio. Complete a table of expiration payoffs and profits for the protective put position, using stock price

---

[17] Of course, if $S_0 + p_0 < c_0 + \frac{K}{(1+r^f)^T}$, then an arbitrage opportunity exists where the investor buys puts and shares of stock while selling calls and risk-free bonds. She enlarges the portfolio, putting upward (downward) pressure on prices on p_0 and S_0 (c_0 and risk-free bonds), until put-call spot parity is restored. She realizes positive initial cash flow and neutral cash flow at expiration, all risk-free.

increments of $5 over a range of [$0, $70]. Plot the payoff and profit functions of stock price over a range of [$0, $70].

At what expiration stock price is the profit equal to zero?

6. Consider the call option in problem 1. Create a covered call portfolio. Complete a table of expiration payoffs and profits for the covered call position, using stock price increments of $5 over a range of [$0, $70]. Plot the payoff and profit functions of stock price over a range of [$0, $70].

At what expiration stock price is the profit equal to zero?

7. Consider the call option in problem 1 and put option in problem 3. Create a long straddle portfolio. Complete a table of expiration payoffs and profits for the long straddle position, using stock price increments of $5 over a range of [$0, $70]. Plot the payoff and profit functions of stock price over a range of [$0, $70].

At which two expiration stock prices is the profit equal to zero?

8. Consider the call option in problem 1 and put option in problem 3. Create a short straddle portfolio. Complete a table of expiration payoffs and profits for the short straddle position, using stock price increments of $5 over a range of [$0, $70]. Plot the payoff and profit functions of stock price over a range of [$0, $70].

At which two expiration stock prices is the profit equal to zero?

9. Consider the call option in problem 1 and put option in problem 3. Create a portfolio that is long the put, long the stock and short the call. Complete a table of expiration payoffs and profits for this portfolio, using stock price increments of $5 over a range of [$0, $70]. Plot the payoff and profit functions of stock price over a range of [$0, $70].

What is the risk-free rate of return, continuously compounded?

CHAPTER 17

Option Valuation: Single Period Binomial Model

In the previous chapter we focused on options at expiration. We examined payoff functions of expiration stock price. We also considered profit functions, taking option premiums, or their prices at date $t = 0$, as exogenous. In this chapter, we begin to explore how to value options, i.e., how investors determine option premiums.

We first explore bounds on American options as a way to reinforce our understanding of the no-arbitrage principle. Afterwards, we create a portfolio consisting of an option and its underlying asset in just the right proportions to generate a constant payoff. Hence, a risk-free rate of return is ensured. From this perfect hedge, we are able value the option in a binomial stock price model. Using an equivalent valuation methodology, we establish a portfolio of stock (the underlying asset) and a risk-free bond to replicate the payoffs of an option, confirming the value calculated via hedging. We see how these models relate to risk-neutral valuation, an important tool in option valuation.

Lastly we derive comparative static results for both calls and puts. We particularly focus heavily on the impact of volatility given its importance.

17.1 Arbitrage and Bounds on Option Premiums

We begin this chapter by placing bounds on a European call option premium, c_0, where the underlying asset is a share of stock that will not pay a dividend prior to expiration. This process allows us the opportunity to further exploit the critically important concept of no-arbitrage.

17.1.1 A European Call Lower Bound

Consider first a lower bound of $\max(0, S_0 - Ke^{-r^f T})$, where the risk-free rate of return is an *APR*, continuously compounded. First, if $S_0 < Ke^{-r^f T}$, then the lower bound equals zero. As the call payoff is non-negative, so must be its premium; otherwise one could generate positive cash flow at $t = 0$ by "buying" a call for $c_0 < 0$. Combined with a guaranteed non-negative payoff at expiration, this represents an arbitrage opportunity.

Now consider the case where $S_0 > Ke^{-r^f T}$. Then $\max(0, S_0 - Ke^{-r^f T}) = S_0 - Ke^{-r^f T} > 0$. Using a contradiction argument, assume that $c_0 = (S_0 - Ke^{-r^f T})f > 0$, for some fraction $f \in (0, 1)$. We argue that this leads to an arbitrage opportunity. Buy the call for $(S_0 - Ke^{-r^f T})f$, buy a risk-free zero coupon bond that matures at date T with face value of K for $Ke^{-r^f T}$ today, and short the stock at S_0. The cash flow today is positive, $S_0 - Ke^{-r^f T} - (S_0 - Ke^{-r^f T})f = (1-f)(S_0 - Ke^{-r^f T}) > 0$.

At expiration, either the option is in-the-money or not. First assume not. Then the call expires worthless, equivalent to $S_T \leqslant K$. The maturing bond generates a cash flow of K, and the shorted stock, with a value of S_T must be returned, requiring cash of S_T.[1] So her expiration cash flow is $K - S_T \geqslant 0$. So she has generated positive cash flow at $t = 0$ equal to $(1-f)(S_0 - Ke^{-r^f T}) > 0$ and non-negative cash flow at $t = T$ equal to $K - S_T \geqslant 0$.

Now consider the other possible outcome, where the call finishes in-the-money. Equivalently, $S_T > K$, so its expiration value is $S_T - K$, as the investor receives a share of stock worth S_T but must pay K. She can return the share that she owes her lender with the share purchased via exercising the call. Finally, the K received from the maturing bond is used to pay her strike price. In short, she has generated positive cash flow at $t = 0$ equal to $(1-f)(S_0 - Ke^{-r^f T}) > 0$ and neutral cash flow at $t = T$.

Summarizing, regardless of whether or not the call expires in-the-money, our investor generates positive, risk-free cash flow(s) at no net cost if $c_0 < \max(0, S_0 - Ke^{-r^f T})$. In a well-functioning capital market, a call premium should not be less than this lower bound. Hence, $c_0 \geqslant \max(0, S_0 - Ke^{-r^f T})$.

17.1.2 A European Call Upper Bound

Consider an upper bound of S_0. Again using a contradiction argument, assume that the call is more expensive than the underlying asset, or $c_0 = S_0(1+x) > S_0$, for some $x > 0$. Consider an investor who sets up a covered call, i.e., short sells the call and buys the stock. Her initial cash flow is $S_0(1+x) - S_0 = xS_0 > 0$. Next, we know

---

[1] This statement implies that the investor does not currently own the stock and enters the market, paying S_T for it. Equivalently, if the investor already owns the stock, she still must surrender it back to her lender, again reducing her portfolio value by S_T, all else equal.

that her payoff at expiration is $\min(S_T, K) \geq 0$, where it is zero only if the expiration stock price equals zero. So her terminal cash value is S_T if the call is not exercised ($S_T \in [0, K]$), as she still owns the share purchased at $t = 0$. If the call is exercised ($S_T > K$), so she delivers the share of stock that she initially purchased and receives $\$K$. So either way, she generates positive cash flow xS_0 at $t = 0$ and non-negative cash flow, $\min(S_T, K) \geq 0$, at expiration, $t = T$.

Summarizing, regardless of whether or not the call expires in-the-money, our investor generates positive, risk-free cash flow(s) at no net cost if $c_0 > S_0$. Hence, in a well-functioning capital market, a call premium should not be more than this upper bound, the stock price S_0.

17.1.3 Summary of Bounds on European Options

Combining previous results for a European call,

$$c_0 \in \left(\max\left(0, S_0 - Ke^{-r^fT}\right), S_0\right), \quad \text{or}$$

$$\max\left(0, S_0 - Ke^{-r^fT}\right) < c_0 < S_0. \tag{17.1}$$

In figure 17.1, we show bounds for a European call option as a function of current stock price, S_0. An upper bound, S_0, is denoted by the dotted line through the origin with a slope of one. We also show its lower bound, $\max(0, S_0 - Ke^{-r^fT})$, denoted by the solid function. Be mindful that the kink in the lower bound in figure 17.1 does *not* correspond to the strike price, assumed to be $K = \$40$, but rather to $Ke^{-r^fT} = 40e^{-4\%(5)} = \$32.75$, assuming that $r^f = 4\%$ and $T = 5$ years. Given an assumed current stock price of $\$50$, we show a violation of the lower bound via a black circle, where $\$10 = c_0 < \max(0, S_0 - Ke^{-r^fT}) = S_0 - Ke^{-r^fT} = 50 - 40e^{-4\%(5)} = \$17.25$. We also

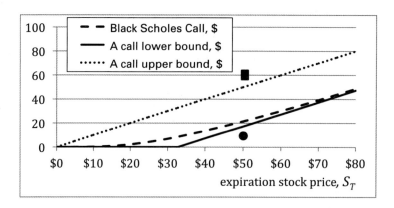

Figure 17.1   Upper and lower bounds on long call premium

show a violation of the upper bound via a black square, where $60 = c_0 > S_0 = \$50$. The astute reader may have noted a dashed curve in figure 17.1. This is the European call value as a function of stock price via the Black-Scholes option pricing model, which we introduce later.[2] Before leaving this section, we present without proof a pair of bounds on a European call premium. The reader is encouraged to confirm these bounds herself utilizing no-arbitrage arguments. For a European put,

$$p_0 \in \left(\max\left(0, Ke^{-r^fT} - S_0\right), Ke^{-r^fT}\right), \quad \text{or}$$
$$\max\left(0, Ke^{-r^fT} - S_0\right) < p_0 < Ke^{-r^fT}. \tag{17.2}$$

17.2 Binomial Stock Price Model

Having developed the bounds for premia of European calls and puts, we are now ready to begin tackling the actual option value. We first need to introduce a binomial stock price model.

Consider a stock with current price S_0 that can take on one of two possible values one period from now, the **up-state price** of S_1^u or the **down-state price** of S_1^d, as shown in figure 17.2. At first, such a model may seem silly, suggesting that one period

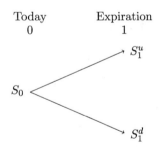

Figure 17.2 Binomial stock price model

from now the stock is limited to just two possible values. However, by shrinking the duration of the period to an infinitesimally small one, then the assumption looks more reasonable.[3] In what follows, we will find it convenient to define

$$u \equiv \frac{S_1^u}{S_0}, \quad \text{and} \quad d \equiv \frac{S_1^d}{S_0}, \tag{17.3}$$

---

[2] In utilizing Black-Scholes, we need a value for the standard deviation of the annualized, continuously compounded rate of return of the underlying asset, the stock. To generate this curve, we assumed that $\sigma = 30\%$.

[3] Indeed it is possible to show that the values of European calls and puts per the Black-Scholes model obtain in the limit as the time period approaches zero in a multi-period equivalent of this binomial model, thus increasing the number of periods accordingly. We explore this multi-period model later.

where we assume that
$$S_1^d < S_1^u \Leftrightarrow d < u. \tag{17.4}$$

Next, for real world probabilities of the two states of π^u and π^d, respectively, the expected price of the stock one period from now is

$$E[S_1] = \pi^u S_1^u + \pi^d S_1^d. \tag{17.5}$$

Finally, the real world expected value one period from now at date $t = 1$ is related to the current price via

$$S_0 = E[S_1] e^{-r^E} = e^{-r^E} \left(\pi^u S_1^u + \pi^d S_1^d \right), \quad \text{and}$$
$$1 = e^{-r^E} \left(\pi^u u + \pi^d d \right) \tag{17.6}$$

where we have expressed the rate of return demanded by equity holders, r^E, as an APr, continuously compounded. Combining equation (17.6) with $\pi^u + \pi^d = 1$, then

$$\pi^u = \frac{e^{r^E} - d}{u - d} > 0, \quad \text{and} \quad \pi^d = \frac{u - e^{r^E}}{u - d} > 0. \tag{17.7}$$

17.2.1 Call Value via Delta Hedge

In this section, we attempt to construct a portfolio consisting of one long call position and shares of the underlying asset (the stock) such that its payoff one period from today is always a constant value. By "always", we mean in each possible state of the world. Given our simple binomial stock price model, there are only two states: up and down. If we can successfully create such a portfolio, then its payoff must be risk-free. Thus, we can discount this certain payoff one period from now back to today's date in order to determine the portfolio's value today. Given that we know the stock's current value, S_0, we can derive the option's value.

Both the position of the stock (long versus short) as well as its magnitude to combine with one long call option is initially unknown. We will let the math tell us the sign and magnitude of the exact position. A necessary requirement for this model to work is to assume that

$$S_1^d < K < S_1^u. \tag{17.8}$$

Recall that from before, $S_0 \in (S_1^d, S_1^u)$. Next, the payoff of the call in the up-state is $c_1^u = \max(0, S_1^u - K) = S_1^u - K > 0$. In the down state, $c_1^d = \max(0, S_1^d - K) = 0$, as $S_1^d - K < 0$. These are summarized in figure 17.3.

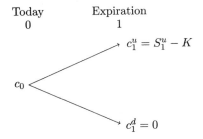

Figure 17.3 Call values in a binomial stock price model

Consider a portfolio with a position of σ shares of the underlying asset and long one call. If σ is positive (negative), then we are long (short) stock, meaning that we initially buy (short sell) stock; a long (short) position implies negative (positive) initial cash flow. At time $t = 0$, the value of the portfolio is $\sigma S_0 + c_0$. At time $t = 1$, its value is either $\sigma S_1^u + c_1^u$ or $\sigma S_1^d + c_1^d$. We summarize in figure 17.4.[4]

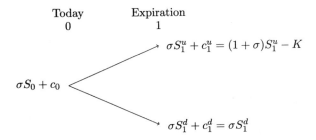

Figure 17.4 Replicating portfolio values in a binomial stock price model

Setting equal the payoffs in the up-state and down-state for the portfolio, then $\sigma S_1^u + c_1^u = \sigma S_1^d + c_1^d$, or $\sigma = -\frac{c_1^u - c_1^d}{S_1^u - S_1^d} = -\frac{\Delta c}{\Delta S}$. As σ is the negative of the ratio of the change in call value per change in stock value, it's the negative of the discrete approximation of the derivative of the call with respect to stock price, $-\frac{\partial c_0}{\partial S_0}$. This concept is extremely important for an option and is thus defined as its **delta**, or

$$\Delta^c \equiv \frac{\partial c_0}{\partial S_0}. \qquad (17.9)$$

Hence in what follows, we denote σ by $-\Delta^c$, even though $\sigma = \frac{\Delta c}{\Delta S}$ is a discrete approx-

---

[4]At time $t = 0$, the portfolio value is its cost (assuming that it is fairly valued), $\sigma S_0 + c_0 < 0$. So the initial cash flow is $CF_0 = -(\sigma S_0 + c_0) > 0$, and $CF_1 = \sigma S_1^d < 0$ as $\sigma = -\Delta^c < 0$.

In contrast, had we shorted the call in figure 17.4, so that value at $t = 0$ equals $\sigma S_0 - c_0 > 0$, then $\sigma = +\Delta^c > 0$, $CF_0 = -(\sigma S_0 - c_0) < 0$, and $CF_1 = \sigma S_1^d > 0$ as $\sigma = +\Delta^c > 0$. Nonetheless, the same call value would have resulted.

imation of $\Delta^c = \frac{\partial c_0}{\partial S_0}$. Substituting $c_1^u = S_1^u - K$ and $c_1^d = 0$, then

$$\Delta^c = \frac{\Delta c}{\Delta S} = \frac{S_1^u - K}{S_1^u - S_1^d} > 0, \tag{17.10}$$

where $\Delta^c \in (0,1)$ follows from $K \in (S_1^d, S_1^u)$. The result that $\Delta^c > 0$ makes intuitive sense. Obviously, a call increases in value as the stock price increases. For a fixed strike price, an increasing stock price implies an increasing value of the option, as the share of stock represents an conditional asset given that the call is exercised. Finally, in the delta hedge portfolio it makes intuitive sense that we must short (Δ^c shares of) stock, as this offsets the positive impact of stock price upon call value.

By setting the portfolio's payoffs in the two states equal to each other via selecting $\sigma = -\Delta^c < 0$ shares of stock for inclusion with one long call, then this payoff is risk-free. So we can discount it by the risk-free rate of return r^f, expressed as an APr, continuously compounded, to derive its current value. Thus, we can set the initial portfolio value $\sigma S_0 + c_0$ equal to the discounted payoff at $t = 1$, or $(\sigma S_1^d + c_1^d)e^{-(1)r^f} = \sigma S_1^d e^{-r^f}$, as $c_1^d = 0$. From $\sigma S_0 + c_0 = \sigma S_1^d e^{-r^f}$, and substituting σ with $-\Delta^c$, then

$$c_0 = \Delta^c \left(S_0 - S_1^d e^{-r^f}\right) = \frac{S_1^u - K}{S_1^u - S_1^d}\left(S_0 - S_1^d e^{-r^f}\right) > 0. \tag{17.11}$$

The inequality follows by an argument that a security with a strictly positive payoff with positive probability and non-negative payoffs in all states of the world must have positive value. Thus, per equation (17.11),

$$S_1^d e^{-r^f} < S_0, \quad \text{or equivalently,} \quad d < e^{r^f}. \tag{17.12}$$

Attempts have also been made to value options via discounting expected payoffs.[5,6]

---

[5]For example, a call theoretically can be valued via $c_0 = e^{-r^c}E[c_1] = e^{-r^c}[\pi^u c_1^u + \pi^d c_1^d] = e^{-r^c}\pi^u(S_1^u - K)$, where $c_1^u = S_1^u - K$ and $c_1^d = 0$, both per the assumptions in expression (17.8), and where we designate r^c as the appropriate discount rate for a call's expected cash flows, expressed as an APr, continuously compounded. Hence, using equation (17.11), $c_0 = \frac{S_0 - S_1^d e^{-r^f}}{S_1^u - S_1^d}(S_1^u - K) = e^{-r^c}[\frac{S_0 e^{r^c} - S_1^d e^{r^c - r^f}}{S_1^u - S_1^d}](S_1^u - K)$. Comparing this latter expression with the initial expression of this footnote, then we can interpret π^u as $\frac{S_0 e^{r^c} - S_1^d e^{r^c - r^f}}{S_1^u - S_1^d}$. Unfortunately, it is difficult to know directly the appropriate value of r^c.

[6]We will later see that options can be valued as if investors are risk-neutral, which means that r^f is the appropriate discount rate for these expressions, even though options are risky. Hence, substituting r^f for r^c into the expression for $\pi^u = \frac{S_0 e^{r^c} - S_1^d e^{r^c - r^f}}{S_1^u - S_1^d}$, we derive the values of risk-neutral probabilities as $pr^u = \frac{S_0 e^{r^f} - S_1^d}{S_1^u - S_1^d}$ and $pr^d = 1 - pr^u$, respectively.

17.2.2 Put Value via Delta Hedge

We now value a put option in the same framework as the call option of the previous section. We again assume that $S_1^d < K < S_1^u$, or $K \in (S_1^d, S_1^u)$. Next, the payoff of the put in the up-state is $p_1^u = \max(0, K - S_1^u) = 0$, as $K - S_1^u < 0$. In the down state, $p_1^d = \max(0, K - S_1^d) = K - S_1^d > 0$. These are summarized in figure 17.5.

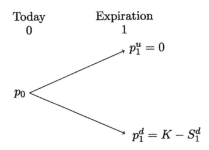

Figure 17.5 Put values in a binomial stock price model

Consider a portfolio with a position of σ shares of the underlying asset and a long position of one put option. At time $t = 0$, the value of this portfolio is $\sigma S_0 + p_0$. At time $t = 1$, its value is either $\sigma S_1^u + p_1^u = \sigma S_1^u$ or $\sigma S_1^d + p_1^d = K - (1 - \sigma)S_1^d$, as summarized in figure 17.6.[7] Setting equal the payoffs in the up-state and down-state for the portfolio, then $\sigma = -\frac{p_1^u - p_1^d}{S_1^u - S_1^d} = -\frac{\Delta p}{\Delta S}$. Analogous to the case involving a call,

$$\Delta^p \equiv \frac{\partial p_0}{\partial S_0} \approx \frac{\Delta p}{\Delta S} = -\frac{K - S_1^d}{S_1^u - S_1^d} \in (-1, 0), \qquad (17.13)$$

where the range of Δ^p follows from $K \in (S_1^d, S_1^u)$.

The result that $\Delta^p < 0$ makes intuitive sense. Obviously, a put decreases in value as the stock price increases. For a fixed strike price, an increasing stock price implies an decreasing value of the option, as the share of stock represents a conditional liability given that the put is exercised. Finally, in the delta hedge portfolio it makes intuitive sense that we must hold long $(-\Delta^p$ shares of) stock, as this offsets the negative impact of stock price upon put value.

We specifically chose $\sigma = -\Delta^p > 0$ shares of stock for inclusion with one long put in our portfolio so that the time $t = 1$ payoff is certain. Hence, as this payoff is

---

[7] At time $t = 0$, the portfolio value is its cost (assuming that it is fairly valued), $\sigma S_0 + p_0 > 0$. So the initial cash flow is $CF_0 = -(\sigma S_0 + p_0) < 0$, and $CF_1 = \sigma S_1^u > 0$ as $\sigma = -\Delta^p > 0$.

In contrast, had we shorted the put in figure 17.6, so that value at $t = 0$ equals $\sigma S_0 - p_0 < 0$, then $\sigma = +\Delta^p < 0$, $CF_0 = -(\sigma S_0 - p_0) > 0$, and $CF_1 = \sigma S_1^u < 0$ as $\sigma = +\Delta^p < 0$. Nonetheless, the same put value would have resulted.

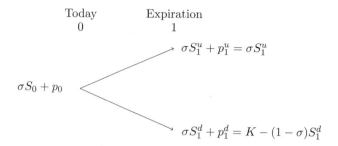

Figure 17.6 Replicating portfolio values in a binomial stock price model

risk-free, then $\sigma S_0 + p_0$ equals $(\sigma S_1^u + p_1^u)e^{-(1)r^f} = \sigma S_1^u e^{-r^f}$, as $p_1^u = 0$. Setting these equal and substituting σ with $-\Delta^p$, then

$$p_0 = -\Delta^p \left(S_1^u e^{-r^f} - S_0 \right) = -\frac{K - S_1^d}{S_1^u - S_1^d} \left(S_1^u e^{-r^f} - S_0 \right) > 0. \qquad (17.14)$$

The inequality follows by an argument that a security with a strictly positive payoff with positive probability and non-negative payoffs in all states of the world must have positive value. Thus, per equation (17.14), $S_0 < S_1^u e^{-r^f}$, or equivalently, $e^{r^f} < u$. Combining this with expression (17.12), then

$$S_1^d < S_0 e^{r^f} < S_1^u, \quad \text{or equivalently,} \quad d < e^{r^f} < u. \qquad (17.15)$$

Put Value per Put-Call Spot Parity

For pedagogical purposes, we derived the put value via delta hedge. We could have derived it from put-call parity as follows. Substituting $c_0 = \frac{S_1^u - K}{S_1^u - S_1^d}\left(S_0 - S_1^d e^{-r^f}\right)$ from equation (17.11) into put-call spot parity, $S_0 + p_0 = c_0 + Ke^{-r^f}$ per equation (16.12), then after a few lines of algebra, $p_0 = -\Delta^p(S_1^u e^{-r^f} - S_0)$, confirming equation (17.14).[8]

17.2.3 Call Replicating Portfolio

In this section and the next, we use a slightly different perspective of the binomial stock price model to value a call and put, respectively. Though these sections deepen one's understanding of option valuation, they may be skipped for brevity.

In this section, we attempt to construct a portfolio of securities, each of which we know how to value, such that its payoffs always replicate exactly that of a call option which expires one period from today. If we can match exactly the payoffs of the call in

---

[8]In equation (16.12) we replace $(1 + r^f)^{-T}$ with e^{-r^f}, assuming $T = 1$ and replacing the discrete rate of return (EAr) with the equivalent APr, continuously compounded.

both the up state as well as the down state, then we can use a no-arbitrage argument to value the call. Specifically, as we can simply value a portfolio of stock and bonds, then we can assign that same value to that of the call. The logic is that if two different baskets of securities have identical payoffs in the future, they must have the same value today.

Recall that we previously constructed a portfolio consisting of stock and a call option to induce a certain payoff at $t = 1$. This allowed us to discount this certain payoff at the risk-free rate to solve for the call's value. In contrast, now we construct a portfolio of stocks and bonds such that the payoffs of this portfolio exactly replicate those of a call. In so doing, we assign the value of the call replicating portfolio to that of the call itself.

By contradiction, if the call price were less than that of the portfolio of stocks and bonds, then one could short sell the latter and buy the call, resulting in a positive initial cash flow. At expiration, as the payoffs of the two are identical regardless of expiration stock price (S_1^u or S_1^d) the the non-negative cash flow generated by the long call position at expiration exactly matches the magnitude of that owed to the lender of the replicating portfolio. The investor realizes a risk-free, cost-free profit. Such an opportunity should not exist in a well functioning capital market.

Analogously, by contradiction if the call price were greater than that of the portfolio of stocks and bonds, then one could buy (go long) the latter and write the call (creating a short position), resulting in a positive initial cash flow. The expiration cash flow would again be zero, resulting in an arbitrage opportunity. In summary, as arbitrage should not be present, we use the no-arbitrage principle to value the call; the value of the call equals that of the replicating portfolio.

We continue to require assumption (17.8), $S_1^d < K < S_1^u$, or $K \in (S_1^d, S_1^u)$. As stock (the underlying asset of the call option that we are trying to value) and bonds are priced via discounting cash flows, we take their prices as given.[9] Thus, they are candidates for our replicating portfolio. Consider a portfolio with a position of σ shares of the underlying asset and a position in zero-coupon, risk-free debt with a face value of

---

[9]Discounting cash flows gives values, which we assume for now equals prices, i.e., that stocks and bonds are priced fairly.

F.[10] Note that we do not assume the signs of the positions, i.e., whether they are long or short. We will let the math tell us. If $\sigma(F)$ is positive, then we are long stock (debt), meaning we initially buy stock (debt) in setting up our call-replicating portfolio; a long position implies negative initial cash flow. If $\sigma(F)$ is negative, then we are short stock (debt), meaning we initially short sell stock (debt) in setting up our call-replicating portfolio; a short position implies positive initial cash flow.

At time $t = 0$, the value of the replicating portfolio is $\sigma S_0 + Fe^{-(1)r^f}$. At time $t = 1$, its value is either $\sigma S_1^u + F$ or $\sigma S_1^d + F$, as summarized in figure 17.7.

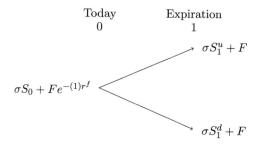

Figure 17.7 Replicating portfolio values in a binomial stock price model

Setting equal the difference between the payoffs in the up-state and down-state for both the call per figure 17.3 and the replicating portfolio per figure 17.7, respectively, then $c_1^u - c_1^d = (\sigma S_1^u + F) - (\sigma S_1^d + F) = \sigma(S_1^u - S_1^d)$. Solving this for σ, then $\sigma = \frac{c_1^u - c_1^d}{S_1^u - S_1^d} = \frac{\Delta c}{\Delta S} = \Delta^c$ for the discrete case.

Equating the payoffs in both the up-state as well as the down-state of the call in figure 17.3 and those of the replicating portfolio in figure 17.7, respectively, then $S_1^u - K = \Delta^c S_1^u + F$ and $0 = \Delta^c S_1^d + F$. Solving these simultaneously,

$$\Delta^c = \frac{\Delta c}{\Delta S} = \frac{S_1^u - K}{S_1^u - S_1^d} > 0, \quad \text{and} \quad F = -S_1^d \frac{S_1^u - K}{S_1^u - S_1^d} = -S_1^d \Delta^c < 0. \qquad (17.16)$$

As both $S_1^u - K > 0$ and $S_1^u - S_1^d > 0$, then $\sigma = \Delta^c > 0$, meaning that the call replicating portfolio is long shares of stock. This makes intuitive sense as previously explained.

---

[10]The assumption of zero-coupon debt is not necessary but simplifies the model. As an example of risk-free debt, consider US Treasuries.

However, the assumption of risk-free debt is potentially problematic if its position in the call replicating portfolio is short, as most investor's cannot issue risk-free debt. But given that we can subsequently set up another portfolio long the call and short the replicating portfolio, a risk-free portfolio can be constructed.

Regarding the zero coupon bond, $F = -S_1^d \Delta^c < 0$, meaning that the portfolio is short debt. The replicating portfolio involves partially financing the long stock position with a short bond position, i.e., in issuing a zero-coupon bond. Obviously the financing is partial as the call value is positive, i.e, as $c_0 = \Delta^c S_0 + Fe^{-(1)r^f} > 0$.

Finally, $c_0 = \Delta^c S_0 + Fe^{-(1)r^f}$, or in terms of exogenous parameters,

$$c_0 = \Delta^c \left(S_0 - S_1^d e^{-r^f} \right) = \frac{S_1^u - K}{S_1^u - S_1^d} \left(S_0 - S_1^d e^{-r^f} \right) > 0, \qquad (17.17)$$

as before per equation (17.11).

17.2.4 Put Replicating Portfolio

We now replicate the payoffs of a put option in the same framework as the call option of the previous section. We again assume that $S_1^d < K < S_1^u$, or $K \in (S_1^d, S_1^u)$.

Analogous to before, consider a portfolio with a position of σ shares of the underlying asset and a position in zero-coupon, risk-free debt with a face value of F. At time $t = 0$, the value of the put replicating portfolio is $\sigma S_0 + Fe^{-(1)r^f}$. At time $t = 1$, its value is either $\sigma S_1^u + F$ or $\sigma S_1^d + F$. These are the same expressions as in figure 17.7. Setting equal the difference between the payoffs in the up-state and down-state for both the put per figure 17.5 and the replicating portfolio per figure 17.7, respectively, then $p_1^u - p_1^d = (\sigma S_1^u + F) - (\sigma S_1^d + F) = \sigma(S_1^u - S_1^d)$. Solving this for σ, then $\sigma = \frac{p_1^u - p_1^d}{S_1^u - S_1^d} = \frac{\Delta p}{\Delta S} = \Delta^p < 0$ for the discrete case.

Equating the payoffs in both the up-state as well as the down-state of the put in figure 17.5 and those of the replicating portfolio in figure 17.7, respectively, then for the up-state: $0 = \Delta^p S_1^u + F$, and for the down-state: $K - S_1^d = \Delta^p S_1^d + F$. Solving these simultaneously,

$$\Delta^p = \frac{\Delta p}{\Delta S} = -\frac{K - S_1^d}{S_1^u - S_1^d} < 0, \text{ and } F = -S_1^u \Delta^p = -S_1^u \frac{K - S_1^d}{S_1^u - S_1^d} > 0. \qquad (17.18)$$

As $\sigma = \Delta^p < 0$, then the put replicating portfolio is short shares of stock. This makes intuitive sense as previously explained. Regarding the zero coupon bond, $F = -S_1^u \Delta^p > 0$, meaning that the put replicating portfolio has a long debt position.

As $p_0 = \Delta^p S_0 + Fe^{-(1)r^f}$, then in terms of exogenous parameters,

$$p_0 = -\Delta^p \left(S_1^u e^{-r^f} - S_0 \right) = \frac{K - S_1^d}{S_1^u - S_1^d} \left(S_1^u e^{-r^f} - S_0 \right) > 0, \qquad (17.19)$$

as before per equation (17.14).

Finally, note the following relation.

$$\Delta^c - \Delta^p = \frac{S_1^u - K}{S_1^u - S_1^d} - \left(-\frac{K - S_1^d}{S_1^u - S_1^d}\right) = 1, \quad \text{or} \quad \Delta^c = 1 + \Delta^p. \tag{17.20}$$

17.2.5 Risk-Neutral Valuation

Ross (1976) shows that options may be modeled via risk-neutral valuation. This means that we can use a binomial stock price model where investors are risk-neutral. As such, we discount all future cash flows by the risk-free rate of return. This also implies that all assets grow in value at this same risk-free rate. For an option with a given underlying asset, or for options with multiple underlying assets of the same volatility return, $\sigma(r)$, a single model suffices. However, a new model is necessary for any option with an underlying asset whose volatility is different from any previously valued.

The intuition behind this important model is given by previous results. As we can set up a portfolio of an option and its underlying asset (in our cases, stock) such that its payoffs are identically the same for each state of the world, then this certain payoff can be discounted at the risk-free rate of return to derive the option's value. As we can always create such a risk-free portfolio, then we can value options as if the world were risk-free.

To figure 17.2, we add **risk neutral probabilities**, pr^u and pr^d shown in figure 17.8.

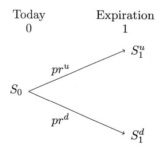

Figure 17.8 Binomial stock price model with risk-neutral probabilities

Next, in terms of these risk-neutral probabilities pr^u and pr^d, then

$$E[S_1] = pr^u(uS_0) + pr^d(dS_0) = S_0 e^{(1)r^f}, \tag{17.21}$$

where the second equality follows from the fact that in a risk-neutral world, the risk-free rate of return is not only the appropriate discount rate for all cash flows, but also the expected growth rate of value for of all assets, regardless of actual risk. Noting that

$pr^d = 1 - pr^u$, then equation (17.21) implies that

$$pr^u = \frac{e^{rf} - d}{u - d}, \quad \text{and} \quad pr^d = 1 - pr^u = \frac{u - e^{rf}}{u - d}. \tag{17.22}$$

Both probabilities are assumed positive, again resulting in the relationships of expression (17.15), repeated here for convenience:

$$S_1^d < S_0 e^{rf} < S_1^u, \quad \text{or equivalently,} \quad d < e^{rf} < u. \tag{17.23}$$

Call Option per Risk-Neutral Valuation

To figure 17.3, we add risk-neutral probabilities, pr^u and pr^d shown in figure 17.9. This is appropriate, as all risky-assets are valued the same way in a risk-neutral framework. Hence, $c_0 e^{(1)rf} = E[c_1] = pr^u(c_1^u) + pr^d(c_1^d) = pr^u(S_1^u - K) = \frac{e^{rf}-d}{u-d}(S_1^u - K)$. Thus,

$$c_0 = \Delta^c S_0 \left(1 - de^{-rf}\right) = \Delta^c \left(S_0 - S_1^d e^{-rf}\right), \tag{17.24}$$

the same as that derived before, i.e., equation (17.11).

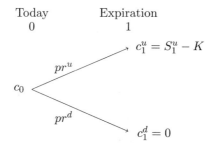

Figure 17.9 Call option via risk-neutral valuation

Put Option per Risk-Neutral Valuation

Analogous to valuing a call, we can value a put option via risk-neutral valuation. To figure 17.5, we add risk-neutral probabilities, pr^u and pr^d shown in figure 17.10. Hence, $p_0 e^{(1)rf} = E[p_1] = pr^u(p_1^u) + pr^d(p_1^d) = pr^d(K - S_1^d) = \frac{u-e^{rf}}{u-d}(K - S_1^d)$. Solving for p_0, then

$$p_0 = -\Delta^p S_0 \left(ue^{-rf} - 1\right) = -\Delta^p \left(S_1^u e^{-rf} - S_0\right), \tag{17.25}$$

the same as that derived before per equation (17.14).

238   **Asset Valuation Theory**

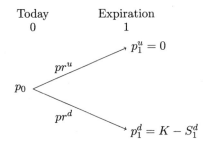

Figure 17.10   Put option via risk-neutral valuation

Risk-Neutral Versus Real World Probabilities

Before leaving risk-neutral valuation, note that from

$$\begin{aligned}S_0 &= e^{-r^E}\left(\pi^u S_1^u + \pi^d S_1^d\right)\\ &= e^{-r^E}\left(E\left[S_1|\pi^u,\pi^d\right]\right) = e^{-r^f}\left(E\left[S_1|pr^u,pr^d\right]\right)\\ &= e^{-r^f}\left(pr^u S_1^u + pr^d S_1^d\right) = S_0,\end{aligned} \qquad (17.26)$$

then

$$\pi^u S_1^u + \pi^d S_1^d = E\left[S_1|\pi^u,\pi^d\right] > E\left[S_1|pr^u,pr^d\right] = pr^u S_1^u + pr^d S_1^d. \qquad (17.27)$$

So $\pi^u - pr^u = \frac{e^{r^E}-d}{u-d} - \frac{e^{r^f}-d}{u-d} > 0$, as $r^E > r^f$. Accordingly, $\pi^u > pr^u \Leftrightarrow \pi^d < pr^d$.

This makes intuitive sense. Consider two worlds, one in which investors are risk-neutral and one in which they are risk-averse. Let's assume that in both worlds, the parameters S_0, u and d (equivalently, S_0, S_1^u and S_1^d) are the same. As the investor in a risk-averse world has a higher discount rate, then she must believe that there is a greater probability of the up-state relative to the corresponding belief of that of an investor. Otherwise, for identical payoffs in each state at date 1 in both worlds, the only way that an investor with a higher discount rate would be willing to pay the same price S_0 as the investor in the risk-neutral world is if she believes that there is higher probability of the up-state and its corresponding higher payoff. Finally, consider the perspective of an investor in a risk-neutral world. Her belief regarding the probability of the down-state (up-state) must higher (lower) than that of a risk-averse investor, given that she is only willing to pay the same price (S_0) and no more, despite their shared beliefs regarding S_1^d and S_1^u.

17.2.6 Comparative Statics

Call Option Comparative Statics

Utilizing equation (17.11) for the value of a call option, or $c_0 = e^{-r^f}(pr^u c_1^u + pr^d c_1^d) = e^{-r^f} pr^u c_1^u$, then we can calculate the following results.

$$\frac{\partial c_0}{\partial S_0} = \frac{\partial (e^{-r^f} pr^u c_1^u)}{\partial S_0} = (e^{-r^f} c_1^u)\frac{\partial pr^u}{\partial S_0} = (e^{-r^f} c_1^u)\frac{e^{r^f}}{S_1^u - S_1^d} = \Delta^c > 0, \quad (17.28)$$

per definition of $\Delta^c \approx \frac{c_1^u - c_1^d}{S_1^u - S_1^d} \in (0,1)$. As expected, as stock, valued S_0, represents a conditional asset given exercise of a call, then the value of a call is increasing in S_0.

Regarding the strike price K,[11]

$$\frac{\partial c_0}{\partial K} = \frac{\partial (e^{-r^f} pr^u c_1^u)}{\partial K} = e^{-r^f} pr^u \frac{\partial c_1^u}{\partial K} = -e^{-r^f} pr^u < 0 \quad (17.29)$$

Not surprisingly, as the strike price (K) represents a conditional liability given exercise of a call, then the value of a call is decreasing in K.

Next, we consider the value of a call as a function of the risk-free rate of return, or

$$\frac{\partial c_0}{\partial r^f} = \frac{\partial (e^{-r^f} pr^u c_1^u)}{\partial r^f} = c_1^u \frac{\partial}{\partial r^f}\left(\frac{S_0 - S_1^d e^{-r^f}}{S_1^u - S_1^d}\right) = \Delta^c S_1^d e^{-r^f} > 0. \quad (17.30)$$

We commented earlier that a feature of risk-neutral valuation is that all assets have an expected rate of return of the risk-free rate, r^f. Recall that $c_0 = e^{-r^f} pr^u c_1^u = e^{-r^f} pr^u(S_1^u - K)$. Thus, as $e^{-r^f} pr^u = \frac{1 - de^{-r^f}}{u - d}$ is increasing in r^f, then so is the call's value. In short, holding fixed S_1^d and S_1^u for a given S_0, then the greater the risk-free rate of return, the higher the discounted probability of the up-state and thus, the greater the value of the call, all else equal.[12]

Impact of Underlying Asset's Volatility of Return upon Call Value

The volatility of the rate of return of the underlying asset, expressed as an APr continuously compounded, is a critically important parameter of option value. To capture this concept in our binomial model, consider two possible pairs of stock prices at time $t = 1$, where the difference between one pair is greater than the other, but where

---

[11]In terms of exogenous parameters, $\frac{\partial c_0}{\partial K} = -\frac{S_0 - S_1^d e^{-r^f}}{S_1^u - S_1^d} < 0$, where the inequality follows from expression (17.15).

[12]In the framework of a call replicating portfolio, which is short risk-free debt with face value $F = -\Delta^c S_1^d < 0$, the higher the risk-free rate of return, the lower is the present value of this liability, $-\Delta^c S_1^d e^{-r^f}$. Hence, call value is increasing in r^f.

240   Asset Valuation Theory

both yield the identical expected stock price one period henceforth. Then all else equal, we will see that an option whose underlying asset has the stock whose price pair with the greater difference has greater value than one whose underlying asset has the stock whose price pair with the smaller difference. In short, we'll show that an option value is increasing in volatility of return of underlying asset.

We attempt to capture this positive impact of volatility of underlying asset return upon call value, $\frac{\partial c_0}{\partial \sigma} > 0$ via $\frac{\partial c_0(S_1^d, S_1^u)}{\partial (S_1^u - S_1^d)}$. Specifically,

$$\frac{\partial c_0\left(S_1^d, S_1^u\right)}{\partial \left(S_1^u - S_1^d\right)} = \left.\frac{\partial c_0}{\partial S_1^u}\right|_{S_1^d} \left[\frac{\partial \left(S_1^u - S_1^d\right)}{\partial S_1^u}\right]^{-1} + \left.\frac{\partial c_0}{\partial S_1^d}\right|_{S_1^u} \left[\frac{\partial \left(S_1^u - S_1^d\right)}{\partial S_1^d}\right]^{-1}$$

$$= \left.\frac{\partial c_0}{\partial S_1^u}\right|_{S_1^d} [1] + \left.\frac{\partial c_0}{\partial S_1^d}\right|_{S_1^u} [-1] = \left.\frac{\partial c_0}{\partial S_1^u}\right|_{S_1^d} - \left.\frac{\partial c_0}{\partial S_1^d}\right|_{S_1^u}, \quad (17.31)$$

or $\frac{\partial c_0(S_1^d, S_1^u)}{\partial (S_1^u - S_1^d)} = \left.\frac{\partial c_0}{\partial S_1^u}\right|_{S_1^d} - \left.\frac{\partial c_0}{\partial S_1^d}\right|_{S_1^u}$. Continuing,[13]

$$\frac{\partial c_0}{\partial S_1^u} = \frac{\partial (e^{-r^f} pr^u c_1^u)}{\partial S_1^u} = e^{-r^f} \frac{\partial (pr^u c_1^u)}{\partial S_1^u} = (S_0 - S_1^d e^{-r^f}) \frac{\partial \Delta^c}{\partial S_1^u}$$

$$= -e^{-r^f} pr^u \Delta^p > 0, \quad (17.32)$$

as $\Delta^p < 0$. Next,[14]

$$\frac{\partial c_0}{\partial S_1^d} = \frac{\partial (e^{-r^f} pr^u c_1^u)}{\partial S_1^d} = e^{-r^f} c_1^u \frac{\partial pr^u}{\partial S_1^d} = -e^{-r^f} pr^d \Delta^c < 0, \quad (17.33)$$

as $\Delta^c > 0$. Thus, combining results (17.31), (17.32) and (17.33), then $\frac{\partial c_0(S_1^d, S_1^u)}{\partial (S_1^u - S_1^d)} > 0$. As this is our crude proxy for $\frac{\partial c_0}{\partial \sigma}$, then we have demonstrated that call value increases in volatility of return of the underlying asset, all else equal.

In order to drive home the previous claim, consider figures 17.11 and 17.12, where the second is a graphical illustration of the first. Specifically, consider five stocks and five call options, one corresponding to each stock. For all five stocks, the current price is the same, $S_0 = \$40$. As we value all five call options in the same risk-neutral world where the risk-free rate of return (an APr, continuously compounded) is 5%, then for all five stocks, the expected value one period (i.e., one year) from today is $E[S_1] = \$40 e^{5\%(1)} = \$42.05$.

---

[13]In terms of exogenous parameters, $\frac{\partial c_0}{\partial S_1^u} = (S_0 - S_1^d e^{-r^f}) \frac{K - S_1^d}{(S_1^u - S_1^d)^2} > 0$, as $K > S_1^d$ per assumption, and $pr^u > 0 \Rightarrow S_0 > S_1^d e^{-r^f}$.

[14]In terms of exogenous parameters, $\frac{\partial c_0}{\partial S_1^d} = -(S_1^u - K) \frac{S_1^u e^{-r^f} - S_0}{(S_1^u - S_1^d)^2} < 0$, as $K < S_1^u$ per assumption, and $pr^d > 0 \Rightarrow S_0 < S_1^u e^{-r^f}$.

stock	S_1^d	S_1^u	pr^u	$E[S_1] = pr^u S_1^u + pr^d S_1^d$	$\sigma(S_1)$	c_1^u	$E[c_1] = pr^u c_1^u$	c_0
A	37.95	42.05	100.0%	100%(42.05) = $42.05	0%	2.05	100.0%(2.05) = $2.05	$1.95
B	30	50	60.25%	60.25%(50) + 39.75%(30)	979%	10	60.25%(10) = $6.03	$5.73
C	20	60	55.13%	55.13%(60) + 44.87%(20)	1989%	20	55.13%(20) = $11.03	$10.49
D	10	70	53.42%	53.42%(70) + 46.58%(10)	2993%	30	53.42%(30) = $16.03	$15.24
E	0	80	52.56%	52.56%(80) + 47.44%(0)	3995%	40	52.56%(40) = $21.03	$20.00

$\sigma(S_1) = \{pr^u(S_1^u - E[S_1])^2 + pr^d(S_1^d - E[S_1])^2)\}^{0.5} = \{pr^u(S_1^u - \$42.05)^2 + pr^d(S_1^d - \$42.05)^2\}^{0.5}$;

$pr^u = \frac{S_0(e^{r^f}) - S_1^d}{S_1^u - S_1^d} = \frac{E[S_1] - S_1^d}{S_1^u - S_1^d} = \frac{\$42.051 - S_1^d}{S_1^u - S_1^d}$, as $S_0 = \$40$, and $r^f = 5\%$;

For all five stocks: $\{A, B, C, D, E\}$), then $E[S_1] = pr^u S_1^u + pr^d S_1^d = \$42.05$;

$c_1^u = S_1^u - K = S_1^u - \$40$, as $K = \$40$;

$c_0 = e^{-r^f}\{E[c_1]\} = e^{-r^f}\{pr^u(S_1^u - K)\} = 0.9512\{pr^u(S_1^u - \$40)\}$;

Figure 17.11 Impact of stock price volatility upon call value

One period from now, stock A's price will be $42.05 with 100% probability, i.e., with certainty, so it is risk-free.[15] Hence, its fair future value (i.e., at $t = 1$) is $E[S_1^A] = \$42.05$. Analogously, one period from now, stock B's (C's, D's, E's) price will be $50 ($60, $70, $80) with 60.25% (55.13%, 53.42%, 52.56%) probability and $30 ($20, $10, $0) with 39.75% (44.87%, 46.58%, 47.44%) probability. In *all fives cases*, $E[S_1] = \$42.05 = S_0 e^{r^f} = pr^{u,1} S_1^{u,i} + pr^{d,i} S_1^{d,i}$, $i \in \{A, B, C, D, E\}$. From $\sigma(S_1) = \{pr^u(S_1^u - E[S_1])^2 + pr^d(S_1^d - E[S_1])^2)\}^{0.5}$, one can confirm that $\sigma(S_1^A) < \sigma(S_1^B) < \sigma(S_1^C) < \sigma(S_1^D) < \sigma(S_1^E)$. In short, in going from stock A to B to C to D to E, volatility of return in strictly increasing.

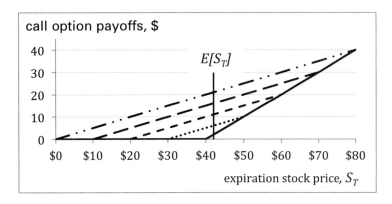

Figure 17.12 Call value is increasing in stock price volatility

Now consider the value of five call options, where each option, which has a strike price of $K = \$40$, has as its underlying asset one of the respective five stocks. Referring back to the final column of figure 17.11, we see that call value is increasing in volatility.

---

[15] This is obviously hypothetical, used for pedagogical purposes, as returns of stocks are not risk-free.

In figure 17.12, we have drawn a vertical line corresponding to the expected stock value at the end of the period, $E[S_1] = \$40e^{(1)r^f} = \$42.05$. The five call payoffs, $E[c_1^i]$, $i \in \{A, B, C, D, E\}$, correspond to where this vertical line crosses the other five non-horizontal lines. First, $E[c_1^A] = \$2.05$ is where the vertical line crosses the 45 degree line of the call option payoff function. The other four call payoff values as shown in figure 17.11, corresponding to the other four stocks, is where the four non-solid lines, each of slope $\frac{1}{2}$, respectively cross the vertical line. Finally, probabilities p^d and p^u for each stock can also be interpreted from figure 17.12. For example, for stock B, pr^d is the ratio of the horizontal distance from $E[S_1] = \$42.05 : \$50 = S_1^u$ to the horizontal distance from $S_1^d = \$30 : \$50 = S_1^u$, or $pr^d = \frac{50 - 42.05}{50 - 30} = 39.75\%$. Also, pr^u is the ratio of the horizontal distance from $S_1^d = \$30 : \$42.05 = E[S_1]$ to the horizontal distance from $S_1^d = \$30 : \$50 = S_1^u$, or $pr^u = \frac{42.05 - 30}{50 - 30} = 60.25\%$. Probabilities pr^u and pr^d for stocks C, D and E can likewise be graphically interpreted.

Impact of Time to Maturity upon Call Value

As is the case with volatility of return of underlying asset, we have no variable to directly capture time to maturity in the single-period binomial stock price model presented thus far. Later, we will see that both call value and put value also increase in time to maturity. Thus, for the impact of time to maturity upon call value, we offer the following intuitive sketch.

All else equal, as duration of time increases, so does volatility of the return of an asset. Intuitively, the range of values that a risky asset may have one day from now is less than that which the asset may have one month from now. From mathematical statistics, variances (and covariances) of returns are linear in duration of time, or

$$\sigma^2(r_{Nt}) = N\sigma^2(r_t), \quad \text{and so} \quad \sqrt{\sigma^2(r_{Nt})} = \sigma(r_{Nt}) = \sqrt{N}\sigma(r_t), \qquad (17.34)$$

where r_t denotes the return for a single period t, and r_{Nt} here denotes the return for a duration of time of N periods. So again, variances (and covariances) of returns are linear in duration of time. Hence, as call option values are increasing in volatility, then they are also increasing in time to maturity, all else equal.

Put Option Comparative Statics

Utilizing equation (17.14) for the value of a put option, or $p_0 = e^{-r^f}(pr^u p_1^u + pr^d p_1^d) = e^{-r^f} pr^d p_1^d$, then we can calculate the following results.

$$\frac{\partial p_0}{\partial S_0} = \frac{\partial (e^{-r^f} pr^d p_1^d)}{\partial S_0} = (e^{-r^f} p_1^d)\frac{\partial pr^d}{\partial S_0} = -(e^{-r^f} p_1^d)\frac{e^{r^f}}{S_1^u - S_1^d} = \Delta^p < 0, \qquad (17.35)$$

per definition of $\Delta^p \approx \frac{p_1^u - p_1^d}{S_1^u - S_1^d} \in (-1, 0)$. As expected, as stock, valued S_0, represents a conditional liability given exercise of a put, then the value of a put is decreasing in S_0.

Regarding the strike price K,[16]

$$\frac{\partial p_0}{\partial K} = \frac{\partial (e^{-r^f} pr^d p_1^d)}{\partial K} = e^{-r^f} pr^d \frac{\partial p_1^d}{\partial K} = e^{-r^f} pr^d(1) > 0. \qquad (17.36)$$

Not surprisingly, as the strike price (K) represents a conditional asset given exercise of a put, then the value of a put is increasing in K.

Next, we consider the value of a put as a function of the risk-free rate of return, or

$$\frac{\partial p_0}{\partial r^f} = \frac{\partial (e^{-r^f} pr^d p_1^d)}{\partial r^f} = p_1^d \frac{\partial}{\partial r^f} \left(\frac{S_1^u e^{-r^f} - S_0}{S_1^u - S_1^d} \right) = \Delta^p S_1^u e^{-r^f} < 0, \qquad (17.37)$$

as $\Delta^p < 0$. Recall that one feature of risk-neutral valuation is that all assets have an expected return of the risk-free rate, r^f. Recall that $p_0 = e^{-r^f} pr^d p_1^d = e^{-r^f} pr^d (K - S_1^d)$. Thus, as $e^{-r^f} pr^d = \frac{ue^{-r^f} - 1}{u - d}$ is decreasing in r^f, then so is the put's value. In short, holding fixed S_1^d and S_1^u for a given S_0, then the greater the risk-free rate of return, the lower the discounted probability of the down-state and thus, the smaller the value of the put.

Impact of Underlying Asset's Volatility of Return upon Put Value

As we did for the call option, we attempt to capture the positive impact of volatility of underlying asset return upon put value, $\frac{\partial p_0}{\partial \sigma} > 0$ via $\frac{\partial p_0(S_1^d, S_1^u)}{\partial (S_1^u - S_1^d)}$. Comparable to equation (17.31),

$$\frac{\partial p_0 \left(S_1^d, S_1^u \right)}{\partial \left(S_1^u - S_1^d \right)} = \left. \frac{\partial p_0}{\partial S_1^u} \right|_{S_1^d} - \left. \frac{\partial p_0}{\partial S_1^d} \right|_{S_1^u}. \qquad (17.38)$$

Continuing,[17]

$$\frac{\partial p_0}{\partial S_1^u} = \frac{\partial (e^{-r^f} pr^d p_1^d)}{\partial S_1^u} = e^{-r^f} p_1^d \frac{\partial pr^d}{\partial S_1^u} = -e^{-r^f} pr^u \Delta^p$$

$$= \frac{\partial c_0}{\partial S_1^u} > 0, \qquad (17.39)$$

---

[16]In terms of exogenous parameters, $\frac{\partial p_0}{\partial K} = \frac{S_1^u e^{-r^f} - S_0}{S_1^u - S_1^d} > 0$, where the inequality follows from expression (17.15).

[17]In terms of exogenous parameters, $\frac{\partial p_0}{\partial S_1^u} = (S_0 - S_1^d e^{-r^f}) \frac{K - S_1^d}{(S_1^u - S_1^d)^2} > 0$, as $K > S_1^d$ per assumption, and $pr^u > 0 \Rightarrow S_0 > S_1^d e^{-r^f}$.

244   Asset Valuation Theory

as $\Delta^p < 0$ per assumption. Interestingly, $\frac{\partial p_0}{\partial S_1^u} = \frac{\partial c_0}{\partial S_1^u} > 0$. Next[18]

$$\frac{\partial p_0}{\partial S_1^d} = \frac{\partial (e^{-r^f} pr^d p_1^d)}{\partial S_1^d} = e^{-r^f} \frac{\partial (pr^d p_1^d)}{\partial S_1^d} = -e^{-r^f} pr^d \Delta^c$$

$$= \frac{\partial c_0}{\partial S_1^d} < 0, \qquad (17.40)$$

as $\Delta^c > 0$. So not only does $\frac{\partial p_0}{\partial S_1^u} = \frac{\partial c_0}{\partial S_1^u} > 0$, but also $\frac{\partial p_0}{\partial S_1^d} = \frac{\partial c_0}{\partial S_1^d} < 0$. Thus, $\frac{\partial p_0(S_1^d, S_1^u)}{\partial (S_1^u - S_1^d)} = \frac{\partial c_0(S_1^d, S_1^u)}{\partial (S_1^u - S_1^d)} > 0$. As this is our crude proxy for $\frac{\partial p_0}{\partial \sigma}$, then we have demonstrated that put value, like call value, increases in volatility of return of the underlying asset.

Comparable to our treatment for a call option, consider figures 17.13 and 17.14, where the second is a graphical illustration of the first. Specifically, we again consider the same five stocks, $\{A, B, C, D, E\}$, shown in figure 17.11, but this time the stocks are underlying assets for five respective put options. As before, all five stocks have the same current price, $S_0 = \$40$. All five put options have the same strike price, $K = \$40$. As we value all five put options in the same risk-neutral world where $r^f = 5\%$, then $E[S_1] = \$40 e^{5\%(1)} = \$42.05 = pr^{u,1} S_1^{u,i} + pr^{d,i} S_1^{d,i}$, $i \in \{A, B, C, D, E\}$. Referring to the final column of figure 17.13, we see that put value, like call value, is increasing in volatility.

stock	S_1^d	S_1^u	pr^u	$E[S_1] = pr^u S_1^u + pr^d S_1^d$	$\sigma(S_1)$	p_1^d	$E[p_1] = pr^d p_1^d$	p_0
A	37.95	42.05	100.0%	100%(42.05) = $42.05	0%	0	0%(2.05) = $0.00	$0.00
B	30	50	60.25%	60.25%(50) + 39.75%(30)	979%	10	39.75%(10) = $3.97	$3.78
C	20	60	55.13%	55.13%(60) + 44.87%(20)	1989%	20	44.87%(20) = $8.97	$8.54
D	10	70	53.42%	53.42%(70) + 46.58%(10)	2993%	30	46.58%(30) = $13.97	$13.29
E	0	80	52.56%	52.56%(80) + 47.44%(0)	3995%	40	47.44%(40) = $18.97	$18.05

Compared to figure 106, only the final three columns differ.
$pr^d = \frac{S_1^u - S_0(e^{r^f})}{S_1^u - S_1^d} = \frac{S_1^u - E[S_1]}{S_1^u - S_1^d} = \frac{S_1^u - \$42.051}{S_1^u - S_1^d}$, as $S_0 = \$40$, and $r^f = 5\%$;
For all five stocks: $\{A, B, C, D, E\}$), then $E[S_1] = pr^u S_1^u + pr^d S_1^d = \$42.05 = S_0 e^{r^f} = \$40 e^{5\%}$;
$p_1^d = K - S_1^d = \$40 - S_1^d$, as $K = \$40$;
$p_0 = e^{-r^f}\{E[p_1]\} = e^{-r^f}\{pr^d(K - S_1^d)\} = 0.9512\{pr^d(\$40 - S_1^d)\}$;

Figure 17.13   Impact of stock price volatility upon put value

In figure 17.14, we have drawn a vertical line corresponding to the expected stock value at the end of the period, $E[S_1] = \$40 e^{(1)r^f} = \$42.05$. The five put payoffs, $E[p_1^i]$, $i \in \{A, B, C, D, E\}$, correspond to where this vertical line crosses the other five non-horizontal lines. First, $E[p_1^A] = \$0$ is where the vertical line crosses the put option payoff

---

[18]In terms of exogenous parameters, $\frac{\partial c_0}{\partial S_1^d} = -(S_1^u - K)\frac{S_1^u e^{-r^f} - S_0}{(S_1^u - S_1^d)^2} < 0$, as $K < S_1^u$ per assumption, and $pr^d > 0 \Rightarrow S_0 < S_1^u e^{-r^f}$.

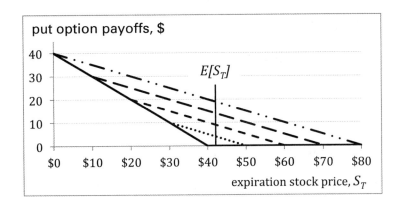

Figure 17.14 Put value is increasing in stock price volatility

function. The other four put payoff values (as shown in figure 17.13) corresponding to the other four stocks, is where the four non-solid lines, each of slope $-\frac{1}{2}$, respectively cross the vertical line. Finally, probabilities pr^d and pr^u for each stock can also be interpreted from figure 17.14 as previously discussed in the discussion for figure 17.12.

Impact of Time to Maturity upon Put Value

For the call option, we argued that as call value is increasing in volatility, then it must also be increasing in time to maturity via $\sigma^2(r_{Nt}) = N\sigma^2(r_t), \Leftrightarrow \sqrt{\sigma^2(r_{Nt})} = \sigma(r_{Nt}) = \sqrt{N}\sigma(r_t)$, where r_t denotes the return for a single period t, and r_{Nt} here denotes the return for a duration of time of N periods.

Though put value is likewise increasing in volatility, the impact of time to maturity upon put value is ambiguous. Generally, put value is increasing in time to maturity. However, a put deeply in-the-money can decrease in time to maturity, all else equal. Intuitively, as stock price generally increases over time, a put deeply in-the-money can lose value if held for a long period of time.

Problems

For this chapter's problem set, a one period (where the period has a duration of one year) binomial stock price model is to be used. Assume that $u = 1.25$ and $d = 0.9$. The initial stock price is $10 and the continuously compounded risk-free rate of return is 6%. Equity holders demand a rate of return of 13%. Any option, either call or put, is a European option, has a strike price of $11 and an expiration date of one year from today.

1. What is the stock price after one period in: (a) the up-state of the binomial model,

S_1^u? (b) the down-state, S_1^d?

2. What is the probability of the up-state in the risk-averse world, π^u?

What would be the probability of the up-state in a hypothetical risk-neutral world, pr^u?

Which one is greater, π^u or pr^u? Explain.

3. What is the expected stock price after one period, $E[S_1]$?

4. What is the value of the call in the: (a) up-state of the model, c_1^u? (b) down-state, c_1^d?

What is the value of the put in the: (a) up-state of the model, p_1^u? (b) down-state, p_1^d?

5. Calculate delta of the call, Δ^c, and delta of the put, Δ^p.

Calculate the difference $\Delta^c - \Delta^p$.

6. Calculate the call option premium, c_0, and the put option premium, p_0.

7. Calculate the sum of the put premium and the initial stock price, $p_0 + S_0$. Calculate the sum of the call premium and the risk-free present value of the strike price, $c_0 + Ke^{-r^f}$. What is the difference of these two sums? Explain this result.

8. Now assume that the initial stock price is $11 per share. Recalculate the call premium. Is it larger or smaller than when the initial stock price was assumed to be $10?

9. Assuming that the initial stock price is $11 per share, recalculate the put premium. Is it larger or smaller than when the initial stock price was assumed to be $10?

10. Return to assuming the original stock price of $10 per share, but assume that the strike price is $12. Recalculate the call premium. Is it larger or smaller than when the strike price was assumed to be $11?

11. Assuming the original stock price of $10 per share, but that the strike price is now $12 per share, recalculate the put premium. Is it larger or smaller than when the strike price was assumed to be $11?

12. Return to the original assumptions ($S_0 = 10$, $K = 11$), but now assume that the risk-free rate of return is 7%. Recalculate the call premium. Is it larger or smaller than

when the risk-free rate was assumed to be 6%?

13. Returning to the original assumptions ($S_0 = 10$, $K = 11$), and given a newly assumed risk-free rate of return of 7%, recalculate the put premium. Is it larger or smaller than when the risk-free rate was assumed to be 6%?

CHAPTER 18

Option Valuation: Multi-period Model

As previously mentioned, it may seem silly to pursue an option pricing model which assumes that a stock price one period henceforth may only take on one of two possible values. However, for a given time to expiration of an option, then by adding more and more periods to the model, we increase the final number of terminal stock prices. This is despite the fact that conditional on a given interim stock price, the next stock price at the end of the upcoming period may still only realize one of two possible values. For each additional period in the model, we add one more possibility regarding expiration price. Correspondingly, as periods are increased for a given expiration date, then the durations of periods shorten.

18.1 Two-period Binomial Stock Price Model

For a given time to expiration T, consider a two-period model, where each period has length $\Delta t = \frac{T}{2}$, as shown in figure 18.1.[1] Given S_0, the prices one period from today corresponding to the up and down states, respectively, are denoted by $S_{T/2}^u$ and $S_{T/2}^d$. So $E[S_{T/2}] = S_0 e^{r^f \Delta t} = pr^u S_{T/2}^u + pr^d S_{T/2}^d$. Comparable to the one-period model,

$$pr^u = \frac{S_0 e^{r^f \Delta t} - S_{T/2}^d}{S_{T/2}^u - S_{T/2}^d} = \frac{e^{r^f \Delta t} - d}{u - d}, \quad \text{and}$$

$$pr^d = 1 - pr^u = \frac{S_{T/2}^u - S_0 e^{r^f \Delta t}}{S_{T/2}^u - S_{T/2}^d} = \frac{u - e^{r^f \Delta t}}{u - d}, \quad (18.1)$$

---

[1] If it is assumed the $ud = du$ as is the case for a so-called **reconnecting tree**, then $S_0 ud = S_T^{ud} = S_T^{du} = S_0 du$, so $E[S_T | S_0] = (pr^u)^2 S_T^{uu} + 2 pr^u pr^d S_T^{ud} + (pr^d)^2 S_T^{dd}$. We assume this to be the case. Otherwise, $ud \neq du$ for non-reconnecting tree.

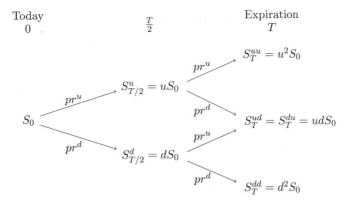

Figure 18.1 Two-period binomial stock price model

where we assume that

$$u = \frac{S^u_{T/2}}{S_0} = \frac{S^{uu}_T}{S^u_{T/2}} = \frac{S^{du}_T}{S^d_{T/2}}, \quad \text{and} \quad d = \frac{S^d_{T/2}}{S_0} = \frac{S^{dd}_T}{S^d_{T/2}} = \frac{S^{ud}_T}{S^u_{T/2}} \quad (18.2)$$

are the same for each period. As r^f is also assumed to be constant for all $t \in [0, T]$, then $e^{r \Delta t} = e^{rT/2}$ is the same each period. Hence, so too pr^u and pr^d are constant each period, regardless of location in the binomial stock price tree.

Regarding the second period, conditional on a stock price of $S^u_{T/2}$, then

$$E[S_T | S^u_{T/2}] = S^u_{T/2} e^{r^f \Delta t} = pr^u S^{uu}_T + pr^d S^{ud}_T. \quad (18.3)$$

Analogously, if the stock price is $S^d_{T/2}$ after one period, then

$$E[S_T | S^d_{T/2}] = S^d_{T/2} e^{r^f \Delta t} = pr^u S^{du}_T + pr^d S^{dd}_T. \quad (18.4)$$

Lastly, unconditionally at time $t = 0$, $E[S_T] = E[S_{T/2}]e^{r^f \Delta t} = S_0 e^{2r^f \Delta t} = S_0 e^{r^f T} = pr^u E[S_T | S^u_{T/2}] + pr^d E[S_T | S^d_{T/2}]$, or

$$E[S_T] = pr^u(pr^u S^{uu}_T + pr^d S^{ud}_T) + pr^d(pr^u S^{du}_T + pr^d S^{dd}_T).$$

Given than $S^{ud}_T = S^{du}_T$ for a reconnecting tree, then $E[S_T] = (pr^u)^2 S^{uu}_T + 2 pr^u pr^d S^{ud}_T + (pr^d)^2 S^{dd}_T$. Running this in reverse, then we can equate the current stock price to future expiration stock prices via

$$S_0 = e^{-r^f T} \left[(pr^u)^2 S^{uu}_T + 2 pr^u pr^d S^{ud}_T + (pr^d)^2 S^{dd}_T \right]. \quad (18.5)$$

Let's return to consideration of values u and d. These are critical, as they are intimately related to the volatility of return of the underlying asset. As we previously saw, volatility positively impacts option value. The annualized volatility of the underlying asset is $\sigma(r)$, where r is an APR, continuously compounded. So for a given period of time duration Δt years, the volatility is $(\Delta t)^{1/2}\sigma(r)$. From $\sigma^2(x) = E[x^2] - (E[x])^2$, then $(\Delta t)\sigma^2(r) = \{pr^u(u^2) + pr^d(d^2)\} - [pr^u u + pr^d d]^2$. Using $pr^u = \frac{e^{r^f \Delta t}-d}{u-d}$, and ignoring terms with orders of Δt greater than one, then approximate solutions are

$$u = e^{(\Delta t)k + \sigma(r)(\Delta t)^{1/2}}, \quad \text{and} \quad d = e^{(\Delta t)k - \sigma(r)(\Delta t)^{1/2}}, \tag{18.6}$$

for some drift factor k. Interestingly, the value of k impacts the rate of convergence of the value of the option as periods are added. However, the limiting value itself remains the same. Hence, a simple solution is to set $k = 0$ as suggested by Cox, Ross and Rubinstein, or

$$u = e^{\sigma(r)(\Delta t)^{1/2}} \quad \text{and} \quad d = e^{-\sigma(r)(\Delta)^{1/2}}. \tag{18.7}$$

Hence, $ud = du = 1$.

18.2 Two-period Binomial Option Pricing Model

Consider the value of a European call in a two-period model. Comparable to our assumption on the strike price (K) shown in expression (17.8), then

$$S_T^{dd} < K < S_T^{uu}. \tag{18.8}$$

Comparable to equation (18.5), which relates expiration stock prices to S_0, payoffs of a European option relate to its value via

$$c_0 = e^{-r^f T}\left[(pr^u)^2 c_T^{uu} + 2pr^u pr^d c_T^{ud} + (pr^d)^2 c_T^{dd}\right]. \tag{18.9}$$

As $c_T^{uu} = \max(S_T^{uu} - K, 0) = S_T^{uu} - K > 0$, $c_T^{ud} = c_T^{du} = \max(0, S_T^{ud} - K)$, and $c_T^{dd} = \max(S_T^{dd} - K, 0) = 0$ per expression (18.8), then

$$\begin{aligned}c_0 &= e^{-2r^f \Delta t}\left[(pr^u)^2 c_T^{uu} + 2pr^u pr^d c_T^{ud}\right]\\&= e^{-r^f T}\left[(pr^u)^2 (S_T^{uu} - K) + 2pr^u pr^d \max\left(0, S_T^{ud} - K\right)\right].\end{aligned} \tag{18.10}$$

Analogously for a European put option, then per expression (18.8), $p_T^{dd} = \max(K - S_T^{dd}, 0) = K - S_T^{dd} > 0$, $p_T^{ud} = p_T^{du} = \max(0, K - S_T^{ud})$, and $p_T^{uu} = \max(K - S_T^{uu}, 0) = 0$. Hence,

$$\begin{aligned}p_0 &= e^{-2r^f \Delta t}\left[(pr^d)^2 p_T^{dd} + 2pr^u pr^d p_T^{ud}\right]\\&= e^{-r^f T}\left[(pr^d)^2 \left(K - S_T^{dd}\right) + 2pr^u pr^d \max\left(0, K - S_T^{ud}\right)\right].\end{aligned} \tag{18.11}$$

An important feature of equations (18.10) and (18.11) is that European option values depend only upon expiration date payoffs. European option values do *not* depend upon interim stock prices. Hence, when valuing a European call or put option, we only need to consider expiration stock prices, as such options may only be exercised at expiration. Later, when we value American options, we will see that one must consider all possible stock prices along the binomial tree, including all interim prices.

18.3 Multi-period Binomial Stock Price Model

For a given time to maturity T, a practitioner chooses either the number of periods N or the period duration, Δt, as the two are related via

$$N = T\Delta t, \quad \text{or} \quad \Delta t = \frac{T}{N}. \tag{18.12}$$

We denote by v the vector that records historical stock price movements. Each element is either u or d reflecting respective past periods' movements, e.g., $v = [uududddudd]$ denotes a given price path over the past 10 periods. Given a reconnecting tree, i.e., $ud = du$, then the order of elements is irrelevant. In other words, after x periods consisting of U upward movements (and hence, $x - U$ downward movements), then vector v contains U and $x - U$ quantities of u and d, respectively. Hence, we denote the stock price after x periods by

$$S^v_{x\Delta t} \equiv S_0 u^U v^{x-U}, \tag{18.13}$$

as it is independent of stock price path taken through the multi-period binomial tree to arrive at $S^v_{x\Delta t}$. Next,

$$\begin{aligned} E[S_{(x+1)\Delta t}|S^v_{x\Delta t}] &= S^v_{x\Delta t} e^{r^f \Delta t} = \left(pr^u u + pr^d d\right) S^v_{x\Delta t} \\ &= pr^u S^{vu}_{(x+1)\Delta t} + pr^d S^{vd}_{(x+1)\Delta t}, \end{aligned} \tag{18.14}$$

where we assume that $d = \frac{S^{vd}_{(x+1)\Delta t}}{S^v_{x\Delta t}}$ and $u = \frac{S^{vu}_{(x+1)\Delta t}}{S^v_{x\Delta t}}$ are constant each period. Rearranging equation (18.14), then

$$pr^u = \frac{S^v_{x\Delta t} e^{r^f \Delta t} - dS^v_{x\Delta t}}{uS^v_{x\Delta t} - dS^v_{x\Delta t}} = \frac{e^{r^f \Delta t} - d}{u - d}, \quad \text{and}$$

$$pr^d = 1 - pr^u = \frac{udS^v_{x\Delta t} - S^v_{x\Delta t} e^{r^f \Delta t}}{uS^v_{x\Delta t} - dS^v_{x\Delta t}} = \frac{u - e^{r^f \Delta t}}{u - d}, \tag{18.15}$$

comparable to previous models.

As before, r^f is also assumed to be constant for all $t \in [0, T]$, and so $e^{r^f \Delta t}$ is constant each period. Also, $d < e^{r^f \Delta t} < u$, where all three terms are assumed to be constant each period.[2] Summarizing,

$$\frac{S^{vd}_{(x+1)\Delta t}}{S^{v}_{x\Delta t}} = d < e^{r^f \Delta t} < u = \frac{S^{vu}_{(x+1)\Delta t}}{S^{v}_{x\Delta t}}. \qquad (18.16)$$

Hence, pr^u and pr^d continue to be constant each period, regardless of location in the binomial stock price tree.

18.4 Multi-period Binomial Option Pricing Model

Next, at time $t = 0$, the prior probability of arriving at a particular expiration stock price S^v_T along *any* stock price path through the binomial tree that terminates at S^v_T is the same as any other such path, equal to $(pr^u)^n (pr^d)^{N-n}$, given n upward and $N - n$ downward movements. Also, the number of paths that terminate at S^v_T is given by the combination function, $\frac{N!}{n!(N-n)!}$, where $n! = 1 \times 2 \times ... \times n$.[3] So the product of these two previous expressions gives the probability of arriving at a particular node, or $prob(S^v_T) = (pr^u)^n (pr^d)^{N-n} \frac{N!}{n!(N-n)!}$. Finally, the conditional payoff of a call given expiration price S^v_T equals $c^v_T = \max(0, S^v_T - K)$.

Summarizing, a European call can be valued via $c_0 = e^{-Tr^f} E[c_T]$, or

$$c_0 = e^{-Tr^f} \sum_{n=1}^{N} \frac{N!}{n!(N-n)!} (pr^u)^n \left(pr^d\right)^{N-n} \max\left(0, S_0 u^n d^{N-n} - K\right). \qquad (18.17)$$

Analogously, for a European put option, then

$$p_0 = e^{-Tr^f} \sum_{n=1}^{N} \frac{N!}{n!(N-n)!} (pr^u)^n \left(pr^d\right)^{N-n} \max\left(0, K - S_0 u^n d^{N-n}\right). \qquad (18.18)$$

Comparable to earlier models, the multi-period call (put) model requires the following assumption:

$$S^{ddd...d}_T < K < S^{uuu...u}_T, \qquad (18.19)$$

so that the call (put) finishes with positive probability in-the-money and with positive probability out-of-the-money.

The multi-period binomial model is very powerful, as it can be used to value essentially any option, not just vanilla European calls and puts as outlined here. The

---

[2] In a richer model, these parameters need not be constant each period.
[3] The combination function is trivially calculated in Excel via the entry $= Combin(N, n)$ for n upward movements and N periods.

option value calculated per this model depends upon number of periods chosen. The model's accuracy is increasing in number of periods, or equivalently, is decreasing in duration of the periods. We will later examine the Black-Scholes model (BS), which accurately values European calls and puts. In the limit, as the number of periods in the binomial model goes to infinity (i.e., as the duration of each period shrinks to infinitesimally short), then the resulting option value approaches that given by BS.

In figure 18.2, we show the impact of number of periods in a binomial model upon European option values, for both a call and a put. To generate these numbers, we use the following parameters: time to maturity $T = 0.5$ years; both call option and put option are issued at-the-money, where $S_0 = K = \$5$; risk-free rate $r^f = 5\%$, expressed as an APr, continuously compounded; the underlying asset has an annualized volatility of return $\sigma(r) = 50\%$, where the return is expressed as an APr, continuously compounded. Furthermore, for each model, we use $u = e^{(\Delta t)^{1/2}\sigma(r)}$ and $d = e^{-(\Delta t)^{1/2}\sigma(r)}$. So pr^u and d are increasing in periods N, while pr^d, u and $e^{r^f \Delta t}$ are decreasing in N. Finally, as a benchmark, we also show the values of both options per BS.

periods	1	2	3	4	5	6	7	8	9
c_0	0.926	0.677	0.814	0.715	0.791	0.728	0.781	0.735	0.775
p_0	0.802	0.554	0.690	0.591	0.667	0.605	0.657	0.612	0.652
periods	10	11	12	13	14	15	16	17	18
c_0	0.739	0.772	0.742	0.769	0.744	0.768	0.746	0.766	0.747
p_0	0.616	0.648	0.619	0.646	0.621	0.644	0.622	0.643	0.623
periods	19	20	21	22	23	24	25	26	**BS**
c_0	0.765	0.748	0.764	0.749	0.764	0.749	0.763	0.750	**0.756**
p_0	0.642	0.624	0.641	0.625	0.640	0.626	0.640	0.626	**0.633**

Figure 18.2   Number of chosen periods impacts binomial model option value

In figure 18.3, we show the results graphically for the call option of figure 18.2. One can see that as the number of periods increases in a binomial model, the call option value approaches the BS value. The results are encouraging, as even with 26 periods, this corresponds to a relatively coarse period duration of one week.[4]

Though not shown, we also calculate the relative volatility of the expiration stock price for each of the 26 models. Specifically,

$$\frac{\sigma(S_T)}{E[S_T]} = \frac{\left(\sum_{n=1}^{N}(pr^u)^n(pr^d)^{N-n}\frac{N!}{n!(N-n)!}\left\{(u)^n(d)^{N-n}S_0 - E[S_T]\right\}^2\right)^{\frac{1}{2}}}{E[S_T]},$$

---
[4]One extension of this model is to shorten the duration of time periods as maturity approaches.

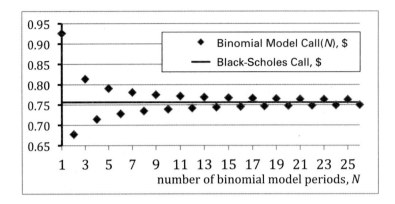

Figure 18.3 European call value as a function of number of periods in a binomial model, from $N = 1$ to $N = 26$ periods

where $E[S_T] = S_0 e^{(T)r^f} = \$5.00 e^{(0.5)5\%} = \$5.13$. With an annualized $\sigma = 50\%$, then the half year volatility, corresponding to $T = 0.5$ years, is $\sigma(T)^{0.5} = 50\%(0.5)^{0.5} = 35.4\%$. Indeed, the calculated values for all 26 models are very close to this hypothetical value, increasing monotonically from 35.0% when $N = 1$ to 36.4% when $N = 26$.

Problems

For this chapter's problem set, use a two-period binomial model. Assume that the volatility of return of the underlying asset, a share of stock, is 50%. Use Cox, Ross and Rubinstein parameters $u = e^{\sigma\sqrt{\Delta t}}$ and $d = e^{-\sigma\sqrt{\Delta t}}$. The initial stock price is $S_0 = \$10$ and the continuously compounded risk-free rate of return is $r^f = 6\%$. Equity holders demand a rate of return of $r^E = 13\%$. Any option, either call or put, is a European option, has a strike price of $K = \$11$ and an expiration date of one half ($T = \frac{1}{2}$) year from today.

1. What is the stock price after one period in the up-state of the binomial model, S_1^u, and the price in the down-state, S_1^d? What are the second period prices: (a) S_2^{uu}, (b) S_2^{ud}, (c) S_2^{du} and (d) S_2^{dd}?

2. What is the probability of the up-state in the risk-averse world, π^u?

What would be the probability of the up-state in a hypothetical risk-neutral world, pr^u?

3. What is the expected stock price after: (a) one period, $E[S_1]$? (b) two periods,

$E[S_2]$?

4. What is the value of the call in each of the following expiration stock price states: (a) c_2^{uu}, (b) c_2^{ud}, (c) c_2^{du} and (d) c_2^{dd}?

What is the value of the put in each of these four states: (a) p_2^{uu}, (b) p_2^{ud}, (c) p_2^{du} and (d) p_2^{dd}?

5. Calculate the initial delta of the call and the initial delta of the put. Calculate the delta of the call and the delta of the put after one period if the: (a) up-state is realized in the first period? (b) down-state is realized in the first period?

For all three sets of delta call and corresponding delta put, calculate the difference $\Delta^c - \Delta^p$.

6. Calculate the call option premium, c_0, and the put option premium, p_0.

7. Calculate the sum of the put premium and the initial stock price, $p_0 + S_0$. Calculate the sum of the call premium and the risk-free present value of the strike price, $c_0 + Ke^{-r^f}$. What is the difference of these two sums? Explain this result.

8. Now assume that the initial stock price is $S_0 = \$11$ per share. Recalculate the call premium, c_0. Is it larger or smaller than when the initial stock price was assumed to be $10?

9. Assuming that the initial stock price is $S_0 = \$11$ per share, recalculate the put premium, p_0. Is it larger or smaller than when the initial stock price was assumed to be $10?

10. Return to assuming the original stock price of $S_0 = \$10$ per share, but assume that the strike price is $K = \$12$. Recalculate the call premium, c_0. Is it larger or smaller than when the strike price was assumed to be $11?

11. Assuming the original stock price of $S_0 = \$10$ per share, but that the strike price is now $K = \$12$ per share, recalculate the put premium, p_0. Is it larger or smaller than when the strike price was assumed to be $11?

12. Return to the original assumptions ($S_0 = 10$, $K = 11$), but now assume that the risk-free rate of return is 7%. Recalculate the call premium, c_0. Is it larger or smaller than when the risk-free rate was assumed to be 6%?

13. Returning to the original assumptions ($S_0 = 10$, $K = 11$), and given a newly assumed risk-free rate of return of 7%, recalculate the put premium, p_0. Is it larger or smaller than when the risk-free rate was assumed to be 6%?

CHAPTER 19

American Binomial Option Pricing Model

Until now, we have focused on European options. We now turn to valuation of American options, which present a greater challenge as they offer the owner greater flexibility. We use the same multi-period binomial stock price tree as before. In addition to the implication of the decision to exercise at expiration, we must now also consider the possibility of early exercise at each node in the binomial tree.

19.1 American Call Option Valuation

The first step in valuation of an American option is to generate a multi-period stock price tree as in section 18.2. Next one generates a binomial tree of option values, where the nodes in this tree map one-to-one to those in the stock price tree. The key to determining these values is **backwards induction**. Starting at an expiration node in the binomial tree, the payoff of an American call is $C_T^x = \max(0, S_T^x - K)$ for terminal node x, a vector whose elements u and d capture any possible series of upward and downward movements to arrive at this node. So one values an American call at all expiration nodes just as she does a European call.

Working backwards one step at a time, consider arrival at a node one period prior to expiration, date $T - \Delta t$. We denote this node with the vector y. The value of the call at this node equals the maximum of the value if exercised, $\max(0, S_{T-\Delta t}^y - K)$, and the value if not exercised, $e^{-r^f \Delta t}[C_T^{yu} pr^u + C_T^{yd} pr^d]$, where yu (yd) is the subsequent node realized if an upward (downward) step ensues. Hence,

$$C_{T-\Delta t}^y = \max\left(\max\left(0, S_{T-\Delta t}^y - K\right), e^{-r^f \Delta t}\left[pr^u C_T^{yu} + pr^d C_T^{yd}\right]\right). \tag{19.1}$$

One values all nodes at the penultimate date of the binomial call accordingly.

One continues to march backwards through the tree, one period at a time using the same logic as that of equation (19.1). Generalizing, the value an American call option at any node z occurring at date t, $t \in \{\Delta t, 2\Delta t, ..., T - \Delta t\}$, i.e., at any node that is *not* an expiration node, is

$$C_t^z = \max\left(\max\left(0, S_t^z - K\right), e^{-r^f \Delta t}\left[pr^u C_{t+\Delta t}^{zu} + pr^d C_{t+\Delta t}^{zd}\right]\right). \tag{19.2}$$

Traveling backwards through the American option tree, when one finally arrives at the single initial node, corresponding to today's date $t = 0$, the value calculated is the value assigned to the American call, C_0.

19.2 American Put Option Valuation

An American put option is valued similarly to that of an American call. After generating a multi-period stock price tree as in section 18.2, one generates an American put value binomial tree. Next, one values an American put at all expiration nodes just as she does a European put. The payoff at each expiration node x is $P_T^x = \max(0, K - S_T^x)$.

One then uses backward induction to value the American put at all other nodes in the tree prior to expiration. The appropriate equation to use for an American put given date t at node z corresponding to equation (19.2) for an American call is

$$P_t^z = \max\left(\max\left(0, K - S_t^z\right), e^{-r^f \Delta t}\left[pr^u P_{t+\Delta t}^{zu} + pr^d P_{t+\Delta t}^{zd}\right]\right). \tag{19.3}$$

Traveling backwards through the American put option tree, when one finally arrives at the single initial node, corresponding to today's date $t = 0$, the value calculated is the value assigned to the American put, P_0.

19.3 Summary of American Option Valuation

To value an American option, one first needs to generate a multi-period stock price tree per section 18.2. Next, an identically shaped binomial tree of American option value is generated via backwards induction. Beginning at expiration date T, option value payoff at each terminal node is calculated via $C_T^x = \max(0, S_T^x - K)$ for a call and $P_T^x = \max(0, K - S_T^x)$ for a put. For an N period binomial model, there are $N + 1$ such nodes.

Moving backwards one period from expiration to date $t = T - \Delta t$, each of these N nodes is evaluated by equation (19.2) (equation (19.3)) for an American call (put). Continuing to work backwards, one calculates the option value at each of the $N - 1$ nodes corresponding to date $t = T - 2\Delta t$ using equation (19.2) (equation (19.3)) for an American call (put). One continues to proceed backwards through the tree, one period at a time, calculating an option value at each node of the tree until the single initial node corresponding to today, date $t = 0$, is reached. The value calculated at this initial node is the value assigned to the American option.

19.4 American Put Valuation: An Example

As an example, consider an American put equivalent to the European put valued in the previous chapter. For convenience, here again are the relevant parameters: time to maturity $T = 0.5$ years; put option is issued at-the-money, where $S_0 = K = \$5$; risk-free rate $r^f = 5\%$, expressed as an APr, continuously compounded; underlying asset has an annualized volatility of return $\sigma(r) = 50\%$, where the return is expressed as an APr, continuously compounded. We will use the binomial model with $N = 26$ periods. Hence, $\Delta t = \frac{T}{N} = \frac{0.5}{26} = 0.01923$ years (one week), $u = e^{(\Delta t)^{1/2}\sigma(r)} = e^{(0.5/26)50\%} = 1.071798$, $d = e^{-(\Delta t)^{1/2}\sigma(r)} = 0.9330117$, $e^{r^f \Delta t} = e^{5\%(0.5/26)} = 1.0009620$, $pr^u = \frac{e^{r^f \Delta t} - d}{u - d} = 48.96\%$ and $pr^d = 51.04\%$.

After calculating the necessary parameters (Δt, u, d, $e^{r^f \Delta t}$, pr^u and pr^d), we generate the stock price tree, shown in two figures due to its size, figures 19.1 (part 1) and 19.2 (part 2).

Next, as outlined in section 19.2, we generate the put price tree, as shown in figures 19.3 (part 1) and 19.4 (part 2). Note that the first node of figure 19.3 has a value of 0.640. Hence, the American put value is calculated as $P_0 = \$0.64$ per this $N = 26$ period binomial model.

19.5 Impact of Ability to Exercise Early

We now explore in more detail the impact upon value of the ability to exercise prior to maturity. Specifically we explore three dimensions. In the next section, we show that value is created from the ability to exercise early. In the subsequent section, we explore where along the binomial stock price tree that an American option is exercised. Finally, we calculate the probability of exercise on or before each date prior to expiration along the binomial stock price tree.

19.5.1 Value Creation

If the calculated conditional value at every node prior to expiration date T given exercise of the option is not greater than that given no exercise, then the incremental flexibility of early exercise of an American option relative to a European option has no value. In such case, an American option has no greater value than a corresponding European option, all else equal. Such an example is a call whose underlying asset is a

260 Asset Valuation Theory

end of period:	0**	1	2	3	4	5	6	7	8
downs*									
0	5.00	5.36	5.74	6.16	6.60	7.07	7.58	8.12	8.71
1		4.67	5.00	5.36	5.74	6.16	6.60	7.07	7.58
2			4.35	4.67	5.00	5.36	5.74	6.16	6.60
3				4.06	4.35	4.67	5.00	5.36	5.74
4					3.79	4.06	4.35	4.67	5.00
5						3.54	3.79	4.06	4.35
6							3.30	3.54	3.79
7								3.08	3.30
8									2.87

end of period:	9	10	11	12	13	14	15	16	17
downs*									
0	9.33	10.00	10.72	11.49	12.32	13.20	14.15	15.16	16.25
1	8.12	8.71	9.33	10.00	10.72	11.49	12.32	13.20	14.15
2	7.07	7.58	8.12	8.71	9.33	10.00	10.72	11.49	12.32
3	6.16	6.60	7.07	7.58	8.12	8.71	9.33	10.00	10.72
4	5.36	5.74	6.16	6.60	7.07	7.58	8.12	8.71	9.33
5	4.67	5.00	5.36	5.74	6.16	6.60	7.07	7.58	8.12
6	4.06	4.35	4.67	5.00	5.36	5.74	6.16	6.60	7.07
7	3.54	3.79	4.06	4.35	4.67	5.00	5.36	5.74	6.16
8	3.08	3.30	3.54	3.79	4.06	4.35	4.67	5.00	5.36
9	2.68	2.87	3.08	3.30	3.54	3.79	4.06	4.35	4.67
10		2.50	2.68	2.87	3.08	3.30	3.54	3.79	4.06
11			2.33	2.50	2.68	2.87	3.08	3.30	3.54
12				2.18	2.33	2.50	2.68	2.87	3.08
13					2.03	2.18	2.33	2.50	2.68
14						1.89	2.03	2.18	2.33
15							1.77	1.89	2.03
16								1.65	1.77
17									1.54

*"downs" indicates the number of downward movements in arriving at a given node.

The number of upward movements is simply the difference between the number of periods that have passed, indicated by the row "end of period:" and the number of downward movements.

** The entry of 0 for "end of period" simply indicates today, date $t = 0$.

A horizontal movement one column to the right across any row corresponds to an upward stock price movement in the binomial stock price tree.

A movement down one row while moving to the right one column corresponds to a downward stock price movement.

Figure 19.1 Stock price tree, $N = 26$ periods, part 1: periods $1 - 17$

Chapter 19 American Binomial Option Pricing Model

end of period:	18	19	20	21	22	23	24	25	26
downs*									
0	17.42	18.67	20.01	21.45	22.99	24.64	26.40	28.30	30.33
1	15.16	16.25	17.42	18.67	20.01	21.45	22.99	24.64	26.40
2	13.20	14.15	15.16	16.25	17.42	18.67	20.01	21.45	22.99
3	11.49	12.32	13.20	14.15	15.16	16.25	17.42	18.67	20.01
4	10.00	10.72	11.49	12.32	13.20	14.15	15.16	16.25	17.42
5	8.71	9.33	10.00	10.72	11.49	12.32	13.20	14.15	15.16
6	7.58	8.12	8.71	9.33	10.00	10.72	11.49	12.32	13.20
7	6.60	7.07	7.58	8.12	8.71	9.33	10.00	10.72	11.49
8	5.74	6.16	6.60	7.07	7.58	8.12	8.71	9.33	10.00
9	5.00	5.36	5.74	6.16	6.60	7.07	7.58	8.12	8.71
10	4.35	4.67	5.00	5.36	5.74	6.16	6.60	7.07	7.58
11	3.79	4.06	4.35	4.67	5.00	5.36	5.74	6.16	6.60
12	3.30	3.54	3.79	4.06	4.35	4.67	5.00	5.36	5.74
13	2.87	3.08	3.30	3.54	3.79	4.06	4.35	4.67	5.00
14	2.50	2.68	2.87	3.08	3.30	3.54	3.79	4.06	4.35
15	2.18	2.33	2.50	2.68	2.87	3.08	3.30	3.54	3.79
16	1.89	2.03	2.18	2.33	2.50	2.68	2.87	3.08	3.30
17	1.65	1.77	1.89	2.03	2.18	2.33	2.50	2.68	2.87
18	1.44	1.54	1.65	1.77	1.89	2.03	2.18	2.33	2.50
19		1.34	1.44	1.54	1.65	1.77	1.89	2.03	2.18
20			1.25	1.34	1.44	1.54	1.65	1.77	1.89
21				1.17	1.25	1.34	1.44	1.54	1.65
22					1.09	1.17	1.25	1.34	1.44
23						1.01	1.09	1.17	1.25
24							0.95	1.01	1.09
25								0.88	0.95
26									0.82

*"downs" indicates the number of downward movements in arriving at a given node.

The number of upward movements is simply the difference between the number of periods that have passed, indicated by the row "end of period:" and the number of downward movements.

A horizontal movement one column to the right across any row corresponds to an upward stock price movement in the binomial stock price tree.

A movement down one row while moving to the right one column corresponds to a downward stock price movement.

Figure 19.2 Stock price tree, $N = 26$ **periods, part 2: periods** $18 - 26$

end of period:	0**	1	2	3	4	5	6	7	8
downs*									
0	0.640	0.494	0.366	0.260	0.174	0.110	0.064	0.034	0.016
1		0.781	0.617	0.469	0.342	0.237	0.154	0.093	0.051
2			0.940	0.759	0.592	0.444	0.317	0.213	0.133
3				1.116	0.921	0.736	0.567	0.417	0.290
4					1.305	1.099	0.900	0.712	0.539
5						1.506	1.293	1.082	0.878
6							1.713	1.497	1.280
7								1.923	1.709
8									2.129

end of period:	9	10	11	12	13	14	15	16	17
downs*									
0	0.006	0.002	0.000	0.000	0.000	0.000	0.000	0.000	0.000
1	0.025	0.010	0.003	0.001	0.000	0.000	0.000	0.000	0.000
2	0.076	0.039	0.017	0.006	0.001	0.000	0.000	0.000	0.000
3	0.188	0.112	0.060	0.027	0.010	0.003	0.000	0.000	0.000
4	0.388	0.262	0.163	0.091	0.044	0.017	0.005	0.001	0.000
5	0.686	0.510	0.357	0.232	0.136	0.069	0.029	0.009	0.002
6	1.064	0.855	0.658	0.479	0.324	0.200	0.108	0.048	0.016
7	1.489	1.267	1.046	0.831	0.628	0.444	0.288	0.165	0.079
8	1.923	1.705	1.481	1.254	1.027	0.805	0.595	0.406	0.248
9	2.321	2.129	1.923	1.702	1.475	1.242	1.007	0.777	0.559
10		2.501	2.321	2.129	1.923	1.702	1.469	1.230	0.988
11			2.668	2.501	2.321	2.129	1.923	1.702	1.465
12				2.824	2.668	2.501	2.321	2.129	1.923
13					2.970	2.824	2.668	2.501	2.321
14						3.106	2.970	2.824	2.668
15							3.233	3.106	2.970
16								3.351	3.233
17									3.462

*"downs" indicates the number of downward movements in arriving at a given node.

The number of upward movements is simply the difference between the number of periods that have passed, indicated by the row "end of period:" and the number of downward movements.

** The entry of 0 for "end of period" simply indicates today, date $t = 0$.

A horizontal movement one column to the right across any row corresponds to an upward stock price movement in the binomial stock price tree.

A movement down one row while moving to the right one column corresponds to a downward stock price movement.

Figure 19.3 American put value tree, $N = 26$ periods, part 1: periods $1 - 17$

end of period:	18	19	20	21	22	23	24	25	26
downs*									
0	0.000	0.000	0.000	0.000	0.000	0.000	0.000	0.000	0.000
1	0.000	0.000	0.000	0.000	0.000	0.000	0.000	0.000	0.000
2	0.000	0.000	0.000	0.000	0.000	0.000	0.000	0.000	0.000
3	0.000	0.000	0.000	0.000	0.000	0.000	0.000	0.000	0.000
4	0.000	0.000	0.000	0.000	0.000	0.000	0.000	0.000	0.000
5	0.000	0.000	0.000	0.000	0.000	0.000	0.000	0.000	0.000
6	0.003	0.000	0.000	0.000	0.000	0.000	0.000	0.000	0.000
7	0.029	0.006	0.000	0.000	0.000	0.000	0.000	0.000	0.000
8	0.128	0.051	0.012	0.000	0.000	0.000	0.000	0.000	0.000
9	0.364	0.203	0.088	0.023	0.000	0.000	0.000	0.000	0.000
10	0.747	0.518	0.314	0.151	0.044	0.000	0.000	0.000	0.000
11	1.220	0.968	0.715	0.471	0.254	0.087	0.000	0.000	0.000
12	1.702	1.465	1.212	0.951	0.681	0.414	0.171	0.000	0.000
13	2.129	1.923	1.702	1.465	1.211	0.939	0.647	0.335	0.000
14	2.501	2.321	2.129	1.923	1.702	1.465	1.211	0.939	0.647
15	2.824	2.668	2.501	2.321	2.129	1.923	1.702	1.465	1.211
16	3.106	2.970	2.824	2.668	2.501	2.321	2.129	1.923	1.702
17	3.351	3.233	3.106	2.970	2.824	2.668	2.501	2.321	2.129
18	3.565	3.462	3.351	3.233	3.106	2.970	2.824	2.668	2.501
19		3.661	3.565	3.462	3.351	3.233	3.106	2.970	2.824
20			3.751	3.661	3.565	3.462	3.351	3.233	3.106
21				3.834	3.751	3.661	3.565	3.462	3.351
22					3.912	3.834	3.751	3.661	3.565
23						3.985	3.912	3.834	3.751
24							4.053	3.985	3.912
25								4.117	4.053
26									4.176

*"downs" indicates the number of downward movements in arriving at a given node.

The number of upward movements is simply the difference between the number of periods that have passed, indicated by the row "end of period:" and the number of downward movements.

A horizontal movement one column to the right across any row corresponds to an upward stock price movement in the binomial stock price tree.

A movement down one row while moving to the right one column corresponds to a downward stock price movement.

Figure 19.4 American put value tree, $N = 26$ periods, part 2: periods 18 – 26

stock that is not expected to pay a dividend prior to expiration; it is never optimal to exercise early an American call option, regardless of stock price path.[1] But generally,

---

[1] A lower bound for a call whose underlying asset pays no dividend is $\max(0, S_0 - Ke^{-r^f T}) \geq \max(0, S_0 - K)$. If exercised, the investor captures the call's intrinsic value, $\max(0, S_0 - K)$. As this is never more than the value of the call (and is usually less than the value of the call), then it is never optimal to exercise early.

value of American option is greater than that of a corresponding European option, as the flexibility to exercise early typically adds value.

Per figure 18.2, we previously calculated the European put option value as $0.626 = p_0 < P_0 = \$0.640$. Taking the difference of the two, we can determine the value of the flexibility to exercise early as $P_0 - p_0 = \$0.014$. This represents the incremental value of the American option relative to the equivalent European option.

As previously mentioned, it is never optimal to exercise early an American call whose underlying asset is a non-dividend paying stock. In contrast, an American put with such an underlying asset may be optimally exercised early. We showed earlier that a lower bound for put value is $\max(0, Ke^{-Tr^f} - S_0) \leqslant \max(0, K - S_0)$, where given $S_0 < Ke^{-Tr^f}$, the weak inequality is strict if $Tr^f > 0$, which is generally the case. Thus, the value of an American put may fall below that of the intrinsic value, which the investor can capture with immediate exercise. Hence, early exercise is possible with an American put, even if its underlying asset is a non-dividend paying stock.

19.5.2 Digging Deeper into Timing

We can determine exactly where in the binomial tree it is optimal to exercise early. At each node x, we simply compare the two values in equation (19.3): $\max(0, K - S_t^z)$ versus $e^{-r^f \Delta t}[pr^u P_{t+\Delta t}^{zu} + pr^d P_{t+\Delta t}^{zd}]$. If the former (latter) is greater, then early exercise is (not) optimal. We did so and the results are shown in figures 19.5 (part 1) and 19.6 (part 2). We highlight the demarcation between choice to exercise or not via underlying the maximum number of downward movements at the end of each period that results in early exercise not being optimal. Equivalently, if one more downward movement is realized than that corresponding to the underlined word <u>not</u> at each date, then early exercise is optimal.

Obviously, once an American option is exercised, subsequent stock prices are irrelevant in determining its value. Nonetheless, we indicate with an "x" in both figures 19.5 and 19.6 the nodes corresponding to the binomial stock price model that would have existed, had the option not been exercised. We do this to give an indication of the probability that the American put is exercised as time passes. Not surprisingly, as time passes, the columns of "x"s grow taller. Nodes with an "x" represent lower stock prices (precisely when puts are more valuable) and later dates. At such nodes, the put is sufficiently in-the-money given the limited remaining time to maturity that early exercise is optimal.

Chapter 19 American Binomial Option Pricing Model   265

end of period:	0**	1	2	3	4	5	6	7	8
downs*									
0	<u>not</u>	not	not	not	not	not	not	not	not
1		<u>not</u>	not	not	not	not	not	not	not
2			<u>not</u>	not	not	not	not	not	not
3				<u>not</u>	not	not	not	not	not
4					<u>not</u>	not	not	not	not
5						<u>not</u>	not	not	not
6							<u>not</u>	<u>not</u>	not
7								exer	<u>not</u>
8									x

end of period:	9	10	11	12	13	14	15	16	17
downs*									
0	not	not	not	not	not	not	not	not	not
1	not	not	not	not	not	not	not	not	not
2	not	not	not	not	not	not	not	not	not
3	not	not	not	not	not	not	not	not	not
4	not	not	not	not	not	not	not	not	not
5	not	not	not	not	not	not	not	not	not
6	not	not	not	not	not	not	not	not	not
7	<u>not</u>	not	not	not	not	not	not	not	not
8	exer	<u>not</u>	<u>not</u>	not	not	not	not	not	not
9	x	x	exer	<u>not</u>	<u>not</u>	<u>not</u>	not	not	not
10		x	x	x	exer	exer	<u>not</u>	<u>not</u>	<u>not</u>
11			x	x	x	x	x	exer	exer
12				x	x	x	x	x	x
13					x	x	x	x	x
14						x	x	x	x
15							x	x	x
16								x	x
17									x

*"downs" indicates the number of downward movements in arriving at a given node.

The number of upward movements is simply the difference between the number of periods that have passed, indicated by the row "end of period:" and the number of downward movements.

** The entry of 0 for "end of period" simply indicates today, date $t = 0$.

A horizontal movement one column to the right across any row corresponds to an upward stock price movement in the stock price tree.

A movement down one row while moving to the right one column corresponds to a downward stock price movement.

Figure 19.5 Optimal early exercise, part 1: periods $1 - 17$

end of period:	18	19	20	21	22	23	24	25	26
downs*									
0	not	not	not	not	not	not	not	not	not
1	not	not	not	not	not	not	not	not	not
2	not	not	not	not	not	not	not	not	not
3	not	not	not	not	not	not	not	not	not
4	not	not	not	not	not	not	not	not	not
5	not	not	not	not	not	not	not	not	not
6	not	not	not	not	not	not	not	not	not
7	not	not	not	not	not	not	not	not	not
8	not	not	not	not	not	not	not	not	not
9	not	not	not	not	not	not	not	not	not
10	not	not	not	not	not	not	not	not	not
11	*not*	*not*	not	not	not	not	not	not	not
12	x	exer	*not*	*not*	*not*	*not*	*not*	*not*	not
13	x	x	x	exer	exer	exer	exer	exer	*not*
14	x	x	x	x	x	x	x	x	x
15	x	x	x	x	x	x	x	x	x
16	x	x	x	x	x	x	x	x	x
17	x	x	x	x	x	x	x	x	x
18	x	x	x	x	x	x	x	x	x
19		x	x	x	x	x	x	x	x
20			x	x	x	x	x	x	x
21				x	x	x	x	x	x
22					x	x	x	x	x
23						x	x	x	x
24							x	x	x
25								x	x
26									x

*"downs" indicates the number of downward movements in arriving at a given node.

The number of upward movements is simply the difference between the number of periods that have passed, indicated by the row "end of period:" and the number of downward movements.

A horizontal movement one column to the right across any row corresponds to an upward stock price movement in the stock price tree.

A movement down one row while moving to the right one column corresponds to a downward stock price movement.

Figure 19.6 Optimal early exercise, part 2: periods 18 − 26

We also consider another perspective from which to consider the where in the binomial tree early exercise is optimal. Figure 19.7 shows how many historical downward movements in stock price are required by the end of each respective period in order to warrant early exercise, consistent with previous figures. This particular American put is never optimally exercised at the end of any of the first six periods. The first possibility of early exercise is at the end of the seventh period, and only if all movements in the first seven periods are downward movements, a highly unlikely event. As noted before, as time passes, the probability of exercise increases, all else equal.

end of period:	1	2	3	4	5	6	7	8	9
downs*	n/o**	n/o	n/o	n/o	n/o	n/o	7	8	8
prob***	n/o	n/o	n/o	n/o	n/o	n/o	0.9%	0.5%	2.3%
end of period:	10	11	12	13	14	15	16	17	18
downs	9	9	10	10	10	11	11	11	12
prob	1.3%	3.8%	2.3%	5.4%	10.3%	6.9%	12.1%	18.9%	13.8%
end of period:	19	20	21	22	23	24	25		
downs	12	13	13	13	13	13	13		
prob	20.5%	15.3%	21.9%	29.5%	37.6%	46.0%	54.2%		

* "downs" indicates the total number of downward movements by the respective period in order to trigger early exercise.
** "n/o" means that it is never optimal to exercise early by the end of the respective period in this particular model.
*** "prob" indicates the probability that early exercise is optimal by the end of this respective period or earlier.

Figure 19.7 Optimal early exercise and its probability

19.5.3 Probability of Exercise as Time Passes

Finally, the more interesting results shown in figure 19.7 are those of the probability of early exercise on or before a given date. As mentioned above, in this particular model, early exercise is never optimal through the first six periods. However, by the end of the seventh period, early exercise is optimal with 0.9% probability. Indeed, the trend is an increasing probability of early exercise on or before a given date as time passes, i.e., as time to maturity decreases. Indeed, *ex-ante* the probability of optimally exercising this particular American put prior to expiration is 54.2%.

Calculation of these percentages is as follows. One needs to generate two more binomial trees. For the first, ignore the possibility of early exercise for the $N = 26$ period model. Determine the prior probability of arriving at any given node via

$(pr^u)^{nu}(pr^d)^{nd}\frac{(nu+nd)!}{nu!nd!}$, where nu (nd) is the number of upward (downward) movements required to arrive at the given node, and where for each date in the tree, $nu+nd$ equals the number of periods that have passed in arriving at that date. To check one's work, the summation of probabilities across all nodes at each given date is one.

Regarding the second tree, for each given date, one simply adds the summation of probabilities corresponding to nodes where early exercise is optimal, i.e., those corresponding to entries of "exer" plus probabilities corresponding to nodes where early exercised has already occurred, i.e, those denoted via "x", shown in figures 19.5 and 19.6. Finally, the probability of early exercise during any given period can be calculated simply as the difference in the probability of early exercise on or before the ending date of the period and the probability of early exercise on or before the beginning date of the period.

The astute reader may have noticed that the probabilities in figure 19.7 are not everywhere non-decreasing, implying negative probabilities of early exercise for periods where the ending date probability is less than that of the beginning date. Specifically, in going from dates 7 to 8, 9 to 10, 11 to 12, 14 to 15, 17 to 18, and 19 to 20, the probabilities decrease. The reason is due to the coarseness of the model. (Accordingly, one will notice in figures 19.5 and 19.6 that the ending date of these same periods do *not* have the entry "exer".) If we were to use an infinite number of periods, each infinitesimally short in duration, then regarding optimal early exercise, the resulting series of probabilities would approach a non-decreasing function. Nonetheless, figure 19.7 drives home the point that for an American put option whose underlying asset is a non-dividend paying stock, the *ex-ante* probability of early exercise is decreasing in time to maturity, i.e., *ex-ante*, early exercise becomes increasingly more likely as the expiration date draws nearer.

Problems

For this chapter's problem set, use a two-period binomial model. Assume that the volatility of return of the underlying asset, a share of stock, is 50%. Use the Cox, Ross and Rubinstein parameters of $u = e^{\sigma\sqrt{\Delta t}}$ and $d = e^{-\sigma\sqrt{\Delta t}}$. The initial stock price is $S_0 = \$10$ and the continuously compounded risk-free rate of return is $r^f = 6\%$. Equity holders demand a rate of return of $r^E = 13\%$. Any option, either call or put, has a strike price of $K = \$11$ and an expiration date of one half $(T = \frac{1}{2})$ year from today.

Chapter 19 American Binomial Option Pricing Model

Except for the fact that we will consider American options in this problem set, this is the same set up as is used for the previous chapter's problem set. Refer to those problems for your calculations of u, d, pr^u, pr^d, S_2^{uu}, S_2^{ud}, S_2^{du}, S_2^{dd}, c_2^{uu}, c_2^{ud}, c_2^{du}, c_2^{dd}, p_2^{uu}, p_2^{ud}, p_2^{du} and p_2^{dd}.

1. Calculate the American call option premium, C_0, and the American put option premium, P_0.

What is the incremental value in being able to exercise the call option early, i.e., what is the difference, American call - European call, $C_0 - c_0$? (The European call premium, c_0, was calculated in problem 6 of the previous chapter's problems.)

What is the incremental value in being able to exercise the put option early, i.e., what is the difference, American put - European put, $P_0 - p_0$? (The European put premium, p_0, was calculated in problem 6 of the previous chapter's problems.)

2. Calculate the sum of the American put premium and the initial stock price, $P_0 + S_0$. Calculate the sum of the American call premium and the risk-free present value of the strike price, $C_0 + Ke^{-r^f}$. What is the difference of these two sums? Explain this result. Does put-call parity hold for American options?

3. Now assume that the initial stock price is $S_0 = \$11$ per share. Recalculate the American call premium, C_0. Is it larger or smaller than when the initial stock price was assumed to be $10?

4. Assuming that the initial stock price is $S_0 = \$11$ per share, recalculate the American put premium, P_0. Is it larger or smaller than when the initial stock price was assumed to be $10?

5. Return to assuming the original stock price of $S_0 = \$10$ per share, but assume that the strike price is $K = \$12$. Recalculate the American call premium, C_0. Is it larger or smaller than when the strike price was assumed to be $11?

6. Assuming the original stock price of $S_0 = \$10$ per share, but that the strike price is now $K = \$12$ per share, recalculate the American put premium, P_0. Is it larger or smaller than when the strike price was assumed to be $11?

7. Return to the original assumptions ($S_0 = 10$, $K = 11$), but now assume that the risk-free rate of return is $r^f = 7\%$. Recalculate the American call premium, C_0. Is it

larger or smaller than when the risk-free rate was assumed to be 6%?

8. Returning to the original assumptions ($S_0 = 10$, $K = 11$), and given a newly assumed risk-free rate of return of $r^f = 7\%$, recalculate the American put premium, P_0. Is it larger or smaller than when the risk-free rate was assumed to be 6%?

Chapter 20: Option Valuation: Black-Scholes Model

We conclude our journey through options with the Black-Scholes model for European option pricing. A detailed derivation is beyond the scope of this textbook. We offer a sketch of an outline of its development, provide its results, and review comparative static results.

The relative (or proportional) stock price path is assumed to follow a generalized Wiener process, a special case of a Markov process, where for the latter the historical price path is irrelevant to future stock price movements. In short, regarding the next stock price in the immediate future, the only relevant stock price is the current one, S_0; no past stock price values are impactful. In contrast to our discrete binomial model of previous chapters, the stock price is now considered a continuous random variable. The relative (or proportional) stock price is modeled via

$$d \ln(S) = \frac{dS}{S} = \mu dt + \sigma dz, \quad (20.1)$$

where t is time; μ is the stock's expected return, an APr, continuously compounded; σ is its volatility (i.e., its standard deviation of return); and dz is a continuous random variable that follows a Wiener process.[1]

The Black-Scholes model abstracts from taxes, transaction costs and trading frictions. Also, securities are perfectly divisible, and the risk-free rate of return is a constant, regardless of maturity. Furthermore, the securities market functions well in the sense that no arbitrage opportunities exist. Next, short selling is not only permitted,

---

[1] In an equivalent discrete model, $\frac{\Delta S}{S} = \mu \Delta t + \sigma \epsilon (\Delta t)^{1/2}$, where ϵ has a standard normal distribution. So if the proportional change in stock price is assumed to be normally distributed, or $\frac{\Delta S}{S}$ is distributed $N(\mu \Delta t, \sigma(\Delta t)^{1/2})$ over period Δt, then the absolute stock price path is lognormally distributed, or S_T is distributed $LN[\ln(S_0) + T(\mu - \frac{\sigma^2}{2}), \sigma(T)^{1/2}]$. Equivalently, $\ln(S_T)$ is normally distributed, $N[\ln(S_0) + T(\mu - \frac{\sigma^2}{2}), \sigma(T)^{1/2}]$.

but also proceeds are immediately available. For ease of exposition, the model further assumes that no dividends are paid prior to the option's expiration.

Using Ito's Lemma for a security's value, $i(S,t)$, then

$$di = \left(\frac{\partial i}{\partial S}\mu S + \frac{\partial i}{\partial t} + \frac{1}{2}\frac{\partial^2 i}{\partial S^2}\sigma^2 S^2\right) dt + \frac{\partial i}{\partial S}\sigma S dz. \tag{20.2}$$

20.1 European Call Option Value

In this section, we use equation (20.2), replacing variable i with c for a call option. Recall that in the delta hedge call option model from chapter 17, we combined one long call option with $-\Delta^c = -\frac{\partial c}{\partial S} < 0$ shares of stock to construct a portfolio whose payoff is independent of ending stock price, i.e., we constructed a portfolio free of risk. Hence, the portfolio's return is that of the risk-free rate of return, r^f, allowing us to value the call option.

Analogously, combining one short call with $\Delta^c = \frac{\partial c}{\partial S} > 0$ long shares of stock, then the portfolio value v^c is

$$v^c = -c + \Delta^c S = -c + \frac{\partial c}{\partial S}S. \tag{20.3}$$

On a differential basis,

$$dv^c = -dc + \Delta^c dS = -dc + \frac{\partial c}{\partial S}dS. \tag{20.4}$$

Substituting both $dS = S(\mu dt + \sigma dz)$ from equation (20.1) and dc from expression (20.2) (including replacement of i with c) into equation (20.4), then after simplification,

$$dv^c = \left(-\frac{\partial c}{\partial t} - \frac{1}{2}\frac{\partial^2 c}{\partial S^2}\sigma^2 S^2\right) dt, \tag{20.5}$$

which by design, lacks the random variable dz. Analogous to what was done in the simple discrete binomial model, by combining Δ^c long shares of stock with one short call eliminates risk over time period dt. Hence the return of such a portfolio is risk-free over dt. As such,

$$dv^c = v^c r^f dt. \tag{20.6}$$

Finally, substituting equation (20.3) for v^c and equation (20.5) for dv^c into equation (20.6), then after simplification,

$$\frac{\partial c}{\partial t} + r^f S\frac{\partial c}{\partial S} + \frac{1}{2}\frac{\partial^2 c}{\partial S^2}\sigma^2 S^2 = r^f c. \tag{20.7}$$

As the independent variables in equation (20.7) are t and S, then the call's payoff $c_T = \max(0, S_T - K)$ is an important boundary condition to differential equation (20.7). The resulting solution is

$$c_0 = S_0 SN(d_1) - Ke^{-r^f T} SN(d_2), \qquad (20.8)$$

where

$$d_1 = \frac{\ln\left(\frac{S_0}{K}\right) + T\left(r^f + \frac{\sigma^2}{2}\right)}{\sigma\sqrt{T}}, \quad \text{and} \quad d_2 = d_1 - \sigma\sqrt{T}, \qquad (20.9)$$

and where $SN(\cdot)$ is the standard normal distribution function of a random variable with a mean of zero and a variance of one.

Figure 20.1 shows the value of a European call per Black-Scholes via dashed curve as a function of stock price. Also shown are the intrinsic value, $\max(0, S_T - K)$, the dotted function, and a lower bound for the European call, $\max(0, S_T - Ke^{r^f T})$, the solid function. As the lower bound is everywhere at least as great as the intrinsic value, then the call option value is always greater that the intrinsic value given $S_T > 0$. Hence it is *never* optimal to exercise early.[2]

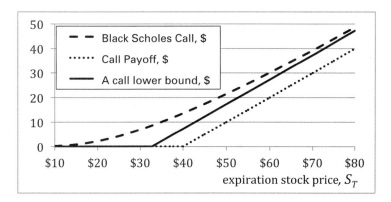

Figure 20.1   Call: premium lower bound and BS value; expiraton payoff

20.2 European Put Option Value

In this section, we use equation (20.2), replacing variable i with p for a put option. Recall that in the delta hedge put option model from chapter 17, we combined one put option with $+\Delta^p = \frac{\partial p}{\partial S} < 0$ shares of stock to construct a portfolio whose payoff is independent of ending stock price, i.e., we constructed a portfolio free of risk. Hence,

---

[2]Note that the Black-Scholes model is for a European option, not an American option. Nonetheless, the above logic applies, as it is never optimal to exercise early an American call whose underlying asset is the same as ours, i.e., a stock that is not expected to pay a dividend prior to expiration.

the portfolio's return is that of the risk-free rate of return, r^f, allowing us to value the put.

Analogously, combining one short put with Δ^p shares of stock, then the portfolio value v^p is

$$v^p = -p + \Delta^p S = -p + \frac{\partial p}{\partial S} S. \tag{20.10}$$

On a differential basis,

$$dv^p = -dp + \Delta^p dS = -dp + \frac{\partial p}{\partial S} dS. \tag{20.11}$$

Substituting both $dS = S(\mu dt + \sigma dz)$ from equation (20.1) and dp from expression (20.2) (including replacement of i with p) into equation (20.11), then after some simplification,

$$dv^p = \left(-\frac{\partial p}{\partial t} - \frac{1}{2}\frac{\partial^2 p}{\partial S^2}\sigma^2 S^2\right) dt, \tag{20.12}$$

which by design, lacks the random variable dz. Just as was done in the simple discrete binomial model, by combining $\Delta^p < 0$ shares of stock with one short put eliminates risk over time period dt. Hence the return of such a portfolio is risk-free over dt. As such,

$$dv^p = v^p r^f dt. \tag{20.13}$$

Finally, substituting equation (20.10) for v^p and equation (20.12) for dv^p into equation (20.13), then after simplification,

$$\frac{\partial p}{\partial t} + r^f S \frac{\partial p}{\partial S} + \frac{1}{2}\frac{\partial^2 p}{\partial S^2}\sigma^2 S^2 = r^f p. \tag{20.14}$$

As the independent variables in equation (20.14) are t and S, then the put's payoff $p_T = \max(0, K - S_T)$ is an important boundary condition to differential equation (20.14). The resulting solution is

$$p_0 = Ke^{-r^f T} SN(-d_2) - S_0 SN(-d_1), \tag{20.15}$$

where d_1 and d_2 are the same as in expressions (20.9).

Figure 20.2 shows the value of a European put per Black-Scholes via dashed curve as a function of stock price. Also shown are the intrinsic value, $\max(0, K - S_T)$, a solid function, and a lower bound for the European call, $\max(0, Ke^{-r^f T} - S_T)$, a dotted function.

In contrast to the case of a call option, put option value crosses beneath intrinsic value. In figure 20.2, this occurs at stock prices less than approximately $S_0 = \$30.50$.

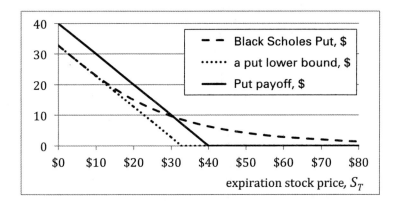

Figure 20.2 Put: premium lower bound and BS value; expiraton payoff

Hence, for a put option whose underlying asset is a non-dividend paying stock, it may be optimal to exercise early if the stock price drops sufficiently.[3]

European Put Option Value per Put-Call Spot Parity

Once we have an expression for a call's value per expressions (20.8) and (20.9), we could derive the "comparable" put's value (i.e., with identical underlying asset, strike price and time to maturity) using put-call spot parity,

$$p_0 = -S_0 + c_0 + Ke^{-r^f T}. \tag{20.16}$$

Substituting c_0 per line (equation (20.8)) into put-call spot parity, then

$$\begin{aligned} p_0 &= -S_0 + \{S_0 SN(d_1) - Ke^{-r^f T} SN(d_2)\} + Ke^{-r^f T} \\ &= -S_0(1 - SN(d_1)) + Ke^{-r^f T}(1 - SN(d_2)) \\ &= Ke^{-r^f T} SN(-d_2) - S_0 SN(-d_1), \end{aligned} \tag{20.17}$$

consistent with equation (20.15), as $1 - SN(x) = SN(-x)$.

Extending Black-Scholes to Include a Continuous Dividend Payout

Stock index funds can be modeled as paying a steady dividend. Assuming a continuous dividend of k, expressed as an APr, then call option value is modified to

$$c_0 = S_0 e^{-kT} SN(d_1) - Ke^{-r^f T} SN(d_2), \tag{20.18}$$

where

$$d_1 = \frac{\ln\left(\frac{S_0}{K}\right) + T\left(r^f + \frac{\sigma^2}{2} - k\right)}{\sigma\sqrt{T}}, \quad \text{and} \quad d_2 = d_1 - \sigma\sqrt{T}. \tag{20.19}$$

---

[3] Upon exercise, the intrinsic value is captured. Note that the Black-Scholes model is for a European option, not an American option. Nonetheless, the above logic applies.

Next, as put-call parity becomes

$$c_0 + Ke^{-r^f T} = S_0 e^{-kT} + p_0, \qquad (20.20)$$

then the comparable put option value becomes

$$p_0 = Ke^{-r^f T} SN(-d_2) - S_0 e^{-kT} SN(-d_1). \qquad (20.21)$$

20.3 Comparative Statics

Comparative statics of calls and puts are given the special name of **Greeks**, as each one is assigned a Greek letter. In this section, in addition to offering expressions for the Greeks, we graphically show European call and put option values as functions of relevant parameters. Throughout this section, we use the following base case parameters: $S_0 = \$50$, $K = \$50$, $r^f = 5\%$, $T = 3$ years and $\sigma = 25\%$. Per the Black-Scholes model, $c_0 = \$11.92$ and $p_0 = \$4.96$ for this base case.

We have already seen that **delta** is defined by

$$\Delta^c \equiv \frac{\partial c}{\partial S} = SN(d_1) \in (0,1) > 0, \quad \text{and}$$

$$\Delta^p \equiv \frac{\partial p}{\partial S} = -SN(-d_1) = \Delta^c - 1 \in (-1, 0) < 0. \qquad (20.22)$$

In figure 20.3 we show both put value and call value as functions of stock price, S_0. Consistent with expressions (20.22), the call (put) is increasing (decreasing) in stock price.

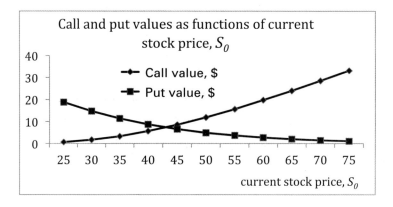

Figure 20.3 Option values as functions of value of underlying asset

Next, the second derivative with respect to stock price is called **gamma**, or

$$\Gamma^c \equiv \frac{\partial^2 c}{\partial S^2} = \frac{Sn(d_1)}{S_0 \sigma \sqrt{T}} > 0, \quad \text{and} \quad \Gamma^p \equiv \frac{\partial^2 p}{\partial S^2} = \frac{Sn(d_1)}{S_0 \sigma \sqrt{T}} > 0, \qquad (20.23)$$

where $Sn(x) = \frac{dSN(x)}{dx}$ is the standard normal density function; hence $Sn(d_1) = \frac{1}{\sqrt{2\pi}} e^{-\frac{(d_1)^2}{2}} > 0$. Note that $\Gamma^c = \Gamma^p > 0$. Generally, the second derivative captures the curvature of a function. As the second derivatives of both the call and put are positive (and equal), then both option value functions are convex in stock price, consistent with the curves in figure 20.3.[4]

Regarding the strike price,

$$\frac{\partial c}{\partial K} = -e^{-r^f T} SN(d_2) < 0, \quad \text{and} \quad \frac{\partial p}{\partial K} = e^{-r^f T} SN(-d_2) > 0. \qquad (20.24)$$

In figure 20.4 we show both put value and call value as functions of strike price. Consistent with expressions (20.24), the call (put) option value is decreasing (increasing) in strike price. Intuitively, given exercise, the strike price is a conditional liability (asset) for the owner of a call (put); hence, the value of the call (put) is decreasing (increasing) in strike price, all else equal.

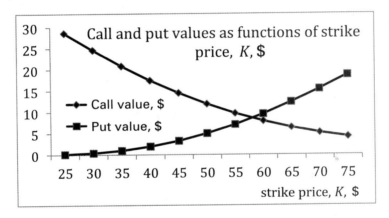

Figure 20.4 Option values as functions of value of strike price

The derivative of option value with respect to risk-free rate is called **rho**, or

$$\rho^c \equiv \frac{\partial c}{\partial r^f} = KTe^{-r^f T} SN(d_2) > 0, \quad \text{and}$$

$$\rho^p \equiv \frac{\partial p}{\partial r^f} = -KTe^{-r^f T} SN(-d_2) < 0. \qquad (20.25)$$

In figure 20.5 we show both put value and call value as functions of the risk-free rate of return, r^f. Consistent with expressions (20.25), the call (put) option value is increasing (decreasing) in risk-free rate of return, r^f. Intuitively, as r^f increases, the expected stock

---
[4]Though not explicitly shown, both option value functions are most curved when the option is at-the-money. Hence, gamma peaks when the option is at-the-money and decreases in distance of the stock price from the strike price.

price at any given future point in time increases per the risk-neutral model. Given exercise, as the stock/underlying asset is a conditional asset (liability) for the owner of a call (put), then the value of the call (put) is increasing (decreasing) in risk-free rate of return, all else equal.

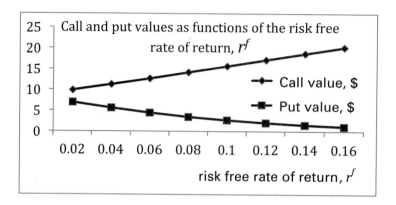

Figure 20.5 Option values as functions of risk-free rate

Next, the derivative of option value with respect to volatility, i.e., standard deviation of return of underlying asset, is called **vega**, or[5]

$$\nu^c \equiv \frac{\partial c}{\partial \sigma} = \nu^p \equiv \frac{\partial p}{\partial \sigma} = S_0 \sqrt{T} S n(d_1) > 0. \tag{20.26}$$

In figure 20.6 we show both the put value and the call value as functions of volatility, σ. Consistent with expression (20.26), the call and put option values are both increasing in volatility, σ.

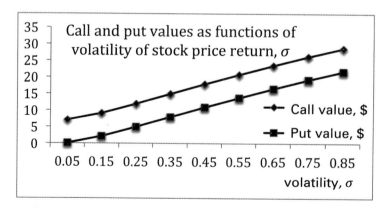

Figure 20.6 Option values as functions of volatility of underlying asset

---

[5]Vega, ν, is *not* actually a letter in the Greek alphabet. Nonetheless, vega, as $\frac{\partial o}{\partial \sigma}$ is considered one of the "Greeks" in the world of options.

As volatility is such an important parameter in option valuation, let's dig deeper. Refer for a moment back to figure 17.12. Recall that this figure is for a series of call options where the underlying assets, all in the context of a binomial price model, represent a series of increasing volatility. Specifically, these underlying assets, consistent with the binomial model, can take on one of two values. Each pair of values in the series represents greater volatility than the previous one, yet the expected value is always the same, $42.05, consistent with the vertical line of figure 17.12.

Now consider an equivalent example, but where expiration stock price returns are modeled via continuous random variables consistent with the Black-Scholes model, as in figure 20.7. Specifically, the solid cumulative distribution function (corresponding to stock A) is a mean-preserving spread of the dashed function (corresponding to stock B). In other words, although stocks A and B both have a mean return of 10%, stock A (B) has a volatility of return of 30% (10%).

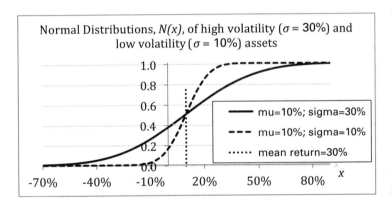

Figure 20.7   Volatilities via distribution functions

It is perhaps easier to demonstrate the desired points via equivalent density functions, shown in figure 20.8. These density functions for stocks A and B, respectively, correspond exactly to the distribution functions of figure 20.7.

Consider two call options, where both are identically the same except for underlying assets. Call A (B) has as its underlying asset stock A (B). Both calls have a strike price corresponding to a rate of return of $r^K = 25\%$, an APr continuously compounded, or $K = S_0 e^{r^K T} = \$50 e^{(25\%)1} = \$64.20$, assuming $T = 1$ year and $S_0 = \$50$. In figure 20.8, $r^K = 25\%$ is shown via vertical dotted line. So call options A and B both finish in-the-money if their respective returns are greater than $r^K = 25\%$, corresponding to expiration stock prices greater than $K = \$64.20$.

Given returns greater than 25% in figure 20.8, the conditional area beneath the

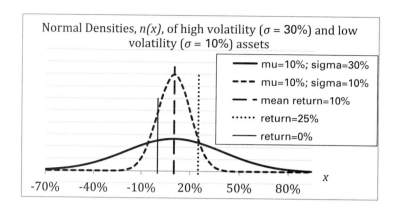

Figure 20.8   Volatilities via density functions

solid curve (corresponding to the more volatile asset A) to the right of $r^K = 25\%$ is greater than the conditional area beneath the dashed curve (corresponding to the lesser volatile asset B) to the right of $r^K = 25\%$. These areas correspond to the probabilities that the respective call options finish in-the-money, where $30.9\% = prob(r^A > 25\%) > prob(r^B > 25\%) = 6.7\%$.[6]

Given returns greater than $r^K = 25\%$, the conditional expected payoffs of the call options are proportional to the respective conditional expected values of stocks A and B. Graphically, these conditional expected values are the "centers of gravity" along the x-axis of the areas beneath the density functions to the right of $r = 25\%$. Accordingly, $44\% = E[r^A | r^A > 25\%] > E[r^B | r^B > 25\%] = 29\%$, where $E[r^i | r^i > 25\%] = \frac{\int_{x=25\%}^{\infty} x f^i(x) dx}{\int_{x=25\%}^{\infty} f^i(x) dx}$, and where f^i, $i \in \{A, B\}$, are the respective normal density functions. In short, given that both calls finish in-the-money, the conditional expected payoff of the call with the more (lesser) volatile asset is greater (smaller).

Summarizing the previous two paragraphs, we assume that calls A and B are identical except for their underlying assets, stocks A and B, respectively. The current prices and expected returns of the stocks are they same, but the volatility of stock A is greater than that of stock B. Hence, not only is the probability that call A finishes in-the-money greater than that of call B, but also given that both A and B finish in the money, the conditional expected payoff of A is greater than that of B. In short, both factors, $prob(r^i > r^K)$ and $E[r^i | r^i > r^K]$, $i \in \{A, B\}$, which favorably impact call option value, are greater (smaller) for the call with the more (less) volatile underlying

---

[6]This follows from $prob(r^A > 25\%) = 1 - prob(r^A \leqslant 25\%) = 1 - SN(\frac{25\% - \mu^A}{\sigma^A}) = 1 - SN(\frac{25\% - 10\%}{30\%}) = 1 - 69.1\% = 30.9\%$. Analogously, $prob(r^B > 25\%)$ is similarly calculated as $1 - SN(\frac{25\% - 10\%}{10\%}) = 1 - 93.3\% = 6.7\%$.

asset, A (B).

Finally, consider two put options, A and B, with these same two underlying assets, A and B, respectively. Let's assume that these puts are issued at-the-money, corresponding to a strike price of $r^K = 0\%$ ($K = \$50$), shown in figure 20.8 via thin horizontal solid line. So the puts finish in-the-money if the returns are negative, $r^i < r^K = 0\%$, $i \in \{A,B\}$, i.e., if the expiration stock prices are $S_T^i < K = \$50$.

Analogous to the previous discussion for calls, given that both puts finish in-the-money, then the conditional area to the left of $r = 0\%$ under the density function of the more volatile underlying asset A (solid curve) is greater than that corresponding to the lesser volatile underlying asset B (dashed curve). So the probability of put A finishing in-the-money is greater than that of put B. In other words, $prob(r^i < r^K)$, $i \in \{A, B\}$, which is increasing in volatility, favorably impacts put option value. Furthermore, given that both puts finish in-the-money, the conditional expected expiration price of stock A is less than that of stock B, implying a greater conditional expected payoff for put A than for put B. (As $E[r^i | r^i < r^K]$ is decreasing in volatility, and as put value is decreasing in $E[r^i | r^i < r^K]$, then increasing volatility also increases put value via this channel.) In summary, the value of the put with the more volatile underlying asset is greater than the value of the put with the less volatile underlying asset, all else equal.

The final Greek to consider is the derivative of option value with respect to time to maturity, called **theta**. Note that in this textbook, Θ is the sensitivity of option value as time to maturity *increases*.[7] Hence,

$$\Theta^c \equiv \frac{\partial c}{\partial T} = \frac{S_0 Sn(d_1)\sigma}{2\sqrt{T}} + r^f K e^{-r^f T} SN(d_2) > 0, \quad \text{and} \tag{20.27}$$

$$\Theta^p \equiv \frac{\partial p}{\partial T} = \frac{S_0 Sn(d_1)\sigma}{2\sqrt{T}} - r^f K e^{-r^f T} SN(-d_2). \tag{20.28}$$

In figure 20.9 we show two different put values and one call value as functions of time to maturity, T. Consistent with expression (20.27), the call option value in figure 20.9 is increasing in time to maturity, T. In other words, as time passes, call option value *decreases*, all else equal.

The impact of time to maturity upon put value is ambiguous, per expression (20.28). In figure 20.9, both puts have parameters $K = \$50$, $r^f = 5\%$ and $\sigma = 25\%$, the same as the call. However, for the call and one of the puts, $S_0 = \$50 = K$ (i.e., at-the-money), whereas the other put is deeply in-the-money, with $\$10 = S_0 <<< K = \$50$.

---

[7] In some textbooks, theta is considered the opposite, i.e., the change in option value as time to maturity shrinks.

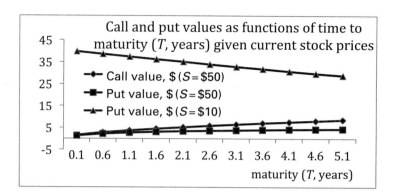

Figure 20.9 Option values as functions of time to maturity

For the put that is at-the-money, the put is increasing in T, consistent with the call option. However, for the put that is so deeply in-the-money, then as time to maturity increases, put value decreases. Intuitively, the intrinsic value for a put so far in-the-money is likely to lose value as time passes, as stock price is likely to increase over time.

Relating Delta, Gamma and Theta

Recall differential equations (20.7) for a call and (20.14) for a put, or

$$\frac{\partial o}{\partial t} + r^f S \frac{\partial o}{\partial S} + \frac{1}{2} \frac{\partial^2 o}{\partial S^2} \sigma^2 S^2 = r^f o, \tag{20.29}$$

where we have substituted o for c and p, respectively, in expressions (20.7) and (20.14). As $\Theta \equiv \frac{\partial o}{\partial T}$, $\Delta \equiv \frac{\partial o}{\partial S}$ and $\Gamma \equiv \frac{\partial^2 o}{\partial S^2}$, then equation (20.29) can be rewritten as a relation between Θ, Δ and Γ, or

$$\Theta + r^f S \Delta + \frac{1}{2} \Gamma \sigma^2 S^2 = r^f o. \tag{20.30}$$

The above differential equation can also be applied to a portfolio. If the portfolio is designed to be Delta neutral, then the term with Δ is eliminated. Analogously, a portfolio can be made to be Gamma neutral, eliminating the term with Γ.

Problems

For this chapter's problem set, assume that the volatility of return of the underlying asset, a share of stock, is 50% and its expected return is 12%. The initial stock price is $10 and the continuously compounded risk-free rate of return is 6%. Equity holders demand a rate of return of 13%. Any option, either call or put, is a European option, has a strike price of $11 and an expiration date of one half ($\frac{1}{2}$) year from today.

Chapter 20 Option Valuation: Black-Scholes Model

1. What is the value of a European call option, c_0, per the Black-Scholes model?

2. What is the value of a European put option, p_0, per the Black-Scholes model?

3. Calculate delta of the call in problem 1, Δ^c, and delta of the put in problem 2, Δ^p.

4. Assuming an initial stock price of $S_0 = \$11$ (versus \$10), what is the European call option's value, c_0? Is this greater or smaller than the value with $S_0 = \$10$ calculated in problem 1? Is the sign of this difference in value, $c_0(S_0 = \$11) - c_0(S_0 = \$10)$, consistent with the call's delta calculated in problem 3?

5. Assuming an initial stock price of $S_0 = \$11$ (versus \$10), what is the European put option's value, p_0? Is this greater or smaller than the value with $S_0 = \$10$ calculated in problem 2? Is the sign of this difference in value, $p_0(S_0 = \$11) - p_0(S_0 = \$10)$, consistent with the put's delta calculated in problem 3?

6. Calculate gamma of the call in problem 1, Γ^c, and gamma of the put in problem 2, Γ^p.

Are they positive or negative? Interpret these results.

7. Calculate the derivative of the call with respect to the strike price, $\frac{\partial c_0}{\partial K}$, of the call in problem 1 and the derivative of the put with respect to the strike price, $\frac{\partial p_0}{\partial K}$, of the put in problem 2.

8. Assuming a strike price of $K = \$12$ (versus \$11), what is the European call option's value, c_0? Is this greater or smaller than the value with $K = \$11$ calculated in problem 1? Is the sign of this difference in value, $c_0(K = \$12) - c_0(K = \$11)$, consistent with $\frac{\partial c_0}{\partial K}$ calculated in problem 7?

9. Assuming a strike price of $K = \$12$ (versus \$11), what is the European put option's value, p_0? Is this greater or smaller than the value with $K = \$11$ calculated in problem 2? Is the sign of this difference in value, $p_0(K = \$12) - p_0(K = \$11)$, consistent with $\frac{\partial p_0}{\partial K}$ calculated in problem 7?

10. Calculate rho of the call in problem 1, ρ^c and rho of the put in problem 2, ρ^p.

11. Assuming a risk-free rate of $r^f = 7\%$ (versus 6%), what is the European call option's value, c_0? Is this greater or smaller than the value with $r^f = 6\%$ calculated in problem 1? Is the sign of this difference in value, $c_0(r^f = 7\%) - c_0(r^f = 6\%)$, consistent with

the call's rho calculated in problem 10?

12. Assuming a risk-free rate of $r^f = 7\%$ (versus 6%), what is the European put option's value, p_0? Is this greater or smaller than the value with $r^f = 6\%$ calculated in problem 2? Is the sign of this difference in value, $p_0(r^f = 7\%) - p_0(r^f = 6\%)$, consistent with the put's rho calculated in problem 10?

13. Calculate vega of the call in problem 1 and vega of the put in problem 2.

14. Assuming a volatility of $\sigma = 60\%$ (versus 50%), what is the European call option's value, c_0? Is this greater or smaller than the value with $\sigma = 50\%$ calculated in problem 1? Is the sign of this difference in value, $c_0(\sigma = 60\%) - c_0(\sigma = 50\%)$, consistent with the call's vega calculated in problem 13?

15. Assuming a volatility of $\sigma = 60\%$ (versus 50%), what is the European put option's value? Is this greater or smaller than the value with $\sigma = 50\%$ calculated in problem 2? Is the sign of this difference in value, $p_0(\sigma = 60\%) - p_0(\sigma = 50\%)$, consistent with the put's vega calculated in problem 13?

16. Calculate theta of the call in problem 1, Θ^c and theta of the put in problem 2, Θ^p.

17. Assuming a time to maturity of $T = 1$ year (versus $\frac{1}{2}$ year), what is the European call option's value, c_0? Is this greater or smaller than the value with $T = \frac{1}{2}$ year calculated in problem 1? Is the sign of this difference in value, $c_0(T = 1) - c_0(T = \frac{1}{2})$, consistent with the call's theta calculated in problem 16?

18. Assuming a time to maturity of $T = 1$ year (versus $\frac{1}{2}$ year), what is the European put option's value, p_0? Is this greater or smaller than the value with $T = \frac{1}{2}$ year calculated in problem 2? Is the sign of this difference in value, $p_0(T = 1) - p_0(T = \frac{1}{2})$, consistent with the put's theta calculated in problem 16?

Solutions to Selected End-of-chapter Problems

Chapter 1

1. Comparing the two prizes at date 0 values, then $PV(\text{Prize 1}) = \$10,000$ and $PV(\text{Prize 2}) = 30,000(1+10\%)^{-10} = \$11,566$. As $PV(\text{Prize 1}) = \$10,000 < PV(\text{Prize 2}) = \$11,566$, you should choose Prize 2.

2. For this problem, we need to compare the project's cost and revenue at the same date, e.g., date 0: $PV(\text{Cost}) = \$10,000$, $PV(\text{Revenue}) = \frac{5,000}{(1+10\%)} + \frac{6,000}{(1+10\%)^2} = \$9504.13$, so intrinsic value $= \$9504 - \$10,000 = -\$496 < 0$. So, you should reject the project.

3. We can set $FV(\text{Cost}) = \sum(FV(\text{Revenues}))$, or $10,000(1+r)^2 = 5,000(1+r) + 6000$. Solving for r, then the internal rate of return is $r = 6.39\%$. Alternatively, we could set $PV(\text{Cost}) = \sum(PV(\text{Revenues}))$, yielding the same answer.

4. You need T years such that $5000(1+8\%)^T = 10,000$. Solving for T, we get $T = \frac{\ln 2}{\ln 1.08} \approx 9$ years.

5. For an annuity of X per year, then the future value is: $X\frac{(1+5\%)^5 - 1}{5\%} = 10,000$. Solving for X, then $X = \frac{10,000 \times 5\%}{(1+5\%)^5 - 1} \approx \$1809.75$.

6. For a growing annuity, intrinsic value is $IV_0 = \frac{20(1+5\%)}{10\%-5\%}\left[1 - \left(\frac{1+5\%}{1+10\%}\right)^5\right] = \$87.16$.

7. For a perpetuity, $P_0 = 1000 = \frac{40}{r}$, so $r = \frac{40}{1000} = 4\%$.

8. For a growing perpetuity, $P_0 = 100 = \frac{10(1+g)}{12\%-g}$, so $g = \frac{12-10}{100+10} \approx 1.8\%$.

Chapter 2

1. $HPR = \frac{100+5}{95} = \frac{105}{95} = 1.11$, and $HPr = HPR - 1 = 11\%$.

2. $HPR = \frac{100+5*3}{98} = \frac{115}{98} = 1.17$, and $HPr = HPR - 1 = 17\%$.

3. $r_{-2} = \frac{25}{20} - 1 = 25\%$, $r_{-1} = \frac{10}{25} - 1 = 60\%$, and $r_0 = \frac{30}{10} - 1 = 200\%$.

4. $AMR = AMr + 1 = \frac{25\% + (-60\%) + 200\%}{3} + 1 = 1.55$. So $AMr = 55\%$.

Next, $GMr = HPR^{\frac{1}{T}} - 1 = \left(\frac{30}{20}\right)^{\frac{1}{3}} - 1 = (1.5)^{\frac{1}{3}} - 1 = 1.14 - 1 = 14\%$.

5. $s^2 = \frac{1}{3-1}[(25\% - 55\%)^2 + (-60\% - 55\%)^2 + (200\% - 55\%)^2] = 1.7576$, and $s = \sqrt{s^2} = \sqrt{1.7576} = 132.57\%$.

6. First, $AMr^x = \frac{(10-15+20+25-30+20)\%}{6} = 5\%$, and $AMr^y = \frac{(20-20-10+30-20+60)\%}{6} = 10\%$.

Next,

Period	r^x	r^y	$(r^x - AMr^x)$	$(r^y - AMr^y)$
-5	$+10\%$	$+20\%$	$+5\%$	$+10\%$
-4	-15%	-20%	-20%	-30%
-3	$+20\%$	-10%	$+15\%$	-20%
-2	$+25\%$	$+30\%$	$+20\%$	$+20\%$
-1	-30%	-20%	-35%	-30%
0	$+20\%$	$+60\%$	$+15\%$	$+50\%$

Thus,
$s(r^x) = \sqrt{\frac{(0.05)^2 + (-0.20)^2 + (0.15)^2 + (0.20)^2 + (-0.35)^2 + (0.15)^2}{6-1}} = \sqrt{0.05} = 0.2236$.

$s(r^y) = \sqrt{\frac{(0.10)^2 + (-0.30)^2 + (-0.20)^2 + (0.20)^2 + (-0.30)^2 + (0.50)^2}{6-1}} = \sqrt{0.104} = 0.3225$.

$s^2(r^x, r^y) = \frac{\sum_{t=-5}^{0}(r_x - AMr_x)r_y}{6-1}$
$= \frac{0.05(0.20) + (-0.20)(-0.20) + 0.15(-0.10) + 0.20(0.30) + (-0.35)(-0.20) + 0.15(0.60)}{6-1}$
$= \frac{0.255}{5} = 0.051$.

Finally, $r(r^x, r^y) = \frac{s^2(r^x, r^y)}{s(r^x)s(r^y)} = \frac{0.051}{0.2236 \times 0.3225} = 0.7072$.

7. First, values are as follows.

Year	V^A	V^B	V^C
-2	$2 \times 5 = 10$	$5 \times 1 = 5$	$3 \times 5 = 15$
-1	$2 \times 6 = 12$	$4 \times 1 = 4$	$3 \times 4.33 = 13$
0	$2 \times 7.5 = 15$	$8 \times 1 = 8$	$3 \times 3 = 9$

Next, $V_{-2}^P = V_{-2}^A + V_{-2}^B + V_{-2}^C = 10 + 5 + 15 = 30$.
Also, $w_{-2}^A = \frac{V_{-2}^A}{V_{-2}^P} = \frac{10}{30} = \frac{1}{3}$, $w_{-2}^B = \frac{V_{-2}^B}{V_{-2}^P} = \frac{5}{30} = \frac{1}{6}$, and $w_{-2}^C = \frac{V_{-2}^C}{V_{-2}^P} = \frac{15}{30} = \frac{1}{2}$.

Analogously, $w_{-1}^A = \frac{12}{29}$, $w_{-1}^B = \frac{4}{29}$, $w_{-1}^C = \frac{13}{29}$, and $w_0^A = \frac{15}{32}$, $w_0^B = \frac{1}{4}$, $w_0^C = \frac{9}{32}$.

Next, $r_{-1}^A = \frac{12-10}{10} = 20\%$, $r_{-1}^B = \frac{4-5}{5} = -20\%$, $r_{-1}^C = \frac{13-15}{15} = -13.33\%$, and

$r_0^A = \frac{15-12}{12} = 25\%$, $r_0^B = \frac{8-4}{4} = 100\%$, $r_0^C = \frac{9-13}{13} = -30.77\%$.

8. $r_{-1}^P = \frac{1}{3}(20\%) + \frac{1}{6}(-20\%) + \frac{1}{2}(-13.33\%) = -3.33\%$, and

$r_0^P = \frac{12}{29}(25\%) + \frac{4}{29}(100\%) + \frac{13}{29}(-30.77\%) = 10.34\%$.

9. $GMr^P = \sqrt{HPR^P} - 1 = \sqrt{R_{-1}^P * R_0^P} - 1 = \sqrt{(1-3.33\%)(1+10.34\%)} - 1 = 3.28\%$.

10. $HPR^P = w_{-2}^A HPR^A + w_{-2}^B HPR^B + w_{-2}^C HPR^C = \frac{1}{3}\frac{15}{10} + \frac{1}{6}\frac{8}{5} + \frac{1}{2}\frac{9}{15} = 1.0667$, and $GMr^P = \sqrt{HPR^P} - 1 = \sqrt{1.0667} - 1 = 3.28\%$.

11. First, shares owned and values are as follows:

Year	sh^A	sh^B	sh^C
-2	$\frac{15}{5} = 3$	$\frac{20}{4} = 5$	$\frac{15}{3} = 5$
-1	$3(1+\frac{5}{10}) = 4.5$	$5(1+\frac{6}{8}) = 8.75$	$5(1+\frac{1}{2}) = 7.5$
0	$4.5(1+\frac{1}{4}) = 5.625$	$8.75(1+\frac{2}{10}) = 10.5$	$7.5(1+\frac{4}{6}) = 12.5$

Year	V^A	V^B	V^C	V^P
-2	15	20	15	$15 + 20 + 15 = 50$
-1	$4.5(10) = 45$	$8.75(8) = 70$	$7.5(2) = 15$	$45 + 70 + 15 = 130$
0	$5.625(4) = 22.5$	$10.5(10) = 105$	$12.5(6) = 75$	$22.5 + 105 + 75 = 202.50$

Then we can calculate returns, variances and standard deviations.

(1) Gross Returns: $R_{-1}^A = \frac{45}{15} = 3$, $R_0^A = \frac{22.5}{45} = 0.5$; $R_{-1}^B = \frac{70}{20} = 3.5$, $R_0^A = \frac{105}{70} = 1.5$; $R_{-1}^C = \frac{15}{15} = 1$, $R_0^C = \frac{75}{15} = 5$; $R_{-1}^P = \frac{130}{50} = 2.6$, $R_0^P = \frac{202.5}{130} = 1.56$.

(2) HPR and HPr: $HPR^A = 3 \times 0.5 = 1.5$, $HPR^B = 3.5 \times 1.5 = 5.25$, $HPR^C = 1 \times 5 = 5$, $HPR^P = \frac{202.5}{50} = 4.05$; $HPr^A = 1.5 - 1 = 0.5$, $HPr^B = 5.25 - 1 = 4.25$, $HPr^C = 5 - 1 = 4$, $HPr^P = 4.05 - 1 = 3.05$.

(3) AMR and AMr: $AMR^A = \frac{3+0.5}{2} = 1.75$, $AMR^B = \frac{3.5+1.5}{2} = 2.5$, $AMR^C = \frac{1+5}{2} = 3$, $AMR^P = \frac{2.6+1.56}{2} = 2.08$; $AMr^A = 1.75 - 1 = 0.75$, $AMr^B = 2.5 - 1 = 1.5$, $AMr^C = 3 - 1 = 2$, $AMr^P = 2.08 - 1 = 1.08$.

(4) GMR and GMr: $GMR^A = \sqrt{1.5} = 1.22$, $GMR^B = \sqrt{5.25} = 2.29$, $GMR^C = \sqrt{5} =$

2.24, $GMR^P = \sqrt{4.05} = 2.01$; $GMr^A = 1.22 - 1 = 0.22$, $GMr^B = 2.29 - 1 = 1.29$, $GMr^C = 2.24 - 1 = 1.24$, $GMr^P = 2.01 - 1 = 1.01$.

(5) $s^2(R)$ and $s(R)$: $s^2(R^A) = \frac{1}{2-1}[(3-1.75)^2 + (0.5-1.75)^2] = 3.125$, $s^2(R^B) = (3.5-2.5)^2 + (1.5-2.5)^2 = 2$, $s^2(R^C) = (1-3)^2 + (5-3)^2 = 8$, $s^2(R^P) = (2.6-2.08)^2 + (1.56-2.08)^2 = 0.54$; $s(R^A) = \sqrt{3.125} = 1.77$, $s(R^B) = \sqrt{2} = 1.41$, $s(R^C) = \sqrt{8} = 2.83$, $s(R^P) = \sqrt{0.5408} = 0.74$.

12. Because dividends were not reinvested, shares owned would be the same as when we bought them. Then the shares are: $sh^A = 3, sh^B = 5, sh^C = 5$. For the portfolio, the weights of each stock are as follows.

Year	w^A	w^B	w^C
-2	$\frac{15}{50} = 0.3$	$\frac{20}{50} = 0.4$	$\frac{15}{50} = 0.3$
-1	$\frac{3 \times 10}{3 \times 10 + 5 \times 8 + 5 \times 2} = \frac{3}{8}$	$\frac{5 \times 8}{3 \times 10 + 5 \times 8 + 5 \times 2} = \frac{4}{8}$	$\frac{5 \times 2}{3 \times 10 + 5 \times 8 + 5 \times 2} = \frac{1}{8}$

Next, we can calculate returns, variances and standard deviations.

(1) Gross Returns: $R^A_{-1} = \frac{10+5}{5} = 3$, $R^A_0 = \frac{4+1}{10} = 0.5$; $R^B_{-1} = \frac{8+6}{4} = 3.5$, $R^B_0 = \frac{10+2}{8} = 1.5$; $R^C_{-1} = \frac{2+1}{3} = 1$, $R^C_0 = \frac{6+4}{2} = 5$; $R^P_{-1} = 0.3 \times 3 + 0.4 \times 3.5 + 0.3 \times 1 = 2.6$, $R^P_0 = \frac{3}{8 \times 0.5} + 0.5 \times 1.5 + \frac{1}{8 \times 5} = 1.56$.

(2) HPR and HPr: $HPR^A = \frac{4+1+5}{5} = 2$, $HPR^B = \frac{10+2+6}{4} = 4.5$, $HPR^C = \frac{6+4+1}{3} = 3.67$, $HPR^P = 0.3 \times 2 + 0.4 \times 4.5 + 0.3 \times 3.67 = 3.5$; $HPr^A = 2 - 1 = 1$, $HPr^B = 4.5 - 1 = 3.5$, $HPr^C = 3.67 - 1 = 2.67$, $HPr^P = 3.5 - 1 = 2.5$.

(3) AMR and AMr: $AMR^A = \frac{3+0.5}{2} = 1.75$, $AMR^B = \frac{3.5+1.5}{2} = 2.5$, $AMR^C = \frac{1+5}{2} = 3$, $AMR^P = \frac{2.6+1.56}{2} = 2.08$; $AMr^A = 1.75 - 1 = 0.75$, $AMr^B = 2.5 - 1 = 1.5$, $AMr^C = 3 - 1 = 2$, $AMr^P = 2.08 - 1 = 1.08$.

(4) GMR and GMr: $GMR^A = \sqrt{2} = 1.41$, $GMR^B = \sqrt{4.5} = 2.12$, $GMR^C = \sqrt{3.67} = 1.92$, $GMR^P = \sqrt{3.5} = 1.87$; $GMr^A = 1.41 - 1 = 0.41$, $GMr^B = 2.12 - 1 = 1.12$, $GMr^C = 1.92 - 1 = 0.92$, $GMr^P = 1.87 - 1 = 0.87$.

(5) $s^2(R)$ and $s(R)$: $s^2(R^A) = \frac{1}{2-1}[(3-1.75)^2 + (0.5-1.75)^2] = 3.125$, $s^2(R^B) = (3.5-2.5)^2 + (1.5-2.5)^2 = 2$, $s^2(R^C) = (1-3)^2 + (5-3)^2 = 8$, $s^2(R^P) = (2.6-2.08)^2 + (1.56-2.08)^2 = 0.54$; $s(R^A) = \sqrt{3.125} = 1.77$, $s(R^B) = \sqrt{2} = 1.41$, $s(R^C) = \sqrt{8} = 2.83$, $s(R^P) = \sqrt{0.5408} = 0.74$.

Chapter 3

1. The expected return and variance of r^x is: $E[r^x] = \int_1^0 1z\,dz = \frac{1}{2}z^2|_1^0 = \frac{1}{2}1^2 - \frac{1}{2}0^2 = \frac{1}{2}$ and $\sigma^2(r^x) = \int_1^0 1(z - \frac{1}{2})^2 dz = \frac{1}{3}z^3 - \frac{1}{2}z^2 + \frac{1}{4}z|_1^0 = \frac{1}{12}$. So $\sigma(r^x) = \sqrt{\sigma^2(r^x)} = \sqrt{\frac{1}{12}}$.

2. The expected return and variance of r^x is: $E[r^x] = -20\% \times 0.2 + 5\% \times 0.5 + 30\% \times 0.3 = 7.5\%$, while $\sigma^2(r^x) = 0.2(-20\% - 7.5\%)^2 + 0.5(5\% - 7.5\%)^2 + 0.3(30\% - 7.5\%)^2 = 0.030625$. So $\sigma(r^x) = \sqrt{\sigma^2(r^x)} = \sqrt{0.030625} = 0.175 = 17.5\%$.

3. The joint density function of these two return variables is: $f_{xy}(z,v) = f_x(z)f_y(z) = 1$. Next, $E(r^x r^y) = \int_{z=0}^{z=1}\int_{v=0}^{v=1}(1)zv\,dv\,dz = (\int_{z=0}^{z=1}f_x(z)z\,dz)(\int_{v=0}^{v=1}f_y(v)v\,dv) = (\frac{1}{2})^2 = \frac{1}{4}$. In problem 1, we know that $E(r^x) = E(r^y) = \frac{1}{2}$. So from $\sigma^2(r^x, r^y) = E(r^x r^y) - E(r^x)E(r^y)$, then $\sigma^2(r^x, r^y) = E(r^x r^y) - E(r^x)E(r^y) = \frac{1}{4} - \frac{1}{2}\frac{1}{2} = 0$.

4. First, $E(r^P) = w^x E(r^x) + w^y E(r^y) = 0.5 \times 10\% + 0.5 \times 20\% = 15\%$. Next, for a correlation coefficient of one, then $\sigma^2(r^P) = (w^x \sigma(r^x))^2 + (w^y \sigma(r^y))^2 = (0.5 \times 0.3)^2 + (0.5 \times 0.6)^2 = 0.1125$. So $\sigma(r^P) = \sqrt{\sigma^2(r^P)} = \sqrt{0.1125} = 0.3354$.

5. From $\sigma^2(r^P) = (w^x \sigma(r^x) + w^y \sigma(r^y))^2 = (0.5 \times 0.3 + 0.5 \times 0.6)^2 = 0.2025$, then $\sigma(r^P) = \sqrt{\sigma^2(r^P)} = \sqrt{0.2025} = 0.45$.

6. From $\sigma^2(r^P) = (w^x \sigma(r^x) - w^y \sigma(r^y))^2 = (0.5 \times 0.3 - 0.5 \times 0.6)^2 = 0.0225$, then $\sigma(r^P) = \sqrt{\sigma^2(r^P)} = \sqrt{0.0225} = 0.15$. The standard deviation of a portfolio is increasing in correlation coefficient of asset returns, as $0.45 = \sigma(r^P|\rho = +1) > \sigma(r^P|\rho = 0) = 0.34 > \sigma(r^P|\rho = -1) = 0.15$.

7. First, $E(r^P) = w^x E(r^x) + w^y E(r^y) + w^z E(r^z) = \frac{1}{3}10\% + \frac{1}{3}20\% + \frac{1}{3}6\% = 12\%$. As the new portfolio has three independent assets, its variance of return is $\sigma^2(R^P) = (w^x \sigma(R^x))^2 + (w^y \sigma(R^y))^2 + (w^z \sigma(R^z))^2 = (\frac{1}{3}0.3)^2 + (\frac{1}{3}0.6)^2 + (\frac{1}{3}0)^2 = 0.05$, and $\sigma(r^P) = \sqrt{\sigma^2(r^P)} = \sqrt{0.05} = 0.2236$. Compared to the two asset portfolio of problem 4, $\sigma(r^P|3 \text{ assets}) = 0.22 < \sigma(r^P|2 \text{ assets}) = 0.34$. Adding an asset whose return has no correlation with the returns of the first two asset returns serves to reduce the portfolio's standard deviation of return, especially given the fact that the newly added asset Z is a risk-free asset.

8. The variance of a portfolio consisting of two assets whose returns are perfectly negatively correlated is $\sigma^2(r^P) = (\sigma(r^P))^2 = (w^x \sigma(r^x) - w^y \sigma(r^y))^2 \geq 0$. To minimize variance, then $\frac{\partial \sigma^2(r^P)}{\partial w^y} = \frac{\partial (w^x \sigma(r^x) - w^y \sigma(r^y))^2}{\partial w^y}$. Respecting the budget condition of $w^x + w^y = 1$, then $\frac{\partial \sigma^2(r^P)}{\partial w^y} = -2\sigma(r^P)[\sigma(r^x) + \sigma(r^y)]$. Setting this equal to zero,

then $\sigma(r^P) = 0 \to (1-w^y)\sigma^x - w^y\sigma^y = 0$, or $w^y = \frac{\sigma(r^x)}{\sigma(r^x)+\sigma(r^y)} = \frac{0.1}{0.1+0.6} = \frac{1}{7}$, and $w^x = 1 - w^y = 1 - \frac{1}{7} = \frac{6}{7}$. Showing a positive second derivative confirms that the variance is minimized, as $\frac{\partial^2 \sigma^2(r^P)}{(\partial w^y)^2} = +2[\sigma(r^x) + \sigma(r^y)]^2 > 0$.

Given that $w^y = \frac{\sigma(r^x)}{\sigma(r^x)+\sigma(r^y)}$ and $w^x = 1 - w^y = \frac{\sigma(r^y)}{\sigma(r^x)+\sigma(r^y)}$, then
$\sigma(r^P) = w^x\sigma(r^x) - w^y\sigma(r^y) = \frac{\sigma(r^y)}{\sigma(r^x)+\sigma(r^y)}\sigma(r^x) - \frac{\sigma(r^x)}{\sigma(r^x)+\sigma(r^y)}\sigma(r^y) = 0$.

9. Given $\rho(R^x, R^y) = 0$, then $\sigma^2(R^P) = (w^x\sigma(R^x))^2 + (w^y\sigma(R^y))^2 > 0$, as $\sigma(R^x) > 0$ and $\sigma(R^y) > 0$. As $\sigma^2(R^P) > 0$, the minimum standard deviation must be positive. As $w^y = 1 - w^x$, then $\sigma^2(R^P) = (w^x\sigma(R^x))^2 + [(1-w^x)\sigma(R^y)]^2 = (w^x)^2 0.3^2 + (1-w^x)^2 0.6^2 = 0.45(w^x)^2 - 0.72w^x + 0.36$. The first order condition is $0.9w^x - 0.72 = 0$. Solving for w^x, then $w^x = \frac{72}{90} = \frac{4}{5}$, and $w^y = 1 - w^x = \frac{1}{5}$. Accordingly, the new minimum standard deviation of this portfolio is $\sigma(R^P) = \sqrt{(w^x\sigma(R^x))^2 + (w^y\sigma(R^y))^2} = \sqrt{(\frac{4}{5}0.3)^2 + (\frac{1}{5}0.6)^2} = 26.83\%$. Note that compared to the result of problem 4 where $w^x = w^y = 0.5$, then $26.83\% = \sigma(R^P|\text{minimized}) < \sigma(R^P|\text{equal weights}) = 33.54\%$. Of course, minimizing risk also reduces reward, as $E[r^P|w^x = \frac{4}{5}] = 12\% < 15\% = E[r^P|w^x = \frac{1}{2}]$.

Whereas the minimum standard deviation of a portfolio of two well-diversified portfolios (see problem 8) can theoretically be zero if the portfolios are perfectly *negatively* correlated (i.e., given a correlation coefficient of $\rho(r^x, r^y) = -1$), it is shown above that given $\rho(r^x, r^y) = 0$, then $\sigma^2(r^P) = 0$ is *not* possible, given positive variance of return of each portfolio. In short, assuming long weights $w^x > 0$ and $w^y > 0$, then $\sigma^2(r^P|\rho(r^x, r^y) = -1) < \sigma^2(r^P|\rho(r^x, r^y) = 0)$, where $\sigma^2(r^P|\rho(r^x, r^y) = -1) = 0$ is possible given the weights shown in problem 8.

Chapter 4

1. Given weights of each asset of w^x, w^y, w^z, and based on conditions given in the problem, we want to maximize the expected return of our portfolio ($E[r^P] = \sum_i w^i E[r^i]$) subject to the budget constraint ($1 = \sum_i w^i$) and the acceptable risk constraint ($\sigma^P = \{\sum_i (w^i\sigma^i)^2\}^{0.5} \leq 0.45$, or $(\sigma^P)^2 = \sum_i (w^i\sigma^i)^2 \leq (0.45)^2$), given zero correlations between pairs of assets). Using the Lagrangian method, $L = [(10\%)w^x + (20\%)w^y + (35\%)w^z] - \lambda[1 - w^x - w^y - w^z] - \mu[(0.45)^2 - (0.3w^x)^2 - (0.5w^y)^2 - (0.7w^z)^2]$. Taking first derivatives, $\frac{\partial L}{\partial w^x} = 0.1 + \lambda + 0.6w^x\mu$, $\frac{\partial L}{\partial w^y} = 0.2 + \lambda + 1w^y\mu$, and $\frac{\partial L}{\partial w^z} = 0.35 + \lambda + 1.4w^z\mu$. Setting these three derivatives to zero and solving the resulting

set of five simultaneous equations (including the budget constraint and acceptable risk constraint), we have $w^x = -0.000181, w^y = 0.438978, w^z = 0.561203$. The expected return is $E[r^P] = 28.419855\%$. Confirming, $\sigma^P = 0.45$. (At the equilibrium solution, $\lambda = -0.100025$ and $\mu = -0.227745$.)

2. Now we have three addtional constraints ($w^x \geq 0$, $w^y \geq 0$, $w^z \geq 0$), The Lagrangian formula becomes $L = [(10\%)w^x + (20\%)w^y + (35\%)w^z] - \lambda[1 - w^x - w^y - w^z] - \mu[(0.45)^2 - (0.3w^x)^2 - (0.5w^y)^2 - (0.7w^z)^2] + \lambda^x[w^x] + \lambda^y[w^y] + \lambda^z[w^z]$. Taking first derivatives, $\frac{\partial L}{\partial w^x} = 0.1 + \lambda + 0.6w^x\mu + \lambda^x$, $\frac{\partial L}{\partial w^y} = 0.2 + \lambda + 1w^y\mu + \lambda^y$, and $\frac{\partial L}{\partial w^z} = 0.35 + \lambda + 1.4w^z\mu + \lambda^z$. Solving, we have $w^x = 0, w^y = 0.438678, w^z = 0.561322$. The expected return is $E(r^p) = 28.419832\%$.

Confirming, $\sigma^P = [(0.5\{0.438678\})^2 + (0.7\{1 - 0.438678\})^2]^{0.5} = 0.45$.

Compared to the case where there were no constraints on short sales (problem 1), the expected return is reduced for the same acceptable risk, or $28.419832\% = E[r^P|\text{short sales prohibited}] < E[r^P|\text{short sales allowed}] = 28.419855\%$.

As is always the case, a constrained optimization is not as optimal as one where at least one of the binding constraints is relaxed.

3. The iso-utility in σr-space is $\frac{dr}{d\sigma}|u = -\frac{du/d\sigma}{du/dr} = -\frac{-2a\sigma}{1} = +2a\sigma$. The slope of the efficient frontier in σr-space is $\frac{dr}{d\sigma} = \frac{4b}{2\sqrt{\sigma}} = \frac{2b}{\sqrt{\sigma}}$. Setting the slopes equal to one another, $2a\sigma^* = \frac{2b}{\sqrt{\sigma^*}}$. So $\sigma^* = (\frac{b}{a})^{\frac{2}{3}}$. Finally, $E[r] = 4b\sqrt{\sigma} + c = 4b[(\frac{b}{a})^{\frac{2}{3}}]^{0.5} + c = 4a^{-\frac{1}{3}}b^{\frac{4}{3}} + c = 4(\frac{b^4}{a})^{\frac{1}{3}} + c$.

4. For parameter a, $\frac{\partial E[r]}{\partial a} = -\frac{4}{3}(\frac{b}{a})^{\frac{4}{3}} < 0$, as a, b and c are positive constants. So $E[r]$ is decreasing in a, as the more risk-averse the investor (i.e., higher a), the lower risk and expected reward the investor accepts in equilibrium. Parameter a can be regarded as a person's level of risk aversion. A larger a means a person is more risk averse. As a risk averse person typically tends to accept a lower expected return to achieve a lower standard deviation of his portfolio, $E[r]$ should be decreasing in a.

For parameter b, $\frac{\partial E[r]}{\partial b} = 4(\frac{4}{3})a^{-\frac{1}{3}}b^{\frac{1}{3}} = \frac{16}{3}(\frac{b}{a})^{\frac{1}{3}} > 0$. So $E[r]$ is increasing in b. Here, parameter b can be regarded as a compensation for a person undertaking risks. This means that a person can get a higher expected return if she is able to accept a higher risk. Therefore $E[r]$ is increasing in b.

For parameter c, $\frac{\partial E[r]}{\partial c} = 1 > 0$. So $E[r]$ is increasing in c. Here, parameter c can be regarded as a risk-free rate of return that can be achieved without taking risks. Therefore a higher risk-free rate of return should enhance the expected return of a portfolio. This means $E[r]$ should be increasing in c.

Chapter 5

1. MRP (market risk premium) $= E[r^m] - r^f = 8\% - 4\% = 4\%$.

2. $MPoR$ (market price of risk) $= \frac{E[r^m] - r^f}{\sigma(r^m)} = \frac{8\% - 4\%}{20\%} = \frac{1}{5} = 0.2$.

3. A well-diversified portfolio has no idiosyncratic risk, so the expected return of portfolio x which includes a well-diversified portfolio and a risk-free asset is $E[r^x] = r^f + \frac{E[r^m] - r^f}{\sigma(r^m)} \sigma(r^x) = 4\% + 0.2(14\%) = 6.8\%$. As portfolio x has a standard deviation of $\sigma(r^x) = [(w^m)^2 \sigma^2(r^m) + (1-w^m)^2 \sigma^2(r^f) + 2w^m(1-w^m)\sigma^2(r^m, r^f)]^{0.5}$, and given that $\rho(r^m, r^f) = 0$ and $\sigma(r^f) = 0$, then $\sigma(r^x) = w^m \sigma(r^m) = w^m(20\%) = 14\%$. Thus, $w^m = \frac{14\%}{20\%} = 0.7$, and $w^f = 1 - 0.7 = 0.3$.

4. The correlation coefficient between portfolio x and the market portfolio is $\rho(r^x, r^m) = \frac{\sigma^2(r^x, r^m)}{\sigma(r^x)\sigma(r^m)} = \frac{\sigma^2(w^m r^m + w^f r^f, r^m)}{\sigma(w^m r^m + w^f r^f)\sigma(r^m)} = \frac{w^m \sigma^2(r^m)}{w^m \sigma^2(r^m)} = 1$.

5. The slope coefficient of a regression of returns of portfolio x on returns of the market portfolio m is $\beta^x = \rho(r^x, r^m) \frac{\sigma(r^x)}{\sigma(r^m)} = 1(\frac{14\%}{20\%}) = 0.7$. Hence the expected return of portfolio x is $E[r^x] = r^f + \beta^x [E[r^m] - r^f] = 4\% + 0.7(8\% - 4\%) = 6.8\%$. The systematic risk is $\beta^x \sigma(r^m) = 0.7(20\%) = 14\%$.

6. Analogous to question 3, a well-diversified portfolio has no idiosyncratic risk, so the expected return of portfolio y which includes a well-diversified portfolio and a risk-free asset is $E[r^y] = r^f + \frac{E[r^m] - r^f}{\sigma(r^m)} \sigma(r^y) = 4\% + 0.2(28\%) = 9.6\%$.

As $\rho(r^m, r^f) = 0$, portfolio y has a standard deviation of $28\% = \sigma(r^y) = [(w^m)^2 \sigma^2(r^m) + (1-w^m)^2 \sigma^2(r^f) + 2w^m(1-w^m)\sigma^2(r^m, r^f)]^{0.5} = w^m \sigma(r^m) = w^m(20\%)$, so $w^m = \frac{28\%}{20\%} = 1.4$.

To achieve a return of 9.6% which is higher than the market return of 8%, we short the risk-free asset which implies that we borrow at the risk-free rate of 4% and combine with your own equity to invest in the risky asset (the market portfolio) at a weight of $1.4 > 1$. Hence our expected portfolio return exceeds that of the market.

7. Replacing y with x in problem 4, then $\rho(r^x, r^m) = 1$. All portfolios along the capital

market line are perfectly positively correlated with each other.

8. Consistent with problem 5, $\beta^y = \rho(r^y, r^m)\frac{\sigma(r^y)}{\sigma(r^m)} = 1.4$. Hence the expected return of portfolio y is $E[r^y] = r^f + \beta^y[E[r^m] - r^f] = 4\% + 1.4(8\% - 4\%) = 9.6\%$. The systematic risk is $\beta^x \sigma(r^m) = 1.4(20\%) = 28\%$.

9. $Sharpe^x = \frac{E[r^x] - r^f}{\sigma(r^x)} = \frac{6.8\% - 4\%}{14\%} = 0.2$; $Sharpe^y = \frac{E[r^y] - r^f}{\sigma(r^y)} = \frac{9.6\% - 4\%}{28\%} = 0.2$; $Sharpe^m = \frac{E[r^m] - r^f}{\sigma(r^m)} = \frac{8\% - 4\%}{20\%} = 0.2$.

As all three portfolios, which involve combinations of the risk-free asset and the market portfolio, fall on the capital market line (CML), then all three have the same Sharpe ratio.

10. $Treynor^x = \frac{E[r^x] - r^f}{\beta(r^x)} = \frac{6.8\% - 4\%}{0.7} = 0.04$; $Treynor^y = \frac{E[r^y] - r^f}{\beta(r^y)} = \frac{9.6\% - 4\%}{1.4} = 0.04$; $Treynor^m = \frac{E[r^m] - r^f}{\beta(r^m)} = \frac{8\% - 4\%}{1} = 0.04$.

As all three portfolios, which involve combinations of the risk-free asset and the market portfolio, fall on the security market line (SML), then all three have the same Treynor ratio.

11. The systematic risk is $\beta^m \sigma(r^m) = 1.0(20\%) = 20\%$.

Chapter 6

For problem 1 to problem 3, there are two systematic factors and three assets, so investors are not optimizing an arbitrage portfolio per se, but rather is simply satisfying three simultaneous equations: two to eliminate two systematic risks and one to ensure that the portfolio is cost-free.

$$z^x \beta_1^x + z^y \beta_1^y + z^z \beta_1^z = 0, \quad (eliminate\ exposure\ to\ SRF_1)$$
$$z^x \beta_2^x + z^y \beta_2^y + z^z \beta_2^z = 0, \quad (eliminate\ exposure\ to\ SRF_2)$$
$$and \quad z^x + z^y + z^z = 0, \quad (cost\ free)$$

where z^x, z^y and z^z are *relative* asset weights. When $I = K + 1$, a simple approach to solving the above is to assume that $|z^x| = 1$ (it is positive when asset x is undervalued and negative when asset x is overvalued), which effectively constrains S. Afterwards, we solve for z^y and z^z (In this case $z^i = w^i$).

1. First, let us see whether portfolio x is overvalued or undervalued. The expected return of portfolio x is $E[r^x] = 5\% + 1.025(2\%) + 1.25(4\%) = 12.05\%$. As $IROR^x =$

$11\% < E(r^x) = 12.05\%$, portfolio x is overvalued. Then we should set $z^x = -1$. Then, the equations become

$$1.025(-1) + 2z^y + 0.7z^z = 0, \quad (eliminate\ exposure\ to\ SRF_1)$$
$$1.25(-1) + 2z^y + 1z^z = 0, \quad (eliminate\ exposure\ to\ SRF_2)$$
$$and \quad (-1) + z^y + z^z = 0. \quad (cost\ free)$$

Solving for z^y and z^z, $z^y = 0.25$ and $z^z = 0.75$. In this case, we will invest $-\$100$ in portfolio x, \$25 in portfolio y and \$75 in portfolio z. This means that we will go long portfolios y and z, and short portfolio x. For each $-\$100$ invested in x, the profit will be $\$100[-1(11\%) + 0.25(17\%) + 0.75(10.4\%)] = \$1.05$.

2. The logic is the same as problem 1. The expected return of portfolio x is $E[r^x] = 5\% + 0.75(2\%) + -0.5(4\%) = 4.5\%$. As $IROR^x = 5\% > E(r^x) = 4.5\%$, portfolio x is undervalued. Then we should set $z^x = +1$. Then, the equations become

$$0.75(1) + 1.5z^y + 1z^z = 0, \quad (eliminate\ exposure\ to\ SRF_1)$$
$$(-0.5)(1) - 0.5z^y - 0.5z^z = 0, \quad (eliminate\ exposure\ to\ SRF_2)$$
$$and \quad (1) + z^y + z^z = 0. \quad (cost\ free)$$

Solving for z^y and z^z, then $z^y = 0.5$ and $z^z = -1.5$. In this case, we will invest $+\$100$ in portfolio x, \$50 in portfolio y and $-\$150$ in portfolio z. This means that we will go long portfolios x and y while we short portfolio z. The profit per \$100 invested in asset x is $\$100[(+1)(5\%) + (0.5)(7\%) + (-1.5)(4.5\%)] = \$1.75$.

3. The logic is the same as problem 1. The expected return of portfolio x is $E[r^x] = 5\% + 2.05(2\%) + 2.5(4\%) = 19.1\%$. As $IROR^x = 18\% < E(r^x) = 19.1\%$, portfolio x is overvalued. So we set $z^x = -1$. Next, the equations become

$$2.05(-1) + 4z^y + 1.4z^z = 0, \quad (eliminate\ exposure\ to\ SRF_1)$$
$$2.5(-1) + 4z^y + 2z^z = 0, \quad (eliminate\ exposure\ to\ SRF_2)$$
$$and \quad (-1) + z^y + z^z = 0. \quad (cost\ free)$$

Solving for z^y and z^z, then $z^y = 0.25$ and $z^z = 0.75$. In this case, we will invest $-\$100$ in portfolio x, \$25 in portfolio y and \$75 in portfolio z. This means that we will go long portfolios y and z, and short portfolio x. The profit per \$100 of portfolio x shorted is $100[(-1)(18\%) + (0.25)(30\%) + (0.75)(15.8\%)] = \$1.35$.

For problems 4 and 5, there are two systematic factors and four assets, so investors are optimizing an arbitrage portfolio and the maximization program is

$$\max_{z^A, z^B, z^C, z^D} IRR^P = \sum_{i=A,B,C,D} z^i(IRR^i - E[r^i]), \text{ subject to}$$

$$z^A\beta_1^A + z^B\beta_1^B + z^C\beta_1^C + z^D\beta_1^D = 0, \quad (no\ SRF1)$$

$$z^A\beta_2^A + z^B\beta_2^B + z^C\beta_2^C + z^D\beta_2^D = 0, \quad (no\ SRF2)$$

$$and \quad z^A + z^B + z^C + z^D = 0, \quad (cost\ free)$$

$$z^i \in [-5, +5], \, i \in \{A, B, C, D\}. \quad (constrain\ S)$$

Such a constrained optimization program can be solved via the Lagrangian method. Let's define $Z \equiv \sum_{long\ i} z^i = -\sum_{short\ i} z^i > 0$, where the equality is due to the cost-free constraint. Then $w^i = \frac{z^i}{Z}, \, i \in \{x, y, z\}$. Finally, for each asset i, $V_0^i = w^i S$.

4. The maximization program is

$$\max_{z^x, z^y, z^z, z^a} IRR^P = \sum_{i=x,y,z,a} z^i(IRR^i - E[r^i]), \text{ subject to}$$

$$0.25z^x + 0.75z^y + 0.5z^z + (-0.25)z^a = 0, \quad (no\ SRF_1)$$

$$0.5z^x + 1.25z^y + (-0.5)z^z + 0.5z^a = 0, \quad (no\ SRF_2)$$

$$and \quad z^x + z^y + z^z + z^a = 0, \quad (cost\ free)$$

$$z^i \in [-5, +5], \, i \in \{x, y, z, a\}. \quad (constrain\ S)$$

Solving for this in Excel, $z^x = -5, z^y = 1.6, z^z = 1.2$ and $z^a = 2.2$. So the weights are $w^x = \frac{-5}{5} = -1, w^y = \frac{1.6}{5} = 0.32, w^z = \frac{1.2}{5} = 0.24$ and $w^a = \frac{2.2}{5} = 0.44$. In this case, we will invest $-\$100$ in portfolio x, \$32 in portfolio y, \$24 in portfolio z and \$44 in portfolio a. This means that we will go long portfolios y, z and a, and short portfolio x. The profit is $\$100[(-1)(7\%) + (0.32)(12\%) + (0.24)(5\%) + (0.44)(7\%)] = \$1.12$ per \$100 of asset x shorted.

5. The logic is the same as problem 4. The maximization program is

$$\max_{z^x, z^y, z^z, z^a} IRR^P = \sum_{i=x,y,z,a} z^i(IRR^i - E[r^i]), \text{ subject to}$$

$$0.25z^x + 0.5z^y + 0.75z^z + 1z^a = 0, \quad (no\ SRF_1)$$

$$1z^x + 0.5z^y + 0.25z^z + 1z^a = 0, \quad (no\ SRF_2)$$

$$and \quad z^x + z^y + z^z + z^a = 0, \quad (cost\ free)$$

$$z^i \in [-5, +5], \, i \in \{x, y, z, a\}. \quad (constrain\ S)$$

Solving for this in Excel, $z^x = -2.22$, $z^y = 5$, $z^z = -3.33$ and $z^a = 0.56$. So the weights are $w^x = \frac{-2.22}{2.22} = -1$, $w^y = \frac{5}{2.22} = 2.25$, $w^z = \frac{-3.33}{2.22} = -1.5$ and $w^a = \frac{0.56}{2.22} = 0.25$. In this case, we will invest $-\$100$ in portfolio x, $\$225$ in portfolio y, $-\$150$ in portfolio z and $\$25$ in portfolio a. This means that we will go long portfolios y and a, and short portfolios x and z. The profit is $\$100[(-1)(9\%) + (2.25)(9\%) + (-1.5)(7\%) + (0.25)(11\%)] = \$3.50$ per $\$100$ of asset x shorted.

Chapter 7

1. See completed figure 7.4 on page 296.

2. See completed figure 7.5 on page 297.

3. The plowback ratio for 2015 is $b = \frac{NI - dividend}{NI} = \frac{\$20,000 - \$3,300}{\$20,000} = 83.5\%$.

Income Statement Entry	2015
Net sales (NS)	198,000
Cost of goods sold ($COGS$)	111,000
Gross profit (GP)	87,000
Selling, general and administrative (SGA) expenses	38,000
Advertising	16,500
Depreciation and amortization ($D\&A$)	3,000
Repairs and maintenance	2,000
Operating Profit ($EBIT^*$)	27,500
Other Income (expense)	
Interest income (II)	500
Interest expense (IE)	(2,000)
Earnings before income taxes (EBT^{**})	26,000
Income taxes	6,000
Net earnings, net income (NI)	20,000
Basic earnings per common share	4.17
Diluted earnings per common share	4.11
$^*EBIT$ stands for earnings before interest income (expenses) and taxes.	
$^{**}EBT$ stands for earnings before taxes (but *after* interest income (expenses)).	
Cash dividends of $\$3,300$ were paid in 2015. All numbers are in $\$$ thousands.	

Figure 7.4   Income statement

Balance Sheet Entry	15/12/31	14/12/31
Assets (A)		
Current Assets (CA)		
Cash	2,500	2,000
Marketable securities (MS)	12,700	8,000
Accounts receivable*	8,000	8,000
Inventories	47,000	36,000
Prepaid expenses	500	700
Total current assets	70,700	54,700
Property, Plant & Equipment: PPE		
Land	800	800
Buildings & leasehold improvements	18,000	11,000
Equipment	21,000	13,000
Gross PPE	39,800	24,800
Less accumulated depreciation & amortization	10,000	7,000
Net PPE	29,800	17,800
Other Assets	800	600
Total Assets, TA	101,300	73,100
Liabilities and Stock holders' Equity		
Current Liabilities (CL)		
Accounts payable (AP)	14,000	7,000
Notes payable to banks (NP)	5,000	6,000
Current maturities of LTD (CM)	2,000	1,000
Accrued liabilities	5,000	6,000
Total current liabilities	26,000	20,000
Deferred Incomes Taxes (DIT)	800	600
Long-Term Debt (LTD)	21,000	16,000
Total liabilities	47,800	36,600
Stock holders' Equity		
Common stock, par value of $1**	4,800	4,500
Additional paid-in capital	900	700
Retained earnings (RE)	52,800	36,100
Less: treasury stock	5,000	4,800
Total Stock holders' Equity	53,500	36,500
Total Liabilities & Stock holders' Equity	101,300	73,100

*This is less allowances for doubtful accounts.

**10,000,000 shares authorized; 4,800,000 shares outstanding in 2015; 4,500,000 shares outstanding in 2014; 4,867,000 diluted shares outstanding in 2015; December 31, 2015 share price equals $10.00 per share.

All numbers are in $ thousands.

Figure 7.5   Balance sheet

4. The dividend payout ratio for 2015 is $1 - b = \frac{dividend}{NI} = \frac{\$3,300}{\$20,000} = 16.5\%$.

5. See completed figure 7.6 on page 298.

Statement of Cash Flows Entry	2015
Operating Cash Flow Activities	
Net income (NI)	20,000
Non-cash adjustments to reconcile net income	
Depreciation & amortization ($D\&A$)	3,000
Deferred income taxes (DIT)	200
Cash provided (used) by working capital	
Accounts receivable	(0)
Inventories	(11,000)
Prepaid expenses	200
Accounts payable	7,000
Accrued liabilities	(1,000)
Operating Cash Flow (OCF)	18,400
Investing Cash Flow Activities	
Additions to property, plant & equipment: PPE	(15,000)
Other investing activities	(200)
Investing Cash Flow (ICF)	(15,200)
Financing Cash Flow Activities	
Sales of common stock	300
Increase (decrease) in short-term borrowings*	(0)
Additions to long-term borrowings	5,000
Reductions of long-term borrowings	(0)
Dividends paid (d)	(3,300)
Financing Cash Flow ($FiCF$)	2,000
Increase (decrease) in cash plus marketable securities	5,200
Cash/MS: beginning of year	10,000
Cash/MS: end of year	15,200

*This includes changes in both CM and NP, or $\Delta(CM + NP)$.
All numbers are in $ thousands.

Figure 7.6   Statement of cash flows

6. The free cash flow for 2015 is $FCF_{2015} = OCF_{2015} + ICF_{2015} + IE_{2015}(1 - T_c) =$ $\$18,400 + (-\$15,200) + \$2,000 \times (1 - \frac{6000}{26,000}) = \$4,738$.

7. The free cash flow to equity holders for 2015 is $FCFE_{2015} = OCF_{2015} + ICF_{2015} + \Delta Debt_{2015-2014} = OCF_{2015} + ICF_{2015} + (\Delta[NP + CMLTD + LTD]) = \$18,400 + (-\$15,200) + (\$[5,000 - 6,000] + \$[2,000 - 1,000] + \$[21,000 - 16,000]) = \$8,200$.

8. The total equity cash flow for 2015 is $TECF_{2015} = Div'd_{2015} +$ net \$ spent on shares$_{2015} = \$3,300 - [\$(4,800 + 900 - 5,000) - \$(4,500 + 700 - 4,800)] = \$3,000$. To confirm, $TECF_{2015} = FCFE_{2015} - \Delta(cash + MS)_{2015-2014} = \$8,200 - \$[(2,500 + 12,700) - (2,000 + 8,000)] = \$3,000$.

Chapter 8

Continue to consider figures 7.4 and 7.5 on pages 83 and 84, respectively, from the previous chapter's problem set.

1. For the common size income statement, see figure 8.13 on page 299.

2. For the common size balance sheet, see figure 8.14 on page 300.

Income Statement Entry	2015
Net sales (NS)	100.0
Cost of goods sold ($COGS$)	56.1
Gross profit (GP)	43.9
Selling, general and administrative (SGA) expenses	19.2
Advertising	8.3
Depreciation and amortization ($D\&A$)	1.5
Repairs and maintenance	1.0
Operating Profit ($EBIT^*$)	13.9
Other Income (expense)	
Interest income (II)	0.3
Interest expense (IE)	(1.0)
Earnings before income taxes (EBT^{**})	13.1
Income taxes	3.0
Net earnings, net income (NI)	10.1
*$EBIT$ stands for earnings before interest income (expenses) and taxes.	
**EBT stands for earnings before taxes (and *after* interest income (expenses)).	
Cash dividends of \$3,300 were paid in 2015.	

Figure 8.13 Common size income statement

Balance Sheet Entry	15/12/31	14/12/31
Assets (A)		
Current Assets (CA)		
Cash	2,500	2,000
Marketable securities (MS)	12,700	8,000
Accounts receivable*	8,000	8,000
Inventories	47,000	36,000
Prepaid expenses	500	700
Total current assets	70,700	54,700
Property, Plant & Equipment: PPE		
Land	800	800
Buildings & leasehold improvements	18,000	11,000
Equipment	21,000	13,000
Gross PPE	39,800	24,800
Less accumulated depreciation & amortization	10,000	7,000
Net PPE	29,800	17,800
Other Assets	800	600
Total Assets, TA	101,300	73,100
Liabilities and Stock holders' Equity		
Current Liabilities (CL)		
Accounts payable (AP)	14,000	7,000
Notes payable to banks (NP)	5,000	6,000
Current maturities of LTD (CM)	2,000	1,000
Accrued liabilities	5,000	6,000
Total current liabilities	26,000	20,000
Deferred Incomes Taxes (DIT)	800	600
Long-Term Debt (LTD)	21,000	16,000
Total liabilities	47,800	36,600
Stock holders' Equity		
Common stock, par value of $1**	4,800	4,500
Additional paid-in capital	900	700
Retained earnings (RE)	52,800	36,100
Less: treasury stock	5,000	4,800
Total Stock holders' Equity	53,500	36,500
Total Liabilities & Stock holders' Equity	101,300	73,100

*This is less allowances for doubtful accounts.

**10,000,000 shares authorized; 4,800,000 shares outstanding in 2015; 4,500,000 shares outstanding in 2014; 4,867,000 diluted shares outstanding in 2015; December 31, 2015 share price equals $10.00 per share.

Figure 8.14 Common size balance sheet

Solutions to Selected End-of-chapter Problems   301

3. For internal liquidity ratios, see figure 8.15 on page 301.

Metric	Statistic	Calculation	Value
Current Ratio	$\frac{CA}{CL}$	$\frac{70{,}700}{26{,}000}$	2.72
Quick Ratio*	$\frac{Cash+MS+AR}{CL}$	$\frac{23{,}200}{26{,}000}$	0.89
Cash Ratio	$\frac{Cash+MS}{CL}$	$\frac{15{,}200}{26{,}000}$	0.58
CF** Liquidity Ratio	$\frac{Cash+MS+OCF}{CL}$	$\frac{33{,}600}{26{,}000}$	1.29
$ARTO^{**}\left(\frac{turns}{year}\right)$	$\frac{NS}{AvgAR}$	$\frac{198{,}000}{8{,}000}$	24.8
Inventory $TO\left(\frac{turns}{year}\right)$	$\frac{COGS}{AvgInv}$	$\frac{111{,}000}{41{,}500}$	2.67
$APTO^{**}\left(\frac{turns}{year}\right)$	$\frac{COGS}{AvgAP}$	$\frac{111{,}000}{10{,}500}$	10.6
Days in AR (DAR)	$\frac{365}{ARTO}$	$\frac{365}{24.8}$	14.7
Days in inventory (DI)	$\frac{365}{Inv.\ TO}$	$\frac{365}{2.67}$	136.7
Days in AP (DAP)	$\frac{365}{APTO}$	$\frac{365}{10.6}$	34.5
Cash conversion cycle, CCC	$DAR+DI-DAP$	$15+137-35$	117

*Quick ratio is also called the acid-test ratio.

**CF: cash flow; AR: accounts receivable; TO: Turnover; AP: accounts payable;

Figure 8.15   Internal liquidity ratios

4. For operating performance ratios, see figure 8.16 on page 302.

5. For financial risk ratios, see figure 8.17 on page 303.

6. For the top half of this contribution margin income statement, see figure 8.18 on page 304.

7. For completed operational risk ratios, see figure 8.19 on page 304.

8. The sustainable growth of equity of this firm, i.e., that which is possible absent external financing, is $g = b(ROE) = 83.5\%(44.4\%) = 37.1\%$.

9. Given a stock price of $10.00 per share, then
  (a) price to sales ratio $= \frac{P}{S} = \frac{\$10/Sh.}{\$198{,}000{,}000/\$4{,}800{,}000 Shs.} = 0.24$;
  (b) price to free cash flow ratio $= \frac{P}{FCF} = \frac{\$10/Sh.}{\$4{,}738{,}000/\$4{,}800{,}000 Shs.} = 10.13$;
  (c) price to book ratio $= \frac{P}{BV} = \frac{\$10/Sh.}{\$53{,}500{,}000/\$4{,}800{,}000 Shs.} = 0.90$; and
  (d) price to earnings ratio $= \frac{P}{E} = \frac{\$10/Sh.}{\$20{,}000{,}000/\$4{,}800{,}000 Shs.} = 2.40$.

Metric	Statistic	Calculation	Value
Efficiency ratios			
Fixed Asset TO^*	$\frac{NS}{AvgnetPPE}$	$\frac{198{,}000}{23{,}800}$	8.32
Total Asset TO $(TATO)$	$\frac{NS}{AvgTA}$	$\frac{198{,}000}{87{,}200}$	2.27
Gross Fixed Asset TO	$\frac{NS}{AvggrossPPE}$	$\frac{198{,}000}{32{,}300}$	6.13
Equity TO	$\frac{NS}{Avgequity}$	$\frac{198{,}000}{45{,}000}$	4.40
Profitability ratios			
GPM^*	$\frac{GP}{NS}$	$\frac{87{,}000}{198{,}000}$	43.9%
OPM^*	$\frac{OP}{NS}$	$\frac{27{,}500}{198{,}000}$	13.9%
NPM^*	$\frac{NI}{NS}$	$\frac{20{,}000}{198{,}000}$	10.1%
Cash Flow Margin	$\frac{OCF}{NS}$	$\frac{18{,}400}{198{,}000}$	9.3%
ROA^*	$\frac{NI}{AvgTA}$	$\frac{20{,}000}{87{,}200}$	22.9%
ROE^*	$\frac{NI}{AvgEquity}$	$\frac{20{,}000}{45{,}000}$	44.4%
Leverage: $\frac{TA}{Eq}$	$\frac{AvgTA}{AvgEquity}$	$\frac{87{,}200}{45{,}000}$	1.94
Dupont ROE	$NPM(TATO)\frac{A.\ TA}{A.\ Eq}$	10.1%(2.27)1.9	44.4%
Cash return on assets	$\frac{OCF}{AvgTA}$	$\frac{18{,}400}{87{,}200}$	21.1%
Return on TC^*	$\frac{NI+IE}{Avg(Eq+D^{**})}$	$\frac{22{,}000}{70{,}500}$	31.2%

*TO:Turnover; GPM, OPM, NPM: gross, operating and net profit margins;

ROA: return on (total) assets; ROE: return on equity; TC: total capital;

**D: debt, both long-term + (short-term), i.e., $D = TD = LTD + (STD) = LTD + (NP + CM)$;

Figure 8.16 Operating performance ratios: efficiency and profitability

Metric	Statistic	Calculation	Value
Leverage ratios			
Debt ratio	$\frac{TL^{\#\#}}{TL+Eq^{***}}$	$\frac{47{,}800}{101{,}300}$	47.2%
LTD^* to total Cap*	$\frac{LTD}{LTD+Eq}$	$\frac{21{,}000}{74{,}500}$	28.2%
Debt to equity	$\frac{TL}{Eq}$	$\frac{47{,}800}{53{,}500}$	0.89
Leverage: $\frac{A}{Eq}$ Lev	$\frac{TA^{***}}{Eq}$	$\frac{101{,}300}{53{,}500}$	1.89
Debt to assets	$\frac{TD^{***}}{TA}$	$\frac{28{,}000}{101{,}300}$	27.6%
Coverage ratios			
Times interest earned	$\frac{EBIT^{*\#}}{IE}$	$\frac{27{,}500}{2{,}000}$	13.75
Cash interest coverage	$\frac{OCF+IE+taxes}{IE}$	$\frac{26{,}400}{2{,}000}$	13.20
Fixed charge coverage	$\frac{EBIT+RentExp^{*\#}}{IE+RentExp}$	N/R**	N/R**
Cash flow adequacy	$\frac{OCF}{CapEx^{\#}+IE+Div^{\#\#}}$	$\frac{18{,}400}{20{,}300}$	90.6%
Cash flow coverage	$\frac{OCF}{AvgTD}$	$\frac{18{,}400}{25{,}500}$	72.2%
Adjusted ROA (for FLI^*)	$\frac{NI+IE(1-T^C)}{AvgTA}$	$\frac{21{,}538}{87{,}200}$	24.7%
FLI^*	$\frac{ROE}{Adj.\ ROA}$	$\frac{44.4\%}{24.7\%}$	1.80

*LTD: long-term debt; Cap: capitalization; FLI: Financial Leverage Index;

**N/R: this calculation is not required for this assignment;

***Eq: equity; TA: total assets; TD: total debt;

*# $EBIT$ is also called operating profit, or OP; Rent Exp: rent expense; (In our example, we ignore rental expenses. In actuality, leasing is a very important consideration. Crudely speaking, leasing is a substitute for debt financing. Such consideration is beyond our scope.)

#CapEx: capital expenditures, or $\Delta GPPE$;

##Div: cash dividends paid; TL: total liabilities;

Figure 8.17 Financial risk ratios: leverage and coverage

304 Asset Valuation Theory

IS Entry	Value	per Unit	Value	Ratio	Value
Net sales (NS)	198,000	price, P	10.00		100.0%
Variable costs (VC)	111,000	UVC	5.61	VCR	56.1%
CM^*	87,000	UCM	4.39	CMR	43.9%
Fixed costs (FC)	59,500		3.01		30.1%
OM^*	27,500	UOM	1.39	OMR	13.9%

$^*CM$: contribution margin; OM: operating margin = $EBIT$ = operating income;

The number of units equals $\frac{revenue}{price} = \frac{\$198,000}{\$10/unit} = 19,800$ units.

For simplicity, it is assumed that $COGS$ is a variable cost, and that all other costs are fixed.

Figure 8.18   Contribution margin income statement

Metric	Statistic	Calculation	Value
Fixed cost ratio, FCR	$\frac{FC}{TC}$	$\frac{130,000}{170,500}$	76.3%
DOL^*	$\frac{NS-VC}{NS-VC-FC}$	$\frac{157,500}{27,500}$	5.73
DOL	$1 + \frac{FC}{EBIT}$	$1 + \frac{130,000}{27,500}$	5.73
DOL	$\frac{CMR}{OMR}$	$\frac{79.5\%}{13.9\%}$	5.73
$CV^*(NS)$	$\frac{\sigma(NS)^{**}}{\mu(NS)^{**}}$	$\frac{32,670}{198,000}$	16.5%
Operations Risk	$\frac{CV(EBIT)^{**}}{CV(NS)^{**}}$	$\frac{40.4\%}{16.5\%}$	2.45

$^*DOL$: degree of operating leverage; CV: coefficient of variation;

$^{**}\sigma(NS) = \$32,670$; $\mu(NS) = \$198,000$; $\sigma(EBIT) = \$11,100$; $\mu(EBIT) = \$27,500$.

Figure 8.19   Operational risk ratios

Chapter 9

1. $WACC = 40\%(9\%)(1 - 30\%) + 60\%(16\%) = 12.12\%$.

2. $EV = \frac{10}{1.1212} + \frac{18}{1.1212^2} + \frac{26}{1.1212^3} + \frac{34}{1.1212^4} + \frac{40}{1.1212^5} + \frac{46}{1.1212^6} + \frac{52}{1.1212^7} + \frac{52(1+4\%)}{12.12\%-4\%}1.1212^{-7} = 431.2973$.

3. $Eq = \frac{7}{1.16} + \frac{13}{1.16^2} + \frac{18}{1.16^3} + \frac{23}{1.16^4} + \frac{23(1+4\%)}{16\%-4\%}1.16^{-4} = 150.0202$.

4. $Eq = \frac{6}{1.16} + \frac{12}{1.16^2} + \frac{17}{1.16^3} + \frac{22}{1.16^4} + \frac{26}{1.16^5} + \frac{29}{1.16^6} + \frac{29(1+4\%)}{16\%-4\%}1.16^{-6} = 164.5715$.

5. $Eq = \frac{2(1.08)}{1.12} + \frac{2(1.08^2)}{1.12^2} + \frac{2(1.08^3)}{1.12^3} + \frac{2(1.08^4)}{1.12^4} + \frac{2(1.08^5)}{1.12^5} + \frac{2(1.08^5)1.03}{12\%-3\%}1.12^{-5} = 28.0615.$

6. 7. (*omitted*)

Chapter 10

1. $ROE_0 = \frac{NI_0}{Eq_{-1}} = \frac{0.24}{2} = 12\%.$

2. $b = 1 - 60\% = 40\%.$

3. $g = ROE(b) = 12\%(40\%) = 4.8\%.$

4. $d_0 = NI_0(1-b) = 0.24(60\%) = \$0.144$ per share.

5. Book value of total equity = book value of equity per share ∗ number of shares outstanding $Eq_0(sharesoutstanding) = Eq_{-1}(1+g)(sharesoutstanding) = 2(1.048)(10) = \$20.96.$

6. $P_0 = \frac{d_1}{r^E - g} = \frac{d_0(1+g)}{r^E - g} = \frac{0.144(1+4.8\%)}{9\%-4.8\%} = \$3.5931.$

7. From $\$3.5931 > \$2.096$, share price is greater than book value per share. This means that the firm has created value for its owners. This is consistent with managers earning more than what owners demand, i.e., $12\% = ROE > r_E = 9\%$.

8. $\frac{P_0}{NI_1} = \frac{P_0}{NI_0(1+g)} = \frac{3.5931}{0.24(1+4.8\%)} = 14.2857.$

9. Five years from yesterday,
   (a) $d_5 = d_0(1+g)^5 = 0.144(1+4.8\%)^5 = \$0.182;$
   (b) $Eq_5 = Eq_{-1}(1+g)^6 = 2.00(1+4.8\%)^6 = \$2.6497;$
   (c) $P_5 = \frac{d_6}{r^E - g} = \frac{d_0(1+g)^6}{r^E - g} = \frac{0.144(1+4.8\%)^6}{9\%-4.8\%} = \$4.5424;$
   (d) $\frac{P_5}{NI_6} = \frac{P_5}{NI_0(1+g)^6} = \frac{4.5424}{0.24(1+4.8\%)^6} = 14.2857.$
   Ten years from yesterday,
   (a) $d_{10} = d_0(1+g)^{10} = 0.144(1+4.8\%)^{10} = \$0.2301;$
   (b) $Eq_{10} = Eq_{-1}(1+g)^{11} = 2.00(1+4.8\%)^{11} = \$3.3497;$
   (c) $P_{10} = \frac{d_{11}}{r^E - g} = \frac{d_0(1+g)^{11}}{r^E - g} = \frac{0.144(1+4.8\%)^{11}}{9\%-4.8\%} = \$5.7423;$
   (d) $\frac{P_{10}}{NI_{11}} = \frac{P_{10}}{NI_0(1+g)^{11}} = \frac{5.7423}{0.24(1+4.8\%)^{11}} = 14.2857,$ the same as $\frac{P_0}{NI_1}.$

10. (a) $P_0(r^E = 15\%) = \frac{d_1}{r^E - g} = \frac{d_0(1+g)}{r^E - g} = \frac{0.144(1+4.8\%)}{15\%-4.8\%} = 1.4795;$
    (b) $\frac{P_0(r^E = 15\%)}{NI_1} = \frac{P_0(r^E = 15\%)}{NI_0(1+g)} = \frac{1.4795}{0.24(1+4.8\%)} = 5.8824.$ In this case, as $\$2.096 > \$1.4795$, book value per share is greater than share price, consistent with the firm having destroyed value for its owners. This is consistent with managers earning less than what

owners demand, i.e., $12\% = ROE < r_E = 15\%$.

11. For $b^1 = 70\%$: (a) $g^1 = ROE(b^1) = 12\%(70\%) = 8.4\%$;
(b) $Eq_1^1 = Eq_0(1 + g^1) = 2.096(1 + 8.4\%) = \$2.2721$;
(c) $P_0^1(b = 70\%) = \frac{d_1^1}{r^E - g^1} = \frac{E_1(1-b^1)}{r^E - g^1} = \frac{Eq_0(ROE)(1-b^1)}{r^E - g^1} = \frac{2.096(12\%)(1-70\%)}{9\% - 8.4\%} = \$12.5760$;
(d) $\frac{P_0^1(b=70\%)}{NI_1} = \frac{1-b^1}{r^E - ROE(b^1)} = \frac{1-70\%}{9\% - 12\%(70\%)} = 50$.
The share price increases as plowback ratio is increased, as $12\% = ROE > r_E = 9\%$. As the firm creates value for owners, they greet the good news of increasing plowback ratio with a price increase.

Chapter 11

1. $EAR(m = 1) = (1 + 12\%)^1 - 1 = 12\%$, $EAR(m = 2) = (1 + \frac{12\%}{2})^2 - 1 = 12.36\%$, $EAR(m = 4) = (1 + \frac{12\%}{4})^4 - 1 = 12.55\%$, $EAR(m = 6) = (1 + \frac{12\%}{6})^6 - 1 = 12.62\%$, $EAR(m = 12) = (1 + \frac{12\%}{12})^{12} - 1 = 12.68\%$, $EAR(m = 24) = (1 + \frac{12\%}{24})^{24} - 1 = 12.72\%$, $EAR(m = 52) = (1 + \frac{12\%}{52})^{52} - 1 = 12.73\%$, $EAR(m = 365) = (1 + \frac{12\%}{365})^{365} - 1 = 12.747\%$, $EAR(m = +\infty) = e^{12\%} - 1 = 12.750\%$.

2. $P = 1000 \frac{8\%/2}{9\%/2}[1 - (1 + \frac{9\%}{2})^{-2(7)}] + 1000(1 + \frac{9\%}{2})^{-2(7)} = 948.89$. As $948.89 < 1000$, this is a discount bond.

3. The nominal yield is the coupon rate, 8%. The current yield is $\frac{annual\ coupon}{price} = \frac{1000(8\%)}{948.89} = 8.43\%$.

4. 5. 6. (*omitted*)

Chapter 12

1. $P(T = 14) = 1000 \frac{8\%/2}{4\%/2}[1 - (1 + \frac{4\%}{2})^{-2(14)}] + 1000(1 + \frac{4\%}{2})^{-2(14)} = 1425.63$. As $1425.63 > 1000$, this is a premium bond.

2. $P(T = 20) = 1000 \frac{8\%/2}{4\%/2}[1 - (1 + \frac{4\%}{2})^{-2(20)}] + 1000(1 + \frac{4\%}{2})^{-2(20)} = 1547.11 > 1425.63$. It is greater than that of problem 1. For a premium bond, as time marches to maturity (in this case, the time to maturity decreasies from 20 to 14), the bond price decreases and approaches the face value F in the limit as time to maturity approaches zero.

3. 4. 5. (*omitted*)

6. $P(r^C = 15\%) = 1000(\frac{15\%}{2})\frac{1-(1+4\%/2)^{-2(14)}}{4\%/2} + 1000(1 + \frac{4\%}{2})^{-2(14)} = 2170.47$. As

2170.47 > 1000, this is a premium bond.

7. (omitted)

Chapter 13

1. $P(4\%) = 100(\frac{8\%}{2})\frac{1-(1+4\%/2)^{-2(3)}}{4\%/2} + 1000/(1+\frac{4\%}{2})^{-2(3)} = 1112.0286$.

2. $P(3.99\%) = 40\frac{1-(1+3.99\%/2)^{-6}}{3.99\%/2} + 1000/(1+\frac{3.99\%}{2})^{-6} = 1112.3276$.
$P(4.01\%) = 40 * \frac{1-(1+4.01\%/2)^{-6}}{4.01\%/2} + 1000/(1+\frac{4.01\%}{2})^{-6} = 1111.7297$.

3. $P(3.99\%) - P(4\%) = 1112.3276 - 1112.0286 = 0.2990 > 0$, or positive. $P(4.01\%) - P(4\%) = 1111.7297 - 1112.0286 = -0.2989 < 0$, or negative. Since $0.2990 > 0.2989$, the price change in the case of yield decrease has the greater magnitude. This is because the yield curve is convex, which means when the yield increases (decreases), the rate of decrease (increase) in absolute bond price is decreasing (increasing).

4. $MaD = [0.5\frac{40}{(1+4\%/2)^1} + 1\frac{40}{(1+4\%/2)^2} + 1.5\frac{40}{(1+4\%/2)^3} + 2\frac{40}{(1+4\%/2)^4} + 2.5\frac{40}{(1+4\%/2)^5} + 3\frac{1040}{(1+4\%/2)^6}]\frac{1}{P(4\%)} = 2.7423$ Years.

5. $MD = \frac{MaD}{1+4\%/2} = 2.6886$.

6. $Conv = [0.5(0.5+0.5)\frac{40}{(1+4\%/2)^1} + 1(1+0.5)\frac{40}{(1+4\%/2)^2} + 1.5(1.5+0.5)\frac{40}{(1+4\%/2)^3}$
$+2(2+0.5)\frac{40}{(1+4\%/2)^4} + 2.5(2.5+0.5)\frac{40}{(1+4\%/2)^5} + 3(3+0.5)\frac{1040}{(1+4\%/2)^6}]*$
$\frac{1}{P(4\%)}\frac{1}{(1+4\%/2)^2} = 8.9403$ Years^2.

7. For first order approximations: $P(y_1) = P_0(y_0)[1-(y_1-y_0)MD]$.
(a) $P(3.99\%) = 1112.0286[1-(3.99\%-4\%)2.6886] = 1112.32759284929$;
(b) $P(4.01\%) = 1112.0286[1-(4.01\%-4\%)2.6886] = 1111.72964277832$.

8. (omitted)

9. For second order approximations:
$P(y_1) = P_0(y_0)[1-(y_1-y_0)MD + \frac{(y_1-y_0)^2}{2}Conv]$.
(a) $P(3.99\%) = 1112.0286[1-(-0.01\%)2.6886 + \frac{(0.01\%)^2}{2}8.9403] = 1112.3276425585$;
(b) $P(4.01\%) = 1112.0286[1-(0.01\%)2.6886 + \frac{(0.01\%)^2}{2}8.9403] = 1111.72969248753$.
For a yield of 3.99%, the first order error is $|1112.32759 - 1112.3276| = 4.97156E-05$, and the second order error is $|1112.32764 - 1112.3276| = 6.39557E-09$. So the second order error is smaller, as expected.
For a yield of 4.01%, the first order error is much $|1111.7296 - 1112.3276| = 4.97028E-$

05, and the second order error is $-1111.7297 - 1112.3276 = 6.39511E - 09$. Again, as expected, the second order error is smaller.

In short, for both cases the second order error is much smaller. This is generally the case whenever we have small to moderate magnitudes of $\Delta y = y_1 - y_0$.

Chapter 14

1. $P(f = 0) = 40\frac{1-(1+4\%/2)^{-28}}{4\%/2} + 1000(1 + \frac{4\%}{2})^{-28} = 1425.63$. As $1425.63 > 1000$, this is a premium bond.

2. Before we calculate the prices, we need to know the fraction f. Here, $f = \frac{3}{6} = 0.5$. So the dirty price is $P(f = 0.5) = (1 + \frac{4\%}{2})^{0.5} P(0) = 1439.81$. The accrued interest is $AI(f = 0.5) = 40(0.5) = 20$. The clean price is $CP(f = 0.5) = P(f = 0.5) - AI(f = 0.5) = 1439.81 - 20 = 1419.81$.

3. 4. 5. 6. 7. (*omitted*)

Chapter 15

1. $SR_{0.5} = 2(\frac{100}{98.02} - 1) = 4.04\%$; $SR_1 = 2[(\frac{100}{95.5})^{\frac{1}{2}} - 1] = 4.66\%$;

$SR_{1.5} = 2\left[\left(\frac{100+100(6\%/2)}{101.01-\frac{100(6\%/2)}{(1+4.04\%/2)^1}-\frac{100(6\%/2)}{(1+4.66\%/2)^2}}\right)^{\frac{1}{3}} - 1\right] = 5.32\%$;

$SR_2 = 2\left[\left(\frac{100+100(9\%/2)}{102.31-\frac{100(9\%/2)}{(1+4.04\%/2)^1}-\frac{100(9\%/2)}{(1+4.66\%/2)^2}-\frac{100(9\%/2)}{(1+5.32\%/2)^3}}\right)^{\frac{1}{4}} - 1\right] = 7.93\%$,

$SR_{2.5} = 2\left[\left(\frac{100+100(8\%/2)}{100.34-\frac{100(8\%/2)}{(1+4.04\%/2)^1}-\frac{100(8\%/2)}{(1+4.66\%/2)^2}-\frac{100(8\%/2)}{(1+5.32\%/2)^3}-\frac{100(8\%/2)}{(1+7.93\%/2)^4}}\right)^{\frac{1}{5}} - 1\right] = 8.00\%$;

Finally, $SR_3 = 2[(\frac{100+100(8.5\%/2)}{99.34-\frac{100(8.5\%/2)}{(1+4.04\%/2)^1}-\frac{100(8.5\%/2)}{(1+4.66\%/2)^2}-\frac{100(8.5\%/2)}{(1+5.32\%/2)^3}-\frac{100(8.5\%/2)}{(1+7.93\%/2)^4}-\frac{100(8.5\%/2)}{(1+8\%/2)^5}})^{\frac{1}{6}} - 1]$
$= 9.00\%$.

2. $_0f_{0.5} = SR_{0.5} = 4.04\%$; $_{0.5}f_1 = 2(\frac{(1+4.66\%/2)^2}{(1+4.04\%/2)^1} - 1) = 5.28\%$;
$_1f_{1.5} = 2(\frac{(1+5.32\%/2)^3}{(1+4.66\%/2)^2} - 1) = 6.64\%$; $_{1.5}f_2 = 2(\frac{(1+7.93\%/2)^4}{(1+5.32\%/2)^3} - 1) = 15.99\%$;
$_2f_{2.5} = 2(\frac{(1+8.00\%/2)^5}{(1+7.93\%/2)^4} - 1) = 8.27\%$; $_{2.5}f_3 = 2(\frac{(1+9.00\%/2)^6}{(1+8.00\%/2)^5} - 1) = 14.06\%$.

3. $_0f_1 = SR_1 = 4.66\%$; $_{0.5}f_{1.5} = 2[(\frac{(1+5.32\%/2)^3}{(1+4.04\%/2)^1})^{\frac{1}{2}} - 1] = 5.96\%$;
$_1f_2 = 2[(\frac{(1+7.93\%/2)^4}{(1+4.66\%/2)^2})^{\frac{1}{2}} - 1] = 11.26\%$; $_{1.5}f_{2.5} = 2[(\frac{(1+8.00\%/2)^5}{(1+5.32\%/2)^3})^{\frac{1}{2}} - 1] = 12.09\%$;

$_2f_3 = 2[(\frac{(1+9.00\%/2)^6}{(1+7.93\%/2)^4})^{\frac{1}{2}} - 1] = 11.15\%$.

4. (*omitted*)

5. (*omitted*)

6. First, we need to calculate the future value of reinvested coupons at a reinvestment rate of 7%, or $FV_{HP}^C = \$1000(\frac{12\%}{2})\frac{(1+7\%/2)^{20\times2}-1}{7\%/2} = \$5073.02$. Next, we need to calculate the selling price of the bond at a new yield-to-maturity of 10%, or $SP_{HP} = \$1000(\frac{12\%}{2})\frac{1-(1+10\%/2)^{-2\times10}}{10\%/2} + \$1000(1+\frac{10\%}{2})^{-2\times10} = \$1124.62$. So the realized holding period return is $rhpy = 2[(\frac{FV_{HP}^C + SP_{HP}}{P_0^B})^{\frac{1}{2\times20}} - 1] = 2[(\frac{5073.02+1124.62}{1114.56})^{\frac{1}{40}} - 1] = 8.77\%$.

Chapter 16

In the problems that follow, the strike price of all options is $K = \$30$. The expiration date of all options is 6 months from now ($T = 0.5$ years), and the current price of the stock (i.e., the underlying asset in all options) is $S_0 = \$29$ per share. The premiums for the call and put are $c_0 = \$1.89$ and $p_0 = \$1.43$, respectively.

1. The long call payoffs and profits are shown in the second and third columns of figure 16.13 on page 310. The corresponding graphs are shown in figure 16.14 on page 310.

Regarding the breakeven stock price for a long call, $0 = S_T^{BE} - K - c_0 = S_T^{BE} - \$30 - \$1.89$, or $S_T^{BE} = \$31.89$.

2. (*omitted*)

3. (*omitted*)

4. The short put payoffs and profits are shown in the last two columns of figure 16.13 on page 310. The corresponding graphs are shown in figure 16.15 on page 311.

Though not requested, regarding the breakeven stock price for a short put, then $0 = K - S_T^{BE} - p_0 = \$30 - S_T^{BE} - \$1.43$, or $S_T^{BE} = \$28.57$.

5. (*omitted*)

6. The long stock and short call (i.e., covered call) payoffs and profits are shown in figure 16.16 on page 311. The corresponding graphs are shown in figure 16.17 on page 312.

The payoff for a covered call is $[S_T - \max(0, S_T - K)]$, so the profit for a covered call

310 Asset Valuation Theory

price	call: problems 1, 2, 6, 7, 8, 9				put: problems 3, 4, 5, 7, 8, 9			
	long position		short position		long position		short position	
	payoff	profit	payoff	profit	payoff	profit	payoff	profit
S_T	c_T	π^c	$-c_T$	$-\pi^c$	p_T	π^p	$-p_T$	$-\pi^p$
0	0	-1.89	0	1.89	30	28.57	-30	-28.57
5	0	-1.89	0	1.89	25	23.57	-25	-23.57
10	0	-1.89	0	1.89	20	18.57	-20	-18.57
15	0	-1.89	0	1.89	15	13.57	-15	-13.57
20	0	-1.89	0	1.89	10	8.57	-10	-8.57
25	0	-1.89	0	1.89	5	3.57	-5	-3.57
28.57	0	-1.89	0	1.89	1.43	0	-1.43	0
30	0	-1.89	0	1.89	0	-1.43	0	1.43
31.89	1.89	0	-1.89	0	0	-1.43	0	1.43
35	5	3.11	-5	-3.11	0	-1.43	0	1.43
40	10	8.11	-10	-8.11	0	-1.43	0	1.43
45	15	13.11	-15	-13.11	0	-1.43	0	1.43
50	20	18.11	-20	-18.11	0	-1.43	0	1.43
55	25	23.11	-25	-23.11	0	-1.43	0	1.43
60	30	28.11	-30	-28.11	0	-1.43	0	1.43
65	35	33.11	-35	-33.11	0	-1.43	0	1.43
70	40	38.11	-40	-38.11	0	-1.43	0	1.43

Figure 16.13   Tabular payoffs and profits for a call and put

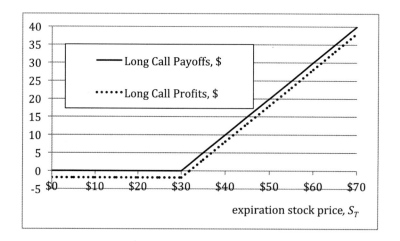

Figure 16.14   Payoff and profit of long call

is $[S_T - \max(0, S_T - K)] - (S_0 - c_0)$. As the call is out-of-the-money (i.e., the call expires worthless) when a covered call breaks even (i.e., the profit function in figure

Solutions to Selected End-of-chapter Problems   311

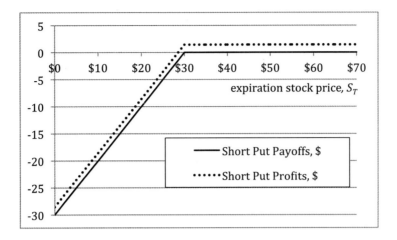

Figure 16.15   Payoff and profit of short put

price	payoffs			profit
S_T	S_T	$-c_T$	CC_T	π^{CC}
0	0	0	0	-27.11
5	5	0	5	-22.11
10	10	0	10	-17.11
15	15	0	15	-12.11
20	20	0	20	-7.11
25	25	0	25	-2.11
27.11	27.11	0	27.11	0
30	30	0	30	2.89
35	35	-5	30	2.89
40	40	-10	30	2.89
45	45	-15	30	2.89
50	50	-20	30	2.89
55	55	-25	30	2.89
60	60	-30	30	2.89
65	65	-35	30	2.89
70	70	-40	30	2.89

Figure 16.16   Tabular payoffs and profits for a covered call

16.17 crosses the zero axis below the strike price of $K = \$30$, or $S_T^{BE} < K$), then $c_T = \max(0, S_T - K) = 0$. Hence, the covered call profit of $[S_T - \max(0, S_T - K)] - (S_0 - c_0)$ becomes $S_T - (S_0 - c_0)$. Finally, setting this profit equal to zero, then the breakeven stock price is $0 = S_T^{BE} - (S_0 - c_0) = S_T^{BE} - (\$29 - \$1.89) = S_T^{BE} - \$27.11$, or $S_T^{BE} = \$27.11$.

7. The long call and long put (and long straddle) payoffs and profits are shown in figure

312   Asset Valuation Theory

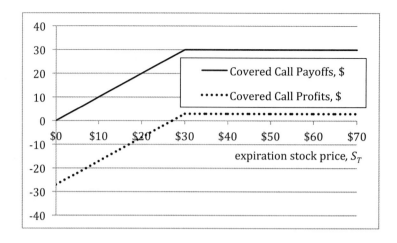

Figure 16.17 Payoff and profit of covered call

16.18 on page 312. The corresponding graphs are shown in figure 16.19 on page 313.

Regarding the two breakeven stock prices, $0 = \max(0, K - S_T^{BE}) + \max(0, S_T^{BE} - K) - (p_0 + c_0) = \max(0, \$30 - S_T^{BE}) + \max(0, S_T^{BE} - \$30) - \$3.32$, or $S_T^{BE} = \$26.68$ and

price	payoffs			profit
S_T	p_T	c_T	LS_T	π^{LS}
0	30	0	30	26.68
5	25	0	25	21.68
10	20	0	20	16.68
15	15	0	15	11.68
20	10	0	10	6.68
25	5	0	5	1.68
26.68	3.32	0	3.32	0
30	0	0	0	-3.32
33.32	0	3.32	3.32	0
35	0	5	5	1.68
40	0	10	10	6.68
45	0	15	15	11.68
50	0	20	20	16.68
55	0	25	25	21.68
60	0	30	30	26.68
65	0	35	35	31.68
70	0	40	40	36.68

Figure 16.18 Tabular payoffs and profits for a long straddle

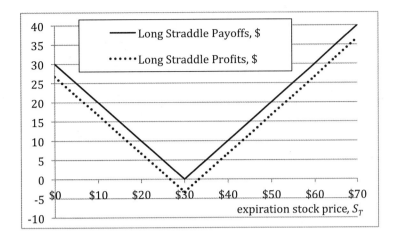

Figure 16.19   Payoff and profit of long straddle

$S_T^{BE} = \$33.32$.

8. (*omitted*)

9. The long stock, long put and short call (and collar) payoffs and profits are shown in figure 16.20 on page 313. The corresponding graphs are shown in figure 16.21 on page 314.

price	payoffs			profit
S_T	p_T	$-c_T$	co_T	π^{co}
0	30	0	30	1.46
5	25	0	30	1.46
10	20	0	30	1.46
15	15	0	30	1.46
20	10	0	30	1.46
25	5	0	30	1.46
30	0	0	30	1.46
35	0	-5	30	1.46
40	0	-10	30	1.46
45	0	-15	30	1.46
50	0	-20	30	1.46
55	0	-25	30	1.46
60	0	-30	30	1.46
65	0	-35	30	1.46
70	0	-40	30	1.46

Figure 16.20   Tabular payoffs and profits for a risk-free collar

Let's solve for the risk-free rate of return, continuously compounded, from put-call parity. From $S_0 + p_0 = c_0 + Ke^{-r^f T}$, or from $\$29 + \$1.43 = \$1.89 + 30e^{-r^f(0.5)}$, then $r^f = -2\ln(\frac{29+1.43-1.89}{30}) = 9.98\%$.

Equivalently, considering the constant payoff at time $t = 1$ year of \$30 in figure 16.20 on page 313 for an intial investment at time $t = 0$ of $S_0 + p_0 - c_0 = \$(29+1.43-1.89) = \$28.54$, then $\$30 = \$28.54 e^{r^f(0.5)}$, or $r^f = 2\ln(\frac{30}{28.54}) = 9.98\%$.

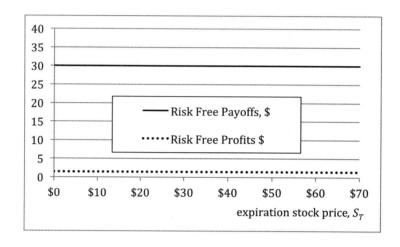

Figure 16.21 Payoff and profit of risk-free collar

Chapter 17

1. (a) $S_1^u = S_0(u) = 10(1.25) = 12.5$; (b) $S_1^d = S_0(d) = 10(0.9) = 9$.

2. The risk-averse up-state probability is $\pi^u = \frac{S_0 e^{r^E} - S_1^d}{S_1^u - S_1^d} = \frac{10e^{0.13}-9}{12.5-9} = 0.6824$. The risk-neutral up-state probability is $pr^u = \frac{S_0 e^{r^f} - S_1^d}{S_1^u - S_1^d} = \frac{10e^{0.06}-9}{12.5-9} = 0.4624$. As $\pi^u > pr^u$, then investors who hold a given risky asset in the risk-averse world must believe that the probability of up-state is greater than that in a risk-neutral world. Holding fixed the initial stock price, the expected stock price in the risk-averse world must be higher, which means that the up-state probability π^u in a risk-averse world must be higher than that in the risk-neutral world, i.e., pr^u.

3. In an risk neutral world, $E[S_1] = S_0 e^{r^f T} = pr^u S_1^u + pr^d S_1^d = 0.4624(12.5) + 0.5376(9) = 10.6184$. Equivalently, note that this equals $S_0 e^{r^f T} = \$10e^{6\%(1)} = \$10.6184$, as 6% is the continuosuly compounded, risk-free rate of return.

Solutions to Selected End-of-chapter Problems   315

4. For a call, (a) $c_1^u = \max(0, S_1^u - K) = \max(0, 12.5 - 11) = 1.5$;
(b) $c_1^d = \max(0, S_1^d - K) = \max(0, 9 - 11) = 0$.
For a put, (a) $p_1^u = \max(0, K - S_1^u) = \max(0, 11 - 12.5) = 0$;
(b) $p_1^d = \max(0, K - S_1^d) = \max(0, 11 - 9) = 2$.

5. Next, $\Delta^c = \frac{S_1^u - K}{S_1^u - S_1^d} = \frac{1.5}{3.5} = \frac{3}{7}$, and $\Delta^p = -\frac{K - S_1^d}{S_1^u - S_1^d} = -\frac{2}{3.5} = -\frac{4}{7}$.
Finally, $\Delta^c - \Delta^p = \frac{3}{7} - (-\frac{4}{7}) = 1$, as is always the case.

6. The call value is $c_0 = \frac{c_u(pr_u) + c_d(pr_d)}{e^{0.06}} = \frac{1.5(0.4624) + 0(0.5376)}{e^{0.06}} = 0.6532$,
and $p_0 = \frac{p_u(pr_u) + p_d(pr_d)}{e^{0.06}} = \frac{0(0.4624) + 2(0.5376)}{e^{0.06}} = 1.0126$.

7. First, $p_0 + S_0 = 1.0126 + 10 = 11.0126$, while $c_0 + Ke^{-r_f} = 0.6532 + 11e^{-0.06} = 11.0126$. The difference between values of these two portfolios is 0.

This illusrates put-call parity, i.e., that the value of a portfolio of a stock plus put option on this stock must equal the value of a portfolio of a call, whose underlying asset is this same stock, plus a risk-free asset whose payoff is the strike price of the call option, which equals the payoff of the strike price of the put options. In short, as both portfolios have the same payoff, they have the same cost of 11.0126 at time 0.

8. 9. 10. 11. 12. 13. (*omitted*)

Chapter 18

1. Parameters: there exist $n = 2$ periods, so $\Delta t = \frac{T}{n} = \frac{0.5}{2} = 0.25$ years. Next, $u|CRR = e^{\sigma\sqrt{\Delta t}} = e^{50\%\sqrt{0.25}} = 1.28403$; $d|CRR = \frac{1}{u} = e^{-\sigma\sqrt{\Delta t}} = e^{-50\%\sqrt{0.25}} = 0.77880$, and $R = e^{-r_f \Delta t} = e^{-6\%(0.25)} = 1.01511$. The first period prices are $S_1^u = uS_0 = 10(1.28403) = 12.8403$, and $S_1^d = dS_0 = 10(0.7788) = 7.7880$. The second period prices are $S_2^{uu} = u^2 S_0 = 10(1.28403^2) = 16.4872$, $S_2^{ud} = S_2^{du} = udS_0 = duS_0 = 10(1.28403)(0.7788) = 10$, and $S_2^{dd} = d^2 S_0 = 10(0.7788^2) = 6.0653$.

2. The risk-averse up-state probability is $\pi^u = \frac{S_0 e^{r_E \Delta t} - S_1^d}{S_1^u - S_1^d} = \frac{10 e^{0.13(0.25)} - 7.7880}{12.8403 - 7.7880} = 0.5032$.
The risk-neutral up-state probability is $pr^u = \frac{R-D}{U-D} = \frac{S_0 e^{r_f \Delta t} - S_1^d}{S_1^u - S_1^d} = \frac{10 e^{0.06(0.25)} - 7.7880}{12.8403 - 7.7880} = 0.4677$. So $0.5032 = \pi^u > pr^u = 0.4677$, as expected.

3. (a) In a risk-neutral world: $E[S_1] = pr^u S_1^u + pr^d S_1^d = 0.4677(12.8403) + 0.5323(7.7880)$
$= 10.1511 = R(S_0) = 1.01511(\$10)$; (b) $E[S_2] = (pr^u)^2 S_2^{uu} + (pr^d)^2 S_2^{dd} + 2pr^u pr^d S_2^{ud}$
$= 0.4677^2(16.4872) + 0.5323^2(6.0653) + 2(0.4677)(0.5323)(10) = 10.3045 = R^2(S_0)$.

4. For a call, (a) $c_2^{uu} = \max(0, S_2^{uu} - K) = \max(0, 16.4872 - 11) = 5.4872$; (b) $c_2^{ud} = \max(0, S_2^{ud} - K) = \max(0, 10 - 11) = 0$; (c) $c_2^{du} = \max(0, S_2^{du} - K) = \max(0, 10 - 11) = 0$; (d) $c_2^{dd} = \max(0, S_2^{dd} - K) = \max(0, 6.0653 - 11) = 0$.

For a put, (a) $p_2^{uu} = \max(0, K - S_2^{uu}) = \max(0, 11 - 16.4872) = 0$; (b) $p_2^{ud} = \max(0, K - S_2^{ud}) = \max(0, 11 - 10) = 1$; (c) $p_2^{du} = \max(0, K - S_2^{du}) = \max(0, 11 - 10) = 1$; (d) $p_2^{dd} = \max(0, K - S_2^{dd}) = \max(0, 11 - 6.0653) = 4.9347$.

5. The initial deltas are: $\Delta^c = \frac{S_1^u - K}{S_1^u - S_1^d} = \frac{12.8403 - 11}{12.8403 - 7.7880} = \frac{1.8403}{5.0523} = 0.3642$ and $\Delta^p = -\frac{K - S_1^d}{S_1^u - S_1^d} = -\frac{11 - 7.7880}{12.8403 - 7.7880} = -\frac{3.212}{5.0523} = -0.6358$. So $\Delta^c - \Delta^p = 0.3642 - (-0.6358) = 1$.

The deltas after one period are: (a) up-state: $\Delta^c = \frac{S_2^{uu} - K}{S_2^{uu} - S_2^{ud}} = \frac{16.4872 - 11}{16.4872 - 10} = \frac{5.4872}{6.4872} = 0.8459$ and $\Delta^p = -\frac{K - S_2^{ud}}{S_2^{uu} - S_2^{ud}} = -\frac{11 - 10}{16.4872 - 10} = -\frac{1}{6.4872} = -0.1541$. Again, $\Delta^c - \Delta^p = 0.8459 - (-0.1541) = 1$.

(b) down-state: $\Delta^c = \frac{S_2^{du} - K}{S_2^{du} - S_2^{dd}} = \frac{10 - 11}{10 - 6.0653} = \frac{-1}{3.9347} = -0.2542$ and $\Delta^p = -\frac{K - S_2^{du}}{S_2^{du} - S_2^{dd}} = -\frac{11 - 6.0653}{10 - 6.0653} = -\frac{4.9347}{3.9347} = -1.2542$. Then $\Delta^c - \Delta^p = -0.2542 - (-1.2542) = 1$.

6. As $c_2^{du} = c_2^{ud} = c_2^{dd} = 0$, then $c_0 = \frac{(pr^u)^2 c_2^{uu}}{e^{r^f T}} = \frac{0.4677^2 (5.4872)}{e^{6\%(0.5)}} = 1.1650$. As $p_2^u = 0$, then $p_0 = \frac{(pr_d)^2 p_2^{dd} + 2 pr_u pr_d p_2^{ud}}{e^{r^f T}} = \frac{0.5323^2 (4.9347) + 2(0.4677)(0.5323)(1)}{e^{6\%(0.5)}} = 1.8399$.

7. First, $p_0 + S_0 = 1.8399 + 10 = 11.8399$, and $c_0 + Ke^{-r^f T} = 1.1650 + 11 e^{-6\%(0.5)} = 11.8399$. The difference is zero. This example illustrates put-call parity. A portfolio of a put and a stock compared with a portfolio of a call and a risk-free asset has the same payoff in half of a year; hence, their costs today must also be equal, i.e., both portfolios cost 11.8399 today, at time 0.

8. 9. 10. 11. 12. 13. (*omitted*)

Chapter 19

1. American options can be executed before the expiration date, so the option payoff at each node could be different. Therefore, the first step is to establish a new payoff tree of a call or put.

For the American call payoffs:
(a) at date 2: $C_2^{uu} = c_2^{uu} = 5.4872, C_2^{ud} = C_2^{du} = c_2^{ud} = 0, C_2^{dd} = c_2^{dd} = 0$;
(b) at date 1: $C_1^u = \max(S_1^u - K, e^{-r^f \Delta t}[pr^u C_2^{uu} + pr^d C_2^{ud}]) = \max(12.8403 - 11, e^{-6\%(0.25)}[0.4677(5.4872) + 0.5323(0)]) = \max(1.8403, 2.5284) = 2.5284$;

$C_1^d = \max(S_1^d - K, e^{-r^f \Delta t}[pr^u C_2^{du} + pr^d C_2^{dd}]) = \max(7.7880 - 11,$
$e^{-6\%(0.25)}[0.4677(0) + 0.5323(0)]) = 0.$

(c) at date 0: $C_0 = \max(S_0 - K, e^{-r^f \Delta t}[pr^u C_1^u + pr^d C_1^d]) = \max(0, 1.1650) = 1.1650.$

For the American put payoffs:

(a) at date 2: $P_2^{uu} = p_2^{uu} = 0, P_2^{ud} = P_2^{du} = p_2^{ud} = 1, P_2^{dd} = p_2^{dd} = 4.9347;$

(b) at date 1: $P_1^u = \max(K - S_1^u, e^{-r^f \Delta t}[pr^u P_2^{uu} + pr^d P_2^{ud}]) = \max(11 - 12.8403,$
$e^{-6\%(0.25)}[0.4677(0) + 0.5323(1)]) = 0.5243;$

$P_1^d = \max(K - S_1^d, e^{-r^f \Delta t}[pr^u P_2^{du} + pr^d P_2^{dd}]) = \max(11 - 7.7880,$
$e^{-6\%(0.25)}[0.4677(1) + 0.5323(4.9347)]) = 3.2120.$

(c) at date 0: $P_0 = \max(K - S_0, e^{-r^f \Delta t}[pr^u P_1^u + pr^d P_1^d]) = \max(1, 1.9258) = 1.9258.$

For the call, the incremental value $C_0 - c_0$ equals zero. For the put, the incremental value $P_0 - p_0$ equals $0.0859 > 0$.

2. $P_0 + S_0 = 1.9258 + 10 = 11.9258$ and $C_0 + Ke^{-r^f T} = 11.8399$. The difference is $0.0859 > 0$. Put-call parity does not hold in this case because the American put is executed before the expiration date, which makes its premium higher. Put-call parity holds for European options, not American options.

3. 4. 5. 6. 7. 8. (omitted)

Chapter 20

1. Per the formula, a European call premium is: $c_0 = S_0 SN(d_1) - Ke^{-r^f T} SN(d_2)$, where $d_1 = \frac{\ln(\frac{S_0}{K}) + T(r^f + \frac{\sigma^2}{2})}{\sigma \sqrt{T}}$ and $d_2 = d_1 - \sigma\sqrt{T}$. Given the conditions in the problem, we then have: $d_1 = \frac{\ln(\frac{10}{11}) + 0.5(6\% + \frac{(50\%)^2}{2})}{50\% \sqrt{0.5}} = -0.00795$ and $d_2 = 0.00795 - 50\%\sqrt{0.5} = -0.3615$. The European call premium is $c_0 = 10 SN(-0.00795) - 11 e^{-6\%(0.5)} SN(-0.3615) = 1.1375.$

2. The European put premium is $p_0 = Ke^{-r^f T} SN(-d_2) - S_0 SN(-d_1) = 11 e^{-6\%(0.5)} SN(0.3615) - 10 SN(0.00795) = 1.8124.$

3. $\Delta^c = SN(d_1) = 0.4968$, and $\Delta^p = -SN(-d_1) = -0.5032$. As always, $\Delta^c - \Delta^p = 1.0000.$

4. Given $S_0 = \$11$, the new parameters are: $d_1 = \frac{\ln(\frac{11}{11}) + 0.5(6\% + \frac{(50\%)^2}{2})}{50\%\sqrt{0.5}} = 0.26163$ and $d_2 = d_1 - \sigma\sqrt{T} = 0.26163 - 50\%\sqrt{0.5} = -0.09192$. So $c_0(S_0 = \$11) = 11 SN(0.26163) - $

$11e^{-6\%(0.5)}SN(-0.09192) = 1.6886$. This is greater than $c_0(S_0 = \$10) = 1.1375$, and the difference is $0.5511 > 0$. This is close to the value of $\Delta^c = 0.4968$, as expected. (As Δ^c increases in S, i.e., $\Gamma^c > 0$, the increase in call premium in going from $\$10$ to $\$11$ is slightly greater than that predicted by $\Delta(S_0 = \$10)$, i.e., that at the lower end of the stock price range of $[\$10, \$11]$.)

5. The new European put premium is $p_0(S_0 = \$11) = 11e^{-6\%(0.5)}SN(0.09192) - 11SN(-0.26163) = 1.3635$. This is smaller than $p_0(S_0 = \$10) = 1.8124$, and the difference is $-0.4489 < 0$. This is close to the value of $\Delta^p = -0.5032$, as expected. (As $\Delta^p < 0$ increases in S, i.e., $\Gamma^p > 0$, the decrease in put premium in going from $\$10$ to $\$11$ is slightly less than that predicted by $\Delta(S_0 = \$10)$, i.e., that at the lower end of the stock price range of $[\$10, \$11]$.)

6. 7. 8. 9. 10. 11. 12. 13. 14. 15. 16. 17. 18. (*omitted*)

References and Suggested Readings

Black, Fischer. "How we came up with the option formula". *Journal of Portfolio Management* 15(2) (1989): 4-8.

Black, Fischer, and Myron Scholes. "The pricing of options and corporate liabilities". *The Journal of Political Economy* 81(3) (1973): 637-654.

Bodie, Zvi, Alex Kane, and Alan J. Marcus. *Essentials of Investments*. McGraw-Hill, 2013.

Brown, Keith C. "The benefits of insured stocks for corporate cash management". *Advances in Futures and Options Research* 2 (1987): 243-261.

Brown, Keith C., ed. *Derivative Strategies for Managing Portfolio Risk*: April 13-14, 1993, Marina Del Rey, California. Association for Investment Management and Research, 1993.

Brown, Keith C., Frank K. Reilly. *Analysis of Investments & Management of Portfolios*. South-Western, 2012.

Chance, Don M., and Roberts Brooks. *Introduction to Derivatives and Risk Management*. Cengage Learning, 2015.

Cox, John C., Stephen A. Ross, and Mark Rubinstein. "Option pricing: A simplified approach". *Journal of Financial Economics* 7(3) (1979): 229-263.

Cox, John C., and Mark Rubinstein. *Options Markets*. Prentice Hall, 1985.

Damodaran, Aswath. *Damodaran on Valuation: Security Analysis for Investment and Corporate Finance* 2E., John Wiley & Sons, 2006.

Elton, Edwin J., Martin J. Gruber, Stephen J. Brown, and William N. Goetzmann. *Modern Portfolio Theory and Investment Analysis*. John Wiley & Sons, 2009.

Fabozzi, Frank J. *Fixed Income Mathematics*. 4E. McGraw-Hill, 2005.

Fabozzi, Frank J. *Bond Markets, Analysis and Strategies*. International 6th Edition, Prentice Hall, 2008.

Fabozzi, Frank J., and Steven V. Mann. *The Handbook of Fixed Income Securities*. McGraw-Hill Professional, 2012.

Fama, Eugene F., and Merton H. Miller. *The Theory of Finance*. Vol. 3. Hinsdale, IL:

Dryden Press, 1972.

Fraser, Lyn M., and Aileen Ormiston. *Understanding Financial Statements*. Prentice Hall, 1998.

Gordon, Myron J. *The Investment, Financing, and Valuation of the Corporation*. RD Irwin, 1962.

Helfert, Erich A. *Techniques of Financial Analysis: A Guide to Value Creation*. McGraw-Hill Professional, 2002.

Hull, John C. *Options, Futures, and Other Derivatives*. 7E. Prentice Hall, 2009.

Koller, Tim, Marc Goedhart, D. Wessels, and T. E. Copeland. "McKinsey & Company. 2010". *Valuation: Measuring and Managing the Value of Companies*. 5E. Hoboken: John Wiley & Sons.

Lintner, John. "Security prices, risk, and maximal gains from diversification". *The Journal of Finance* 20(4) (1965): 587-615.

Macaulay, Frederick, R., "Some Theoretical Problems Suggested by the Movements of Interest Rates, Bond Yields and Stock Prices in the United States since 1856". 1938. New York: NBER.

Maginn, John L., Donald L. Tuttle, Dennis W. McLeavey, and Jerald E. Pinto, eds. *Managing Investment Portfolios: A Dynamic Process*. Vol. 3. John Wiley & Sons, 2007.

Malkiel, Burton G. "Expectations, bond prices, and the term structure of interest rates". *The Quarterly Journal of Economics* 76(2) (1962): 197-218.

Markowitz, Harry. "Portfolio selection". *The Journal of Finance*, 7(1) (1952): 77-91.

Markowitz, Harry. "Portfolio selection: Efficient diversification of investments". *Cowles Foundation Monograph*, no. 16 (1959).

Merton, Robert C. "The relationship between put and call option prices: Comment". *Journal of Finance* 28(1) (1973): 183-184.

Mossin, Jan. "Equilibrium in a capital asset market". *Econometrica: Journal of the Econometric Society* 34(4) (1966): 768-783.

Navin, Robert L. *The Mathematics of Derivatives: Tools for Designing Numerical Algorithms*. Vol. 373. John Wiley & Sons, 2007.

Pinto, J., E. Henry, T. Robinson, and J. Stowe. *CFA, Equity Asset Valuation*, John Wiley & Sons, 2010.

Reilly, Frank K., and Rupinder S. Sidhu. "The many uses of bond duration". *Financial Analysts Journal* 36(4) (1980): 58-72.

Rendleman, Richard J., and Brit J. Bartter. "Two-state option pricing". *The Journal of Finance* 34(5) (1979): 1093-1110.

Ross, Stephen A. "The arbitrage theory of capital asset pricing". *Journal of Economic Theory* 13(3) (1976): 341-360.

Ross, Stephen A. "Return, risk and arbitrage", in *Risk and Return in Finance* (I. Friend and JL Bicksler, Eds.). Balinger, Cambridge, MA, 1977.

Sharpe, William F. "Capital asset prices: A theory of market equilibrium under conditions of risk". *The Journal of Finance* 19(3) (1964): 425-442.

Sharpe, William F. "Factor models, CAPMs, and the ABT". *The Journal of Portfolio Management* 11(1) (1984): 21-25.

Sharpe, William F. *Investors and Markets: Portfolio Choices, Asset Prices, and Investment Advice*. Princeton University Press, 2011.

Stoll, Hans R. "The relationship between put and call option prices". *The Journal of Finance* 24(5) (1969): 801-824.

Stowe, John D., Thomas R. Robinson, Jerald E. Pinto, and Dennis W. McLeavey. *Analysis of Equity Insvestment: Valuation*. Association for Investment Management and Research, 2002.

Tuckman, Bruce, and Angel Serrat. *Fixed Income Securities: Tools for Today's Markets*. Vol. 626. John Wiley & Sons, 2011.

Williams, John Burr. *The Theory of Investment Value*. Vol. 36. Cambridge, MA: Harvard University Press, 1938.

Yates, James W., and Robert W. Kopprasch. "Writing covered call options: Profits and risks". *The Journal of Portfolio Management* 7(1) (1980): 74-79.

Index

absolute valuation, 108
accrued interest, 180, 181
accrued liabilities, 72
accumulated depreciation, 72
adjusted present value method, 128
annuity, 7
    growing, 7
APT
    arbitrage, 56
    assumptions, 55
    beta, 56
    cost-free, 57
    how to profit, 60
    idiosyncratic risk-free, 58
    implementation, 62–66
    loading factor, 56
    risk premium, 56
    systematic risk-free, 58
arbitrage, 56, 221
arbitrage pricing theory, APT, 55
arbitrageur, 56
arithmetic mean return, 12

balance sheet, 72, 74
balance sheet ratios, 114
balance sheet relations, 113
basics, 1, 3, 10
beta, 47
    APT, 56
bond cash flow timeline, 147
bonds
    basis point, 175
    bootstrapping, 187
    callable, 198

convexity, 168
discount bond, 153
dollar duration, 175
expected cash flows, 149
fixed coupon payments, 152
forward rates, 190
forward rates, multi-period, 192
interest on interest, 149
maturity impacts price, 155
other yield metrics, 199
par bond, 152
par value, 152
partial period timeline, 177
premium bond, 153
price-yield curve, 151
price-yield estimate
    first order, 171
    second order, 171
price-yield metrics, 175
price-yield relations, 166
pricing between coupon dates, 177
promised cash flows, 149
rate and yield metrics, 187
sources of return, 148
spot rates, 187
total return, 149
yield spread, 199
yield to first call, 198
yield to second call, 199
yield to worst, 198, 199
z-spread, 200
bootstrapping, 187
break-even output, 100

business risk, 102

callable bonds, 198
capital asset pricing model, CAPM, 48
capital market line, CML, 43
cash, 72
cash flow
    debt, 81
    financing, 76
    investing, 76
    operating, 76
    present value, 5
cash flows
    expected, 4
    future value, 5
    promised, 4
    timeline, 3
clean price, 180, 181
coefficient of variation, 14
common size balance sheet, 87
common size income statement, 86
common size statements, 86
contribution margin, 98, 99
contribution margin ratio, 99
convexity, 168
correlation coefficient, 15, 32
cost of debt, 124
cost of goods sold, COGS, 71
coupon rate, 147
covariance, 14, 29
coverage ratios, 98
current assets, 72
current liabilities, 72
current maturities of LSD, 72
current yield, 151

DCF techniques, 125
    adjusted present value method, 128
    dividend discount model, 126
    enterprise value, 125
    equity value, 126
    FTE method, 126
    Gordon dividend discount model, 127
    impacts of WACC and FCF growth, 130
    multi-stage dividend discount model, 127
    total equity CF model, 126
    WACC method, 125
debt cash flow, 81
debt maturity date, 147
debt tax shield, 97, 129
degree of operating leverage, 101
demanded rate of return, 59
depreciation, 71
dirty price, 178
diversification, 30, 48
diversified portfolio, 48
dividend discount model, 126
dividend payout ratio, 74
dividend reinvestment, 11

earnings before taxes, EBT, 71
earnings multiplier model, EMM, 135
earnings yield, 106
earnings, net income, 71
EBIT, operating profit, 71
EBT, earnings before taxes, 71
effective annual rate, EAr, 145
effective convexity, 173
effective duration, 172
effective periodic rate, 145
efficiency ratios, 92
efficient frontier, 39
efficient portfolio, 39
EMM
    comparative statics, 137
        equity holders' r^E, 138
        inital equity, 138
        plowback ratio, b, 139
        ROE, 139

dividends, 136
equity value, 135
net income, 135
price, 136
price-to-earnings ratio, 136
EMM, earnings multiplier model, 135
empirical duration, 174
enterprise value, 125
equity valuation, 69
equity value, 126
expected rate of return, 29, 32, 59
external liquidity ratios, 102

face value of debt, 147
Fama French 3-factor model, 55
financial accounting statements, 71
financial basics, 3
financial risk ratios, 94
financial statement analysis, 85
financing cash flow, 76
firm-specific risk, 32, 46
fixed costs, 99
flow variable, 4
flow variables, 71
flows-to-equity method, 126
forward contract, 208
free cash flow, 82
free cash flows, 78
free cash flows to equity, 78
frontier of portfolios, 33
fundamental risk, 46
future value, 5, 8

geometric mean return, 12
global minimum variance portfolio, 38
Gordon dividend discount model, 127
gross PPE, 72
gross profit, 71
gross return, 10
portfolio, 16

growing annuity, 7
future value, 8
growing perpetuity, 7
growth rates, 109
absolute, 109
relative, 109

historical return, 11
historical returns, 10
holding period return, 13

idiosyncratic risk, 32, 46, 50
implied rate of return, 48, 59
income statement, 71
income statement ratios, 111
income statement relations, 110
income taxes, 71
interest coupons, 147
interest expense, 71
internal liquidity ratios, 88
intrinsic value, 7, 59
bonds, 148
intrinsic value Vs. price, 60
investing cash flow, 76
investment opportunity set, 33
investor preferences, 39
invoice price, 178
iso-utilities, 39

law of large numbers, 32
leverage, 94
leverage ratios, 98
long-term debt, 72

Macaulay duration, 166
Malkiel results, 158
absolute price change, 158
coupon rate, 162
discrete analysis, 160
relative price change, 158
summary, 164

time to maturity, 163
yield to maturity, 158
march to maturity, 155
market model, 47
market portfolio, 46
market price of risk, 46
market risk premium, 46
marketable securities, 72
Markowitz Theory, 36
MM proposition II, 122
modified duration, 167
multi-factor model, 55
multi-stage dividend discount model, 127

net income, earnings, 71
net PPE, 72
net working capital, 89
nominal yield, 151
notes payable, 72

operating cash flow, 76
operating performance ratios, 92
operating profit, EBIT, 71
operational risk ratios, 98
operations risk, 102
optimal investment opportunity set, 39
Options, 203
    American, 204, 206
    arbitrage, 203, 221, 225
        contradiction, 225
    at-the-money, 207, 210
    binomial model, 203, 204, 227
        American call value, 257
        American option early exercise, 264
        American option summary, 258
        American option value, 259
        American options, 257
        American put example, 259
        American put value, 258
        arbitrage, 233
        backward induction, 257–259
        call option value, 253
        call premium, 230, 235
        Call valuation, 257
        call value, 237
        call volatility, 239–242
        comparative statics, 239, 242
        contradiction, 233
        delta hedge, 228
        delta of call, 229
        delta of put, 231
        down-state, 227, 252
        efficacy, 253
        multi-period, 204
        multi-period call, 252
        multi-period model, 248, 252
        multi-period put, 252
        period duration, 251
        probabilities, 228, 238, 251
        probability of early exercise, 267
        put premium, 232
        put replicating portfolio, 235
        put value, 235
        put volatility, 243–245
        put-call spot parity, 232
        reconnecting tree, 248
        replicating portfolio, 232
        risk-free rate, 239, 243
        risk-neutral probabilities, 236, 237
        risk-neutral valuation, 236, 237
        state of the world, 228
        stock price, 239, 242
        stock price tree, 259
        strike price, 239, 243
        strike price assumption, 228, 252
        time to maturity, 242, 245
        two-period model, 248, 250
        up-state, 227, 252
        up-state, down-state, 249

Index   327

value of early exercise, 259
Black-Scholes, 204
    put value, 273
Black-Scholes model, 271
    assumptions, 271
    call value, 273
    comparative statics, 276
    continuous dividend, 275
    Delta, 276
    delta hedge, 272, 274
    differential equation, 272, 274
    early exercise, 274
    European call, 272
    Gamma, 276
    Ito's Lemma, 272
    put value, 274–276
    put-call spot parity, 275, 276
    Rho, 277
    risk-free return, 272, 274
    stock price model, 271
    strike price, 277
    Theta, 281
    time to maturity, 281
    Vega, 278
    volatility, 278–281
bounds on value, 203
call, 206
call profit, 207
collar
    payoff, 218
    profit, 218
collar, bull spread, 218
covered call, 215
    payoff, 215
    profit, 215
delta hedge, 203
European call, 224, 225
    bounds, 226
    lower bound, 224

    upper bound, 225
European put
    bounds, 227
exercise decision, 206
expiration, 203
expire worthless, 206
expiry, expiration date, 205
in-the-money, 207, 210
insurance, 214
kink point, 207, 208, 211
long call, 206
long call payoff, 207
long call profit, 207
long put, 210
long put payoff, 211
long put profit, 211
long straddle, 216
    payoff, 216
    profit, 216
make delivery, 206
naked call, 216
no arbitrage, 226
out-of-the-money, 207, 210
owner, buyer, 205
payoffs, 203
portfolios of, 214
premium, 203, 205
    call, 207
profits, 203
protective put, 214
    payoff, 214
    profit, 214
put, 206
put premium, 212
put-call spot parity, 203, 220
replicating portfolio, 203
risk-neutral valuation, 203
seller, 205
short call, 208

short call payoff, 209
short call profit, 209
short put payoff, 212
short put profit, 212
short straddle, 217
    payoff, 218
    profit, 218
strike price, 205
take delivery, 206
underlying asset, 205
writer, 203
zero-sum game, 206, 209, 212

perpetuity, 7
plowback ratio, 74
portfolio
    arithmetic mean return, 17
    diversified, 48
    efficient, 39
    market, 46
    two-asset, 32
    variance, 17
portfolio holding period return, 16
portfolio optimization, 38
portfolio returns, 15
portfolio theory, 25, 36
portfolio weights, 16
PPE, gross, 72
PPE, net, 72
present value, 5
price-to-book ratio, 105
price-to-cash flow ratio, 105
price-to-earnings ratio, 106
price-to-sales ratio, 104
price-yield approximations, 170
price-yield curve, 151
pro-forma balance sheet, 118
pro-forma future cash flows, 119
pro-forma income statement, 118
pro-forma statement of cash flows, 119

pro-forma statements, future, 118
probability
    density function, 27
    discrete random variable, 28
    discrete variance, 28
    distribution function, 27
profitability ratios, 92
promised cash flows, 149
property, plant, equipment, PPE, 72

quoted price, 181

rate of return, 10
    continuously compounded, 17
    coupon rate, 147
    demanded, 59
    demanded by all-equity firm investors, 124
    demanded by debt holders, 124
    demanded by equity holders, 121
    effective annual rate, EAr, 145
    expected, 27, 29, 59
    forward rates, 190
    forward rates, multi-period, 192
    future, 27
    historical, 10
    implied, 48, 59
    net, 10
    portfolio, 15
    realized holding period yield, 194–197
    required, 59
    spots and yields, 187
    variance, 14, 27, 30
    yield to maturity, 150
    z-spread, 200
realized holding period yield, 194–197
relative valuation, 85, 103
required rate of return, 59
retained earnings, 72
return

gross, 10
returns
    historical portfolio, 18
reward, 25
risk, 25
    idiosyncratic, 50
    systematic, 50
    total, 50
risk and reward, 39
risk aversion, 45
risk minimization, 38
risk premium, 56
risk-averse, 39

security market line, SML, 48
SGA expenses, 71
single factor model, 56
spot rates, 187
statement of cash flows, 75, 76
stock holders' equity, 75
stock variable, 4
stock variables, 71
sustainable growth, 102
systematic risk, 32, 46, 47, 50
systematic risk factor, 47
systematic risk factor, SRF, 55

timeline, 71
    bond cash flows, 147
    bond partial period, 177
    historical, 11
timeline of cash flows, 3
total bond return, 149
total equity cash flow, 82
total equity CF model, 126
total risk, 50
Treynor ratio, 48
turnover ratio, 90
two-asset portfolio, 32

unit contribution margin, 99
unit fixed cost, 99
unit variable cost, 99
unlevered firm value, 128
utility function, 39

value additivity, 6
variable costs, 99
variance, 14, 27, 30, 32
variance discrete random variable, 28

weighted average cost of capital, WACC, 119
weights
    portfolio, 16

yield to maturity, 150
yield to worst, 198

北京大学出版社教师反馈及教辅申请表

　　北京大学出版社本着"教材优先、学术为本"的出版宗旨，竭诚为广大高等院校师生服务。为更有针对性地提供服务，请您认真填写以下表格并经系主任签字盖章后反馈给我们，我们将按照您填写的联系方式免费向您提供相应教辅资料，以及在本书内容更新后及时与您联系邮寄样书等事宜。

书名		书号	978-7-301-	作者	
您的姓名				职称职务	
校/院/系					
您所讲授的课程名称					
每学期学生人数	____人		____年级	学时	
您准备何时用此书授课					
您的联系地址					
邮政编码			联系电话（必填）		
E-mail（必填）			QQ		
您对本书的建议：			系主任签字 盖章		

我们的联系方式：

北京大学出版社经济与管理图书事业部

北京市海淀区成府路 205 号，100871

联 系 人： 周莹

电　　话： 010-62767312 /62757146

传　　真： 010-62556201

电子邮件： em@pup.cn　em_pup@126.com

Q Q： 5520 63295

微信： 北大经管书苑（pupembook）

新浪微博： @北京大学出版社经管图书

网　　址： http://www.pup.cn